AFRICAN DEVELOPMENT REPORT
2005

AFRICA IN THE WORLD ECONOMY
PUBLIC SECTOR MANAGEMENT IN AFRICA
ECONOMIC AND SOCIAL STATISTICS ON AFRICA

PUBLISHED FOR THE AFRICAN DEVELOPMENT BANK
BY
OXFORD UNIVERSITY PRESS

OXFORD
UNIVERSITY PRESS

Great Clarendon Street, Oxford OX2 6DP
Oxford University Press is a department of the University of Oxford.
It furthers the University's objective of excellence in research, scholarship,
and education by publishing worldwide in

Oxford New York
Auckland Cape Town Dar es Salaam Hong Kong
Karachi Kuala Lumpur Madrid Melbourne
Mexico City Nairobi New Delhi Shanghai Taipei Toronto

With offices in
Argentina Austria Brazil Chile Czech Republic France Greece
Guatemala Hungary Italy Japan Poland Portugal Singapore
South Korea Switzerland Thailand Turkey Ukraine Vietnam

Oxford is a registered trade mark of Oxford University Press
in the UK and in certain other countries

Published in the United States
by Oxford University Press Inc., New York

British Library Cataloguing in Publication Data
Data available
Library of Congress Cataloging-in-Publication Data
Data available
ISBN 0-19-928084-3   978-0-19-928084-1

Typeset by Hope Services, Abingdon, Oxon
Printed in Great Britain
on acid-free paper by
Ashford Colour Press Limited, Gosport, Hampshire

FOREWORD

The *African Development Report*, prepared annually by the staff of the Development Research Department of the Bank, provides an in-depth review of recent macro-economic performance and structural issues in Africa, viewed from continental, regional and national perspectives. It also assesses the prospects of the African economy in the context of recent global developments. In addition, it provides an in-depth analysis of a topical issue that is critical to Africa's development — with this year's focus being on *Public Sector Management in Africa*.

With respect to Africa's economic performance in 2004, the Report notes that it improved markedly. The region's GDP growth rate reached an average of 5.1 percent from 4.4 percent in 2003, resulting in a per capita GDP growth of 2.8 percent. This is the highest GDP growth rate recorded for the continent since 1996, and considerably above the average of 3.7 percent for the previous five years. It is also noteworthy that this is the first time in over two decades that the continent has recorded growth rates exceeding 4 percent per annum for two consecutive years. As was the case in the past, growth in 2004 exhibited a considerable variation across individual countries, although the trend, overall, was quite positive. Some 20 countries achieved GDP growth rates exceeding 5 percent and 14 others recorded growth rates of between 3 and 5

percent. Only three countries witnessed negative growth rates, compared with six in the preceding year.

Several factors, both external and internal, contributed to this strong overall economic performance. Externally, Africa's terms of trade improved considerably — by 6.7 percent — largely due the rise in oil prices and the further strengthening of the prices of major non-fuel commodities, particularly metals. In addition, the rebound in the global economy along with strong demand from Asia for the region's primary export commodities also boosted the Continent's exports. As a result, Africa's current account improved significantly in 2004, recording a surplus of over $5 billion. Improved export performance and debt relief measures have contributed to a continuing decline in the debt service ratio for the Continent, which reached 11.8 percent in 2004, the lowest in some two decades. Similarly, Africa's total debt in relation to its GDP continued its trend decline, reaching 43 percent from a high of 76 percent in 1994.

On the domestic front, most African countries made good progress towards sound macroeconomic policies and management. And although much remains to be done, many countries continued to pursue their programs of reforms, including privatization of state-owned enterprises, public sector reforms, and the strengthening of regulatory frameworks. Significant strides in creating a better environment for private sector participation and for attracting foreign direct investment were thus made, with many adopting policies to promote small and medium enterprises.

This combination of policies has resulted in strikingly improved key macro-economic indicators. For the first time, Africa's average fiscal position produced a balanced outcome in 2004, thanks to the fiscal surpluses achieved by many countries and prudent policies in most. Monetary growth was also quite restrained. These two factors contributed to an average inflation rate of 7.7 percent, the lowest in over two decades.

While welcoming the improved economic performance of the African economy, it should nonetheless be noted that the overall GDP growth rate is still below the 6–8 percent required to achieve the Millennium Development Goals (MDGs). Indeed, on current trends only the countries of North Africa, South Africa and Mauritius are likely to attain the goal of halving by 2015 the number of people living below the poverty line, although a number of others may meet some of the education and health MDGs. Clearly, African countries would need to build on the achievements of the recent past and accelerate their economic and social progress. This would require a number of policy measures.

First, it is essential that peaceful and stable conditions are maintained or restored. Second, countries would need to sustain the prudent macroeconomic policies that they have begun to implement as well as deepen their reform programs. In particular, financial sector and governance reforms are critical to create a more favorable climate for the growth of the private sector. Third, in an era of globalization, it is imperative that African countries strengthen their regional cooperation and integration arrangements, particularly in the context of the NEPAD initiative. And fourth, African countries would need to give high priority to combat the HIV/AIDS pandemic.

In all such efforts, African countries will continue to need the support of the international community. Such support is particularly critical with respect to official development assistance (ODA), debt reduction, and enhanced market access for Africa's exports. With respect to ODA, there have been sizeable increases in ODA to Africa in recent years, although much of it was accounted for by debt relief. Despite these developments — and as the recent report of the UN Millennium Project makes clear — ODA still falls short of what is required for Africa to be on course towards attaining the MDGs. It is, however, essential that the donor community takes further action to increase ODA in line with the pledges it had made earlier at Monterrey and other fora.

Progress has also been made in terms of reducing Africa's external debt burden — in part due to the HIPC initiative — but more needs to be done. In this regard, the recent decision by the G8 member countries to cancel the debts owed by post-completion HIPC countries to the international financial institutions is commendable. And with respect to external trade, the WTO July 2004

Framework holds the promise of elim- inating the tariff and non-tariff barriers for Africa's exports as well as reducing the trade-distorting agricultural subsidies of industrial countries.

Meeting the development challenges of Africa requires the state to be an effective regulator, facilitator and provider — the topic that the *African Development Report* deals with extensively this year. The Report addresses these and other public sector management reform issues in Africa and provides a number of recommendations.

The Report notes that a development-oriented state needs a strong administrative capacity, with an efficient, open, and accountable public service. This is critical for designing and implementing sound policies, managing the public sector, regulating the private sector and providing key services — particularly in public health, education and some infrastructure services — where the private sector may be reluctant to invest. To perform these essential development functions more effectively, African governments would need to build a public service capable of understanding the challenges of develop- ment, evaluating development policy proposals, and effectively implementing them.

Clearly, these tasks are best performed under conditions of good political and economic governance. By contrast, lack of accountability and transparency, and corruption often serve to undermine competitiveness, economic growth and development. Despite the significant progress that most African countries have made in the past decade in developing and

institutionalizing democratic institutions much remains to be done. In particular, African governments would need to redouble their efforts to fight corruption.

In assessing public sector management reforms in Africa, the Report finds that good progress has been made in a number of countries. Nonetheless, the process of rationalizing the role of the state and adapting it to the requirements of a modern competitive economy remains a major challenge in many. A number of factors have contributed to this state of affairs. Past approaches to public sector management reforms have often relied heavily on strategies that failed to take account of the historical legacies and peculiarities of individual countries. Reform efforts have also often over-emphasized one facet of reform over others.

Given the limited success of such approaches, the Report recommends the adoption of a broader and long-term approach that takes into account the specificities of each country. Of critical importance in this regard is the need to mobilize political support among all stakeholders. In addition, success in public sector management reform requires a clarity of vision, the development of well-trained and professional administrators, and effective collaboration with all relevant stakeholders. A critical challenge in this regard is developing an effective incentive system to attract and retain skilled administrative officials. Clearly, when the incentive structures in the public service remain unattractive, its efficiency as well as ability to effect policies will remain very low.

As in past years, this year's *African Development Report* provides rich reference material on the African economy and on public sector management reforms in Africa. I am confident that policy makers, researchers, and representatives of the civil society and the private sector on the continent and elsewhere will find the information and analysis useful.

Omar Kabbaj
President
African Development Bank

ACKNOWLEDGEMENTS

The *African Development Report 2005* has been prepared by a staff team in the Development Research Department under the direction of Henock Kifle.

The research team was led by Mohamed Nureldin Hussain and comprised Mohammed Salisu, Barfour Osei, Bernhard Gunter, Audrey Verdier-Chouchane and Christina Okojie (consultant) from the Research Division.

The Economic and Social Statistics on Africa were prepared by the Statistics Division led by Charles L. Lufumpa and comprised André Portella, Beejaye Kokil, Maurice Mubila and Koua Louis Kouakou.

Rhoda R. Bangurah provided production services and Richard Synge editorial services.

Preparation of the *Report* was aided by the background papers listed in the bibliographical note. Comments from within and outside the Bank are noted with appreciation. From the Bank, Claudius Bamidele Olowu; and from outside, Janine Aron of the Centre for the Study of African Economies, University of Oxford; Goran Hyden of the University of Florida; Ladipo Adamolekun, an Independent Scholar; Charlotte Vaillant, an Independent Consultant; Joseph Ayee of the University of Ghana all made comments and suggestions to improve the *Report*. Dominic Byatt and Claire Croft at Oxford University Press oversaw the editiorial and publication process.

ABBREVIATIONS

AAF-SAP	African Alternative Framework to Structural Adjustment Programs
AAPAM	African Association for Public Administration and Management
APPER	Africa's Priority Programme for Economic Recovery
ADB	African Development Bank
ADF	African Development Fund
ACP	African, Caribbean and Pacific
ADR	African Development Report
AFRACA	African Rural and Agricultural Credit Association
AFROSAI	African Organization of Supreme Audit Institutions
AGOA	African Growth and Opportunity Act
AIDS	Acquired Immune Deficiency Syndrome
ANC	African National Congress
APC	Adaptable Program Credit
APL	Adaptable Program Loan
APRM	African Peer Review Mechanism
AsDB	Asian Development Bank
ATLE	Africa's Ten Largest Economies
AU	African Union
BAC	Botswana Accountancy College
BCC	Banque Centrale du Congo
BCEAO	Banque Centrale des Etats de l'Afrique de l'Ouest
BEAC	Banque des Etats d'Afrique Centrale
BEST	Business Environment Strengthening in Tanzania
BNA	Banco Nacional de Angola
BoB	Bank of Botswana
BoM	Bank of Mauritius
BOO	Build-Own-Operate
BOT	Build-Operate-Transfer
BOU	Bank of Uganda
CAR	Central African Republic
CDF	Comprehensive Development Framework
CFA	Communaute Financiere Africaine
CFAA	Country Financial Accountability Assessment
CGP	Country Governance Profile
CIDA	Canadian International Development Agency
CIP	Competitive Industrial Performance
CITI	Corruption Index of Transparency International

COMESA	Common Market of East and Southern Africa
CPAR	Country Procurement Assessment Report
CPMS	Computerized Personnel Management System
CSO	Civil Society Organization
DAC	Development Assistance Committee
DANIDA	Danish International Development Agency
DFID	Department for International Development
DMO	Debt Management Office
DPSA	Department of Public Service Administration
DRC	Democratic Republic of Congo
EAC	East African Community
EBRD	European Bank for Cooperation and Development
EC	European Commission
ECA	UN Economic Commission for Africa
ECZ	Electoral Commission in Zambia
EIB	European Investment Bank
EPZ	Export Processing Zone
ERP	Economic Recovery Program
ESAAG	East and Southern Association of Accountants General
EU	European Union
FAO	UN Food and Agriculture Organization
FDI	Foreign Direct Investment
FMOC	Financial Markets Operations Committee
GCA	Global Coalition for Africa
GDP	Gross Domestic Product
GENA	Global Education Network for Africa
GTZ	Technische Zusammenarbeit
HIV	Human Immunodeficiency Virus
IADB	Inter-American Development Bank
ICPC	Independent Corrupt Practices Commission
ICT	Information and Communications Technology
IDA	International Development Association
IDB	Islamic Development Bank
IDF	Institutional Development Facility
IFAD	International Bank for Agricultural Development
IMF	International Monetary Fund
IRIS	Integrated Risk Information System
ITD	International Tax Dialogue
KACA	Kenya Anti-Corruption Authority
KUBI	Kenyan Urban Bribery Index

LIL	Learning and Innovation Loan
LNAT	Learning Networks for African Teachers
MCPC	Monetary and Credit Policy Committee
MDBs	Multilateral Development Banks
MENA	Middle East and North Africa
MFA	Multi-Fiber Agreement
MFIs	Multilateral Financial Institutions
MFN	Most Favored Nations
MHT	Medium and High Technology
MITI	Ministry of International Trade and Industry
MMD	Movement for Multiparty Democracy
MOU	Memorandum of Understanding
MP	Member of Parliament
MTEF	Medium Term Expenditure Framework
MVA	Manufacturing Value Added
NAI	National Audit Institution
NDF	Nordic Development Fund
NEPAD	New Economic Partnership for Africa's Development
NIB	Nordic Investment Bank
NIE	New Institutional Economics
NGO	Non-Governmental Organization
NPM	New Public Management
O&M	Organization and Methods
OAU	Organization for African Unity
ODA	Official Development Assistance
OECD	Organization for Economic Cooperation and Development
OPEC	Organization of Petroleum Exporting countries
PA	Public Administration
PAC	Public Accounts Committee
PBRS	Performance Based Reward System
PCT	Public Choice Theory
PE	Public Enterprises
PEM	Public Expenditure Management
PER	Public Expenditure Review
PMS	Performance Management System
PPP	Public Private Partnership
PRGF	Poverty Reduction and Growth Facility
PRSP	Poverty Reduction Strategy Paper
RDBs	Regional Development Banks
RMC	Regional Member Country

RMP	Reserve Money Program
SAC	Structural Adjustment Credit
SACU	Southern African Customs Union
SADC	Southern African Development Community
SAL	Structural Adjustment Loan
SAP	Structural Adjustment Program
SAPRI	Structural Adjustment Programs Review Initiatives
SARB	South African Reserve Bank
SASE	Selective Accelerated Salary Enhancement
SES	Senior Executive Service
SFH	Société Forestière Hazim
SIDA	Swedish International Development Agency
SIPs	Sector Investment Programs
SMB	Seychelles Marketing Board
SOE	State Owned Enterprises
SPA	Strategic Partnership with Africa
SSA	Sub-Saharan Africa
STAP	Scientific Technical Advisory Panel
SWAP	Sector-Wide Approach
TA	Technical Assistance
TI	Transparency International
TOR	Tema Oil Refinery
UDB	Ugandan Development Bank
UEMOA	Union Economique et Monetaire Ouest Africaine
UMA	Union du Magreb Arabe
UN	United Nations
UNCCA	UN Common Country Assessment
UNCTAD	United Nations Conference on Trade and Development
UNDAF	UN Development Assistance Framework
UNDP	United Nations Development Program
UNESCO	United Nations Educational, Scientific and Cultural Organization
UNIDO	United Nations Industrial Development Organization
UNIFEM	United Nations Fund for Women
UNSIA	UN Special Initiative for Africa
UK	United Kingdom
US	United States
USAID	United States Agency for International Development
VAT	Value Added Tax
WAEMU	West African Economic and Monetary Union
WB	World Bank

WBI   World Bank Institute
WFP   World Food Program
WITS   Work Improvement Teams
WTO   World Trade Organization
ZCCM   Zambia Consolidated Copper Mines

CONTENTS

PART ONE: AFRICA IN THE WORLD ECONOMY

PART TWO: PUBLIC SECTOR MANAGEMENT IN AFRICA

PART THREE: ECONOMIC AND SOCIAL STATISTICS ON AFRICA

BOXES

Text Figures

Text Tables

PART ONE

AFRICA IN THE WORLD ECONOMY

CHAPTER 1
The African Economy in 2004

Introduction

Africa's economic growth rate in 2004 was 5.1 percent, higher than in any year since 1996. This encouraging performance resulted from a combination of factors: a rise in demand for many African raw materials and commodities, improved trade access for African exports, greater macro-economic stability in the majority of countries, further easing of debt burdens and, equally importantly, a lessening of some of the continent's major conflicts. Africa's 2004 growth rate equaled the rate recorded for the global economy as a whole but was below the rates for other developing regions. While Africa's per capita growth rate has so far remained too low to bring about significant reduction of overall poverty levels, it has been improving year on year — although few African countries now seem likely to reach the Millennium Development Goals by 2015.

Africa's Ten Largest Economies (ATLEs), which recorded growth near to the continental average in 2004, continued to register a relatively strong macroeconomic performance. Indeed, the continent as a whole recorded improved overall macro-economic stability, which was manifested by a continuing slackening of inflation rates, a reduction in fiscal imbalances, and a positive external position. Debt service ratios were well down on previous years, and national savings levels also began to rise.

This chapter provides an overview of the performance of the African economy in 2004. The first part evaluates overall growth and macroeconomic performance. It also highlights sub-regional growth perform-ances (their performances are discussed in greater detail in Chapter 2). It analyzes the performance of the ATLEs, which account for three-quarters of total African GDP, and surveys the performance of major sectors, including agriculture, industry, services and energy.

In the second part of the chapter, some of the factors influencing African economic performance are examined. The impact of external factors on the African economy is discussed, particularly in the light of the high commodity and oil prices and the depreciation of the US dollar in 2004. The role of domestic macroeconomic manage-ment, and regional policies, in Africa's growth performance for 2004 is also reviewed. The chapter concludes with medium-term prospects for the African economy, based on a projected global growth scenario.

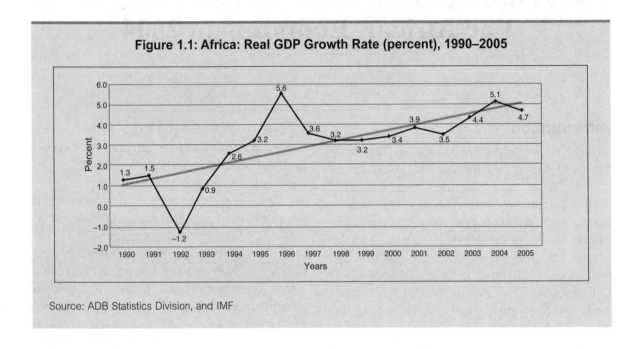

Figure 1.1: Africa: Real GDP Growth Rate (percent), 1990–2005

Source: ADB Statistics Division, and IMF

Performance of the African Economy[1]

Stronger Growth Amid Global Recovery

Real GDP growth in Africa in 2004 rose to 5.1 percent, from 4.4 percent in 2003, following a continued upward trend since 1999 (see Figure 1.1 and Table 1.1). This is the highest rate of growth Africa has experienced since 1996, and has occurred against a backdrop of global recovery and improved terms of trade for Africa. Underlying the improvement is a greater demand for commodities and oil at higher prices with improved world growth, greater macroeconomic stability in African coun-

tries, some improved access for African exports, and further easing of debt burdens in some countries under the Heavily Indebted Poor Countries (HIPC) initiative. Several countries rebounded in 2004 from severe droughts in 2003, although some Southern African countries experienced poor weather conditions in 2004. Other countries expanded oil production, benefiting from the rapid rise in international oil prices. Finally, conflict was reduced in several regions, though conflict in the Darfur region in Sudan together with renewed conflict in Côte d'Ivoire, and continued economic and political instability in Zimbabwe all remain causes for concern.

Africa's growth rate in 2004 translates into a real per capita growth rate of 2.8 percent, up from 2.1 percent in the

---

[1] The cut-off date for the 2004 data used in this chapter is 28 February 2005. The estimates provided may, therefore, change slightly as they are firmed up in the course of the year.

Table 1.1: Africa: Macroeconomic Indicators, 2000– 2004[a]

		2000	2001	2002	2003	2004[b]
1.	Real GDP Growth Rate	3.4	3.9	3.5	4.4	5.1
2.	Real Per Capita GDP Growth Rate	1.1	1.6	1.2	2.1	2.8
3.	Inflation (%)	13.5	10.5	9.1	10.0	7.7
4.	Investment Ratio (% of GDP)	18.9	19.6	20.1	20.0	20.1
5.	Fiscal Balance (% of GDP)	–0.5	–2.2	–3.0	–1.4	0.0
6.	Growth of Money Supply (%)	17.9	19.3	18.5	18.0	15.6
7.	Export Growth, volume (%)	9.3	0.8	1.0	7.2	4.6
8.	Import Growth, volume (%)	2.5	4.2	4.5	5.8	7.2
9.	Terms of Trade (%)	14.8	–3.5	1.0	3.8	6.7
10.	Trade Balance ($ billion)	24.8	10.2	6.7	15.6	8.7
11.	Current Account ($ billion)	5.0	–1.5	–6.2	1.3	5.1
12.	Current Account (% of GDP)	0.9	–0.3	–1.1	0.2	0.7
13.	Debt Service (% of Exports)	16.2	16.6	17.2	13.2	11.8
14.	National Savings (% of GDP)	18.9	18.4	18.4	19.7	19.8
15.	Net Capital Inflows ($ billion)	15.4	21.8	25.7	35.6	...
16.	FDI ($ billion)	14.5	33.7	19.9	24.3	...
17.	FDI (% of FDI to developing countries)	5.8	15.4	12.6	14.1	...

Notes: [a] Calendar year
         [b] Preliminary estimates
         ... Not available
Source: ADB Statistics Division and IMF.

previous year, on an improving trend from 1999 (when per capita growth measured 0.9 percent). However, this fairly modest per capita growth improvement has to be seen in the context of the MDGs, which call for reducing the proportion of people living on less than $1 a day to half the 1990 level by 2015 — from 27.9 percent of all people in low and middle income economies to 14.0 percent. The goal of halving the incidence of poverty by 2015 requires a sustained growth in per capita income. On average, African countries require per capita growth rate of 4.6 percent per annum, translating into a GDP growth rate of more than 7 percent, to be able to achieve the MDGs.

However, there is considerable variation in the growth requirement across countries, ranging from Benin which needs less than 1 percent per capita annual growth, to Guinea-Bissau, where poverty has worsened in the last decade, and which requires nearly 12 percent per capita annual growth. The weighted average per capita growth target for resource rich economies is 4.1 percent a year, but for conflict-torn economies, like Democratic Republic of Congo (DRC), Liberia and Sierra Leone, per capita incomes must now grow at over 8 percent a year (UNIDO, 2004).

Improvements in Growth and Per Capita Growth Distribution

Apart from the growth level variations across countries, there can also be considerable volatility in individual countries' growth rates over time. Because of their vulnerability to external shocks of various kinds, and to conflict in some regions, it has proved difficult for many African countries to sustain higher growth rates at levels postulated by the MDGs. Agriculture, the mainstay of GDP in many African countries, is especially vulnerable to changing climatic conditions and drought. In 2004, however, agricultural recovery after droughts in the 2002/03 season accounted for sharply improved performance in Ethiopia, Malawi and Rwanda while, on the other hand, Lesotho and Swaziland were seriously affected by poor weather in 2004. Variable export prices affect producers with a strong dependence on one or a few commodities in their export baskets. Large increases in oil production in Angola, Chad, and Equatorial Guinea, at much increased oil prices, elevated growth. Higher metal commodity prices benefited South Africa and other metal exporters; but poor cocoa prices impacted badly on Côte d'Ivoire. Conflict also seriously affects growth and its abatement in several countries has improved their performance in 2004 (e.g.

Central African Republic [CAR] and Burundi). However, the spillover effects of conflict are substantial and protracted, with displacement of people both internationally, as refugees, and internally within a war-torn country. Demobilization, repatriation and resettlement is a slow and costly process, and also accounts for much of the poor growth and food insecurity currently in Africa, as discussed below.

The variation in the growth performance of African countries has not altered greatly from 2003, but overall there has been an improvement (see Table 1.2). Notably, the number of countries in the category of negative growth fell from six in 2003 to three in 2004. Those remaining are Cote d'Ivoire, Zimbabwe and the Seychelles (see Table 1.3). In 2004, a total of 20 countries (as opposed to 25 in 2003) had growth in excess of 5 percent. Five countries placed in this category in 2003 moved down to the 3–5 percent growth category in 2004 (Botswana, Burkina Faso, Cape Verde, Morocco, and Nigeria), while four countries moved further down to the 0–3 percent group (Lesotho, Libya, Mali, and Niger). In contrast, Angola, Burundi, Ethiopia, and Uganda moved up from the 3–5 percent or lower categories in 2003 to the over 5 percent growth category in 2004. Angola's improved performance benefited from oil production increases and high oil prices, but the big improved performers were Burundi and Ethiopia. Both countries moved up from the negative growth category to the growth category above 5 percent; there was a reduction of conflict in Burundi, and Ethiopia has rebounded after devastating drought.

Figure 1.2: Africa and the MDGs: Differences between Current and Required GDP Growth Rates for Countries to Reach the Millennium Development Goals by 2015

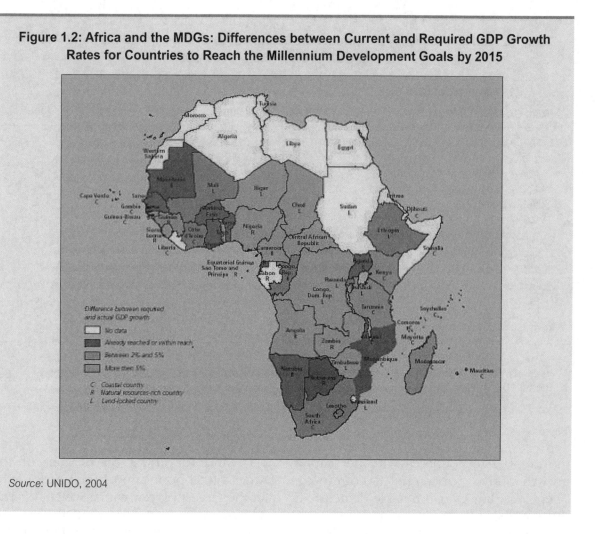

Source: UNIDO, 2004

The 0–3 and 3–5 percent growth categories had equal numbers of countries in both 2003 (ten) and 2004 (fourteen) — an increase of 4 countries in each group. Surprisingly, with the exception of Djibouti, all the new entrants into the 0–3 percent growth category in 2004 were countries which experienced growth rates in excess of 5 percent in 2003. Similarly, of all the new entrants into the 3–5 percent growth category in 2004, only Kenya had an upward mobility.

The per capita growth distribution exhibits a slightly different pattern from that of GDP growth. There was virtually little or no variation in the distribution of countries in all categories between 2003 and 2004 (see Table 1.2). The number of countries with negative per capita growth remained unchanged (12 countries), as was

Table 1.2: Africa: Frequency Distribution of Countries According to Real GDP and Real Per Capita GDP Growth Rates, 2000–2004

Number of Countries **Real GDP Growth Rate (%)**	**2000**	**2001**	**2002**	**2003**	**2004**[a]
Negative	11	4	6	6	3
0–3	13	15	15	10	14
Above 3 to 5	11	13	19	10	14
Above 5	16	19	11	25	20
Not available	2	2	2	2	2
Total	53	53	53	53	53
Real Per Capita GDP Growth Rate (%)					
Negative	18	12	15	12	12
0–1.5	10	12	10	6	5
Above 1.5 to 5	18	20	19	25	26
Above 5	5	7	7	8	8
Not available	2	2	2	2	2
Total	53	53	53	53	53

Note: [a] Preliminary estimates
Source: ADB Statistics Division.

the number of countries with per capita growth above 5 percent (8 countries). There was, however, a notable decrease in the number of countries in the 0–1.5 percent per capita growth category (from 6 in 2003 to 5 in 2004). In consequence, there was an additional one country in 2004 in the 1.5–5 percent per capita growth category.

Performance of Africa's Ten Largest Economies

The group of Africa's Ten Largest Economies (ATLEs) accounts for over 77 percent of total African GDP (see Table

1.4), and for about 55 percent of the Africa's total population. South Africa is by far the largest player, with a weight of over 27 percent in total African GDP. The next three, in order of size, are Algeria, Egypt and Nigeria — together they account for nearly 30 percent of African GDP. Since 2003, Algeria and Egypt, and also Libya and Tunisia, have swapped rankings in the table.

The ATLE countries saw a marginal fall in the weighted real growth rate from 4.8 to 4.4 percent, between 2003 and 2004, below the continental average of 5.1 percent. In all but four of these economies, the growth

Table 1.3: Country Growth Categories, by Real GDP Growth Rates, 2003–2004

Real GDP Growth Rate (%)	2003	2004
Negative	6	3
	Burundi (–1.2 %), Côte d'Ivoire (–1.7 %), Ethiopia (–3.9 %), Seychelles (–6.3 %), CAR (–7.0 %), Zimbabwe (–10.3 %)	Côte d'Ivoire (–2.0 %), Seychelles (–2.0 %) and Zimbabwe (–4.8 %)
0–3	10	14
	Eritrea (3.0%), South Africa (2.8 %), Gabon (2.8%), Swaziland (2.4 %), Comoros (2.1 %), Kenya (1.8 %), Guinea (1.2 %), Rwanda (0.9%), Congo (0.8 %), Guinea Bissau (0.6%)	Benin (2.2%), Togo (2.9 %), Guinea (2.5 %), CAR (0.9 %), Comoros (1.9 %), Eritrea (1.8%), Gabon (1.6%), Swaziland (2.1 %), Guinea Bissau (1.0%), Lesotho (2.3 %), Niger (1.0%), Libya (0.9%), Mali (2.1%), Djibouti (3.0%)
Above 3 to 5	10	14
	Uganda (4.7%), Benin (3.0%), Malawi (3.9 %), Mauritius (4.3%), Cameroon (4.3 %), Namibia (3.7 %), Djibouti (3.5%), Angola (3.4%), Egypt (3.2 %), Togo (4.4%)	Burkina Faso (4.0 %), Cameroon (4.1 %), Rwanda (4.0%), Mauritius (4.1%), Nigeria (3.7%), Congo (4.0 %), Egypt (4.3 %), South Africa (3.8 %), Malawi (4.3 %), Namibia (4.4 %), Morocco (3.5 %), Kenya (3.1%), Botswana (4.4%), Cape Verde (4.0%)
Above 5	25	20
	Equatorial Guinea (11.0%), Nigeria (10.7%), Madagascar (9.8%), Chad (12.5%), Burkina Faso (8.0%), Tanzania (7.1%), Mozambique (7.1%), Algeria (6.9%), Gambia (6.7%), Sierra Leone (8.6%), Senegal (6.5%), Sudan (6.0%), Mali (7.4 %), DRC (5.7%), Tunisia (5.6%), Botswana (5.2 %), Cape Verde (5.3%), Morocco (5.5 %), Zambia (5.1 %), Niger (5.3%), Ghana (5.2%), Sao Tome & Principe (5.5%), Libya (5.3%), Mauritania (6.6%), Lesotho (5.2%)	Chad (31.3%), Equatorial Guinea (59.8%), Ethiopia (11.5 %), Angola (10.9%), Mozambique (7.8%), Gambia (7.7%), Sierra Leone (7.4%), Sudan (7.3%), Sao Tome & Principe (6.1%), DRC (6.8%), Tanzania (7.4%), Senegal (6.0%), Algeria (5.4%), Uganda (5.9%), Tunisia (5.5%), Burundi (5.5 %), Madagascar (5.3%), Ghana (5.8%), Mauritania (5.2%), Zambia (5.1%)
Not available	2	2
	Liberia and Somalia	Liberia and Somalia
Total	53	53

Source: ADB Statistics Division

rate fell. In some oil producers, such as Angola, Sudan and Tunisia, growth rates exceeded 5 percent, given the surge in oil prices and increased oil production in all, save for Tunisia. The sharp rise in the Angola's growth rate relative to 2003, from 3.4 to 10.9 percent, can be accounted for by a big expansion in the value of oil production as well as the post-conflict dividends. Sudan witnessed the second highest growth rate in the ATLE zone, at 7.3 percent in 2004 (up from 6.0 percent in 2003). It too benefited from the high oil production and prices. Egypt also experienced improved economic performance in 2004; growth accelerated to 4.3 percent, up from 3.2 percent in 2003 recovery from effects of both the war in Iraq and lower tourism receipts. South Africa's growth rate

recovered from 2.8 percent in 2003 to 3.8 percent in 2004 owing to increased mining production and a rebound in the manufacturing and services sectors, despite the appreciation of the rand.

The decline in overall growth of ATLEs is accounted for by the deterioration in growth in four of the biggest players: Algeria, Morocco, Nigeria and Libya. Algeria — a member of OPEC, with increased oil production in 2004 — experienced a deceleration in growth (from 6.9 percent in 2003 to 5.4 percent in 2004). The slowdown in real growth in Algeria was partly on account of a slower expansion of hydrocarbon output and partly due to slower agriculture growth following the 2003 bumper crop. Morocco too experienced a slowdown in growth —

Table 1.4: Africa's Ten Largest Economies (ATLEs), 2004

Country	GDP at current US$ (Billions)	Population (Millions)	GDP Growth Rate (%)	Country Weight in total African GDP (%)
SOUTH AFRICA	214.2	45.21	3.8	27.0
ALGERIA	82.4	32.34	5.4	10.4
EGYPT	75.5	73.39	4.3	9.5
NIGERIA	72.3	127.12	3.7	9.1
MOROCCO	50.2	31.06	3.5	6.3
LIBYA	30.4	5.66	0.9	3.8
TUNISIA	28.2	9.94	5.5	3.6
SUDAN	20.5	34.33	7.3	2.6
ANGOLA	20.3	14.08	10.9	2.6
CAMEROON	16.0	16.30	4.1	2.0
TOTAL ATLE	**610.0**	**389.4**	**4.4**	**77.0**

Source: ADB Statistics Division, UN and IMF.

Table 1.5: Macroeconomic Indicators for ALTE*, 2000–2004

Indicators	2000	2001	2002	2003	2004
1. Real GDP Growth Rate	4.0	3.5	3.6	4.8	4.4
2. Real Per Capita GDP Growth Rate	2.0	1.4	1.6	2.8	2.4
3. Inflation (%)	2.9	3.7	5.0	4.6	4.4
4. Investment Ratio (% of GDP)	19.1	19.8	21.2	20.5	20.6
5. Fiscal Balance (% of GDP)	0.4	−1.9	−2.6	−1.2	0.3
6. Growth of Money Supply (%)	14.4	17.8	19.5	14.7	8.7
7. Export Growth, volume (%)	10.5	0.2	−0.4	7.2	3.6
8. Import Growth, volume (%)	3.4	3.9	6.7	4.1	7.4
9. Terms of Trade (%)	20.7	−3.2	0.1	4.1	9.5
10. Trade Balance ($ billion)	26.8	15.9	8.3	22.1	36.0
11. Current Account ($ billion)	17.1	8.2	−1.5	9.3	17.3
12. Current Account (% of GDP)	3.8	1.9	−0.4	1.9	3.1
13. Debt Service (% of Exports)	15.8	16.5	15.4	13.6	12.0
14. National Savings (% of GDP)	22.9	21.1	20.4	21.6	22.4
15. Net Capital Inflows ($ billion)	1.3	7.1	11.6	11.0	...
16. FDI ($ billion)	5.6	15.6	7.5	9.4	...
17. FDI (% to developing countries)	2.2	7.1	4.8	5.5	...

* ALTE: South Africa, Algeria, Egypt, Nigeria, Morocco, Libya, Tunisia, Sudan, Angola and Cameroon.
... Not available
Source: ADB Statistics Division and IMF.

from 5.5 percent in 2003 to 3.5 percent in 2004 — due to slower growth in cereal production. Nigeria, however, recorded the biggest deceleration in growth in the ATLE zone; GDP growth rate declined sharply from 10.7 in 2003 to 3.7 percent in 2004, following a series of work stoppages and disruptions in oil production. Libya, in 2004, witnessed its slowest growth performance since 1999; growth rate decelerated to 0.9 percent in 2004, down from 5.3 percent in 2003. With the fall in real GDP growth for the ATLEs, there was also a marginal fall in the per capita growth rate, from 2.8 to 2.4 percent (see Table 1.5).

The fiscal performance, however, has improved in these economies. The overall fiscal deficit to GDP ratio has declined since 2002, from 2.6 percent to 1.2 percent in 2003, and in 2004, the fiscal balance turned into a surplus of 0.3 percent of GDP. The overall fiscal performance mirrored the situations in individual ATLE countries; all countries witnessed improved fiscal balance, except Sudan and Egypt. Four ATLE countries (Algeria, Cameroon, Libya and Nigeria) recorded fiscal surpluses of varying degrees in 2004, while the rest had manageable fiscal deficits. Only Egypt had a fiscal deficit, which was rather excessive and rising; 6.0 percent of GDP in 2004, up from 5.4 percent of GDP in 2003. Sudan too saw its fiscal deficit rise, albeit modestly, from 0.4 percent of GDP in 2003 to 1.2 percent in 2004. All the other ALTE countries that recorded fiscal deficits witnessed significant improvements in 2004. For instance, Angola's fiscal deficit declined to 3.5 percent of GDP (from 6.6 percent of GDP in 2003), while fiscal deficits in Morocco, South Africa and Tunisia fell to 2.5 percent of GDP or lower.

The improved fiscal performance of the ATLEs in 2004 translated into a slower growth in consumer prices. Inflation in these countries declined, from 4.6 to 4.4 percent. Again, this reflected the falling inflation in all but three ATLE countries; Algeria, Egypt and Tunisia are the only countries with rising inflation. The overall performance of the ATLE countries played a crucial role in the trend in Africa's overall inflation, which decelerated from 10.0 percent in 2003 to 7.7 percent in 2004.

As a result of increases in oil receipts, the trade balance for the ATLEs rose very strongly to $36.0 billion from $22 billion in 2003, and more than four times the value in 2002. Consequently the current account registered an improvement from 1.9 percent of GDP in 2003 to 3.1 percent in 2004. Both exports and imports, in volume terms, grew in 2004 the growth of the latter accelerated while that of the former decelerated. The rapid increase in import growth largely reflects growth in domestic demand.

National savings rates for ATLEs, at 22.4 percent of GDP in 2004, were slightly below their level in 2000 (22.9 percent), but

have been fairly steady in the last few years. ATLE rates are higher than the African average of 19.8 percent. The North African ATLE countries had the highest savings ratios and South Africa the lowest. Data on compensatory 'foreign saving' in the form of net capital inflows, particularly FDI, are available only for 2003. They indicated an increase over the previous year, but were still below the 2001 levels.

Sub-Regional Growth Performances

Regional variations in growth rates are shown in Table 1.6, both for the geographical sub-regions and for a variety of sub-regional economic groupings. Three of the geographical sub-regions experienced improvements in real GDP growth between 2003 and 2004, in each case quite substantial. Growth in Central Africa rose from 5.0 to 14.4 percent. That of East Africa rose from 2.3 to 6.8 percent. Southern Africa experienced a more modest improvement from 2.6 to 4.0 percent. In contrast, Northern Africa experienced a slight decline from 5.1 to 4.6 percent; while the weighted growth figure for West Africa fell sharply from 7.0 to 3.4 percent. Details on the performance of each sub-region are given in Boxes 1.1–1.5.

There is a striking variability in sub-regional growth rates. Conflict in Central Africa caused very low growth in 2000 but since then there has been a rebound in growth, with sustained high rates for a few years, and a sharp increase in 2004, aided by increases in commodity and oil prices. East Africa experienced unusually low rates of growth in 2002 and 2003, following severe droughts, but has since recovered. Growth has also been volatile in West Africa, because of external commodity price shocks, conflict and drought. Growth fell from 3.9 to 2.5 percent between 2001 and 2002, then rose to 7.0 percent and fell again to 3.4 per cent in the subsequent two years. Southern Africa is wholly dominated by the performance of the South African economy, and has shown minimal variability since 2001 (between 2.7 and 4.0 percent), despite volatile performances by some of the other countries in this sub-region.

Table 1.6: Real GDP Growth Rates by Sub–Region, 2000–2004

	2000	2001	2002	2003	2004[a]
ADB Geographical sub–regions					
Central Africa	1.1	7.7	5.3	5.0	14.4
Eastern Africa	4.0	5.3	2.2	2.3	6.8
Northen Africa	3.8	4.0	3.5	5.1	4.6
Southern Africa	3.3	2.7	3.8	2.6	4.0
Western Africa	3.4	3.9	2.5	7.0	3.4
ADB Operational groupings					
ADF–eligible countries (incl. Blend countries)	2.6	4.1	3.5	4.7	5.5
ADF–only Countries	2.7	4.8	4.3	4.0	6.4
Blend countries	2.6	1.9	0.2	7.4	2.3
Non–ADF countries	3.9	3.8	3.5	4.2	4.8
Regional & economic groups					
AMU	2.3	4.0	3.4	6.1	4.4
CAEMC	5.0	13.1	5.6	5.7	19.9
COMESA	3.5	3.5	3.4	2.7	5.4
ECCAS	1.5	6.8	7.2	4.7	13.6
ECOWAS	3.4	3.9	2.5	7.0	3.4
FRANC ZONE	2.3	7.9	3.4	4.7	9.9
SADC	3.0	2.7	3.9	3.0	4.3
WAEMU	0.5	4.4	1.8	4.0	1.9
HIPC Countries	3.8	6.2	4.0	4.3	7.0
Net Oil Exporters	4.3	4.1	3.7	5.9	6.1
Net Oil Importers	2.9	3.8	3.3	3.3	4.4
ALL RMCs	**3.4**	**3.9**	**3.5**	**4.4**	**5.1**

Note: [a] Preliminary estimates.
Source: ADB Statistics Division.

Box 1.1. Sub-Regional Highlights — Central Africa

Central Africa's growth in 2003 surged to 14.4 percent from 5.0 percent in 2003, far exceeding the average for 2000–03 of 4.7 percent. The sub-region has ten countries and the smallest share of African GDP at 5.9 percent and contributes 7.4 percent of Africa's exports, with about 12 percent of the total African population. There was great variation in the performance of individual countries.

Star performers in 2004 growth rates were the following countries: Equatorial Guinea (59.8 percent), Chad (31.3 percent), Democratic Republic of Congo (6.8 percent), and São Tomé and Príncipe (6.1 percent). Growth in Equatorial Guinea and Chad was largely driven by increased oil production, while growth in the DRC was a result of post-conflict dividends. Burundi grew at 5.5 percent while Rwanda, another post-war country, saw growth at 4.0 percent, up from the 0.9 percent in 2003, but down from the 2000–03 average of 5.8 percent, and far below its high growth rates of 1995–2000. Both Cameroon and Gabon improved growth to 4.1 and 1.6 percent, respectively. Growth in both countries decelerated during 2004. The Central African Republic rebounded from two successive years of negative growth (–0.6 and –7.0 percent in 2002 and 2003 respectively). Thus the growth rate of 0.9 percent the country recorded in 2004 represented an improvement in economic performance.

Box 1.2. Sub-Regional Highlights — East Africa

East Africa saw a sharp rise in the growth rate of real GDP, from 2.3 percent in 2003 to 6.8 percent in 2004, far exceeding the average for 2000–03 of 3.4 percent. East Africa has the smallest share of African exports at 5.2 percent, and the second smallest share (behind Central Africa) of African GDP, measuring 6.8 percent. Yet East Africa, with 11 countries, is relatively populous with almost a quarter share of the total African population. Again there is considerable variation in the performance of individual countries. Kenya's economy is the largest in the sub-region, contributing around 2 percent of total African GDP. It is no longer the tenth but now the eleventh largest economy in Africa, as of 2004. Kenya's growth rate rose to 3.1 percent, up from 1.8 percent in 2003, buoyed by improved tourism receipts. By contrast, the economies of Tanzania and Uganda grew by over 5 percent each, at 7.4 and 5.9, respectively, exceeding their 2000–03 averages.

The star performer of the region was Ethiopia, with a growth rate of 11.5 percent, rebounding from negative growth under severe drought conditions in 2002/03, and exceeding its 2000–03 average of 2.7 percent. Madagascar, reversed its negative growth of 2002, occasioned by a political crisis, achieving 9.8 percent growth in 2003, and a strong 5.3 percent in 2004, larger than its 1995–2002 growth rate. Both Mauritius and Djibouti improved growth to 4.1 and 3.0 percent, respectively. Comoros, with 1.9 percent growth, maintained its steady low growth rate trend, at just over 2 percent in the last five years. Seychelles growth remained disappointingly negative, and averaged negative growth in 2000–03, hit hard by tourism competition from South Asia and the Caribbean. Post-war Eritrea grew at 1.8 percent, down from 3 percent in 2003, and exceeding the negative average for 2000–03. No data are available for Somalia, which has a humanitarian crisis, and widespread destitution.

Box 1.3. Sub-Regional Highlights — North Africa

The seven countries of North Africa account for the largest share of the African economy at 36.5 percent, and contribute a similar proportion of its exports, largely oil and gas. Real GDP growth for 2004 in the sub-region was 4.6 percent, down from 5.1 percent in 2003, but exceeding the 2000–2003 average of 4 percent. The sub-region accounts for 22.1 percent of the total African population.

Most countries in the sub-region grew by over 5 percent in 2004, with the exceptions of Egypt, Libya and Morocco, and most are oil producers, benefiting from expanded production and high oil prices. Growth decelerated in Morocco (from 5.5 to 3.5 percent in 2004), Libya (from 5.3 to 0.9 percent in 2004), Mauritania (6.6 to 5.2 percent), and Algeria (6.8 to 5.8 percent in 2004). The high weight of Algeria's economy in the sub-region (with 11 percent of African GDP alone), accounts for the marginal fall in overall sub-regional growth. In 2004, Sudan was the top performing economy in the region, with growth rate accelerating to 7.3 percent, up from 6.0 percent in 2003.

Tunisia continued to maintain a healthy growth rate, above 5 percent, as the country witnessed bumper harvests for the second year running in the agricultural sector. The Egyptian economy has somewhat recovered from effects of the war in Iraq and lower receipts in the tourism sector. Growth at 4.3 percent is up from 3.2 percent in 2003, but well below the average of 5.2 percent for 1995–2000.

Box 1.4. Sub-Regional Highlights — Southern Africa

More than a third of African GDP and 30.4 percent of African exports were generated in Southern Africa, with by far the largest contributor being South Africa (with a weight alone of over a quarter of African GDP). Output growth in Southern Africa rose from 2.6 percent in 2003 to 4.0 percent in 2004, also exceeding the 2000–03 average of 3.1 percent. Southern Africa, with ten countries, is relatively under-populated, with a share of Africa's population of 14 percent. The sub-region has been ravaged by HIV/AIDS in the last decade, experiencing the most serious incidence rates in all Africa.

High performers achieving growth rates in excess of 5 percent in 2004 included Angola at 10.9 percent, benefiting from high oil prices, and Mozambique, maintaining the exceptionally high growth it has recorded over an eight-year period, with output increasing by 7.8 percent in 2004. Zambia recorded the third highest growth rate in the region, at 5.1 percent due to the strengthening of copper and metal prices. Botswana and Namibia each grew at 4.4 percent in 2004. Botswana's growth, however, continues to be highly affected by the HIV/AIDS pandemic; its growth rate has been on a declining trend since 2002. South Africa grew at 3.8 percent, up from 2.8 percent in 2003, matching its performance in 2002 and exceeding its average growth in 1995-2001 of 2.85 percent.

Lesotho experienced a major drought in 2004, which decelerated its growth to 2.3 percent in 2004, down from 5.2 percent in 2003. Swaziland's growth has fallen since 2002 and registered 2.1 percent in 2004. The food security situation throughout Swaziland is serious, following a drought that reduced the 2004 cereal harvest by a third. Zimbabwe registered negative growth for the sixth year in a row, at −4.8 percent.

Box 1.5. Sub-Regional Highlights — West Africa

West Africa's sub-regional average growth of 3.4 percent fell below the 7.0 percent rate achieved in 2003, and also just below the 2000–2003 average of 4.2 percent. The sub-region produces just over a fifth of Africa's exports and has a 16.5 percent share of African GDP. It is the most populous region with 28.9 percent of the total African population, in 15 countries. The largest population by far is in Nigeria and numbers 127 million. Nigeria is also the largest economy in the region, and contributing 8 percent of Africa's GDP.

Star growth performers in the region were The Gambia (7.7 percent), Sierra Leone (7.4 percent), Senegal (6.0 percent), and Ghana (5.8 percent), and almost all surpassing their good performance in 2003. Post-war Sierra Leone is reaping the benefits of reconstruction and restoration of political stability in the country.

Nigeria's growth rate fell to 3.7 percent from 10.7 percent in 2003, largely caused by oil disruptions in the Niger Delta (oil producing area) and by economy-wide work stoppages to protest against domestic oil price increases. Given its weight in Africa's GDP, this helps explain the decline in regional growth. Benin, Burkina Faso,

Cape Verde, Mali, Niger, and Togo all experienced a decline in their GDP growth rate. Benin's growth has fallen to 2.2 percent from 3.9 percent in 2003, and far below its average growth, well in excess of 4 percent, in the preceding three years. Burkina Faso's growth also declined relative to 2003 and its earlier higher growth rates. Mali's growth has been rather volatile in the last four years — partly explained by the adverse impact of the crisis in Côte d'Ivoire, and registered a mere 2.1 percent growth in 2004. Guinea more than doubled its growth rate to 2.5 percent.

Côte d'Ivoire, experiencing significant civil disturbance since 2002, continued to register negative growth. A very modest growth perform-ance was recorded by Guinea-Bissau at 1 percent, up from 0.6 percent in 2000–2003. Guinea Bissau and Niger jointly had the second lowest growth in the region, after Cote d'Ivoire. There are no data for war-torn Liberia. In general, growth in the Francophone West African countries was much lower than that in the Anglophone countries, partly due to the appreciation of the CFA franc and partly due to the effects of the conflict in Cote d'Ivoire, their major trading partner in the region.

Macroeconomic Stability Has Generally Improved

Improved real GDP growth and real per capita growth in 2004 were accompanied by strengthened macroeconomic funda-mentals (see Figures 1.3 and 1.4). The fiscal outlook improved, with the fiscal deficit to GDP ratio declining since 2002, from 3.0 percent, through 1.4 percent in 2003, to zero percent in 2004. This result is to a degree driven by higher export receipts in the oil and commodity exporting econo-

mies, some of which dominate total African GDP. The fiscal position continues to be better than for developing and emerging countries as a whole.

The average inflation rate for Africa fell to halve of its 2000 rate, and from 10.0 to 7.7 percent relative to 2003, starting to close the gap with other developing and emerg-ing countries The African Economic Out-look, produced jointly by the ADB and OECD, projects a further fall in inflation to 7.1 percent in the coming year. While

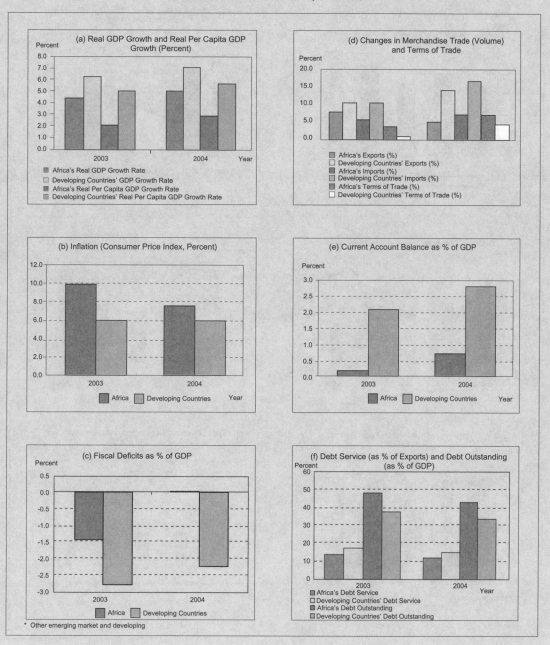

Figure 1.3: Developing and Other Emerging Market Countries* vis-à-vis Africa's Major Performance Indicators, 2003–2004

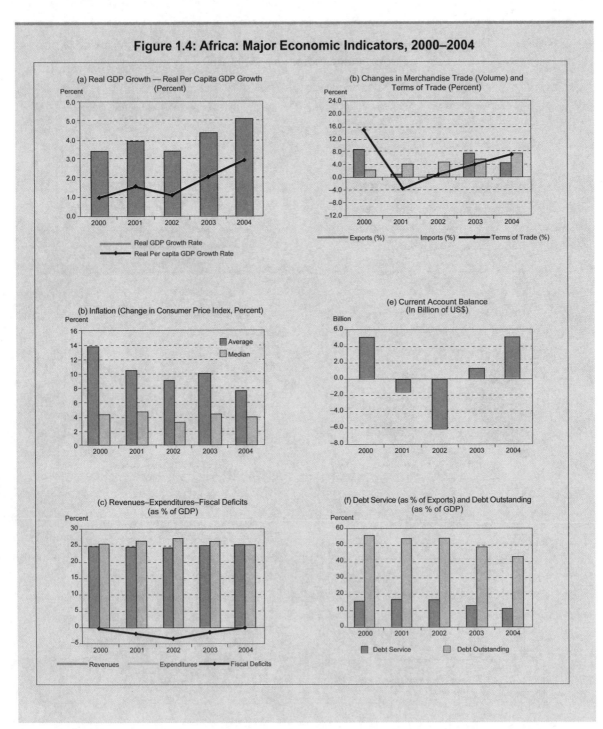

Figure 1.4: Africa: Major Economic Indicators, 2000–2004

macroeconomic stability has generally improved, there are inflationary pressures apparent in several countries such as Angola, Chad, Egypt, Gambia, Guinea, Kenya, Nigeria, Rwanda, Sao Tome & Principe, Zambia, and Zimbabwe. The fiscal and monetary policy issues are discussed below.

In North, Central and East Africa, all countries recorded inflation below 10 percent. In the West African sub-region, there was double-digit inflation in The Gambia, Ghana (improving), Guinea, Liberia and Nigeria. In Southern Africa, South Africa's inflation, at 2.6 percent, has been reduced to below the 3-6 percent inflation-targeting band, and all other countries in the sub-region recorded inflation below 10 percent, except Angola (improving to 43.5 percent), Zambia (worsening to 17.8 percent) and Zimbabwe (worsening to 350 percent). Unsurprisingly, given political instability and severe economic problems, Zimbabwe is the worst inflation performer in Africa, with triple digit inflation twice its average 2000–03 inflation rate. This is causing serious hardships to millions of its citizens, along with food shortages from sharply contracted output.

Investment and Savings

The African gross national investment to GDP ratio has been fairly static, at around 20 percent throughout the last three years, though this clearly masks considerable country variations. In North Africa, investment ratio has averaged around 23 percent of GDP since 2000. Egypt and Libya are the only countries with an investment ratio below 20 percent in 2004

(16.7 and 12.6 percent, respectively). High gross national savings ratios to GDP are also common in this region, with an average of 27.6 percent. The two largest oil-producing countries in the region, Algeria and Libya, registered the highest savings ratios of 40.7 percent and 33.8 percent, respectively, in 2004. In contrast, Sudan had the lowest savings ratio of 13.5 percent, up from the 5.9 percent recorded in 2003.

Southern Africa, which was the worst performing region in terms of national investment ratio during 2000–03 (17.5 percent), witnessed a significant improvement in 2004; average investment to GDP ratio rose to 20 percent. High investment ratios were posted by Mozambique (44.3 percent), Angola (33.4 percent), and Lesotho (31.4 percent). The sub-region's savings ratio was 15.1 percent, marginally better than that of the weakest performer, East Africa. Botswana was the strongest performer with a savings ratio of 36.9 percent, followed by Namibia, with 28.3 percent. Zimbabwe, with a negative savings ratio of 4 percent (evidence of dissaving in the economy) was the weakest link, followed by Malawi with a meager savings ratio of 1.0 percent (up from a negative rate of 0.4 percent in 2003). The other countries had savings ratio ranging from 11.8 percent (Zambia) to 25.1 percent (Lesotho).

The remaining three sub-regions had average investment ratios in the region of 18 to 20 percent. Saving ratios averaged 18.5 percent in Central Africa, driven by the extremely high rate of savings in Gabon (37 percent). In West Africa, the savings ratio averaged 18 percent, with only two countries, Ghana and Nigeria, achieving over 20 percent. The worst performing African sub-region in terms of savings was East Africa, with a savings-to-GDP ratio for 2004 of only 14.7 percent. Rates were uniformly low, except for Mauritius (26.1 percent) and Uganda (18.7 percent).

Terms of Trade

Probably the most striking statistic for 2004 is the significant improvement in the terms of trade for Africa as a whole, which grew at 6.7 percent in 2004 relative to about 4 percent average growth during 2000–2003, and 3.8 percent growth in 2003. In 2001, the terms of trade had actually deteriorated (negative growth in the terms of trade), while terms of trade growth was very low at 1 percent in 2002. In 2004, high oil and commodities prices favored oil and metals exporters, but penalized oil importers. More detail is provided on the net gainers and losers amongst African countries, in the latter part of this chapter.

Regionally, North Africa sustained a terms of trade growth improvement, from 5.4 percent in 2000–2003 to 6.5 percent in 2004, with big gains for the oil exporters. However, the improvement was positive though small for Egypt, while Mauritania, Morocco and Tunisia witnessed deterioration. Central Africa experienced a growth in the terms of trade of 12.5 percent in 2004 with particularly large growth for Chad (32.9 percent), Equatorial Guinea (59.6 percent), Gabon (12.4) and Republic of Congo (10.8 percent). The terms of trade deteriorated for most of the other countries. For East Africa, the terms of trade worsened

on average, though the Seychelles and Djibouti gained to a degree. Southern Africa's terms of trade grew at 7.4 percent in 2004 relative to 2 percent during 2000-2003. The biggest drivers in sub-regional performance were the oil producer Angola (31.6 percent), metals exporter South Africa (2.9 percent) and the copper exporter Zambia (10.3 percent). Most of the other countries in the sub-region saw worsening terms of trade. Finally, in West Africa, the terms of trade growth, at 12 percent in 2004 relative to 6.8 percent in 2000–2003, was largely due to the oil producer, Nigeria (19.7 percent), and also Benin (12.6 percent), Mali (7.1 percent) and Togo (13.9 percent). All the other West African countries experienced worsening terms of trade in 2004.

Following an increasing trend since 2000, the volume of imports grew strongly in 2004, at 7.2 percent (5.8 percent in 2003). Export volume growth, however, fell from 7.2 percent in 2003 to 4.6 percent in 2004. However, the trade balance recorded a sizeable surplus of $8.7 billion though much lower than the $15.6 billion in 2003. The current account as a percentage of GDP also showed a small improvement from 0.2 percent to 0.7 percent relative to 2003, largely due to the terms of trade improvement. Debt service continued its decline from a high of 17.2 percent of exports in 2002 to 11.8 percent in 2004.

Major Developments by Sector

The performance of key sectors of the African economy is shown in Table 1.7. All sectors grew in 2004 relative to 2003, with overall real GDP growth of 5.1 percent.

Agriculture contributes about 20 percent of African GDP, industry (including mining, quarrying and energy) about 32 percent and services the remainder. Industry had the largest growth rate, with a rebound in manufacturing growth from 2003. The sectors are discussed in turn.

Agriculture

In 2004, agricultural growth increased to 5.0 percent relative to 3.8 percent in 2003 and 2.7 percent in 2002. This was almost wholly because of higher prices for agricultural commodities, with cereal production static in Central Africa and falling in all other regions in 2004. Total cereal production fell to 127.8 million tonnes from 129.5 million between 2003 and 2004 (see Table 1.8). This was in part due to continued political instability in several countries, including in Zimbabwe and Côte d'Ivoire, severe drought in other cases, locust damage and shortages of key agricultural inputs.

Table 1.7: Sector Growth Rates, 2001–2004 (Percentage changes from preceding year)

	2001	2002	2003	2004[a]
Agriculture	5.2	2.7	3.8	5.0
Industry	3.7	2.8	4.3	6.0
Manufacturing	3.4	2.7	1.2	3.3
Services	3.7	4.2	4.6	4.4
GDP at Constant Market Prices	**3.9**	**3.5**	**4.4**	**5.1**

Note: [a] Preliminary estimates
Source: ADB Statistics Division

Table 1.8: Africa's Cereal Production, 2001–2004 (In million tonnes)

	2001	2002	2003	2004
North Africa	32.9	31.2	41.1	40.9
Eastern Africa	22.5	21.7	21.2	20.8
Southern Africa	17.6	18.8	19.2	18.3
Western Africa	36.9	39.0	42.8	42.5
Central Africa	5.1	5.0	5.2	5.2
Africa	**115.0**	**115.7**	**129.5**	**127.8**

Source: Adapted from FAOSTAT, December 2004.

Food Security by Sub-Region

Twenty-three African countries face exceptional food emergencies as of December 2004. The FAO's report on the food supply situation and crop prospects in SSA highlighted the predominant, and catastrophic, role of civil conflict in causing food crises, through the direct effects of conflict, the effects on neighboring countries of the flood of refugees (Chad, DRC, Guinea and Tanzania), and through the absorption of returnees at the cessation of conflict (Angola, Burundi, Eritrea and Sierra Leone). A number of these 23 countries, especially in Southern and Eastern Africa, have experienced drought or partial drought, while Mauritania suffered a locust plague. Zimbabwe continues to experience economic disruption with serious consequences for food production.

In **Southern Africa**, cereal production in 2004 was estimated at 22 million tonnes, slightly lower than the previous year. The cereal import requirement for 2004/05 of about 7 million tonnes, can largely be met by cereal surpluses in South Africa and Zambia, and by trade, but substantial food aid is still required to assist food insecure and HIV/AIDS-affected populations in the sub-region. Angola has absorbed large numbers of internally displaced persons and refugees. Even with above-average cereal output, it could meet only half of the country's total cereal requirement. Almost three-quarters of a million people are highly vulnerable to food insecurity. Lesotho experienced a major drought in 2004, and the food supply situation remains precarious. The cereal imports required can mostly be covered through trade, but poverty for a large section of the population has created a major problem of food insecurity. In Madagascar, rice and maize production exceeded the previous year's harvests. However, high rice prices, due to high world prices and devaluation of the local currency, have impacted accessibility to food. Further, poor weather, expensive oil imports and the depressed prices of its main exports such as vanilla and shrimp have created some food security problems. In Malawi, cereal output declined by about 14 percent from the near-average production of 2003. Over one million vulnerable people require emergency food assistance due to crop failures and the HIV/AIDS pandemic. Rising maize prices are expected to increase this number.

Mozambique has shown continued steady recovery in agricultural production over several years. Food aid is still required to compensate for the lasting impact of past floods and droughts, and the HIV/AIDS

problem. The food security situation throughout Swaziland is serious, following a drought that reduced the 2004 harvest of main season cereals by a third. Swaziland is self-sufficient only in one third of its cereal requirement, and heavily dependent on food imports. The incidence of HIV/AIDS is one of the highest in Africa, and food aid is required primarily to ameliorate its impact.

Zambia, by contrast, has experienced two consecutive good cereal harvests, and an export surplus of about 150,000 tonnes is expected during the 2004/2005 marketing year. The situation in Zimbabwe is difficult. Farmers have suffered seed, fertilizer, fuel, spare parts and draught power shortages. Prices of the food staple maize have soared due to shortages and hyper-inflation (an annual rate of 350 percent in 2004). High unemployment has created considerable food insecurity. According to the FAO, about 2.3 million people in rural areas will not cover their food needs, and possibly just as many will not do so in urban areas.

In **East Africa**, the aggregate sub-regional output is expected to be lower than 2003 because of drought, erratic rainfall and conflict. Severe drought conditions in parts of Somalia, Eritrea, Kenya and south-eastern Ethiopia are a cause for serious concern. In Eritrea, the food supply situation remains tight as a result of consecutive poor harvests and the lingering effects of its past war with neighboring Ethiopia. High cereal prices continue to affect purchasing power and the food security of large numbers of people, and food assistance is supplied to about 600,000 people affected by crop failure. Emergency food needs have also risen in Ethiopia, with 7.8 million people now requiring aid. Kenya's maize crop is well below the average of the previous five years, and is expected to result in an acute maize shortfall. Food assistance will be provided to about 2.3 million people affected by drought. Somalia's protracted insecurity and extreme poverty has led to a humanitarian emergency. Recent nutrition surveys in parts of the country indicate serious malnutrition rates. Uganda's food supply situation remains stable but prices (especially maize prices) are relatively high. Civil unrest in the north, seriously constrains the food situation, and food distribution occurs for over 1.4 million vulnerable people. Tanzania's 2004 cereal crop, mainly maize, is over 20 percent above the previous five years' average. However, sharp price increases were observed due partly to the increased cereal demand from neighboring countries like DRC and Malawi, which suffer major deficits.

West African agricultural production in the Sahel is expected to be close to the five-year average, but drought and locusts caused severe localized damage to crops. In Burkina Faso, cereal output in 2004 was estimated to be above the average for the previous five years, though the output of sorghum, the most important cereal crop, fell. Poor rains and locust infestation caused severe damage to crops and pastures in the northern areas. Cape Verde saw a big fall in the maize, beans and potato crops. Most food is imported, but rural areas may face food vulnerability. Chad's cereal production is estimated to be 30 percent lower than 2003 following inadequate rains.

In Côte d'Ivoire, escalating violence drove refugees into Liberia. Persistent insecurity, population displacement and the prolonged partition of the country have all served to constrain agricultural production. Cotton production is about half of the previous year's level, and marketing has been seriously disrupted. The sugar industry is about to collapse, since three of the four sugar growing areas and processing plants are in the crisis area. Despite the repatriation of Sierra Leonean refugees, Guinea still hosts over 80,000 refugees, mostly from Liberia (but also Côte d'Ivoire and Sierra Leone), in addition to 80,000 internally displaced persons and 100,000 returnees from Côte d'Ivoire. In Guinea-Bissau, cereal production was 72 percent above last year's level; and rice, the main crop, is expected to increase by over 90 percent. In Liberia, the crisis in Côte d'Ivoire led to an influx of over 19,000 refugees. The end of the civil war and the return of displaced farmers should promote agricultural production in 2004 from its low level in 2003 (although seed and tool shortages are reportedly impeding cultivation). Repatriation of over 300,000 Liberian refugees, scattered across West Africa, and demobilization of ex-combatants has begun. In Mali, crop loss due to locusts was significant in affected areas, but good crop production in the most important southern producing areas ameliorated the impact.

In Niger, due to a fall in grain output, some 3.6 million people are estimated to be at risk of food shortage. Senegal suffered similarly due to inadequate rainfall combined with severe desert locust infestations in several areas. With scarce pasture and water, the southern movement of livestock herds has started far earlier than usual, which may lead to confrontations. In Sierra Leone, rice production is expected to further increase this year, reflecting an improved security situation, increased plantings following the return of refugees and farmers previously displaced, as well as improved availability of agricultural inputs. An estimated 1 million internally displaced people have been resettled. In The Gambia, there were good harvests.

In **Central Africa,** civil strife and insecurity continue to undermine food security in several countries. In Burundi, while cereal production for 2004 is about 3 percent higher than last year, total food production remains below the average of pre-civil war period (1988–93). Insecurity continues to be reported in some areas of the country causing disruptions in the repatriation and resettlement of the refugees (over 200,000 Burundian refugees have returned since 2002). In spite of good weather and seed distributions, a strong agricultural recovery is not expected in CAR this year due to persistent insecurity. Most of the 230,000 internally displaced persons have returned home, but Chad still hosts an estimated 41,000 refugees.

In the Congo, following the peace agreement between the Government and the rebels in March 2003, disarmament and demobilization has been set in motion, while displaced persons have returned home. However, the security situation remains volatile and hampers humanitarian

aid. In the Democratic Republic of Congo, the relative improvement in the security situation in the country and the assisted absorption of internally displaced persons and returning refugees may have a positive impact. However, insecurity is still a major constraint to food production and food security. In Rwanda, the production of cereals in 2004 is estimated to match the five-year average, but up to 400,000 chronically food insecure people in vulnerable areas require food aid.

In **North Africa**, there were bumper harvests for the second year running, in some cases at record levels of output. Favorable weather conditions, larger areas sown and adequate availability of agricultural inputs helped drive these results. Algeria was aided by the implementation of the Agricultural Development Plan set up by the Government in 2000. In both Algeria and Morocco, intensive and large scale control operations during the 2003/04 agricultural season brought the widespread desert locust infestation under control, limiting damage to agriculture. Cereal output in Algeria is provisionally estimated at 3.95 million tonnes, similar to the bumper crop harvested last year and 75 percent above average. Egypt's output of the wheat crop (largely irrigated) is estimated at 7.18 million tonnes, up 5 percent from the above average production of 2003. Barley output is estimated to have almost doubled to a record 264,000 tonnes, driven by an expansion in the area sown. However, the prospect of future conflict with neighboring countries due to serious projected water shortages for irrigation in the Nile Basin has recently been brought to world attention. In Morocco, with a second consecutive year of bumper harvests, cereal production is estimated at a record 8.47 million tonnes, in 2004.

In Tunisia, cereal output is estimated at 2.5 million tonnes. This was the second successive year of good production, somewhat below the previous harvest, but far above the average for the last five years. In Mauritania, food shortages are serious. Following drought and widespread desert locust infestations, cereal output is estimated at about 44 percent below last year's output and 36 percent below the previous five years' average. Pastures have also been severely affected. This follows several years of drought and poor harvests. In Sudan, a humanitarian crisis on an enormous scale prevails in Greater Darfur, where conflict has forced more than 1.2 million people from their homes and farms, with large numbers fleeing to neighboring Chad. Agricultural production and humanitarian assistance are exceedingly difficult under these conditions. Southern Sudan will likely face a decline in the current season's cereal harvest; and similarly in central and northern Sudan, due to erratic rainfall and civil unrest. Food assistance is currently provided to more than 2 million people affected by war and drought.

Industry

Structural transformation — specifically the growth of manufacturing and of services — is a pre-requisite for rapid and sustainable poverty reduction in SSA. The region has shown industry growth rates of 2.8 percent, 4.3 percent and 6.0 percent in 2002, 2003

and 2004 respectively. These rates reflect the growth in energy (oil) and mining activities over the last two years, aided by buoyant oil and commodity prices. For manufacturing alone, growth fell to 1.2 percent in 2003 from 2.7 percent in 2002, but increased again to 3.3 percent in 2004, helped by the recovery in world demand.

A comparison of the levels and growth of industrialization between Africa and other regions can be made using the levels of the dollar value added of manufacturing (MVA) per capita and recent growth rates in MVA and MVA per capita. These are shown in Table 1.9.

SSA seriously lags behind other developing regions in terms of industrialization. The average per capita value of MVA (shown in the last column) for South East Asia is $363, while that for Latin America is $663. Yet per capita MVA only averages $68 for Africa as a whole (excluding South Africa), $195 for North Africa, $29 for Central Africa, $29 for West Africa and $34 for East and Southern Africa (excluding South Africa).

Apart from South Africa and Mauritius, MVA per head in the 15 most industrialized SSA countries is extremely low (see Table 1.10). Such low levels of MVA per head starkly illustrate the underdevelopment of African manufacturing.

UNIDO (2004) report emphasizes the highly skewed distribution of manufacturing activity. Only ten out of 45 countries in SSA have an MVA of $1 billion or more, while just one country, South Africa, accounts for just over one quarter of the sub-continent's total MVA. The top ten producers of manufactures account for 45

Table 1.9: Annual Growth of MVA, 1993–2003 and Per Capita MVA, 2003[a/]

Country Group or Country /Area	Total MVA								Per capita MVA						
	Growth Rate (percentage)		Index (1995=100)						Growth Rate (percentage)		Index (1995=100)				
	1993–1998	1998–2003	2000	2001	2002[b/]	2003[c/]			1993–1998	1998–2003	2000	2001	2002[b/]	2003[c/]	2003[c/]
Africa	4.2	3.9	125	128	132	139			1.6	1.5	111	111	112	116	68
North Africa	4.1	4.5	129	132	137	143			2.2	2.5	117	118	121	124	195
UMA	1.8	2.6	113	115	118	121			0.1	1	104	104	106	106	224
Central Africa	1.0	5.1	117	124	136	141			-1.4	2.4	103	107	114	115	29
West Africa	4.7	2.0	115	117	117	125			1.8	-0.6	100	100	98	101	29
East and Southern Africa	5.1	2.8	121	124	126	137			2.4	0.6	107	107	107	113	34
Latin America	2.7	0.7	113	111	111	114			1.0	-0.8	104	101	99	101	663
South and East Asia	7.5	7.8	139	144	155	168			5.9	6.4	129	132	141	151	363
West Asia and Europe	5.7	3.3	124	122	129	141			3.4	1.1	111	107	110	119	611
World	3.4	2.7	118	117	120	125			2.0	1.4	111	108	110	113	1 181

Notes: [a/] At constant 1995 prices.
[b/] Provisional.
[c/] Estimates.
Source: ADB Statistics Division

percent of total MVA and the top 15 are responsible for almost half (49 percent) of the total.

Shares of MVA in GDP for the top 15 MVA per capita countries in 2001 are also shown in Table 1.10. Swaziland's strong performance is partly the result of the expansion of its manufacturing sector a decade earlier, when companies 'disinvested' from South Africa to Swaziland, under trade sanctions in the apartheid era. It has also benefited from programs to promote manufacturing exports. The share of manufacturing in GDP is also high in Mauritius due to the strength of its successful export processing zone, specializing in clothing exports. Other countries with high MVA shares in GDP in 2001 are South Africa, Côte d'Ivoire, and Zimbabwe — attributed by the UNIDO report to European settler communities that led to an expansion of industry, often supplemented by government protection, to satisfy settler needs. In SSA as a whole, 33 countries have manufacturing shares in GDP of less than 12.5 percent.

Growth of total African MVA in the last decade exceeded the world average but was far below the growth rate achieved in South and East Asia. However, in per capita terms, growth in the last decade fell below the world average. North and Central Africa performed better than the African average in MVA growth (and also in per capita MVA growth) in the five years to 2003, with Central Africa improving dramatically on the growth of the previous five years. West, East and Southern Africa regions, the latter excluding South Africa, performed worse between 1993–98 and 1998–2003. In per capita terms, MVA growth was actually negative in West Africa, and in all three regions, below the African average.

The UNIDO report suggests that the top eight SSA performers in MVA growth tend also to be the best performers in terms of MVA per capita growth, though high population growth excluded Rwanda from the per capita MVA top ten in the decade to 2001 (see Table 1.11).

However, two countries with relatively large populations by SSA standards, Ethiopia and Uganda, made the top ten in the last decade. By about 2000, the share of the top ten fastest growers in MVA was 17 percent of the total MVA in SSA (excluding South Africa). It is notable that there are several small economies in the top ten. UNIDO emphasizes that policy to prioritize industrial exports in countries like Mauritius, and more recently Lesotho, has undoubtedly played a larger role in the success of several of the smaller economies.

Services: Tourism

Services contribute a substantial proportion to African GDP. The services sector grew at an estimated 4.4 percent in 2004 compared with 4.6 percent in 2003. However, the services sector stands to gain in the medium-term from increased FDI flows, particularly to retail and wholesale industries.

A big contributor to services growth in 2004 was international tourism. Globally this was a very strong year for tourism, with positive results for all regions. The strong rebound of growth has followed three years where accumulated tourism growth measured less than 1 percent. In 2003, the Iraq war affected tourism demand in North

Table 1.10: Top 15 Countries in Sub-Saharan Africa by MVA, MVA Per Capita and Share of MVA in GDP, 2001

MVA Rank	Country	MVA ($ million)	Per capita MVA ($)
1	South Africa	26418	597
2	Sudan	3606	112
3	Cote d'Ivoire	2930	185
4	Cameroon	2248	146
5	Nigeria	2120	18
6	Zimbabwe	1779	139
7	Senegal	1133	118
8	Kenya	1057	34
9	Ethiopia	1009	15
10	Mauritius	1004	842
11	Burkina Faso	898	72
12	Ghana	880	44
13	Uganda	692	26
14	Zambia	625	59
15	Angola	525	41

MVA Per Capita and Share of MVA in GDP

Rank	Country	Per capita MVA ($)	Country	Share of MVA in GDP (percent)
1	Mauritius	842	Swaziland	28.8
2	Seychelles	669	Mauritius	21.7
3	South Africa	597	Cote d'Ivoire	21.6
4	Swaziland	362	South Africa	19.3
5	Gabon	307	Zimbabwe	19.1
6	Namibia	216	Burkina Faso	18.2
7	Botswana	192	Chad	16.1
8	Cote d'Ivoire	185	Rwanda	15.7
9	Cameroon	146	Zambia	15.0
10	Zimbabwe	139	Cameroon	14.9
11	Senegal	118	Senegal	13.6
12	Sudan	112	Lesotho	12.4
13	Cape Verde	109	Seychelles	12.4
14	DRC	78	Madagascar	10.8
15	Burkina Faso	72	Kenya	10.4

Source: UNIDO (2004)

Table 1.11: Top Performers in Sub-Saharan Africa by MVA Growth and MVA Per Capita Growth, 2001

Average growth rates of MVA (percent)

Rank	Country	1981–1991	Country	1991–2001
1	Swaziland	17.9	Uganda	13.5
2	Lesotho	13.1	Ethiopia	9.1
3	Mauritius	11.0	Equat. Guinea	8.3
4	Cape Verde	9.6	Burkina Faso	7.7
5	Seychelles	8.9	Cape Verde	6.2
6	Botswana	8.7	Mauritius	5.9
7	Gambia	7.2	Lesotho	5.5
8	Mali	7.1	Seychelles	5.4
9	Ghana	6.2	Rwanda	5.4
10	Burundi	5.6	Benin	5.3

Average growth rates of MVA Per Capita (percent)

Rank	Country	1981–1991	Country	1991–2001
1	Swaziland	14.1	Uganda	10.1
2	Lesotho	10.8	Ethiopia	7.1
3	Mauritius	10.1	Equat. Guinea	5.4
4	Seychelles	7.8	Burkina Faso	5.2
5	Cape Verde	7.6	Mauritius	4.9
6	Botswana	5.4	Seychelles	4.9
7	Mali	4.4	Cape Verde	3.7
8	Gambia	3.1	Lesotho	3.5
9	Guinea	2.7	Botswana	2.6
10	Somalia	2.6	Benin	2.3

Source: UNIDO (2004)

Africa, and in particular Morocco, Tunisia and Egypt. The constraints posed by political considerations later began to fade as consumer and business confidence improved. For Africa as a whole, international tourism arrivals grew at 7.0 percent in the first eight months of 2004, surpassing growth in Europe (see Table 1.12).

For North Africa, growth was 17 percent, while that of SSA was a mere 1.0 percent. Morocco and Tunisia had growth rates of 17 and 19 percent respectively. Strong performers in SSA were Uganda (41 percent), Madagascar (48 percent) and Kenya (18 percent).

Under the auspices of the NEPAD,

tourism ministers met in the Seychelles in May 2004 to approve a detailed plan on tourism, endorsed by the AU in July 2004.

Energy

Estimated total world crude oil supply in 2004 was 72.5 million barrels per day (mb/d), increasing from 69.3 mb/d in 2003

Table 1.12: International Tourism Arrivals by Sub–region

	International Tourism Arrivals (million)				Market Share (%)		Average annual growth (%)			
	2000	2002	2003	2004	2003	2004	02/01	03/02	04[a]/03	90–00
Africa	20.0	30.0	31.0	33.0	4.5	4.3	2.2	3.1	7.0	6.3
North Africa	7.3	10.0	11.0	13.0	1.6	1.7	–2.6	4.6	17.0	1.8
Subsaharan Africa	12.7	19.0	20.0	20.0	2.9	2.7	5.0	2.4	1.0	10.2
Americas	128.0	117.0	113.0	124.0	16.4	16.3	–4.5	–3.1	10.0	3.2
North America	91.0	83.0	77.0	85.0	11.2	11.1	–3.6	–7.0	9.0	2.4
Caribean	17.0	16.0	17.0	18.0	2.5	2.4	–4.8	6.2	6.0	4.2
Central America	4.0	5.0	5.0	6.0	0.7	0.8	6.5	4.2	17.0	8.4
South America	15.0	13.0	14.0	16.0	2.0	2.1	–12.8	7.9	15.0	6.8
Asia and the Pacific	115.0	131.0	119.0	153.0	17.3	20.2	8.8	–9.0	29.0	7.2
North–East Asia	63.0	74.0	68.0	88.0	9.8	11.5	12.6	–8.8	30.0	8.4
South– East Asia	37.0	42.0	36.0	48.0	5.3	6.3	5.6	–13.7	33.0	5.6
Oceania	9.0	9.0	9.0	10.0	1.3	1.3	0.8	–1.0	13.0	6.5
South Asia	6.0	6.0	6.0	8.0	0.9	1.0	0.4	9.0	20.0	6.8
Europe	390.0	397.0	399.0	414.0	57.7	54.6	2.5	0.4	4.0	3.4
Northen Europe	47.0	46.0	47.0	51.0	6.9	6.7	3.5	2.1	7.0	3.8
Western Europe	140.0	138.0	136.0	139.0	19.7	18.3	1.6	–1.4	2.0	2.3
Central and Eastern Europe	62.0	66.0	68.0	73.0	9.8	9.6	3.2	3.4	8.0	4.8
Southern/ Mediterranean Europe	141.0	148.0	148.0	152.0	21.4	20.0	2.7	0.1	3.0	4.0
Middle East	24.0	28.0	29.0	35.0	4.2	4.6	16.1	3.4	20.0	9.5
World	**686.0**	**703.0**	**691.0**	**760.0**	**100.0**	**100.0**	**2.8**	**–1.7**	**10.0**	**4.2**

Notes: [a] Provisional data
Source: World Tourism Organization, January 2005.

Table 1.13 Crude Oil Production[a/], 1995–2004 (Thousand Barrels per Day)

Country	1995	1997	1998	1999	2000	2001	2002	2003	2004*
Algeria	1,202	1,277	1,246	1,202	1,254	1,310	1,306	1,611	1,672
Angola	646	714	735	745	746	742	896	903	1,047
Cameroon	111	124	121	100	116	110	104	98	94
Congo	188	253	265	270	280	255	249	229	242
Congo (Democratic Republic)	30	28	26	22	26	24	23	25	28
Cote d'Ivoire	8	19	20	15	11	11	15	21	24
Egypt	920	856	834	852	748	698	631	618	597
Equatorial Guinea	5	52	83	102	118	195	231	265	350
Gabon	365	370	352	331	315	270	251	241	239
Libya	1,390	1,446	1,390	1,319	1,410	1,367	1,319	1,421	1,507
Nigeria	1,993	2,132	2,153	2,130	2,165	2,256	2,118	2,241	2,521
Sudan	n.a.	5	10	69	186	209	245	280	324
Tunisia	89	84	80	83	79	70	76	66	69
Other Countries	8	6	24	32	52	12	230	314	329
Africa	**6,954**	**7,368**	**7,340**	**7,272**	**7,507**	**7,529**	**7,693**	**8,337**	**9,044**
OPEC	**26,004**	**27,710**	**28,774**	**27,579**	**29,262**	**28,344**	**26,370**	**28,006**	**30,101**
World Total	**62,335**	**65,690**	**66,921**	**65,848**	**68,342**	**67,942**	**66,842**	**69,252**	**72,537**

na: Not available
* Estimates
a/ Crude Oil (Including Lease Condensate)
Sources: International Energy Agency, Energy Intelligency Administration, Economist Intelligence Unit, Etudes et Statistiques BEAC and ADB Statistics Division estimates

(see Table 1.13). African non-OPEC countries supplied 3.3 mb/d and African OPEC producers (Algeria, Libya and Nigeria) supplied 5.7 mb/d. Africa's contribution to global supplies in 2004 was 9.0 mb/d or 12 percent. Production rose significantly in Angola and Sudan. Among the small-to-medium producers, including Cameroon, Congo, Equatorial Guinea, Gabon, Sudan and Tunisia, production was fairly static, falling somewhat in Cameroon and Gabon.

The African Economy and the External Environment

In general, African countries are vulnerable to external shocks in the global demand for their exports, to changing terms of trade for their exports (largely agricultural, mining and oil commodities) and their imports (predominantly manufactured goods and oil for non-oil producers), and to net capital inflows (both private flows and official development assistance). The resilience of different countries to external shocks through these channels depends on a range of factors, including their macro-economic stance, their level of dependence on external flows, the linkage of production with higher technology imports, and the extent of their export diversification.

In 2004, there was a strong global expansion and higher demand for commodities at increased prices. As noted earlier, global growth rebounded to 5.1 percent in 2004 from 3.9 percent in the preceding year, following an upward trend since 2001 (see Table 1.14). The improved growth was widespread, both in the advanced economies (at 3.4 percent up from 2.0 percent) and in emerging markets. Asian growth reached 8.1 percent, resulting in a big rise in demand for African commodities from China and other parts of Asia. China's share of world trade has trebled since the early 1990s. Increased demand for African exports, coupled with higher commodity prices, fostered Africa's growth performance.

High Oil and Commodity Prices

Improved trade performance, particularly amongst the oil and metals exporters, was a major factor in improved African growth in 2004. For Africa as a whole, the terms of trade growth increased significantly to 6.7 from 3.8 in the preceding year. In 2004, oil prices and many commodity prices rose strongly as a result of increased global demand, especially in China and Asia. Oil prices in 2004 averaged US$38.3 per barrel (Brent crude), a rise of nearly 60 percent from the 2001 level of US$24.4 per barrel.

The oil price rise is due more to rising global demand than to supply-side factors, but supply constraints in several major oil producers (including Iraq, Russia and Venezuela) also contributed. Big increases in oil production were seen in Angola, Chad and Equatorial Guinea, and OPEC quotas were raised four times in 2004 for the three African members. Higher prices of oil and commodities, coupled with a growth in export volume in many oil and commodities exporters, drove up export value.

Most other commodity prices also rose strongly in 2004 relative to 2003, with the marked exception of cocoa prices, falling nearly 12 percent from 175.1 to 155 cents per kg, and impacting negatively on Côte d'Ivoire's performance. Arabica coffee saw a 25 percent rise in price, tea an 11 percent rise, rice and soybeans around 168 percent and wheat over 7 percent. Prices for robusta coffee fell slightly, while those for sugar and cotton were almost static (a small fall, after strong rises in 2003 for cotton). Metals and minerals achieved huge rises in 2004: of over 70 per cent for lead and tin, over 60 percent for copper and over 40 percent for nickel, of 36 percent for silver, nearly 27 percent for zinc, 20 percent for aluminium, and finally, almost 13 percent for gold (see Table 1.15).

Africa's growth is largely dependent on changes in prices of primary commodities. For instance, the IMF has estimated for SSA, the net impact of commodity price changes on trade balances relative to GDP, assuming unchanged trade volumes. Large net gains of more than 3 percent are expected for Angola, Chad, Congo, Gabon, Nigeria

Table 1.14: Selected International Economic Indicators, 2000–2004 (Percentage changes from preceding year, except otherwise specified)

	2000	2001	2002	2003	2004[a]
Changes in output					
World	4.7	2.4	3.0	3.9	5.1
Advanced economies	3.8	1.2	1.6	2.0	3.4
Other emerging market and developing countries	5.9	4.0	4.8	6.3	7.1
– Central and eastern Europe	4.9	0.2	4.4	4.6	6.0
– Commonwealth of Independent States	9.1	6.4	5.4	7.9	7.8
– Asia	6.8	5.6	6.6	7.9	8.1
– Western hemisphere	3.9	0.5	–0.1	2.1	5.3
– Africa[b]	3.4	3.9	3.5	4.4	5.1
Changes in Consumer Price Index					
Advanced economies	2.2	2.1	1.5	1.8	2.0
Developing countries	7.1	6.6	5.9	6.0	5.8
– Central and eastern Europe	22.9	19.5	14.8	9.2	6.8
– Commonwealth of Independent States	24.6	18.7	13.8	12.0	10.3
– Asia	1.9	2.7	2.1	2.6	4.3
– Western hemisphere	6.7	6.1	8.9	10.6	6.6
– Africa[b]	13.5	10.5	9.1	10.0	7.7
Changes in Merchandise Trade (volume)					
World Trade	13.2	–0.4	3.5	5.5	10.5
Advanced economies					
– Exports	12.6	–1.5	2.0	2.9	8.6
– Imports	12.4	–1.6	2.7	4.4	9.0
Developing countries					
– Exports	15.4	3.1	7.0	10.5	13.8
– Imports	15.7	3.4	6.5	10.5	16.5
Africa[b]					
– Exports	9.3	0.8	1.0	7.2	4.6
– Imports	2.5	4.2	4.5	5.8	7.2
Changes in terms of trade					
Advanced economies	–3.1	0.4	1.1	1.4	0.1
Developing countries	7.3	–3.2	1.0	0.9	3.9
– Asia	–4.5	–0.8	0.8	–0.6	–0.9
– Africa[b]	14.8	–3.5	1.0	3.8	6.7
Changes in FDI					
World	27.7	–41.1	–17.0	–17.6	...
Developed countries	33.8	–48.4	–14.3	–25.2	...
Developing countries	8.9	–13.0	–28.3	9.1	...
– Asia	29.7	–23.4	–15.6	13.5	...
– Western hemisphere	–9.2	–9.6	–41.7	–3.2	...
– Africa[b]	–24.7	124.8	–39.9	27.6	...

cont. overleaf

Table 1.14: *Cont.*

	2000	2001	2002	2003	2004[a]
FDI (as percent of global FDI flows)					
Developed countries	79.8	69.9	72.2	65.5	...
Developing countries	18.2	26.9	23.2	30.7	...
–Asia	10.5	13.7	13.9	19.1	...
–Latin American and Caribbean countries	7.0	10.8	7.6	8.9	...
–Africa[b]	0.6	2.4	1.7	2.7	...

Notes: [a] Preliminary estimates
[b] ADB Regional Member Countries.
Sources: IMF, *World Economic Outlook*, September 2004 and ADB Statistics Division.

Table 1.15: Selected Commodity Prices

Commodity	Unit	2002	2003	2004
Crude Oil, Brent	$/bbl	25.0	28.9	38.3
Agricultural Commodities				
Wheat, US, HRW	$/mt	148.1	146.1	156.9
Rice, Thai, 5 percent	$/mt	191.9	197.6	237.7
Soybeans	$/mt	212.7	264.0	306.4
Sugar, world	Cents/kg	15.2	15.6	15.8
Coffee, Arabica	Cents/kg	135.7	141.5	177.3
Coffee, robusta	Cents/kg	66.2	81.5	79.3
Cocoa	Cents/kg	177.8	175.1	155.0
Tea, average (3) auctions	Cents/kg	150.6	151.7	168.5
Cotton A Index	Cents/kg	101.9	139.9	136.6
Metals and Minerals				
Aluminum	$/mt	1,349.9	1,431.3	1,715.5
Copper	$/mt	1,559.5	1,779.1	2,865.9
Gold	$/toz	310.0	363.5	409.2
Iron ore	cents/dmtu	29.3	32.0	37.9
Lead	cents/dmtu	45.3	51.5	88.7
Nickel	$/mt	6,771.8	9,629.5	13,823.2
Silver	cents/toz	462.5	491.1	669.1
Tin	cents/kg	406.1	489.5	851.3
Zinc	cents/kg	77.9	82.8	104.8

Source: Adapted from World Bank, Commodity Price Data (Pink Sheets), January 2005.

and Zambia. The greatest gains are expected to accrue to the oil producers and to a lesser extent to metals exporters. Moderate net gains of 1–3 percent are expected for DRC, Mali, Mauritania and Sudan. Countries with net losses (–1 percent or less) include Côte d'Ivoire, Guinea Bissau, Kenya and Swaziland, largely because of higher oil import bills and, in Côte d'Ivoire, a sharp decline in cocoa prices. The remaining countries are roughly balanced. The oil market remains vulnerable to shocks, and higher and more volatile oil prices will impinge on growth in poor countries.

If rapid growth in China, and in due course in India, is sustained for two decades or more, as the IMF suggests it might, a 'commodity supercycle' may be entered, with persistently high commodity prices. The larger inflows due to metals exporters, like South Africa, may then induce a 'permanent' real appreciation in the floating exchange rate, which will have to be accommodated, as it will not be a temporary phenomenon. Already in 2004, the prolonged strength of the South African rand impacted on the cost effectiveness of some mining operations.

Financial Flows and Doing Business

Africa's economic performance is also linked to the volumes of net capital inflows comprising both Official Development Assistance (ODA) and private capital flows. After declining through most of the 1990s, total net ODA to Africa has begun to recover, rising from a total $15.8 billion in 2001 to $24.7 billion in 2003. SSA accounted for about two-thirds of the increase in ODA. In principle, these inflows can provide essential resources to augment domestic investment.

Foreign direct investment (FDI) in Africa increased from $19.9 billion in 2002 to $24.3 billion in 2003 — an increase of over 22 percent. As a result, Africa's share of developing country FDI increased from 12.6 percent in 2002 to 14.1 percent in 2003, but still below the 2001 peak of 15.4 percent. A number of factors have contributed to the recovery in FDI inflows to Africa, but the key ones include the continued liberalization of FDI policies, improved macroeconomic management by many countries and increased investments in oil production and other natural resources. These factors explain why the increased FDI in the continent was more "broad-based than in any year since 1999, with 22 countries receiving more than $100 million compared to 16 in 2001" (UNCTAD, 2004).

The largest recipients of FDI in 2003, in order of size of receipts, were South Africa, Egypt, Morocco, Nigeria and Algeria. The survey of investment promotion agencies places the following countries next in order of attractiveness for FDI in 2004–2005: Kenya, Libya, Tunisia, Angola, Equatorial Guinea, Namibia, Ghana and Mozambique. FDI inflows to Africa have been heavily concentrated in natural resources exploitation. Flows are directed to Angola, Algeria, Gabon, Nigeria and Sudan for oil and gas projects, and in South Africa and Tanzania in mining. The primary sector was the largest recipient of accumulated FDI to Africa, with a 55 percent share for the period 1996–2000.

The main investors in Africa are South Africa and China, and their investment is more widespread and less focused on specific countries, than that of traditional investor countries, the UK and France. The resources that can be made available to support investment are also constrained by the volume of outstanding external debt and the resources needed to service it. Debt burdens for several countries eased under the HIPC initiative in 2004. In general, debt servicing as a percentage of exports, has continued a downward trend.

In much of Africa, cumbersome regulation stifles productive activity by removing the flexibility of companies to respond to market conditions. Regulation is more cumbersome in all aspects of business activity, than for other regions. Yet growth stagnates or is inadequate in many African countries, there are few new jobs and poverty has risen. African countries reformed the least of all countries in 2003. Yet if greater ease of doing business can help growth, which the report claims to demonstrate, this suggests African countries should give a high priority in the coming years to simplifying business regulation and adopting the best practices, following other successful reformers (like Botswana).

The African Economy and the Domestic Policy Environment

Fiscal Policy

The positive outcome for the fiscal deficit in 2004 for Africa, and especially for the ATLE countries, was discussed above. For the first time in over two decades, the ATLE fiscal balance in 2004 registered a modest surplus, and these gains were behind the fiscal strengthening for Africa as a whole. This historic fiscal performance was made possible by the progress that most African countries made in implementing sound macroeconomic policies and strengthening the management of their economies. Although much remains to be done, many countries pursued, with vigor, their programs of reforms, including privatization of state owned enterprises, public sector reforms, as well as the strengthening of regulatory frameworks. It is important that African countries continue to sustain the prudent macroeconomic policies they have begun to implement and deepen their reform programs, as these are critical to improve the region's growth and development prospects.

Monetary Policy

For the ATLE countries, growth in money supply has slowed since 2001, and more sharply in 2004. For Africa as a whole the pattern is similar and yet the fall in the growth in money supply from 2003 to 2004 is not really informative on the monetary stance in Africa. This is because it is an aggregate figure, conflating outcomes for countries like South Africa, and other countries where money supply growth can be a proxy for fiscal policy. Given South Africa's high weight in African GDP, the African money supply figure needs to be disaggregated by groups of countries following different monetary policy rules to help shed light on fiscal behavior in different countries.

In South Africa, given extensive domestic financial liberalization in the 1980s, money targets ceased to be of much use in controlling inflation, and were supplemented in the early 1990s by a range of other indicators. Liberalization of the capital market in 1995, and a huge increase in net inflows, further weakened reliance on money targets. In 2000, South Africa formally adopted inflation targeting as a monetary policy rule. Short-term changes in the broad money aggregate in South Africa today reflect a host of factors, including asset price effects, interest rate effects, and changing precautionary behavior by investors and consumers.

On the other hand, for countries with thin financial markets, money supply growth is likely to be a good indicator of fiscal imbalances and aid disbursement, and hence pressures of excess demand, ultimately feeding into inflation. In many African countries, monetary policy largely amounts to fiscal management and operates through a monetary targeting regime. Price stability is indirectly pursued by ensuring that the growth in money supply is equilibrated with demand. However, as seen in South Africa, with greater sophistication of financial systems and increasingly more open economies, the monetarist view of a simple connection between money supply and inflation is rendered increasingly dubious. Box 1.6 discusses monetary policy operation in Uganda, the drawbacks with monetary targeting given extensive financial liberalization, and suggests possibilities for future monetary policy.

Several African countries are looking to inflation targeting (or a hybrid monetary rule, e.g. weighting growth, employment or income, as well as inflation), to overcome the problems associated with setting monetary targets.

As stated earlier, inflationary risks vary across countries and regions, and mostly appear moderate, except for North Africa and Nigeria. In North Africa, worrying inflationary pressures were evident in all the countries (save for Morocco and Sudan), with 2004 inflation significantly higher than 2000–03 inflation in many cases. In West Africa, mild inflationary pressures are present in Cape Verde and Sierra Leone. Serious inflation was evident in Nigeria. All other countries posted low inflation and modest inflation falls relative to 2000–03. In Central Africa, inflationary pressures are evident only in Congo, Equatorial Guinea, Gabon and Rwanda, relative to 2000–2003, with a good record of macroeconomic stability for the other countries in the region. In East Africa, inflationary pressures were evident in Ethiopia, the Seychelles and Uganda. Elsewhere, macroeconomic stability was sustained, and inflation was halved in Eritrea. In Southern Africa, there were mild inflationary pressures in South Africa and Zimbabwe has been experiencing hyperinflation.

The African Economy and Regional Policy

Africa's regional policy is increasingly affected by the New Partnership for Africa's Development (NEPAD). Since its launching in October 2001, NEPAD has focused on: advocacy and outreach; preparation and implementation of NEPAD priority

Box 1.6: The Conduct of Monetary Policy in Uganda

The Bank of Uganda (BOU), despite its legal independence, like many other central banks in Africa, does not *de facto* have full independence. There is a degree of fiscal dominance in that the fiscal authority chooses a deficit, which the central bank has to finance. Further, the embryonic state of financial markets, which weakens the effectiveness of monetary policy, requires not only that fiscal policy be coordinated with monetary policy, but also that some degree of accommodation of fiscal policy is inevitable to ensure that price stability is maintained. Although government securities were surrendered to the BOU to be used solely for monetary policy purposes, the government pays for the interest cost on these instruments, so that the BOU cannot claim full instrument independence.

The BOU is entrusted with the role of maintaining price stability and a sound financial system, but it perceives the former as the primary objective of monetary policy. To conduct monetary policy, the BOU adopted the Reserve Money Program (RMP) under the auspices of an IMF-supported financial program, in the early 1990s. Under this monetary targeting framework, price stability is indirectly pursued by ensuring that the growth in money supply is equilibrated with the demand. The RMP is a flow of consolidated assets and liabilities of the central bank, which provides a framework for assessing liquidity conditions so that changes in the monetary authorities' balance sheet do not result in undesirable changes in broader aggregates. Intermediate targets include the broad money aggregate, M3 (including both the liabilities in domestic currency and those in foreign currency), and targets on net international reserves, net domestic assets and net domestic credit, to ensure that the private sector is not crowded out. The operational target, base money, was adopted as a performance benchmark in 2002 under the IMF-supported financial program.

The RMP assumes underlying economic relationships between base money, broader monetary aggregates, economic growth, and inflation, the final target for monetary policy. However, following domestic financial liberalization in the latter part of the 1990s, and a more open economy after full capital market liberalization in 1997, this partly monetarist view of a simple connection between money supply and inflation has been challenged. The effects of external shocks, and more sophisticated markets has led to increased interaction between domestic money markets and the foreign exchange market. Dollarization has also become an important phenomenon. These factors have implications for the volatility of the demand for money and the predictability of money growth consistent with the inflation targets.

Consequently, some flexibility has been introduced in the RMP. Rather than solely using deviations of actual base money from the desired level, developments in other macroeconomic indicators such as exchange rates, interest rates and inflation have increasingly become important in guiding the monetary policy actions.

Operational Issues

There are three major steps in the implementation of monetary policy at the BOU. The first is the derivation of monetary targets that are consistent with the overall macro-economic objectives. The second step involves determining the instruments mix to manage liquidity in such a manner that the monetary targets are not breached. This is carried out by the Monetary and Credit Policy Committee (MCPC). The third step is in implementing the MCPC decisions and interacting with the markets. This is executed by the Financial Markets Operations Committee (FMOC), comprised of the Domestic Financial Markets Department, the External Operations Department, the Supervision Department and the Research Department.

The MCPC agrees upon the mix of the sterilization instruments (Treasury bills, Treasury

Box 1.6: *cont.*

bonds and daily sales of foreign exchange), which is not expected to change through the quarter unless there has been a shock to the system that requires otherwise. While the FMOC uses the flexible repurchase instrument (repo) to address the short-term movements in liquidity and intra-auction liquidity surges, it would have to seek permission from MCPC in order to adjust the sterilization instruments mix.

Challenges for the BOU

The four decades of central banking experience for BOU have contributed to building a strong foundation for monetary management, but several challenges persist, while others have emerged. For instance, there are high intermediation costs; and excess reserves in the banking sector have been created because of reluctance by banks to expose themselves beyond the prime borrowers. A high cash ratio and segmentation of the banking system also constrain the transmission of policy signals and the forecasting ability for monetary aggregates.

The size of aid inflows, the disbursement pattern and expenditure composition of the current poverty reduction program all heavily constrain monetary policy. Some types of aid create excess domestic demand, while others help expand supply in the medium-run, with greater long-run benefits. The optimal choice and mix of instruments should strive to minimize the adverse effects of real appreciation on the private sector, as well as to minimize instrument volatility that is potentially damaging to macroeconomic stabilization. Nonetheless, this is a balance that has proved difficult to achieve.

While primary issues of Treasury bills, surrendered by government to the BOU in 1992, have been used to manage liquidity, the need for development of secondary market based instruments cannot be over-emphasized. Under the primary market-based system of instruments (both Treasury bills and Treasury bonds), the fiscal authorities directly meet the interest cost of monetary policy. This limits the flexibility and independence of monetary policy. Furthermore, primary market-based instruments are not as flexible in liquidity management as they have to be planned, issued within specific schedule, and announced in advance. Yet, the repo market, introduced in 2000 to improve the flexibility of monetary policy, is still thin, implying that any short-run changes in the instruments and liquidity conditions result in volatile interest rates.

The instability of money demand supports the notion that monetary policy should focus explicitly on inflation movements rather than on base money growth. However, a shift to an inflation targeting framework requires building technical capacity in economic modeling, forecasting and analysis, as well as ensuring availability of high frequency real sector data.

Source: Sebudde and Mutambi, 2004

programs; implementation of the African Peer Review Mechanism (APRM); promoting the integration of NEPAD principles and programs in national and regional development plans, including Poverty Reduction Strategy Papers (PRSPs); and engaging the industrialized countries and multilateral institutions on development issues (NEPAD Annual Report 2003/04).

African heads of state and government have continued to champion NEPAD both in Africa and internationally. Several

African countries have established national NEPAD Steering Committees with representation from civil society and business.

NEPAD has focused on strengthening co-operation with development partners, including FAO, WFP, World Bank, USAID and the ADB. National governments are giving increased priority to agriculture and to the preparation of integrated agricultural and rural development plans. The FAO is supporting the preparation of medium-term development plans, which include the identification of bankable projects in more than 49 African countries. The World Bank has also earmarked $500 million for boosting agricultural research and technology development through the implementation of a Multi-Country Agri-cultural Productivity Program.

Since 2002, the ADB has financed twelve NEPAD projects amounting to $520 million. Most of these projects were in transport and water supply and sanitation sectors. Among the transport projects were: the transport sector adjustment program in Morocco, road project in Tunisia, and road project in Zanzibar Island of Tanzania. Examples of the water and sanitation projects include water and sanitation project in Morocco, small towns water supply and sanitation project in Uganda, and the Rift Valley water supply and sanitation in Kenya. The World Bank has also financed a number of scientific technical advisory panel (STAP) projects. One of the most important projects under the STAP scheme was the interconnection of power pools in West and Southern Africa.

The African challenge of maintaining 'effective governments that provide policy certainty, effective law enforcement and delivery of public goods and services' has been underlined by the African Peer Review Mechanism (APRM). The overall objective of the APRM is to ensure that the policies and practices of participating states conform to agreed political, economic, and corporate governance values, codes, and standards. The APRM is defined as 'a system of voluntary self-assessment and constructive peer dialogue and persuasion'. The APRM Panel, consisting of six Eminent Persons appointed to take charge of implementing the mechanism, was inaugurated in July 2003 in Cape Town, South Africa. Partner institutions are the ADB, the AU, ECA and UNDP.

The 23 member states of the AU that have signed the APRM memorandum of understanding are: Algeria, Angola, Benin, Burkina Faso, Cameroon, Republic of Congo, Egypt, Ethiopia, Gabon, Ghana, Kenya, Lesotho, Malawi, Mali, Mauritius, Mozambique, Nigeria, Rwanda, Senegal, Sierra Leone, South Africa, Tanzania and Uganda. Several other countries have indicated an interest. Although the APRM experienced delays in the preparatory phase, reviews were set in motion in four countries: Ghana, Kenya, Mauritius and Rwanda. The aim is to produce two reviews per quarter. Detailed technical assessments on political, economic and corporate governance, as well as development policies and practices, will be undertaken by independent experts. The results will be published and used for mutual learning and cooperation on governance and development issues amongst countries. The transparency of the process will hopefully encourage compliance with good governance standards, especially from the stakeholders in the country.

Africa's Economic Prospects

The African economy is influenced, to a large extent, by developments in the world economy. It is therefore necessary to highlight the global economic prospects first before discussing the economic outlook for the continent. Global economic growth in 2004 was impressive and unusually widespread and well balanced. The US continues to be one of the main drivers of global economic growth. The US trade deficit has been a major symptom of the US's role in sustaining world demand in the past few years. It is to be hoped that domestic demand growth in rapidly-growing Asian countries, and elsewhere, will compensate for a somewhat weaker growth impetus from the US in the coming few years.

A number of projections, including the IMF's *World Economic Outlook* (IMF, 2004) and the UN's *World Economic Situation and Prospects* (UN, 2005), have forecasted a slower global economic growth for 2005 — largely based on the current trends in world oil prices and expected slow down in economic activities in the industrial countries. A forecast growth rate of 3.5 percent is anticipated for the world economy in 2005. In the United States, growth is expected to decelerate to 3 percent in 2005 given the hesitant recovery in employment, gradual upward trend in

interest rates, and waning of fiscal stimuli. In Japan, resurgence in economic activity is expected in 2005 as the financial sector continues to strengthen and deflation is reversed. Current macroeconomic policies in the EU zone remain largely supportive of growth, but structural fiscal deficits are large, and restrictive fiscal policy stance is expected in 2005. Thus, real GDP growth in 2005 in the EU zone is likely to remain at their current levels. Commodity-driven growth in the Commonwealth of Independent States (CIS) will moderate in 2005 slowing down below the 7 percent recorded in 2004.

Given the high degree of globalization of Asia, particularly East Asia, the outlook for 2005 would be slower growth. The interplay between several factors, especially higher oil prices and mixed effects of the phasing out of the multi-fiber arrangement on textiles and clothing on individual countries in the region, would play a decisive role in growth prospects in the region. Growth in China is expected to slightly decelerate to 8.7 percent (9 percent in 2004), slightly reducing Asia's regional growth to 6.5 percent in 2005. Growth in Latin America in 2005 will continue to remain heavily dependent on the external environment, although the adverse effects may be offset by stronger domestic demand in the larger economies in the region. On average, growth in Latin America is expected to be 4 percent in 2005.

Growth rate in Africa for 2005 was forecast at 4.7 percent, compared with the 5.1 percent recorded in 2004. The lower economic outlook for 2005 was based on the assumptions of slower global growth forecast and lower oil prices. Both of these factors will have moderating effects on demand and economic growth in Africa, despite the expected gains from macro-economic management, improved political stability and governance, easing of regional conflicts, and increased agricultural production.

A projected path of raised prices for most metals, minerals and oil commodities, especially if China's high rates of growth are sustained for a decade or more, and if Indian growth burgeons, would have a substantial impact on Africa's economies. Real currency appreciation might take the edge off the bonanza, but there would be large gains to certain African countries, in line with the analysis earlier in this chapter. An important challenge, influencing medium- and long-term outcomes, will be to establish and enforce prudent fiscal rules to smooth surplus export receipts over time, invest them for future growth and avoid the wastage that has characterized past oil and commodities booms.

Another challenge for these countries and other primary-commodity dependent exporters, is the greater diversification of exports, which would help reduce the large growth variability to which most African countries are prey. Any global strategy aimed at reducing poverty in Africa has to take seriously the trade barriers these countries face in marketing their products. Greater access to European and world markets would give a significant impetus to primary and value-added African exports.

Manufacturing is a key diversification sector. Thus the widening productivity gap between agriculture and manufacturing and between manufacture and economy-wide productivity indicates that SSA has moved backwards in the past three decades. While manufacturing output shares grew between 1960 and 1970 in Africa, they declined steadily thereafter. Manufacturing employment shares rose between 1960 and 1980 and have declined since then. Further, average manufacturing labor productivity relative to aggregate labor productivity is lower now than it was in 1970. The implication is that SSA has 'deindustrialized' since 1970.

The significant turnaround required in SSA's economies, to reach the MDGs, is dependent in part upon a resuscitation of the manufacturing industry, continent-wide. On current trends, only a few countries are likely to reach these goals. Governments should continue to deregulate for a friendly business environment to foster both domestic and foreign invest-ment, while government itself redirects investment largely into infrastructure and skills development.

Substantial financial and technical assistance has been promised, with a focus on Africa through the UK's Africa Commis-sion, the UK's current leadership of the G8 countries, and ongoing international commitments to meeting the MDGs. Better coordinated aid, more debt relief, eliminat-ing barriers to exports, especially of agricultural goods, will all be to the good of African countries.

Apart from the impact of exceptional external conditions, Africa's growth gains have also been attributed to its good macroeconomic   stability,   improved governance and the coordinated regional efforts to address Africa's problems (e.g. through NEPAD).

Sustaining macroeconomic stability performance, with the credibility that accompanies it, is of key importance. African countries should aim for more transparent fiscal and monetary polices, following the lead of South Africa. It is argued that future monetary policy in many African countries, which have liberalized domestic financial markets and the capital account, may well have to look beyond money targeting. A move to a rule such as inflation targeting will require greater monetary and fiscal transparency, an improved understanding of the monetary transmission process in these countries, and a modeling effort to forecast inflation and growth.

Moreover, the challenges posed for monetary policy in the presence of thin financial markets, by positive and negative commodity price shocks, and especially by huge aid inflows, deserve far more attention. The blockage of financial intermediation, through the difficulties of absorbing excess liquidity generated by these inflows, is damaging monetary policy transmission in these countries, and investment and growth.

In general, as this chapter has emphasized, savings rates and investment ratios to GDP in the continent, with the possible exception of North Africa, still fall far short of what is needed to foster domestic investment and growth. This leads to far more dependence of compensatory 'foreign savings' in the form of FDI or shorter-term inflows, which can introduce further external volatility into these economies. This is an area that deserves much closer policy attention.

CHAPTER 2

Regional Economic Profiles

Introduction

In addition to providing an overview of the performance of each sub-region, this chapter discusses individual country performances in some detail, highlighting the major changes that occurred during the year. The analysis focuses on recent trends in the domestic economy (growth and inflation), public finance and structural reforms, and recent trends in the external sector (current account developments and external debt), as well as giving a brief economic outlook for 2005.

Of Africa's five sub-regions, Central and East Africa were the strongest economic performers in 2004, with real GDP growth rates of 14.4 percent and 6.8 percent respectively. Growth in Central Africa was largely explained by post-conflict dividends and rapidly rising oil production in some countries. East Africa's growth recovery in 2004 reflected bumper harvests, as agriculture — the backbone of the sub-region's economy — recovered from two consecutive years of drought.

Southern Africa also performed better in 2004 than it did during the period 2000–03 because of improved economic activity in South Africa, the lead country in the sub-region. Growth in North Africa, the largest sub-regional wealth contributor, was relatively robust, at 4.6 percent. West Africa, after being the best performer in the continent in 2003 as a result of exceptional cereal harvests, saw its growth decelerate to 3.4 percent in 2004 because of the difficulties faced by the two largest economies of the sub-region, Nigeria and Côte d'Ivoire, following a series of disruptions to oil production in Nigeria and lingering conflict in Côte d'Ivoire. These trends highlight the many disparities that exist across Africa's sub-regional groupings. The five sub-regions' real GDP growth rates, as well as their shares in Africa's GDP, trade and population are summarized in Table 2.1.

Central Africa

Central Africa encompasses ten countries: Burundi, Cameroon, Central African Republic (CAR), Chad, the Democratic Republic of Congo (DRC), Congo, Equatorial Guinea, Gabon, Rwanda and São Tomé & Príncipe. Five are oil producing/exporting countries (Cameroon, Congo, Gabon, Equatorial Guinea and Chad) while the rest are endowed with agricultural and mineral resources. Central Africa has not fully exploited its resources mainly because of a long history of conflict and political instability, especially in the Great Lakes Region. However, the winding down of conflict over recent years contributed to accelerated growth in 2004. Even so, the sub-region remains a small contributor to Africa's GDP, at 5.9 percent. Cameroon is by far the largest economy in

Table 2.1: A Sub-Regional Overview of African Economies

	Average Real GDP Growth 2000–2003	2004[a/]			
		Real GDP Growth	Share in Africa's GDP	Share in Africa's Exports[b/]	Share in Total Population
Central Africa	4.8	14.4	5.9	7.4	12.2
Eastern Africa	3.4	6.8	6.8	5.2	22.6
Northen Africa	4.1	4.6	36.5	36.4	22.1
Southern Africa	3.1	4.0	34.3	30.4	14.1
Western Africa	4.2	3.4	16.5	20.7	28.9
Franc Zone	4.6	9.9	10.2	12.0	13.5
Net Oil Exporters	4.5	6.1	43.1	55.6	33.2
Net Oil Importers	3.3	4.4	56.9	44.4	66.8
ALL RMCs	**3.8**	**5.1**	–	–	–

Notes: a/ Preliminary estimates
    b/ Exports of goods and non-factor services
Source: ADB Statistics Division, 2004

the sub-region and contributed about 34.5 percent of its GDP in 2004.

The total population of Central Africa was 104.9 million in 2004, equivalent to 12.2 percent of the continental total. Economic growth in the sub-region failed to match that of the population through most of the 1990s, but since 2002 the resumption of growth in post-conflict countries has led to an encouraging increase in per capita GDP. The sub-region's GDP per capita averaged $442 in 2004, against a continental average of $848. This hides wide disparities, however, with GDP per capita in Gabon and Equatorial Guinea reaching $5,062 and $8,740 respectively, compared with $95 in Burundi, $121 in DRC and $207 in Rwanda in 2004.

There were some significant political developments in the sub-region during the year 2004. A coup attempt took place in the DRC in June 2004 and instability persisted in the east of the country, resulting in the take-over of Bukavu by former rebel troops in the same month. Despite this, the transitional government in DRC remained on track and elections are scheduled to take place in 2005. Efforts to improve relations between Rwanda and DRC intensified although tension resurfaced between the two countries in December 2004. General elections in Burundi, initially scheduled for November 2004, were delayed to April 2005. In Cameroon, elections were held in October 2004 and President Paul Biya was re-elected. A coup attempt involving South African mercenaries was foiled in Equatorial Guinea in March 2004.

Recent Trends in the Domestic Economy

Economic Growth

Growth in Central Africa, at 14.4 percent, outpaced continental growth by 5.1 percentage point in 2004, reflecting good performances in Chad and Equatorial Guinea (see Table 2.2). Other countries in the sub-region, including DRC and São Tomé & Príncipe performed relatively well,

while others showed slow economic growth (Figure 2.1). Peace consolidation and increased stability in **Burundi** resulted in improved real GDP growth of 5.5 percent in 2004. Despite adverse weather conditions causing limited agricultural growth, the end of the fighting in most of the country allowed growth in manufacturing while donor-funded projects boosted the construction sector. In addition, in January 2004, the IMF approved a three-year $104 million arrangement under the PRGF.

Growth in **Cameroon** accelerated in 2004 to 4.1 percent, but still lower than the

Table 2.2: Central Africa: GDP and Export Performances

Country	Real GDP Growth Rate (%)		GDP Per Capita (US$)		Real Exports[c] Growth (%)		Exports[b] Per Capita (US$)	
	Average 2000–2003	2004[a]	Average 2000–2003	2004[a]	Average 2000–2003	2004[a]	Average 2000–2003	2004[a]
BURUNDI	1.1	5.5	100	95	5.3	−17.0	8	9
CAMEROON	4.5	4.1	697	982	0.2	4.8	199	221
CENTRAL AFRICAN REP.	−1.4	0.9	274	353	−4.6	45.3	34	47
CHAD	7.7	31.3	233	481	14.2	218.1	63	251
CONGO	4.5	4.0	877	1,148	6.6	10.3	744	937
CONGO, DEM. REP. OF	0.1	6.8	102	121	−3.2	8.3	27	30
EQUATORIAL GUINEA	23.4	59.8	4,241	8,740	29.9	13.1	6,076	8,540
GABON	0.7	1.6	3,988	5,062	3.7	12.8	2,603	3,266
RWANDA	5.8	4.0	213	207	6.9	5.8	15	16
SAO TOME & PRINCIPE	4.4	6.1	333	424	17.3	12.8	142	150
CENTRAL AFRICA	**4.8**	**14.4**	**323**	**442**	**3.1**	**18.7**	**144**	**193**

Notes: [a] Preliminary estimates
[b] Exports of goods and non-factor services
[c] Real exports of goods growth
Source: ADB Statistics Division, 2004

Figure 2.1 : Central Africa: Selected Economic Indicators, 2000–2004

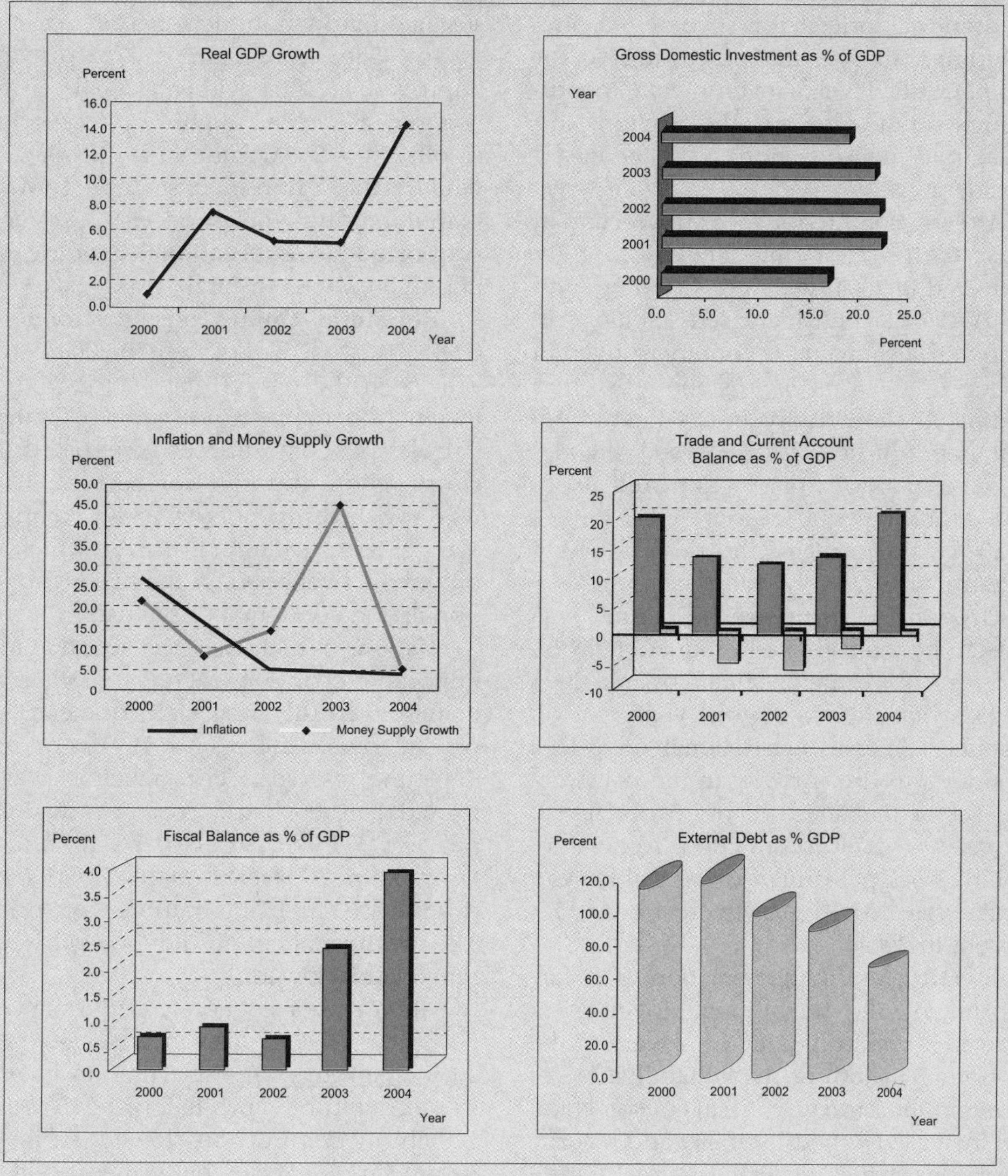

Real GDP Growth

Gross Domestic Investment as % of GDP

Inflation and Money Supply Growth

Trade and Current Account Balance as % of GDP

Fiscal Balance as % of GDP

External Debt as % GDP

Source: ADB Statistics Division, 2004

yearly average of 4.5 percent during 2000–03. Economic performance benefited from strong agricultural output and high international prices for several exports, including oil. The manufacturing sector also performed well. Government expenditure rose in the run-up to the elections and household consumption also increased considerably.

After a contraction of 7.0 percent in 2003, **CAR**'s economic activity slightly recovered in 2004, with a real GDP growth rate of 0.7 percent. Increased stability and improved security in the country resulted in higher food crops as resident that fled fighting in the country in 2003 returned. Mining production also resumed slightly. However, cotton production fell from 14,000 tonnes in 2003 to only 1,500 tonnes in 2004 as a result of the destruction of infrastructure, notably cotton factories.

Growth performance in **Chad** was boosted by the rise in oil production, as oil fields in Doba came on stream by mid-2003 (2004 was the first full year of oil production), and international oil prices continued to rise. Activity in the construction sector remained strong, especially in the case of road construction. Agriculture and livestock performance was stable. As a result, real GDP growth reached 31.3 percent in 2004.

In **DRC**, the implementation of policy reforms by the transitional government allowed a stabilization and recovery of the economy, including the rehabilitation of transport infrastructure, fiscal consolidation and increased political stability and security conditions (which facilitate internal trade). Economic performance improved, with real

GDP growth rising to 6.8 percent in 2004, resulting largely from a recovery in mining production, particularly of diamonds, and sustained growth in the services sector.

In **Congo**, economic performance improved in 2004 with real GDP growth rising to 4 percent. High oil prices helped to offset for the decline in oil production, while the non-oil sector (notably manufacturing and services) recovered, supported by international funding and improved access to rural areas.

Equatorial Guinea posted strong real GDP growth of 59.8 percent in 2004. Strong activity in the oil and gas sector, with oil production rising to an average 300,000 barrels per day in 2004, boosted the construction and services sectors. There was new investment by a US oil company, Marathon. Agriculture, however, which still provides a livelihood for the majority of the population continued to stagnate.

Gabon, which is the second most important economy in the region, relies heavily on oil, although domestic oil production has fallen since 1997 because of depleting reserves. Oil production in 2003 totaled 266,900 barrels per day, against a peak of 371,000 barrels per day in 1997. Growth in 2004 slowed to 1.6 percent, despite the high international oil prices. The performance of the non-oil sector remained lackluster.

After a poor economic performance in 2003, real GDP growth in **Rwanda** rose to 4.0 percent in 2004, reflecting an increase in agricultural production. However, activity in construction slowed, while the manufacturing sector performed poorly as a result of an electricity shortage.

Growth in **São Tomé & Príncipe** accelerated to 6.1 percent in 2004 as a result of a recovery in cocoa production, increased government consumption, and foreign investment in the oil and tourism sectors.

Prices and Exchange Rates

Inflation in Central Africa averaged 3.1 percent in 2004, against a continental average of 7.7 percent. This reflected tight monetary and fiscal policies in the CFA zone — which comprises Cameroon, CAR, Chad, Congo, Equatorial Guinea and Gabon — and macroeconomic stabilization in DRC. The strengthening of the CFA franc against the US dollar since 2003 has also helped to dampen inflationary pressure in the sub-region, and kept the lid on fuel prices.

Monetary policy in the Central African CFA zone is dictated by the regional central bank, Banque des Etats d'Afrique Centrale (BEAC) and aims at controlling inflation and maintaining the peg of the CFA franc with the euro. However, the BEAC's inter-bank and money market has lacked effectiveness, because of the region's excess liquidity and poor regional financial integration. Statutory reserve requirements for commercial banks were introduced in September 2001 and tightened in March 2003. Interest rate adjustments remain rare and limited, although the BEAC cut its rediscount rate from 6.30 percent to 6 percent in December 2003, in the context of falling regional inflation and lower world interest rates.

Foreign reserves are pooled together in an operation account held at the French Public Treasury, which in turn guarantees the stability and convertibility of the regional currency. In line with the euro, the CFA franc appreciated against the US dollar for the second consecutive year, from an average of CFA581:US$1 in 2003 to CFA535:US$1 in 2004.

Inflation in **Cameroon** declined to 0.2 percent in 2004, from 2.7 percent in 2003. In **CAR**, consumer prices fell by 2.1 percent in 2004, as a result of improved security and food crops, as well as tight regional monetary policy. Inflation pressures resulting from increased oil revenue in **Chad** were more than compensated by a fall in food prices due to rising agricultural production, with inflation standing at 8.7 percent in 2004. Inflation in **Congo** rose to a low 3.3 percent in 2004. Oil activity in **Equatorial Guinea** allowed a rise in government expenditure resulting in an increase of inflation to 7.9 percent. Tight regional monetary policy and low demand pressure resulted in an average inflation of 2 percent in **Gabon** in 2004.

In **Burundi**, inflation in 2004 rose to 7.0 percent *vis-à-vis* 2003 as a result of rising international prices, poor food crops and an increase in government spending. Nonetheless, this figure is lower than the 10.7 percent recorded during the period 2000–2003. Monetary policy in Burundi is based on inflation targeting. The country's central bank has been gradually switching to indirect monetary instruments by adopting weekly liquidity auctions and reducing banks refinancing ceilings. There was a further relaxation in exchange control, and the differential between the official and parallel exchange rate market narrowed. The depreciation of the Burundi franc against the US dollar slowed down in 2004, as a result of a weak US dollar and tighter monetary policy.

Inflation in **DRC** decelerated to 7.9 percent in 2004, against a massive yearly average of 176.3 percent during 2000–03. The Banque Centrale du Congo (BCC) aims to achieve price stability within the framework of a floating exchange rate system that was introduced in May 2001. The bank continued to pursue a relatively prudent monetary policy in 2004. Despite lower inflation, the bank kept its refinancing rate unchanged in 2004, after cutting it to 8 percent in November 2003. The BCC made substantial progress in facilitating monetary transactions in Congolese francs by gradually introducing higher value banknotes. The growth of credit to the private sector remained robust. The Congolese franc depreciated by 19.4 percent against the US dollar in 2004 (end-September) against a small appreciation of 1 percent in 2003 (end-September).

In **Rwanda**, inflation accelerated to 8.2 percent in 2004, as a result of deteriorating food supply conditions after poor harvests in 2003. This also reflected a tightening in the central bank's monetary stance. The Rwanda franc continued to depreciate against the US dollar, albeit at a slower rate of 3.9 percent in 2004 (end-September) as opposed to the 14.2 percent observed in 2003 (end-September).

Inflation in **São Tomé & Príncipe** accelerated to 14.0 percent in 2004, against an average 7.4 percent during 2000–03. There has been a marked improvement in money aggregates since 1998, as a result of

a tightening in reserve requirements, and a substantial fall in net bank credit to the government. The discount rate, which fell from 43 percent in 1997 to 15 percent in 2002, has remained largely unchanged in the past two years, averaging 14.5 percent in 2004. The dobra continued to depreciate slightly against the US dollar in 2004.

Public Finance and Structural Reforms
Fiscal Developments

Central Africa's fiscal position principally reflects fluctuations in government earnings from the oil sector. Overall, the sub-region achieved a fiscal surplus equivalent to 3.9 percent of GDP in 2004, thanks to firm oil prices, increased donor support in post-conflict recovering countries and improved fiscal performances, notably in Gabon and Congo (see Table 2.3).

In **Burundi**, the government's fiscal balance showed a surplus of 18.3 percent of GDP in 2004, despite election-related expenditure, an increase in social spending, stemming from the resettlement of refugees, and the cost of military demobilization, which began in 2003. However, progress in fiscal consolidation was made, and in April 2004, the transaction tax was extended to all domestic transactions, in preparation for the introduction of VAT in 2005.

Cameroon's overall government balance has remained in surplus since 2000, reflecting rising government earnings from the oil sector (mostly as a result of rising world prices) and efforts to widen the tax base. Although expenditure,

Table 2.3: Central Africa: Macroeconomic Management Indicators

Country	Inflation (%)		Fiscal Balance as % of GDP		Gross Domestic Investment		Gross National Savings	
					as % of GDP			
	Average 2000–2003	2004[a/]	Average 2000–2003	2004[a/]	Average 2000–2003	2004[a/]	Average 2000–2003	2004[a/]
BURUNDI	10.7	7.0	–3.7	18.3	8.7	12.4	2.1	–2.6
CAMEROON	2.7	0.2	2.4	0.8	15.9	15.3	13.5	15.4
CENTRAL AFRICAN REP.	3.1	–2.1	–2.1	–1.2	8.2	6.8	4.8	3.8
CHAD	4.9	–8.7	–5.6	–4.1	39.5	22.9	10.9	8.9
CONGO	0.8	3.3	–1.8	5.0	23.5	22.9	24.5	24.2
CONGO, DEM. REP. OF	176.3	7.9	–3.4	–4.8	12.3	12.3	4.6	15.7
EQUATORIAL GUINEA	6.7	4.0	14.7	28.5	41.1	13.6	21.2	18.6
GABON	0.8	–0.7	6.5	8.8	28.6	29.5	35.4	37.0
RWANDA	3.5	8.2	–0.9	–0.1	17.8	20.3	11.3	23.3
SAO TOME & PRINCIPE	7.4	14.0	–15.4	–17.2	33.8	48.0	11.5	0.0
CENTRAL AFRICA	**12.2**	**3.1**	**1.1**	**3.9**	**20.3**	**18.4**	**16.5**	**18.5**

Note: [a/] Preliminary estimates
Source: ADB Statistics Division, 2004

including social spending, were higher than projected in the run-up to the October elections (this delayed IMF payments under the PRGF), rising oil receipts and an increased share of non-oil revenue resulted in a surplus of 0.8 percent of GDP in 2004, against 2.4 percent of GDP during 2000–03.

The government's fiscal position in **CAR** remained precarious in 2004, despite some commitment to strengthen public finance management. Although increased security allowed for some recovery in economic activity, this was not enough to have a significant impact on tax collection. The fiscal deficit stood at 1.2 percent of

GDP in 2004, but the government continued to face difficulties in paying civil servants wages, despite some donor support notably from France and China.

The government of **Chad** has shown strong commitment to sound oil revenue management, since measures agreed with the World Bank were passed into law in 2003. As a result, a total of CFAfr5 billion was credited to a stabilization account and the fiscal deficit declined to 4.1 percent of GDP in 2004.

The fiscal deficit in **DRC** declined to 4.7 percent of GDP in 2004, vis-à-vis 2003, but still higher than the 3.8 percent recorded during 2000–03. The government is committed to reducing extra-budgetary spending and enhancing revenue collection. It also pursued its main objective of reorienting public spending from military costs towards priority sectors, particularly health and education. A supplementary budget was adopted in June 2004 to cover the cost of preparing presidential and legislative elections scheduled in June 2005. Revenues from trade and the oil sector increased, while corporate taxes were revised and the government also made progress in preparing for the introduction of VAT in 2005.

The government in **Congo** remained committed to pursuing a prudent fiscal policy in 2004, as part of its negotiations with the IMF to obtain a PRGF. The government took measures to strengthen fiscal discipline, hiring an independent auditing company in the oil sector to enhance transparency in oil revenue management. Rising oil prices and revenues, coupled with a slight increase in public revenues in the non-oil sector, helped to keep the fiscal surplus at 5.0 percent of GDP in 2004.

Equatorial Guinea retained a strong fiscal surplus of 28.5 percent of GDP in 2004, up from a yearly average 14.7 percent of GDP in 2000–03, encouraging little discipline from the government. Revenue benefited from rising oil production and prices — foreign oil firms in the country operate under production sharing agreements. Recurrent expenditure and capital spending increased sharply. Transparency in the management of oil revenues was still lacking.

Gabon continued its efforts to strengthen non-oil revenue and curtail recurrent expenditure to compensate for shrinking oil revenue. The value added tax (VAT) was raised from 18 percent to 25 percent while, in April 2004, measures were introduced to contain the wage bill. The fiscal surplus increased to 8.8 percent of GDP in 2004, up from an average 6.5 percent of GDP during 2000–03.

Income tax reforms introduced in 2003 helped to increase revenue in **Rwanda** in 2004. The share of recurrent expenditure in the budget remained high, although external financial assistance supported an increase in recurrent and capital spending in priority sectors. A supplementary budget was passed in August 2004 to allow for an increase in expenditure resulting from higher energy cost and the impact of the strengthening of the euro on the external debt burden. The fiscal deficit in 2004 fell from 0.9 percent of GDP during 2000–03 to 0.1 percent of GDP in 2004.

In **São Tomé & Príncipe,** the government increased civil servants' wages by 33 percent in May 2004, against a recommended 23 percent by the IMF. As a result, the fiscal deficit widened in 2004 to 17.2 percent of GDP. Preparations were made for the management of future oil revenues and, in August 2004, the National Assembly adopted an oil revenue management law in line with a World Bank recommendation.

Structural Reforms

The pace of structural reforms in 2004 remained slow for most oil-producing countries in Central Africa, despite government pledges to increase transparency in the oil sector. The extent and nature of reform efforts in the non-oil producing countries in the region have varied.

In **Burundi** the government announced an ambitious program of structural reforms in 2004. This involved the privatization of Onatel (telecommunications), Cotebu (textiles), Sosumo (sugar), Sodeco and Ocibu (coffee), Brarudi (breweries), Socabu (insurance) and the dissolution of the Burundi Tea Board. Some progress was made in the liberalization of the telecommunications sector, with a Chinese firm awarded a mobile phone license in April 2004. The government also remained committed to reforms in the judiciary, although progress was slow.

Despite nominal commitment by **Cameroon**'s government to push through structural reforms, no progress was made in the privatisation of SNEC (water), Camtel (telecommunications) and Cameroon Development Corporation (banana, rubber and palm oil). The government also failed to meet IMF recommendations to put into liquidation the national air company, Camair, and restructure the post office savings bank, CEP. Both have been in financial difficulties for many years.

Structural reforms in **CAR** remained stalled, although some efforts were made to improve the financial position of the telecommunications company, Socatel. Public utilities mooted for privatisation include Socatel, Enerca (energy) and SNE (water). Even so, the difficult business environment has kept strategic investors away from the country.

In **Chad**, the privatization program made little progress in 2004. The privatization of the cotton company, Cotontchad, has yet to start. Other enterprises targeted for sale include Air Chad and Sotel Chad (telecommunications).

The government in **DRC** made some progress in structural reforms in 2004. It was notably committed to finalize audits for the main utilities (water, electricity, communications and transport) and in January 2005 launched a call for an expression of interest in the audit of the diamond mining company, Miba. Plans for restructuring the banking sector were finalized in March 2004 — seven commercial banks were to undergo restructuring, before being open to private capital, while two banks were to be liquidated. Meanwhile, the restructuring of the oil parastatal, Cohydro, remained stalled.

In 2004, the government of **Congo** made some progress in revenue transparency in the oil sector, but experienced some new setbacks in its program of privatization. Annual audits in the national oil company, SNPC, continued with oil accounts now consolidated and reviewed on a quarterly basis. The sale of the railway company, CFCO, collapsed in August 2004, after talks with two pre-selected bidders fell through. The electricity utility, SNE, whose privatization was abandoned in 2001 for lack of interest from strategic investors, has yet to be restructured.

In the case of **Equatorial Guinea**, although the government has made a nominal commitment to privatization, no program was drawn up in 2004.

In **Gabon** the government renewed its commitment to structural reforms in 2004.

The country's privatization program has been stalled for many years. This has hindered private sector activity and postponed a much-needed diversification away from the oil sector. In June 2004, the government launched a restrictive bid, involving the three companies that had qualified in a previous bid in 2003, for a 50 percent stake in Gabon Télécom. The restructuring of the airline company, Air Gabon, gathered momentum in preparation for its divestiture. Other companies slated for sale include Hevegab (rubber) and Agrogabon (palm oil and soap).

Rwanda undertook reforms in 2004. The state-owned tea estate, Pfunda, was sold to a UK company in July 2004. Two commercial banks, the Banque Commerciale du Rwanda and Banque Continentale Africaine, were also privatized, as part of reforms to strengthen the banking sector. Negotiations with potential buyers for a 98 percent share in the telecommunications utility, Rwandatel, began in April, with the sale scheduled for completion in 2005.

São Tomé and Príncipe has made preparations for the sale of EMAE (water and electricity).

Recent Trends in the External Sector

Current Account Developments

Central Africa's external position improved markedly in 2004, with the current account balance turning into a small surplus of 0.2 percent of GDP, compared with a deficit of 3.6 percent of GDP during 2000–03 (see Table 2.4). The main development in the region in 2004 was in Chad, where oil exports replaced cotton and livestock as the main source of foreign exchange earnings for the first time. São Tomé & Príncipe should also start producing oil in the years to come. Only Cameroon currently has a relatively wide export base, although this mostly entails crude oil and low value-added agricultural products. The terms of trade for oil-exporting countries in Central Africa improved in 2004, with world oil prices rising from an already high $28.9 per barrel in 2003 to $38.3 per barrel in 2004. The continued strengthening of the CFA franc against the dollar contributed to sluggish export performance in some of the non-oil CFA zone countries in 2004.

In **Burundi**, the current account deficit widened to 15.1 percent of GDP in 2004, mostly reflecting movements in the trade balance. Coffee export earnings declined, while the demand for imports increased with economic growth. Buoyant official transfers — coupled with concessional lending — continued to pay for the country's balance of payments deficit.

Cameroon's trade surplus rose to 2.4 percent of GDP in 2004 — higher oil international prices more than compensated falling production — while earnings from non-oil exports (notably coffee, cocoa, and timber) remained significant. There was a decline in the current account deficit to 2.1 percent of GDP in 2004, against a yearly average of 3.8 percent of GDP during 2000–03.

Net trade in goods and services has usually recorded a deficit in **CAR**, because of heavy freight costs. Export earnings, mostly from diamond, timber, and to a lesser extent, cotton, are nonetheless high

Table 2.4: Central Africa: The External Sector

Country	Trade balance as % of GDP		Current Account as % of GDP		Terms of Trade (%) of GDP		Total External Debt as % Exports		Debt Service as % of	
	Average 2000–2003	2004[a]	Average 2000–2003	2004[a]	Average 2000–2003	2004[a]	Average 2000–2003	2004[a]	Average 2000–2003	2004[a]
BURUNDI	−11.5	−20.8	−7.4	−15.1	−11.8	−0.3	184.9	184.8	59.2	408.5
CAMEROON	3.8	2.4	−3.8	−2.1	10.2	2.4	67.6	40.6	10.3	10.4
CENTRAL AFRICAN REP.	2.5	2.0	−3.4	−2.8	0.9	−7.8	89.7	90.7	2.9	13.1
CHAD	−18.1	28.4	−35.9	−18.3	15.4	32.9	40.5	20.9	9.2	1.0
CONGO, DEM. REP. OF	1.0	−6.4	−2.9	−3.0	−0.5	−5.2	232.7	160.6	145.9	4.1
CONGO, REPUBLIC OF	51.6	51.0	1.1	1.6	18.8	10.8	188.5	50.6	7.8	13.6
EQUATORIAL GUINEA	37.6	76.7	−17.7	18.3	8.8	59.6	11.8	5.0	4.0	1.1
GABON	39.0	42.3	11.4	11.6	2.7	12.4	61.4	51.3	26.4	12.5
RWANDA	−9.3	−12.5	−6.5	−6.8	−4.2	−10.0	79.2	86.3	27.3	29.4
SAO TOME & PRINCIPE	−39.6	−46.5	−46.0	−59.9	3.2	−3.4	514.9	405.9	40.2	109.0
CENTRAL AFRICA	**14.0**	**20.5**	**−3.6**	**0.2**	**6.4**	**12.5**	**105.6**	**62.0**	**25.7**	**9.4**

Note: a/ Preliminary estimates
Source: ADB Statistics Division, 2004

enough for the country to occasionally post a small trade surplus in FOB terms. In 2004, the current account deficit narrowed to 2.8 percent of GDP in 2004 because of depressed imports and a slight recovery in timber and diamond exports.

Increased oil production in **Chad** meant that exports of goods in volume terms increased by an estimated 218 percent in 2004. High oil prices boosted export earnings. At the same time, the completion of the pipeline since 2003 and a slowdown in oil-related investment caused imports of capital and intermediate goods to fall. As a result, Chad's trade deficit turned into a

surplus of 28.4 percent of GDP in 2004. The current account deficit shrank from 35.9 percent of GDP during 2000–2003 to 18.3 percent in 2004.

DRC has abundant natural resources and a well-diversified export base, comprising diamonds, crude oil, copper, cobalt and coffee. The trade balance deteriorated in 2004 as import growth outpaced export growth. Exports benefited from increased diamond earnings and higher international metal prices, while imports rose substantially as ongoing externally-financed projects increased capital goods imports. Despite rising net official transfers, the current account balance turned from a small surplus in 2003 to a deficit of 3 percent of GDP in 2004.

Congo's external position improved for the third consecutive year in 2004, in the context of rising international oil prices. Up to 90 percent of the country's export earnings come from oil, while the demand for imports remains relatively small, with occasional rises in capital spending mostly reflecting foreign investment in the country. The trade surplus increased to 51 percent of GDP in 2004 and the deficit in the invisible balance (notably profit remittances from oil companies and external debt payment services) remained roughly unchanged. The current account surplus increased from 1.1 percent of GDP during 2000–03 to 1.6 percent in 2004.

The current account balance in **Equatorial Guinea** turned from a deficit of 17.7 percent of GDP during 2000–03 to a surplus of 18.3 percent of GDP in 2004. Oil exports surged with fast-rising production and high international oil prices, while the demand for imports slowed with investment. Freight costs were lower, although profit remittances remained significant, with the invisible deficit reaching 58.4 percent of GDP in 2004, as against a trade surplus of 76.7 percent of GDP.

Gabon's external position strengthened for the second consecutive year in 2004, with the current account balance recording a surplus equivalent to 11.6 percent of GDP. The increase in the trade surplus to 42.3 percent of GDP mostly reflected the impact of rising world prices, but oil production continued to decline. The

domestic demand for imports remained modest by comparison with the level of Gabon's oil-based GDP.

Rwanda's export base is relatively narrow but increased production and rising world prices for coffee and tea — the country's main export commodities — boosted exports, while strong tin prices also boosted cassiterite exports. Import growth in 2004 reflected higher oil prices and the demand for imports fuelled by donor activity. Substantial official transfers helped to contain the current account deficit at 6.8 percent of GDP in 2004.

São Tomé & Príncipe's export base is also very narrow (mostly cocoa beans), while imports comprise food, oil and capital equipment. Exports rose in 2004 as a result of higher cocoa production and high cocoa prices. Capital investment in the oil sector increased imports. Transport and freight insurance also rose significantly, bringing the invisible deficit to 13.4 percent of GDP. The current account deficit increased to nearly 60 percent of GDP in 2004, up from an annual average of 46 percent of GDP during 2000–03.

External Debt

Central Africa's external debt burden is the highest in Africa. Debt amounted to 62 percent of the sub-region's GDP in 2004, down from an average 105.6 percent of GDP during 2000–03. Only five out of the eight low-income countries in the region have qualified for debt relief under the HIPC initiative. Not all governments in the region have regularized relations with external creditors and/or concluded an IMF-sponsored PRGF.

Foreign direct investment has increased significantly but is largely confined to the oil sector — political instability being the main hindrance to FDI elsewhere. According to UNCTAD's *World Investment Report, 2004*, FDI inflows to the sub-region totaled $3.1 billion in 2003, of which $1.4 billion and $837 million went respectively to Equatorial Guinea and Chad. The CFA zone countries created a regional stock market in Libreville, Gabon, in July 2003, although it is not yet operational.

The external debt burden in **Burundi** remains unsustainable. The debt service ratio rose to 408.5 percent in 2004. In 2004, the debt-to-GDP ratio fell to 184.8 percent in 2004, following the approval of a PRGF with the IMF in January 2004. Debt relief was granted in March, with the Paris Club approving a $4.4 million cancellation and $81 million rescheduling. The country is expected to reach decision point under the HIPC initiative by mid-2005.

A decline in **Cameroon**'s external debt burden has resulted from an improved fiscal position and a prudent borrowing policy, combined with successive debt relief deals with the Paris Club and interim debt relief under the enhanced HIPC initiative. The country is now expected to reach its HIPC completion point in 2005, assuming a new PRGF is approved by the IMF. In 2004, the external debt-to-GDP ratio decreased to 40.6 percent, while the debt service ratio declined to 10.4 percent.

CAR's external debt is mostly made up of highly concessional, multilateral, long-term loans. The country has yet to qualify for debt relief under the enhanced HIPC initiative, reflecting the continued accumulation of multilateral and bilateral debt payment arrears and delays in securing an IMF financial deal. The debt-to-GDP ratio fell to 90.7 percent in 2004, reflecting improved growth, while the debt service ratio totaled 13.1 percent.

External debt in **Chad** continued to decline rapidly to 20.9 percent of GDP in 2004, reflecting a double digit economic growth, debt relief, and access to non-debt capital inflows. Chad qualified for the HIPC initiative in May 2001, which could pave the way for debt relief of $260 million when completion point is met. As oil reached full production, the debt service ratio declined dramatically to 1 percent in 2004.

DRC reached decision point under the enhanced HIPC initiative in July 2003. Debt relief from bilateral and multilateral creditors will amount to approximately $10 billion in nominal terms, after the country reaches completion point. The debt-to-GDP ratio was estimated at 160.6 percent in 2004, while the debt service ratio represented 4.1 percent.

Congo has inherited a heavy debt burden because of excess borrowing against future oil earnings in the past. However, external debt in 2004 declined to 50.6 percent of GDP while the debt service ratio doubled to 13.6 percent. This reflected the government's resumption of its current external debt obligations and clearance in non-rescheduling debt payment arrears. Multilateral lenders subsequently resumed their assistance to the country, and following the IMF approval of a new three-year PRGF to the country in December 2004, the Paris Club agreed to debt relief of $3 billion and a rescheduling deal.

Equatorial Guinea is not eligible for concessional assistance, being a middle-income economy. As a result, most of the country's external public debt has been contracted on a bilateral basis. The debt burden remained low in 2004, with total debt falling further to 5 percent of GDP due to remarkable growth performances, while the debt service ratio declined to 1.1 percent, because of rising oil export earnings.

Following a standby agreement signed with the IMF in May 2004, the **Gabon** government negotiated a $711 million debt arrears rescheduling deal with the Paris Club, and negotiations were under way with the London Club of commercial banks. This, coupled with previous debt rescheduling deals and relatively prudent borrowing policy in recent years, led to a further decline in the country's external debt to 51.3 percent of GDP in 2004. Meanwhile, the debt service ratio fell considerably from 26.4 percent during 2000–03 to 12.5 percent in 2004. Gabon does not qualify for HIPC debt relief, being classified as a middle-income economy.

Rwanda's external debt amounted to $1.49 billion, an equivalent 86.3 percent of GDP, at end-2004, while the debt service ratio increased slightly to 29.4 percent. The country qualified for debt relief under HIPC in May 2001, but failures to meet benchmarks under the 2002–05 PRGF since late 2003 have delayed completion point. The government continued to depend on interim debt relief from its creditors to meet its debt payment obligations.

While falling to 405.9 percent in 2004, **São Tomé & Príncipe**'s external debt-to-GDP ratio remained the highest in Africa.

The country qualified for the HIPC initiative in December 2000, paving the way for a nominal debt relief of $200 million at completion point. About 65 percent of the country's debt is owed to multilateral lenders. The government is expected to negotiate a new PRGF and interim debt relief with the IMF in 2005. The debt service ratio increased to 109 percent in 2004, up from 40.2 percent during 2000–03.

Outlook

Central Africa's sub-regional GDP is forecast to grow by 4.1 percent in 2005, compared with 14.4 percent in 2004, assuming deceleration in growth in Chad to 10.8 percent in 2005 (from 31.3 percent in 2004), as oil production reaches its full capacity of 250,000 barrels per day. Lower oil prices and a slower growth in average annual oil production will nonetheless cause real GDP growth to slow down in 2005. Growth in Burundi is expected to remain strong in 2005, assuming satisfactory weather conditions. Rising donor assistance will support the country's reconstruction efforts while the approval of a new PRGF in January 2004 will allow the country to benefit from interim debt relief under the HIPC initiative. In Cameroon, the approval of a new PRGF with the IMF, expected for 2005, and strengthened macroeconomic policy, will support annual growth rates of 4–5 percent. Economic recovery in CAR will hinge on success in fostering security and political stability, leading to the gradual resumption in donor support.

Presidential and legislative elections in DRC are to be held in 2005, although delays may occur. Growth is expected to remain robust, driven by increased foreign-financed investment and the implementation of structural reforms. Instability in the east of the country may rise in the run-up to the elections, however, hindering post-war reconstruction efforts. Real GDP growth in Congo is expected to accelerate to 9–10 percent in 2005, following the approval by the IMF of a PRGF (2004–07) in December 2004. This will support rising investment and activity in the non-oil sector, as the pace of structural reforms accelerates. Growth performance will remain exceptionally strong in Equatorial Guinea, as oil production continues to expand, notably in offshore fields, Zafiro, Ceiba and Alba, situated to the north of Bioko island. Economic growth in Gabon will continue to be modest as a result of falling oil production although new development programs — and reforms to diversify the economy — will support recovery in the non-oil sector next year. The government is expected to complete its PRSP in early 2005. In Rwanda, annual growth rate of around 6 percent is expected to be achieved in 2005, on the back of donors' continued support and progress in structural reforms, and assuming satisfactory weather conditions. Increased investment in petroleum exploration and infrastructure development will continue to drive economic performance in São Tomé & Príncipe. However, the start of oil production, initially forecast in 2006, is not expected before 2008.

East Africa

The East African sub-region is made up of 11 countries: Comoros, Djibouti, Eritrea, Ethiopia, Kenya, Madagascar, Mauritius, Seychelles, Somalia, Tanzania and Uganda. East Africa's GDP accounted for 6.8 percent of the continent's output in 2004. Most countries in the sub-region thrive on tourism and exports of primary commodities, notably tea and coffee. Other countries, like Mauritius, have been more successful in diversifying their export base away from traditional products. East Africa is a net importer of oil. Kenya is the largest economy of the zone, followed by Tanzania, Ethiopia, and Uganda. Taken together, these four countries generated 72.1 percent of sub-regional GDP in 2004.

The population of East Africa was estimated at 204.5 million in 2004, representing about 22.6 percent of the continent's population. Seychelles and Mauritius are middle-income countries, their GDP per capita being estimated at $8,375 and $5,158 respectively in 2004. By contrast, Eritrea and Ethiopia are among the poorest countries in Africa, with a per capita income below $220. The region's GDP per capita remains the lowest in Africa, averaging $276 in 2004.

In Somalia, the peace process has made good progress. A 275-member Somali transitional parliament was set up in Kenya in August 2004 and Colonel Abdullahi Yusuf Ahmed was elected as Somali president in October for a five-year mandate. Although in September 2004 the UN extended the mandate of the UN Mission in Ethiopia and Eritrea for another six months, there was rising concern over the stalled border dispute between the two countries. In Comoros, the slow transition to a new federal system was completed, with elections of the national and island assemblies taking place in March–April 2004, and the installation of a federal government in July. In the Seychelles, Albert René stepped down as president after spending 27 years in power.

Recent Trends in the Domestic Economy

Economic Growth

After two years of subdued economic activity, mostly resulting from the severe drought that hit the Horn of Africa in 2002 and 2003, the worst in many years, East Africa recovered in 2004, with growth accelerating to 6.8 percent, against an average 3.4 percent during 2000–03 (see Table 2.5 and Figure 2.2).

Table 2.5: East Africa: GDP and Export Performances

Country	Real GDP Growth Rate (%)		GDP Per Capita (US$)		Real Exports[c] Growth (%)		Exports[b] Per Capita (US$)	
	Average		Average		Average		Average	
	2000–2003	2004[a]	2000–2003	2004[a]	2000–2003	2004[a]	2000–2003	2004[a]
COMOROS	2.3	1.9	324	454	–6.5	14.5	54	75
DJIBOUTI	2.2	3.0	854	932	8.4	4.0	395	461
ERITREA	–0.1	1.8	172	215	9.9	–3.5	28	19
ETHIOPIA	2.7	11.5	94	112	10.5	12.0	15	19
KENYA	1.0	3.1	385	445	7.2	11.2	101	128
MADAGASCAR	2.0	5.3	273	239	9.5	–5.8	66	67
MAURITIUS	5.0	4.1	4,045	5,158	6.4	7.4	2,321	2,732
SEYCHELLES	–0.7	–2.0	8,014	8,375	15.6	4.3	6,429	7,112
SOMALIA	...	...	...	...	6.1	6.1	...	...
TANZANIA	6.4	7.4	268	288	15.7	8.8	41	50
UGANDA	5.5	5.9	235	274	5.4	5.2	29	35
EAST AFRICA	**3.4**	**6.8**	**247**	**276**	**7.2**	**7.9**	**61**	**72**

Notes: [a] Preliminary estimates
[b] Exports of goods and non-factor services
[c] Real exports of goods growth
Source: ADB Statistics Division, 2004

Figure 2.2: East Africa: Selected Economic Indicators, 2000–2004

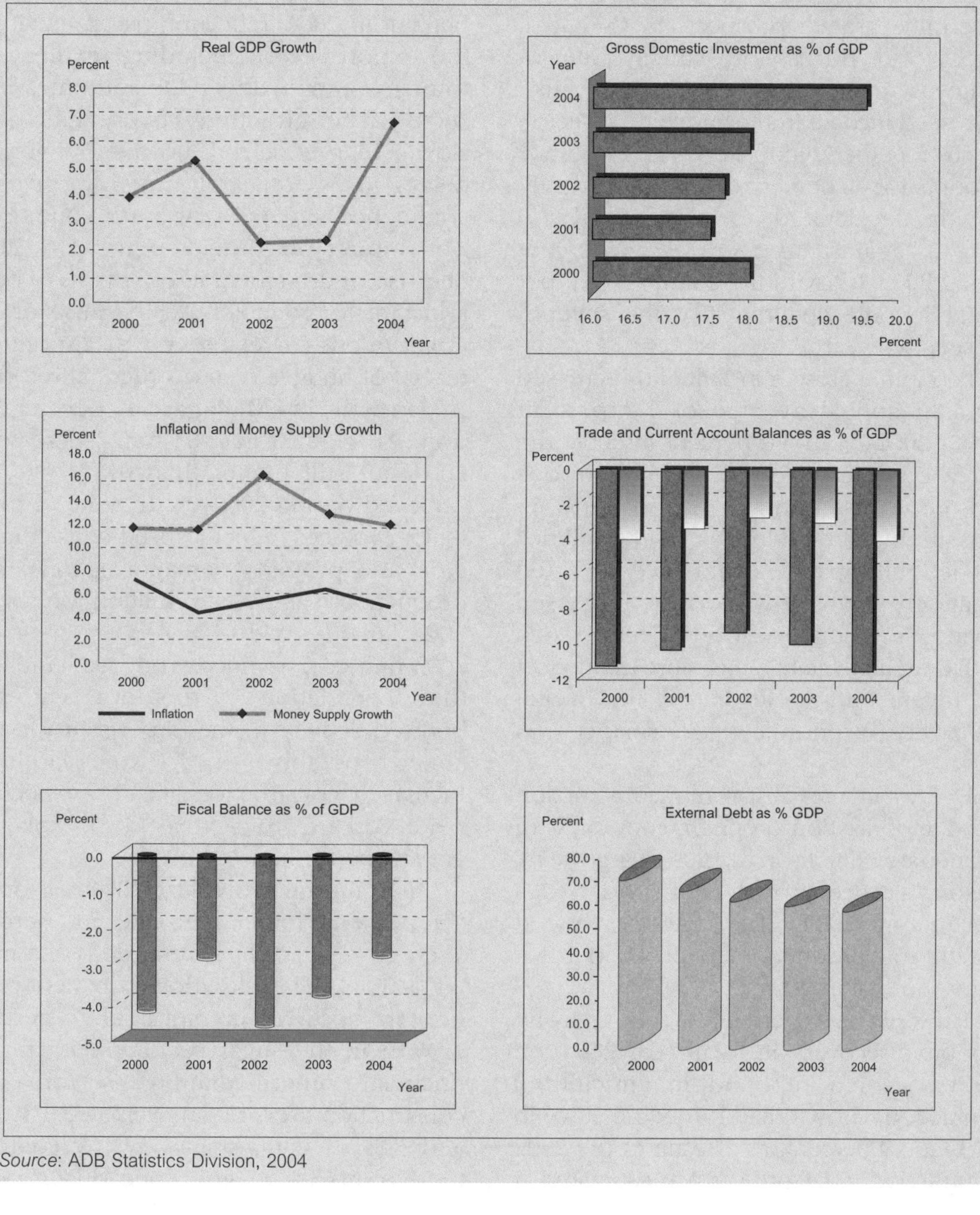

Real GDP Growth

Gross Domestic Investment as % of GDP

Inflation and Money Supply Growth

Inflation   Money Supply Growth

Trade and Current Account Balances as % of GDP

Fiscal Balance as % of GDP

External Debt as % GDP

Source: ADB Statistics Division, 2004

Unsettled disputes over competencies and resources between the islands and central administration have continued to undermine growth prospects in **Comoros**. Low world prices for vanilla, one of Comoros' main export crops, have also depressed income in the agricultural sector, which (together with fisheries and forestry) accounts for 42 percent of GDP. As a result, growth decelerated to a subdued 1.9 percent, against an average 2.3 percent during 2000–03, with the country's real per capita income declining for the seventh consecutive year.

Economic growth in **Djibouti** increased from an annual average of 2.2 percent during 2000–03 to 3.0 percent in 2004; the increased presence of foreign troops boosted consumption. The decline in transshipment activity, as port facilities reached full capacity, could have impacted negatively on growth. But increased private investment in projects, such the Doraleh oil facility, has more than offset the adverse effects, leading to the overall improved economic performance in 2004.

Delays in the post-war reconstruction and demobilization program, coupled with inadequate rainfalls in the 2003/04 growing season, slashed growth in **Eritrea** to 1.8 percent in 2004. The FAO estimated agricultural production to be 60 percent below normal in 2004.

Ethiopia experienced a strong economic recovery in fiscal year 2004, on the back of a rebound in agricultural production. Growth had turned negative in 2003, at 3.9 percent, as a result of the 2002 drought. Real GDP growth was estimated at 11.5 percent in 2004, with agricultural output growing by 18.9 percent.

Economic growth in **Kenya** rose to 3.1 percent in 2004, reflecting rising activity in the export sector, including textiles and tourism, and in the telecommunications sector. The growth recovery has been slower than expected, however, owing to delays in essential reforms, low investor confidence and poor weather conditions. Agriculture performed poorly in 2004 because of drought, and donors have been reluctant to frontload aid, because of the government's relatively disappointing record of budgetary and structural reforms.

Growth in **Madagascar** decelerated from 9.8 percent in 2003 to 5.3 percent in 2004 but still higher than the 2 percent achieved during 2000–03. In spite of three major cyclones, which caused considerable crop and property damage, national rice production was put at 3 million tonnes for 2004, an increase of 8 percent over the 2003 figures. Sustained world demand and the depreciation of the local currency boosted activity in the exports processing zone, notably in textiles/clothing. Increased construction activity, especially road works in rural areas, also explained growth performance.

In **Mauritius** growth for 2004 was put at 4.1 percent, lower than the 5.0 percent average growth recorded during 2000–2003. The slowdown in economic growth occurred in spite of 7 percent growth in the sugar sector. Tourism, the financial intermediation sector and construction grew by an estimated 1.1, 2.6, and 3.8 percent respectively. By contrast, the Exports Processing Zone (EPZ) sector registered negative growth for the second consecutive year.

Real GDP in **Seychelles** declined by 2 percent in 2004, slightly less than the 5.1 percent fall registered in 2003. Extensive government intervention and rigidities in the foreign exchange market have created bottlenecks in the economy, while high prices have depressed domestic consumption and tourism.

Economic performance in **Tanzania** remained strong in 2004 (2003/04 in national statistics). Growth in mining, construction, tourism, transport and telecommunications and manufacturing largely explained the overall growth rate of 7.4 percent. Despite progress towards economic diversification, the country is still highly vulnerable to external shocks. The agricultural sector is responsible for 40–50 percent of GDP but food security remains a concern. Cereal crop production (mainly maize) was estimated at about 4.9 million tonnes, more than 20 percent above the previous year's output.

Real GDP growth in **Uganda** increased from 5.5 percent in 2003 to 5.9 percent in 2004 (2003/04 in national statistics). Improved weather conditions contributed to a recovery in the agricultural sector, while the construction and telecommunications sectors continued to register high rates of growth.

Prices and Exchange Rates

After accelerating to 5.4 percent during 2000–03, as a result of severe food shortages, average consumer price inflation in East Africa slowed down slightly to 5.0 percent in 2004. Improved food supply

conditions and also a marked improvement in some of the countries' monetary and fiscal policy helped to compensate for the impact of a more than 30 percent rise in world oil prices. Inflation differentials with the rest of the world remain significant, although the depreciation of the main currencies in the sub-region decelerated in 2004, as a result of the weak US dollar. All countries — except Comoros and Seychelles — operate a floating exchange rate system.

Strong price stability was the objective of monetary policy in **Comoros**, with the Comoros franc being firmly pegged to the euro. Consumer prices rose by an average 5.0 percent in 2004, against an average 2.2 percent during 2000–03.

Djibouti's relatively sound monetary and exchange rate policy has helped to keep inflation under control. The local currency remains in effect pegged to the US dollar. Inflation in 2004 averaged 2 percent, against an average 1.9 percent during 2000–03, mostly reflecting price movements in oil and food import.

Tight food supply conditions in **Eritrea** have continued to push up cereal prices. Lax monetary policy also contributed to inflationary pressures. Inflation averaged 9 percent in 2004. The FAO and WFP jointly approved an emergency operation in July 2004 to bring food assistance to about 600,000 people.

Improved food supply conditions dampened inflation in **Ethiopia** in 2004. Inflation fell from 14.6 percent in 2003 to 7.5 percent in 2004. Although food prices declined in most regions, domestic prices for petroleum products and construction materials increased, reflecting rising world oil prices and activities under donor-funded reconstruction programs (including housing and road building). The National Bank of Ethiopia (central bank) maintained a relatively sound monetary policy, centered around restricted government borrowing, sterilization of excess liquidity (mostly stemming from aid inflows and remittances), and a market-determined exchange rate system, with the birr depreciating slightly against the US dollar in 2004.

Tight food supply conditions, high oil and transport prices, and higher-than-targeted money supply contributed to inflation in **Kenya** in 2004. The average rate accelerated to 11.6 percent in 2004, from an average 6.9 percent during 2000–2003, despite the government efforts at tighter fiscal control. A decline in interest rates helped to stimulate private sector lending, whilst a relatively healthy foreign exchange reserve position enabled the Central Bank of Kenya to intervene in the market to keep in check the depreciation of the Kenya shilling against most international currencies.

Inflation in **Madagascar** accelerated to 5.0 percent in 2004 (up from a negative 1.4 per cent the previous year), as a result of high world prices for oil and rice (an estimated 100,000 tons of rice still need to be imported every year) and the sharp depreciation of the local currency. The Central Bank of Madagascar used balance of payments support and raised interest rates and reserve requirements to stop the currency's fall by mid-2004. A continuous 'Reuters Dealing' methodology was adopted to replace the auction-based foreign exchange trading system, while the euro quotation of the Malagasy franc was extended to the US dollar. The euro value of the local currency — which is gradually to be changed to the ariary — depreciated by 40 percent in the first half of the year, before remaining broadly unchanged in the second half.

The Bank of **Mauritius** continued to pursue a relatively sound monetary policy in 2003/04, with inflation decelerating slightly to 3.4 percent, from an average 5.0 percent during 2000–03. An automatic adjustment mechanism for the prices of petroleum products was introduced in April 2004. The BoM increased its Lombard Rate by 25 basis points in October 2004, from 9.5 percent to 9.75 percent, to stem inflationary pressure and keep its domestic financial instruments attractive. The rupee, on average, appreciated slightly against the US dollar, but depreciated against the euro.

The introduction of a goods and services tax in 2003 has fuelled inflationary pressures in **Seychelles**. Consumer prices increased by 7 percent in 2003 and 4.2 percent in 2004. In December, the Seychelles parliament enacted a bill assuring the autonomy of the central bank.

Average inflation in **Tanzania** accelerated to 5.7 percent by mid-2004, fuelled by rising prices for food and petroleum products, but slowed down in the second part of the year, to average a yearly 3.8 percent. The Tanzania shilling depreciated slightly against the US dollar in nominal terms but remained roughly unchanged in real effective terms in 2003/04.

Inflation in **Uganda** decelerated to 1.9 percent in 2004 as a result of improved food supply conditions. The relative stability of the Uganda shilling in real effective terms contributed to price stability. Stronger than projected currency demand prompted the Bank of Uganda to loosen its monetary stance by increasing sales of foreign exchange at the beginning of the year. In addition, long-term treasury bonds were introduced in January 2004.

Public Finance and Structural Reforms
Fiscal Developments

East Africa's fiscal deficit declined in 2004 to 3.0 percent of GDP, reflecting continued efforts by governments in the region to enhance revenue and tighten expenditure control. However, the region's fiscal deficit continues to be high by continental standards, reflecting the poor state of public finances in Eritrea as well as Kenya's expansionary fiscal stance in recent years (see Table 2.6).

Table 2.6: East Africa: Macroeconomic Management Indicators

Country	Inflation (%)		Fiscal Balance as % of GDP		Gross Domestic Investment		Gross National Savings	
					as % of GDP			
	Average 2000–2003	2004[a]	Average 2000–2003	2004[a]	Average 2000–2003	2004[a]	Average 2000–2003	2004[a]
COMOROS	2.2	5.0	−3.6	−0.3	11.6	10.4	10.9	9.0
DJIBOUTI	1.9	2.0	−2.2	1.0	11.7	20.6	5.4	10.0
ERITREA	18.8	9.0	−31.8	−22.1	28.1	32.2	17.6	12.3
ETHIOPIA	1.9	7.5	−8.6	−5.0	18.6	19.5	13.9	16.6
KENYA	6.9	11.6	−0.7	−1.7	14.1	13.7	12.2	8.8
MADAGASCAR	8.3	5.0	−4.2	−3.3	15.9	22.4	19.6	15.1
MAURITIUS	5.0	3.4	−5.7	−5.3	23.0	25.0	26.4	26.1
SEYCHELLES	3.9	4.2	−8.8	7.9	27.7	18.5	13.7	16.2
SOMALIA	5.8	..	..	..	..	..	..	..
TANZANIA	4.9	5.7	−1.2	−2.9	18.1	21.4	13.7	13.8
UGANDA	2.0	1.9	−4.4	−1.7	19.7	21.7	12.3	18.7
EAST AFRICA	**5.4**	**5.0**	**−3.9**	**−3.0**	**17.8**	**19.5**	**14.9**	**14.7**

Note: [a] Preliminary estimates
Source: ADB Statistics Division, 2004

The implementation of coherent budget policies in **Comoros** remains difficult. The holding of elections, coupled with low donor support and a high public sector wage bill (strikes prompted a significant increase in salaries in 2003), led to a continued accumulation in domestic and external payment arrears in 2004, although reduced government spending and larger aid flows helped to keep the fiscal deficit (on a commitment basis) at 0.3 percent of GDP.

Djibouti's fiscal balance turned into a slight surplus of 1 percent of GDP in 2004. Tax administration and revenue collection improved, except for petroleum products receipts. Efforts to settle domestic payment arrears continued (the government used revenue from new military arrangements with the US and France to accelerate settlement in 2003), but non-priority spending remained higher than budgeted. New provisions on budget preparation and monitoring came into force in April 2004.

The lack of budget support and rising defense expenditures have forced the government in **Eritrea** to rely on domestic credit financing and payment arrears to finance its budget deficit, which was estimated at 22.1 percent of GDP in 2004.

Fiscal policy in **Ethiopia** has continued to focus on enhancing revenue collection (notably with regard to the functioning of a large taxpayer unit, and computerization of VAT), strengthening public expenditure management, and restricting recurrent outlays (including wages and defense outlays). Fiscal decentralization and the reorientation of spending programs towards poverty-related activities were also

major planks of the government's budgetary program. Resumed economic growth pushed up tax revenues in 2004. Increased donor budget support also contributed to a decline in the overall government deficit to 5.0 percent of GDP in 2004.

There was a marked improvement in the state of **Kenya**'s public finances in 2003/04, reflecting tighter control over expenditures in the post-electoral period and resumed donor assistance. Concerns about lack of transparency were, however, raised by some donors. Public domestic borrowing has remained high and the government has yet to pursue reforms to reduce the public sector wage bill. The Kenyan government was committed to adopting a common external tariff with Tanzania and Uganda by January 2005. The budget deficit rose to 1.7 percent of GDP in 2004, compared with 0.7 percent of GDP during 2000–03.

The authorities in **Madagascar** have initiated a series of budgetary measures to strengthen revenue collection and expenditure management. VAT was levied on non-capital goods and the remaining tax exemptions granted in September 2003 were not renewed. There was an increase in cyclone-related capital expenditures and capital spending in priority sectors, mostly education, transport and rural infrastructure. Increased aid inflows largely filled the financing gap, with the budget deficit estimated at 3.3 percent of GDP in 2004.

The overall fiscal deficit in **Mauritius** declined slightly to 5.3 percent of GDP in 2003/04, down from 5.7 percent during 2000–03. While tax and non-tax revenue increased, expenditures (mainly government subsidies and transfers) and capital outlays in education and infrastructure remained unsustainably high. The deficit was largely financed from domestic borrowing, with the IMF projecting public debt to reach 73 percent of GDP by mid-year. The financial situation of a number of state-owned utilities continued to deteriorate in the first half of 2004.

The fiscal balance in **Seychelles** remained in surplus for the second consecutive year, to reach an estimated 7.9 percent of GDP in 2004 as a result of rising tax receipts and the reduction in government outlays. The government successfully negotiated a new fishing agreement with the EU, with new proceeds expected for the period 2005–08. Measures to reduce custom duties and eliminate import permits were included in the 2005 budget.

The government of **Tanzania** exceeded its 2003/04 revenue performance target, with total revenue (excluding grants) rising to 12.9 percent of GDP by mid-year, against a targeted 12.4 percent. There were improvements in tax administration, tightened control over tax evasion in the petroleum sector and buoyancy of revenue in fast-growing sectors. Although parliament approved a supplementary budget in February 2004 and drought-related expenditures were accounted for, the fiscal deficit was contained at 2.9 percent of GDP, against a targeted deficit of 3.8 percent of GDP. This reflected high inflows of grants, but also improvements in expenditure planning and implementation. Spending allocation and the 13 percent rise in public sector wages in 2003/04 were in line with the government's poverty reduction strategy.

The **Uganda** government broadly met its 2003/04 budgetary targets, despite strong pressure for greater spending on defense and public administration. The fiscal deficit, including grants, declined to an estimated 1.7 percent of GDP. Strong performance in income tax collection more than offset a VAT shortfall, the latter indicating scope for improvement in the operations of the Uganda Revenue Authority. The composition of expenditure was meanwhile shifted away from the Poverty Eradication Action Plan priorities because of additional spending to meet security needs, provide support to the presidency and cover salary shortfalls. Meanwhile, there was an accumulation of new payments arrears.

Structural Reforms

The pace of structural reforms in East Africa as a whole was slow, although most governments remain committed to pushing through measures to improve public finances and create an environment conducive to private sector development. Progress was most apparent in Djibouti, Ethiopia, and Madagascar.

The **Comoros** government is nominally committed to pursuing a program of structural reforms, mostly involving the restructuring and privatization of major utilities (telecommunications, petroleum distribution and the port). The difficult process of political reconciliation since 2001 has, however, switched the focus away from reforms.

The government in **Djibouti** has agreed to an ambitious structural reform program under the 2004 IMF Staff Monitored

Program. A new free trade law was adopted in June 2004 and the labour and investment codes were due to be revised by end-year, after some delays. The latter involved the unification and simplification of the tax exemption regime. A strategy for small and medium enterprise development was put forward, with a new regulatory framework for micro-finance adopted ahead of schedule. Other reforms mooted for 2004 included a revised banking law and central bank charter and a new restructuring plan for the water and energy sector.

Eritrea's program of structural reforms made little progress in 2004. Trade and business regulations remained burdensome and plans to launch mobile phone services have been delayed. Structural transformation largely hinges on post-reconstruction projects, including in 2004 the launch of a World Bank-funded electrification program and an African Development Bank-sponsored education program.

The program of structural reforms in **Ethiopia** has made good progress and received positive feedback from the IMF and World Bank in 2004. Progress was notably made in streamlining regulatory procedures (following revision of the investment code in 2003), pressing ahead with fiscal decentralization, and restructuring the financial sector. The government has plans to revive the program of privatization (including the liberalization of the telecommunications sector) and accelerate the country's application for WTO membership.

The IMF delayed completion of its first review of **Kenya**'s program under the Poverty Reduction and Growth Facility, which it approved in November 2003, because of delays in essential reforms with regard to the fight against corruption and privatization. The government has nonetheless taken preliminary steps to liberalize the telecommunication sector, privatize the national railway and announced in its 2004/05 budget extensive restructuring of the financial sector, including the sale of two banks. Nonetheless, much more needs to be done to accelerate the country's economic revival. The government successfully completed its final PRSP in May 2004, providing an articulated strategy to reach the Millennium Development Goals (MDGs).

The government in **Madagascar** has shown strong commitment to policy measures aimed at liberalizing the economy and improving the business climate. After much delay, the sale of Telma (telecommunications) to Chinese Distacom was finalized in mid-2004. Preparations for the divestiture of Jirama (power), Sirama (sugar), Hasyma (cotton) are underway. Other essential reforms taken since 2003 include the establishment of an anti-corruption commission, trade liberalization, and amendments in the property act and land registry system.

Reforms in **Mauritius** are essential to restore the economy's external competitiveness. The sugar and textile sectors are soon to suffer from increased competition, as the Multi-Fiber Agreement (MFA) comes to an end and the EU sugar protocol is dismantled. A number of EPZ firms were forced to close down in 2004 and more than 6,000 workers were laid off in the first seven months of the year. The Mauritius government has plans to improve the enabling environment for the private sector, by streamlining business and investment regulations and establishing a secondary stock exchange market for small and medium enterprises.

The new government of **Seychelles** plans to accelerate the macroeconomic reform program. Measures to liberalize trade, reduce custom duties and eliminate import permits were announced in the 2005 budget; reforms in public administration (including privatization) and the Seychelles Marketing Board (SMB) are also expected. Foreign exchange controls could ease, but a devaluation of the currency remains unlikely.

A second wave of structural reforms focusing on fiscal consolidation and the business climate has begun in **Tanzania**, although the fight against corruption, the privatization of the National Microfinance Bank, and the restructuring and rehabilitation of Tanesco (electricity) remains high on the government's agenda. A new income tax bill became effective in July 2004 and the coverage of the Large Taxpayer Department has increased significantly. Business licensing reform and labor law reform were initiated in 2004, under the Business Environment Strengthening in Tanzania (BEST) program. The revised Land Act was signed into law in April 2004.

The pace of structural reforms in **Uganda** has remained slow. After much delay, the government decided in March 2004 on the divesture option for the Ugandan Development Bank (UDB), which is now to be merged with the Development Finance Department of the Bank of Uganda, and up to 30 percent of its shares will be sold. The government plans to divest the National Insurance Corporation, Kinyara Sugar Works, and to sell a 20 percent stake of New Vision Printing and Publishing in 2005. Meanwhile, the government has approved a preliminary agenda of reform for the public pension scheme.

Recent Trends in the External Sector
Current Account Developments

All countries in East Africa, except Comoros, Djibouti, Mauritius and Seychelles, recorded deteriorations in their terms of trade in 2004, as world oil prices increased by more than 30 percent throughout the year. Coffee (arabica) and tea exporting countries benefited from higher international prices for their commodities, but other countries, like Comoros and, to a lesser extent, Madagascar registered a steep export revenue loss, as a result of declining international prices for their export products. There was, however, a slight recovery in tourism, although potentials in this sector remain largely unexplored. As a result, the current account deficit increased to 3.9 percent of the regional GDP in 2004, against an average 1.5 percent of GDP during 2000–03 (see Table 2.7).

Meanwhile, there were signs of good progress on sub-regional integration. All East African countries, except Somalia and Tanzania, are members of COMESA. Kenya,

Table 2.7: East Africa: The External Sector

Country	Trade Balance as % of GDP		Current Account as % of GDP		Terms of Trade (%)		Total External Debt as % of GDP		Debt Service as % of Exports	
	Average 2000–2003	2004[a/]	Average 2000–2003	2004[a/]	Average 2000–2003	2004[a/]	Average 2000–2003	2004[a/]	Average 2000–2003	2004[a/]
COMOROS	−10.6	−6.9	−1.7	−2.2	54.0	0.0	103.4	83.3	7.2	6.0
DJIBOUTI	−35.4	−44.7	−6.3	−10.7	−1.6	5.1	66.9	67.5	6.6	5.4
ERITREA	−62.2	−66.4	−6.7	−9.9	−4.4	−0.1	71.8	97.1	17.2	29.7
ETHIOPIA	−19.1	−23.0	−4.8	−3.8	−14.4	−7.0	85.9	74.0	48.1	16.0
KENYA	−10.0	−11.4	−2.3	−7.7	−2.2	−7.6	43.4	37.9	17.7	10.9
MADAGASCAR	−2.4	−9.3	−4.7	−8.6	1.7	−8.0	99.5	112.8	17.6	8.0
MAURITIUS	−6.7	−5.3	2.5	2.6	0.0	1.1	22.3	17.8	8.5	6.3
SEYCHELLES	−20.9	−10.1	−12.5	1.0	7.5	8.3	74.1	81.9	12.6	13.3
SOMALIA	−8.7	−5.7	−3.2	−1.9	−0.1	−0.1	87.4	55.8	100.7	88.2
TANZANIA	−7.4	−8.7	−4.2	−5.2	0.9	−10.1	67.0	58.6	22.7	10.7
UGANDA	−8.3	−9.5	−5.6	−1.2	−2.7	−3.6	56.4	58.8	22.2	17.4
EAST AFRICA	**−10.4**	**−11.8**	**−3.5**	**−4.3**	**−1.5**	**−3.9**	**62.9**	**55.9**	**19.8**	**11.9**

Note: a/ Preliminary estimates
Source: ADB Statistics Division, 2004

Uganda and Tanzania signed a trade protocol in June 2004, establishing a customs union with a three-band common external tariff within the East African Community (EAC) and providing for the elimination of international trade barriers within five years. The protocol came into force in January 2005.

Comoros' external position failed to improve in 2004, as a result of a higher oil import bill (despite a weak US dollar), sluggish export performance and depressed world prices for the country's main export crops, vanilla and cloves.

Tourism earnings (despite great potentials) and aid inflows (under the multi-donor trust fund) have remained low, but workers remittances have helped partly to compensate for the trade deficit.

Djibouti's external current deficit increased to 10.7 percent of GDP, in large part reflecting movements in the trade balance. There was however a marked increase in net services and income, as a result of rising public and private transfers and receipts from freight and travel.

Eritrea's current account deficit increased to 9.9 percent of GDP in 2004 as a result of post-reconstruction activities and large-scale food imports. The country's export base, consisting of salt, hides and skins, and livestock, remains relatively narrow and external assistance has remained well below anticipated levels, owing to continued political uncertainty and the absence of an IMF program.

Ethiopia's external current account deficit fell to 3.8 percent of GDP in 2004, down from 4.8 per cent during 2000–03, due to strong growth in exports following higher world coffee prices and improved harvests. The growth in real exports, at 12 percent in 2004, helped to offset most of the import bills associated with the fleet expansion program of the Ethiopian Airlines and strong demand for imported capital goods. Private transfers and grants, project loan disbursements and balance of payments support were more than sufficient to bridge the financing gap, with external reserves estimated at $618 million in 2004.

Kenya's external current account deficit rose to 7.7 percent of GDP in 2004, up from 2.3 percent of GDP during 2000–03, due to high growth in oil and non-oil imports, which offset strong performance in major export categories, such as horticulture, tea, coffee, and textiles. The services and income account surplus increased slightly, however, because of increased tourism receipts and current transfers.

Madagascar's external current account deficit increased to 8.6 percent of GDP in 2004. The import bill surged in local currency terms, owing to the currency depreciation and high world oil prices. Import volumes nonetheless increased

quite significantly, fuelled by increased purchases of capital goods. The rise in exports was largely explained by a rebound in EPZ activity, despite an anticipated decrease in the export volume of vanilla. The government is committed to diversifying the country's export base, taking advantage of preferential trading arrangements for which the country qualifies.

Mauritius' exports grew by 7.4 percent in 2004. High world oil prices and the depreciation of the rupee inflated the import bill, while the demand for imported raw materials and capital goods also increased. Nonetheless, the trade deficit declined from 6.7 percent of GDP during 2000–03 to 5.3 percent in 2004. A 26 percent rise in tourism receipts helped Mauritius to retain a small current account surplus of 2.6 percent of GDP.

Seychelles' current account balance turned into a surplus of 1 percent of GDP in 2004, reflecting declining demand for imports (subject to licensing), rising exports of canned tuna, and oil re-exports. In addition, despite a drop in the number of visitors, tourism receipts increased for the second consecutive year in 2004, owing to the recent upgrading of its five-star hotel industry. Seychelles pulled out of SADC in 2004.

Tanzania's trade deficit widened slightly to 8.7 percent of GDP in 2003/04, largely due to strong growth in imports, driven by an increase in the volume and price of petroleum products and food imports. Imports of capital goods and industrial raw materials were also on the increase, reflecting strong economic activity. Export performance was mixed, with substantial growth recorded in non-traditional exports (gold and manufactured products), while traditional exports continued to stagnate, despite signs of recovery in the world prices of coffee, cotton, tea and cashew nuts. Tourism receipts rose to $515 million, which, coupled with lower debt service payments and rising current transfers (equivalent to 4.6 percent of GDP), helped to contain the country's current account deficit at 5.2 percent of GDP in 2003/04.

Export earnings in **Uganda** increased by an estimated 10.7 percent in US dollar terms in 2003/04, led by strong growth in non-coffee export volumes and improved terms of trade, notably for tea and cotton. There was no significant increase in the oil import bill. High flows of private and official transfers also largely contributed to a decrease in the external current account deficit to 1.2 percent of GDP in 2003/04, down from 5.6 percent during 2000–03.

External Debt

The external debt burden in East Africa continued to decline in 2004. Ethiopia and Madagascar reached completion point under the enhanced HIPC initiative in 2004. At the same time, the stock of external debt continued to increase rapidly in some countries, including Eritrea and Seychelles. Total external debt averaged 55.9 percent of the regional GDP in 2004, with the debt service ratio declining to 11.9 percent.

The stock of external debt in **Comoros** totaled $230 million by end-2004, an equivalent debt-GDP ratio of 83.3 percent, making it unsustainable. External payment

arrears (the debt service (paid) ratio stood at 6.0 percent in 2004) and the absence of a program with the IMF prevented Comoros to qualify for debt relief under the HIPC Initiative.

Djibouti's debt-to-GDP ratio rose to 67.5 percent in 2004. The government cleared all its external payment arrears owed to multilateral organizations in 2004 and a bilateral donor roundtable has been scheduled for 2005.

Initially, **Eritrea** had no external debt. But since the end of the war with Ethiopia, it began to borrow to finance development. Given the low level of its GDP, the debt burden rose to 97.1 percent of GDP in 2004, up from 71.8 percent during 2000–03. The debt service also rose from 17.2 percent (2000–03) to 29.7 percent (2004). The authorities are committed to borrowing on mainly long-term, concessional terms.

Ethiopia reached completion point under the enhanced HIPC initiative in April 2004, with multilateral and bilateral creditors committing to a total debt service relief of $3.3 billion. Despite significant debt relief and the government's prudent borrowing policy, debt sustainability may not be achieved because of the country's high vulnerability to external shocks. The IMF and World Bank consequently called for a substantial increase in external assistance to the country in the form of grants. External debt was estimated at $5.67 billion in 2004, equivalent to 74 percent of GDP.

Kenya is not eligible for debt relief under the enhanced HIPC initiative. The IMF and World Bank conducted a debt sustainability analysis in 2003 and in

January 2004, the Paris Club of official bilateral creditors agreed to a rescheduling of $350 million of arrears and maturities falling due between 2004 and 2006. The country's external debt stock — of which 58 percent is multilateral and 38 percent bilateral — was put at 37.9 percent of GDP in 2004. By comparison, domestic public debt rose to 26 percent of GDP by mid-2004.

Madagascar reached completion point under the enhanced HIPC initiative in October 2004, paving the way for a total nominal debt relief of US$1.9 billion from all creditors. The full delivery of HIPC assistance will reduce the debt-to-exports ratio to 137 percent in net present value terms. The country's total stock of external debt was estimated at $3.57 billion in 2004, an equivalent 112.8 percent of GDP. The government has actively wooed foreign investors from Europe and Asia, with non-debt foreign capital flows expected to rise as a result.

Mauritius' external debt is low. The debt-to-GDP ratio fell to 17.8 percent in 2004, down from 22.3 percent during 2000–03. Foreign direct and portfolio investments continued to flow into the country, with net foreign exchange reserves representing up to ten months of imports by end-September 2004.

Seychelles' public external debt (including that of state parastatals) rose to $580 million in 2004, equivalent to 81.9 percent of GDP. Half of the country's external debt is owed to commercial lenders and/or on foreign currency terms. Seychelles attracts a small, albeit regular, stream of foreign investment every year,

mostly reflecting offshore investment opportunities.

Tanzania has continued to benefit from high inflows of official program loans and grants, as well as continued debt relief under the enhanced HIPC initiative since reaching completion point in 2001. FDI was estimated at 2.4 percent of GDP in 2003/04. The debt-to-GDP ratio declined to 58.6 percent of GDP in 2004, as a result of further implementation of Paris Club bilateral agreements. The debt service ratio in 2004 was estimated at 10.7 percent, down from an average 22.2 percent during 2000–03.

Uganda's stock of public external debt fell to an equivalent 58.8 percent of GDP. About 90 percent of the external debt is owed to multilateral donors, 9 percent to non-Paris club creditors, and 1 percent to Paris Club creditors. Uganda was the first country in Africa to reach completion point under the enhanced HIPC initiative in May 2000. Net inflows of private capital and donor support remained sufficient to cover the country's financing gap in 2003/04, with gross international reserves estimated at 6½ months of imports as of end-June 2004. The debt service ratio was reduced to 17.4 percent in 2004, indicating robust export growth.

Outlook

East Africa's growth prospects for 2005 are mixed. Abundant rains since mid-2004 have improved prospects for the 2004/05 cereal crops in the Horn of Africa. Growth is projected to accelerate in Kenya assuming a stronger commitment to reforms. Mauritius will face a more challenging environment, as a result of eroding preferential access to the EU and US markets. The impact of the Tsunami tidal wave has yet to be fully estimated in the region. Much infrastructure, including roads, bridges, and buildings, was destroyed in Somalia, Kenya, Tanzania, and the region's island economies: Comoros, Seychelles and Madagascar. Hardship has been reported particularly in the already impoverished populations of Comoros and Somalia. Seychelles, which relies heavily on beach tourism, also faced costly damage, and in January 2005, the Paris Club of official bilateral creditors announced its decision to freeze debt payments for the country. Overall though real GDP in East Africa is expected to grow by 5.2 percent in 2005 — a 1.6 percentage point below the 2004 growth rate.

North Africa

North Africa, which comprises seven countries — Algeria, Egypt, Libya, Mauritania, Morocco, Sudan and Tunisia — is the largest sub-regional contributor to the continent's wealth, accounting for 36.5 percent of its GDP in 2004. Whereas merchandise exports from Algeria, Libya and Sudan are dominated by oil and gas, export composition tends to be wider in other countries. Egypt, Morocco and Tunisia export both traditional products and manufactured goods, notably textiles, electronic and equipment goods. Tourism is also a major source of foreign exchange earnings in the region. Algeria is the largest economy of the region, generating an equivalent 28.6 percent of its GDP in 2004.

The region is home to 189.7 million people, representing 22.1 percent of the continent's population. Per capita GDP averaged $1,521 in 2004, which is roughly twice as high as the continental's average. All countries are classified as middle-income countries, except for Mauritania and Sudan. Sparsely populated Libya is the wealthiest country, with an income per head of $5,364.

The outbreak of fighting between rebel and government forces in the region of Darfur, Sudan, drew much of the international attention on Africa from January 2004. The UN Security Council voted a resolution in July 2004 calling on the government to disarm pro-government militias and allow the free flow of humanitarian aid, as killings of civilians continued unabated. In the meantime, a peace deal between the government and the southern-based Sudan People's Liberation Movement was signed in May 2004. Concerns over security remained a key issue elsewhere in the region. The UN envoy to Western Sahara, James Baker, resigned in June 2004 after seven years in office, while another alleged coup attempt was foiled in Mauritania in September 2004, the third in 15 months. The re-election of President Abdelaziz Bouteflika in Algeria passed off peacefully in April 2004, which contrasted with the violence that marred the 2002 legislative elections. In Tunisia, President Zine al-Abedine Ben Ali and his party were re-elected by a landslide in October 2004. In the meantime, Libya continued to thaw its relations with the West, with a number of European heads of state paying visits to the country and the US and EU lifting remaining trade sanctions in September 2004.

Recent Trends in the Domestic Economy

Economic Growth

North Africa's growth performance remained strong in 2004, at 4.6 percent, largely reflecting strong performance in oil producing countries. Real GDP growth already accelerated markedly as a result of higher oil output and prices. Economic performance has strengthened in Egypt and Morocco in recent years (see Table 2.8 and Figure 2.3).

Growth in **Algeria** decelerated slightly from 6.9 percent in 2003 to 5.4 percent in 2004, but still higher than the yearly average of 3.9 percent during 2000–03. The Algerian economy is not highly diversified, with the oil and gas sector contributing more than 30 percent of its annual GDP. An increase in oil production to near capacity, 1.3 million b/d, and continued private investment in the gas sector were largely responsible for growth in 2004. Construction also performed relatively well, despite supply bottlenecks in the publicly-owned cement industry, while growth in agriculture decelerated slightly from its 2003 peak. Despite stronger growth performance since 2002, the social situation in Algeria remains tense, with the rate of unemployment estimated at 24 percent in 2003.

Table 2.8: North Africa: GDP and Export Performances

Country	Real GDP Growth Rate (%)		GDP Per Capita (US$)		Real Exports[c] Growth (%)		Exports[b] Per Capita (US$)	
	Average 2000–2003	2004[a]	Average 2000–2003	2004[a]	Average 2000–2003	2004[a]	Average 2000–2003	2004[a]
ALGERIA	3.9	5.4	1,866	2,548	3.8	5.5	714	1,041
EGYPT	3.8	4.3	1,310	1,029	7.6	−1.4	239	282
LIBYA	3.6	0.9	4,931	5,364	2.3	14.9	1967	3,148
MAURITANIA	5.1	5.2	367	422	−6.9	11.6	135	138
MOROCCO	4.0	3.5	1,230	1,615	2.5	7.9	399	514
SUDAN	6.3	7.3	452	598	31.3	6.3	63	102
TUNISIA	4.2	5.5	2,206	2,836	8.0	0.9	988	1,235
NORTH AFRICA	**4.1**	**4.6**	**1,379**	**1,521**	**5.0**	**5.5**	**405**	**550**

Notes: [a] Preliminary estimates
[b] Exports of goods and non-factor services
[c] Real exports of goods growth
Source: ADB Statistics Division, 2004

Figure 2.3: North Africa: Selected Economic Indicators, 2000–2004

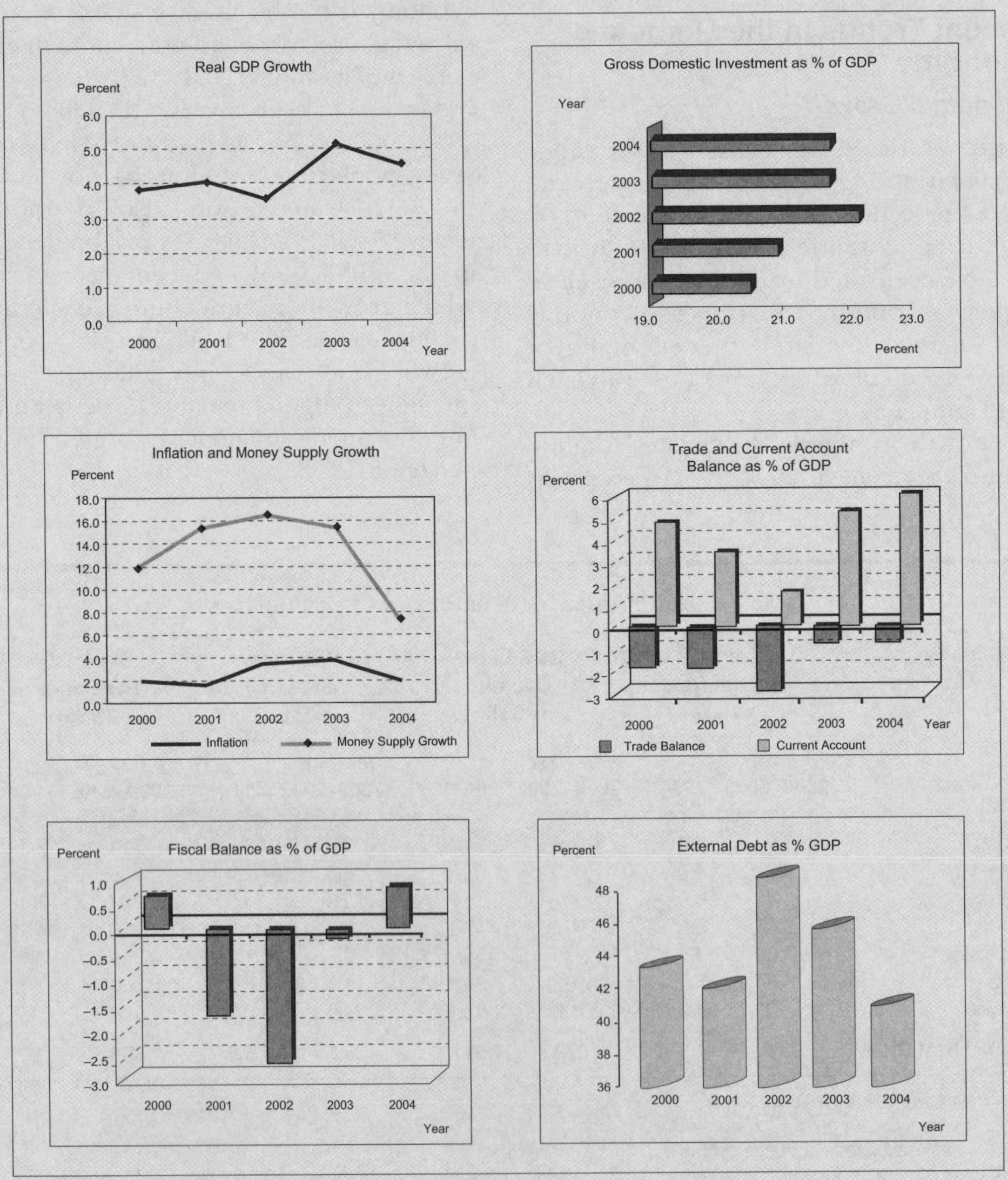
Real GDP Growth
Percent
6.0
5.0
4.0
3.0
2.0
1.0
0.0
2000
2001
2002
2003
2004
Year
Gross Domestic Investment as % of GDP
Year
2004
2003
2002
2001
2000
19.0
20.0
21.0
22.0
23.0
Percent
Inflation and Money Supply Growth
Percent
18.0
16.0
14.0
12.0
10.0
8.0
6.0
4.0
2.0
0.0
2000
2001
2002
2003
2004
Inflation
Money Supply Growth
Trade and Current Account Balance as % of GDP
Percent
6
5
4
3
2
1
0
−1
−2
−3
2000
2001
2002
2003
2004
Year
Trade Balance
Current Account
Fiscal Balance as % of GDP
Percent
1.0
0.5
0.0
−0.5
−1.0
−1.5
−2.0
−2.5
−3.0
2000
2001
2002
2003
2004
Year
External Debt as % GDP
Percent
48
46
44
42
40
38
36
2000
2001
2002
2003
2004
Year

Source: ADB Statistics Division, 2004

Economic performance in **Egypt** has improved since mid-2003, reflecting the short-lived impact of the war in Iraq, the steep depreciation of the pound and the country's consequent gains in external competitiveness. Real GDP growth accelerated from 3.8 percent in 2002/03 to 4.3 percent in 2003/04. Growth was driven by a recovery in tourism and rising manufactured exports. The government aims to speed up reforms to strengthen economic growth and create employment. Private sector growth has remained subdued, however, despite the improved availability of foreign currency.

Economic growth in **Libya** rapidly decelerated to 0.9 percent in 2004, from 5.3 percent the previous year, despite rising oil production and receipts. Also, OPEC raised Libya's production quota from 1.26 million b/d in April 2004 to 1.45 million b/d in November 2004.

Mauritania's economy suffered from a severe desert locust invasion in 2004, after experiencing three consecutive years of drought. Cereal production in 2004 was 44 percent lower than in the previous year. Services, which account for roughly half of GDP, performed relatively well, however, and so did manufacturing and mining. Activity was notably buoyant in construction and public works (led by the ongoing expansion of the state mining company's production capacity) and oil exploration. The real GDP grew by 5.2 percent in 2004, in line with the yearly average of 5.1 percent during 2000–03.

After accelerating to 5.5 percent in 2003, mainly because of exceptionally good cereal harvests, real GDP growth in **Morocco** slowed down to 3.5 percent in 2004. Weather conditions remained good during the growing season 2003/04, with the primary sector recording a small increase as a result. There was a surge in activity in tourism and a rise in mining and energy production, which helped to compensate for lower activity in construction and manufacturing. The rate of GDP growth, however, remains insufficient to significantly reduce unemployment and poverty.

The humanitarian crisis in Darfur has had a limited impact on overall growth performance in **Sudan**. Rising oil production, improved peace prospects in the south, continued flows of FDI and reasonably good performance in livestock and agriculture supported a 7.3 percent GDP growth in 2004, up from 6 percent in 2003. Sudan's estimated oil reserves have doubled since 2001, with crude production reaching an estimated 345,000 b/d by mid-2004.

Growth in **Tunisia** was strong for the second consecutive year in 2004, averaging 5.5 percent. All sectors except textile and clothing performed well, with a marked recovery in tourism, strong agricultural output, a revival in industrial activity (fuelled by agro-processing and electricity and machinery production), and a dynamic telecommunications sector. Although Tunisian economy is well diversified and relatively resilient to external shocks, private domestic investment is still insufficient in the modern sector, where tax-privileged foreign investment dominates.

Prices and Exchange Rates

Monetary policy in the region strongly focused on maintaining competitive exchange rates and liberalizing foreign exchange markets. Inflation in North Africa has remained roughly stable in recent years; inflation in 2004 remained at the yearly average of 2.7 percent during 2000–03.

Rapid growth in money and credit continued to fuel liquidity in the banking sector in **Algeria**, with inflation rising to 4.0 percent in 2004. Although the Central Bank of Algeria mopped up some excess liquidity through the use of auctions and reserve requirements, the persistence of unsterilized foreign currency deposits generated by robust oil and gas sales reflected a largely accommodating monetary policy and the need for stronger credit regulation and financial supervision. There was a slight depreciation of the Algerian dinar against the euro in 2004.

Inflationary pressures in **Egypt** mounted in 2003/04, largely as a result of the steep depreciation of the Egyptian pound. Consumer prices increased by an average 9.7 percent in 2003/04. Although efforts were made to strengthen monetary policy, after a new banking law was introduced in 2003, central bank credit to the government continued to increase. A free float exchange rate system was introduced in January 2003, two years after the peg to the US dollar was formally abandoned, but policies to support the float and reduce exchange controls have not been fully effective, leading to the persistence of a dual foreign exchange market. The Egyptian pound depreciated

by a yearly average of 16 percent against the US dollar in 2002/03 and 2003/04.

The **Libyan** government has initiated steps to liberalize the economy since 2003. In June 2003, the Central Bank of Libya proceeded with the elimination of the Great Man-Made River exchange tax, as previously levied on private foreign exchange transactions, and finalized the unification of the dual exchange rate system by devaluing the official exchange rate by 15 percent. Cheaper imports, as a result of slashed import tariffs and the lifting of import licensing requirements, kept the average inflation rate at a subdued 2.2 percent in 2004.

Mauritania's central bank pursued a relatively prudent monetary policy in 2004, with inflation decelerating to 6.7 percent. The real effective exchange rate of the ouguiya depreciated by an estimated 11.8 percent in 2004. There was still a differential between market and parallel rates, as a result of the central bank's heavy intervention on the market, which maintained the ouguiya at an artificially high value.

Morocco's pegged exchange rate system has helped to maintain price stability, with inflation averaging 1.5 percent in 2004. The authorities adjusted the fixed exchange rate for the first time in 11 years in April 2001, when the currency basket, to which the dirham is pegged, was modified to reflect the growing importance of the euro area in Morocco's trade. There was hardly any inflation in 2004. The inter-bank money rate fell to 2.3 percent by September 2004. There was a slight depreciation in the effective nominal exchange rate in 2004, which helped to maintain Morocco's external competitiveness. Abundant liquidity continued to characterize the country's banking system in 2004, as a result of the positive balance of payments and proceeds from privatization. Credit to the economy increased only modestly and frequent money market interventions by the Bank Al-Maghrib helped to mop up excess liquidity.

The Central Bank of **Sudan** managed to sterilize the larger than expected foreign exchange earnings stemming from private capital flows and oil sales. The Bank also maintained a tightly managed floating exchange rate system. Inflationary pressures were kept under control, as a result, notwithstanding rising demand for consumer goods and capital equipment, and a food shortage in Darfur. Inflation averaged 5.0 percent in 2004, down from 7.1 percent during 2000–03.

A reduction in oil price subsidies and higher import prices put upward pressure on domestic prices in **Tunisia** in 2004. Exchange rate stability and a relatively prudent monetary and fiscal policy helped to keep inflation under control, from an average 2.6 percent in 2000–03 to 3.6 percent in 2004. The central bank kept its key interest rate unchanged as a result, with credit to the economy rising by 4.8 percent in the first nine months of 2004. In line with the objective of maintaining a constant real exchange rate, the Tunisian dinar depreciated slightly against the US dollar, but roughly kept the same value against the euro in 2004.

Public Finance and Structural Reforms

Fiscal Developments

The fiscal position in North Africa is relatively healthy compared with the rest of the continent. This has permitted governments in the region to adopt pro-cyclical policies and delay unpopular civil service reforms. The regional fiscal balance showed a surplus of 0.9 percent of GDP in 2004, as opposed to a fiscal deficit of 0.9 percent during 2000–03 (see Table 2.9).

Fiscal policy in **Algeria** has taken an expansionary stance since the Economic Recovery Program was initiated in 2001. Higher-than-projected oil revenues in 2004 largely compensated for rising capital and recurrent expenditures and the gradual decline in custom tariffs in the context of trade liberalization and Algeria's negotiation for its entry to the WTO. There was a 25 percent rise in the minimum wage, while capital expenditures covered the remaining cost of reconstruction following the May 2003 earthquake and some of the country's pressing needs for social and physical infrastructure. As a result, the budget surplus rose to 5.6 percent of GDP in 2004. Quasi-fiscal operations by public banks remained unrecorded, however, with public sector borrowing continually crowding out investment in the private sector.

The budget deficit in **Egypt** rose to 6.0 percent of GDP in 2004, due to an increase in interest payments associated with the tightening of monetary policy and a rise in price subsidies and budgetary transfers. In September 2004, the government

Table 2.9: North Africa: Macroeconomic Management Indicators

Country	Inflation (%)		Fiscal Balance as % of GDP		Gross Domestic Investment		Gross National Savings	
					as % of GDP			
	Average 2000–2003	2004[a/]	Average 2000–2003	2004[a/]	Average 2000–2003	2004[a/]	Average 2000–2003	2004[a/]
ALGERIA	2.2	4.0	4.6	5.6	27.6	28.8	40.6	40.7
EGYPT	2.7	9.7	−5.4	−6.0	18.3	16.7	18.8	20.7
LIBYA	−1.8	2.2	6.2	16.6	12.5	12.6	23.2	33.8
MAURITANIA	4.6	−6.7	1.4	1.0	23.5	37.7	18.0	14.6
MOROCCO	1.6	1.5	−3.2	−2.5	23.1	22.8	25.7	24.8
SUDAN	7.1	5.0	−0.4	−1.2	18.0	20.4	5.9	13.5
TUNISIA	2.6	3.6	−2.8	−1.5	26.5	24.7	22.6	21.8
NORTH AFRICA	**2.7**	**2.7**	**−0.9**	**0.9**	**21.3**	**21.7**	**25.1**	**27.6**

Note: [a/] Preliminary estimates
Source: ADB Statistics Division, 2004

announced its decision to lower custom tariffs from 14.9 percent to 9 percent. Other mooted tax reforms include lowering income taxes and transforming the general sales tax into VAT. The measures are expected to stimulate economic activity, which, coupled with reforms to phase out existing tax incentives and strengthen revenue collection, will help to compensate for the loss in custom revenues. Further fiscal consolidation is also needed in the context of persistent off-budget outlays and rising net public debt resulting from domestic borrowing.

Oil resources in **Libya** account for approximately 75 percent of government receipts. The Libyan government continued to pursue an expansionary fiscal stance in 2004 in the context of rising oil production and world prices. In accepting IMF Article VII obligations, the government has committed to proceed with tax and custom reforms, which involve gradually phasing out widespread tax exemptions for state-owned enterprises and price subsidies on products of primary necessity, as well as gradually reducing tariffs and non-tariff barriers. Despite rising spending, the overall budget balance registered a substantial surplus of 16.6 percent of GDP in 2004.

Ongoing reforms in tax and custom administration, and the strengthening of public expenditure management have helped the government in **Mauritania** to maintain a relatively prudent fiscal stance in recent years. The budget surplus as a percentage of GDP declined from an average of 1.4 percent in 2000–03 to an estimated 1.0 percent in 2004. Final budget figures for 2004 may point to a deficit, however, with the introduction of new taxes in that year only partly compensating for the 28 percent public sector pay rise, effective from January 2004. The target for HIPC-related social expenditures was set at 11.3 percent of GDP for 2003.

Morocco's fiscal deficit declined to 2.5 percent of GDP in 2004, after increasing from 4.6 percent of GDP in 2002 to 5.4 percent in 2003. The increase in the fiscal deficit in 2003 stemmed from salary increases, security-related spending, and weaker import tariff revenues. Ongoing tax reforms in 2004 budgeted a 5.8 percent decline in custom revenues as a result of trade liberalization, which a 4.7 percent rise in VAT receipts and a 9.7 percent rise in non-fiscal receipts helped to compensate. The government is committed to fiscal consolidation, which implies reducing tax exemptions, reinforcing tax administration and cutting down the public sector wage bill. The government had to curtail its investment spending in 2004 due to higher-than-projected recurrent expenditures.

Fiscal revenues in **Sudan** increased with oil production and world prices in 2004. Some of the export-related oil revenues were saved in the government oil savings account. Non-oil revenues were lower than expected, indicating an array of tax exemptions and room for enhanced revenue collection. Public expenditures also rose significantly, as a result of expansionary policies, which included an increase in civil service salaries. At 0.4

percent of GDP during 2000–03, the budget deficit turned accelerated to 1.2 percent of GDP in 2004.

Tunisia's central government budget deficit declined from 2.8 percent of GDP during 2000–03 to 1.5 percent of GDP in 2004. Public debt declined slightly to less than 60 percent of GDP in 2004, while the impact of higher-than-projected world oil prices on price subsidies was partly reduced by an upward adjustment in retail prices in the first half of the year. Ongoing measures to widen the tax base and strengthen VAT collection helped to compensate for falling custom revenues, but receipts from privatization were lower than envisaged. The government's fiscal position remains sound, despite structural rigidities on the expenditure side, with the wage bill absorbing roughly two-thirds of total recurrent expenditures.

Structural Reforms

The pace of structural reforms in North Africa accelerated somewhat in 2004, as governments in Egypt, Libya, and Morocco took important steps to liberalize their economies and encourage private sector activities.

Structural reforms in **Algeria** have proved difficult, although progress has been made in trade liberalization and the liberalization of the telecommunication sector. This reflects the complexity of the task (there are more than 1,000 state-owned enterprises) and strong resistance from trade unions. The government has recently sought to adopt a more pragmatic approach to privatization and in September 2004 announced the partial sale of 11 state-owned enterprises on the stock market. Plans to liberalize the hydrocarbon sector have been frozen since December 2003. The financial sector, which is mostly state-owned following the collapse of the country's two largest private banks in 2003, is in dire need of restructuring; most of the lending currently goes to loss making public companies.

In **Egypt**, the government has revived plans to liberalize the economy and improve the business climate. In September 2004, it announced a decision to cut customs duties and to reduce bureaucratic impediments. A new program of structural reforms was unfolded, with priority given to the restructuring of the financial sector and the privatization of state-owned banks. A total of 192 out of 306 state-owned enterprises had already been sold in the 1990s, but key public services, such as telecommunications, water and energy remain under state control.

The government of **Libya** has moved away from a state-centred economic policy since 2003, when President Muammar Qadhafi announced plans to privatize some 360 public enterprises and banks. The government controls almost the entire economy and private sector activities outside the foreign-owned oil sector are restricted to small-scale activities in retailing and agriculture. Two state-owned banks have now been privatized, and there are plans to set up a stock market. The trade regime has also been greatly simplified following the country's application for WTO membership.

The pace of structural reforms in **Mauritania** has slowed down since 2002.

The privatization program has almost reached completion point, with the electricity company, Somelec, being the only public utility yet to be privatized Other reforms include restructuring the National Social Security Fund and liberalizing the banking sector, but little progress was made in 2004.

In **Morocco**, the long-awaited sale of a 16 percent share in Maroc Telecom went to Vivendi of France in November 2004. Another 15 percent share in Maroc Telecom was floated (and largely oversubscribed) on the stock market in December 2004. A 20 percent share in the Banque Centrale Populaire was floated on the stock exchange market in June 2004. Trade liberalization in Morocco (a WTO-member) also made good progress and custom duties were further reduced in 2004 under the European Union Association Agreement. The program of structural reforms also includes pension reform, the strengthening of the financial sector, and support for the private sector. The labour code was modified in 2003 and there are plans to reform the judicial system and streamline administrative procedures.

The government of **Sudan** has drawn up a program of privatization, which includes the sale of key public utilities. Private participation has increased in the construction, tourism, telecommunication and banking sectors and in 2004, negotiations started with private stakeholders in the United Arab Emirates for the sale of a majority share in Sudan Airways. The government has maintained a relatively open trade regime, following the abolition of import and export licensing in the late

1990s and the simplification of the custom tariffs structure to an average tariff rate of 22.7 percent. The country formally applied for WTO membership in October 2004.

In **Tunisia**, the government showed further commitment to improving the business environment for the domestic private sector, completing the privatization process and accelerating trade liberalization in 2004. Custom tariff rates were reduced and there was a slight relaxation in foreign exchange control in November 2004, as a first step towards achieving full exchange rate convertibility. Tunisia's trade regime is relatively restrictive and complex, with the level of the MFN tariff averaging a still high 32.7 percent by mid-2004. The government also issued new tenders for the sale of a number of state-owned companies, including that of a 34 percent share in the state-owned Banque du Sud, but most failed to attract successful bidders. Tunisie Telecom has yet to be opened to private participation, and little progress was made in streamlining administrative procedures and relaxing business and labor regulations, although plans for reforming the Social Security Fund were announced in early 2004.

Recent Trends in the External Sector

Current Account Developments

North Africa's external position strengthened in 2004, on the back of rising oil prices and improved external competitiveness. In surplus for the fifth consecutive year, the current account balance rose to 5.9 percent of GDP, against a yearly average of 3.7 percent during 2000–03 (see Table 2.10).

North African countries have faced rising external competition for their manufactured exports, because of eroding preferential access to the EU markets and still tightly managed foreign exchange systems. Most North African countries, except Mauritania, Morocco and Tunisia, are oil exporters. Other primary commodities that the region exports include cotton, iron ore, phosphate rock, and fish. Tourism is also a major source of foreign exchange earnings in Egypt, Morocco, and Tunisia.

All countries in North Africa, except Algeria and Mauritania, are members of the Community of Sahel-Saharan States (CEN-SAD). The Arab Maghreb Union comprising Algeria, Libya, Mauritania, Morocco and Tunisia, which has largely remained moribund, was revived in 2001.

Hydrocarbons earnings account for 98 percent of total export volumes in **Algeria**. Exports increased by 12 percent in the first nine months of 2004, reflecting rising oil prices and higher crude oil exports under OPEC, while the import bill in US dollars increased by more than 30 percent over the same period, as a result of the strong demand for imported machinery. The current account surplus increased slightly to an estimated 13.1 percent of GDP in 2004, compared with an average of 12.7 percent of GDP during 2000–2003.

Egypt's external position strengthened significantly in 2004, reflecting the country's improved competitiveness as a result of the sharp depreciation of the Egyptian pound since January 2003.

Table 2.10: North Africa: The External Sector

Country	Trade Balance as % of GDP		Current Account as % of GDP		Terms of Trade (%)		Total External Debt as % of GDP		Debt Service as % of Exports	
	Average 2000–2003	2004[a]	Average 2000–2003	2004[a]	Average 2000–2003	2004[a]	Average 2000–2003	2004[a]	Average 2000–2003	2004[a]
ALGERIA	17.2	19.3	12.7	13.1	15.4	11.9	40.8	26.1	21.3	14.8
EGYPT	–9.6	–9.9	0.5	3.2	5.9	1.5	31.5	40.6	11.8	11.5
LIBYA	–0.5	–0.2	10.6	21.3	10.5	13.8	21.4	19.3	0.0	0.0
MAURITANIA	–5.6	–23.5	–5.5	–23.1	5.2	–9.8	193.4	158.7	18.4	16.8
MOROCCO	–9.2	–12.1	2.6	0.2	–2.0	–2.9	45.2	31.8	22.5	13.9
SUDAN	–1.9	0.2	–12.1	–6.8	4.7	11.5	151.6	125.1	8.2	10.7
TUNISIA	–10.7	–8.8	–3.8	–2.8	–1.0	–0.3	62.1	56.5	17.6	19.3
NORTH AFRICA	**–2.0**	**–0.3**	**3.7**	**5.9**	**5.4**	**6.5**	**44.6**	**40.9**	**15.4**	**12.0**

Note: a/ Preliminary estimates
Source: ADB Statistics Division, 2004

Exports increased in both volume and value terms, reflecting the impact of the pound's depreciation, and there was a gradual opening of the country's economy to bilateral and multilateral trade. Despite higher dollar-denominated foreign debt service payments, the current account balance turned into a surplus in 2003 and increased by 1 percentage point of GDP to an equivalent to 3.2 percent of GDP in 2004.

Libya heavily relies on oil exports, which account for over 95 percent of total export revenues. Despite booming oil receipts, the trade balance has been in deficit since 2003, as a result of a surge in imports following the elimination of import licensing requirements. The current account balance, however, recorded a surplus of 21.3 percent of GDP in 2004, up from 10.6 per cent during 2000–03.

Mauritania's external current account deficit remained high in 2004, rising to the equivalent of 23.1 percent of GDP, as a result of large-scale food and commercial imports (despite humanitarian assistance) and rising oil-related machinery and equipment imports. Export performance is set to improve in 2005, as the iron mining company expands its export capacity. Rising FDI inflows in the oil sector have helped to finance the external gap since 2002.

Morocco's current account balance has turned into a surplus since the devaluation of the Moroccan dirham in 2001. The boost in export competitiveness has subsided, however, with the current account surplus falling to a low 0.2 percent of GDP by 2004. This also reflected a rising oil import bill and the recovery in demand for equipment and semi-finished manufactured imports. Export growth in 2004 was driven by an increase in sales for phosphate rock, olive oil, and energy. Strong foreign investment inflows and private sector lending, coupled with rising tourism receipts and workers remittances helped to improve the overall balance of payments.

Sudan's current-account deficit declined to 6.8 percent of GDP in 2004, in large part reflecting higher exports of oil. While the trade deficit turned into a surplus in 2004, services and income outflows were high, because of oil-related payments and expenses.

Tunisia's external trade position continued to strengthen in 2004, on the back of rising exports in processed agricultural products, mining, machinery, and electricity. Tourism receipts made a strong recovery, increasing by 16.1 percent in the first nine months of 2004, while workers' remittances increased by 13 percent over the same period. As a result, the external current account deficit declined from an average 3.8 percent of GDP during 2000–03 to 2.8 percent in 2004.

External Debt

The region's external debt burden is low by African standards. The total debt stock in 2004 stood at 40.9 percent of regional GDP. Mauritania is the only country eligible for debt relief under the Enhanced HIPC initiative.

The structure of North Africa's capital account indicates greater access to international capital markets. Egypt, Morocco, and Tunisia have secured favorable ratings from several credit rating agencies, enabling their governments and commercial banks to borrow externally from private lenders. Non debt-creating capital inflows are significant in North Africa. The bulk of foreign participation is oil-related, but also reflects stakes in strategic utilities and in the banking, export and tourism sectors. Morocco, Egypt and Tunisia have opened their stock markets to foreign investors, attracting small amounts of foreign portfolio investment.

The government of **Algeria** has taken advantage of booming oil-driven foreign reserves to make early repayments on its external debt. As a result, the country's external debt stock declined to 26.1 percent of GDP in 2004. The government has plans to seek a sovereign rating to facilitate its return to international capital markets. Foreign investment outside Algeria's hydrocarbons sector remains minimal, reflecting slow progress in restructuring the public sector and enhancing the business climate for investors. The debt service ratio declined to 14.8 percent in 2004, reflecting rising oil receipts.

In **Egypt**, the government's prudent external borrowing policy has kept the debt-to-GDP ratio at 40.6 percent in 2004, up an average 31.5 percent in 2000–2003. The debt service ratio stood at 11.5 percent, reflecting rising export earnings. Greater integration into global capital markets was achieved in June 2001, when Egypt successfully issued eurobonds. Egypt is the largest recipient of FDI in the region. The country has made considerable progress in liberalizing and simplifying its investment regime and steps are being taken to accelerate the pace of privatization and to relax foreign exchange regulations in order to promote greater foreign participation outside the oil and gas sector.

Libya is poorly integrated in the world financial markets, having little need for external financing. External debt totaled an estimated 19.3 percent of GDP in 2004.

The debt-to-GDP ratio in **Mauritania** declined to a still high 158.7 percent in 2004. The country reached completion point under the enhanced HIPC in June 2002, paving the way for debt service relief equivalent to $1.1 billion. Despite declining foreign reserves, the government has maintained a relatively prudent borrowing policy, mostly contracting loans on long-term, concessional terms. The debt service ratio in 2004 fell to 16.8 percent, down from an average 18.4 percent in 2000–03.

Morocco's stock of external debt declined to 31.8 percent of GDP in 2004. The government has attempted to reduce its external debt burden over the years by negotiating debt-for-equity swaps and debt buy-back measures. Total government debt was officially projected at 67.6 percent of GDP in 2004, 16.2 percent of which were owned to external creditors.

Despite the oil export boom, **Sudan** has not adequately addressed its debt problem, as the strong foreign investment inflows in the oil sector have failed to bridge the external gap. In addition, official development has remained low, owing to Sudan's external arrears to its main creditors, which has prevented the resumption of new disbursements. The debt-to-GDP ratio declined to a still high 125.1 percent of GDP in 2004, with the debt service ratio at 10.7 percent.

The stock of external debt in **Tunisia** declined to 56.5 percent of GDP in 2004, reflecting an improvement in the current account balance and strong foreign direct investment inflows. Tunisia's FDI stock as a percentage of GDP is the highest in the sub-region, with the bulk of FDI taking place in the manufacturing sector.

Outlook

Economic growth in North Africa is forecast to remain relatively strong in 2005, with GDP growth rate projected at 4.8 percent. Export earnings from the oil and gas sector will continue to support expansionary policies in Libya and Sudan, while structural reforms in Egypt, Mauritania and Morocco start paying off in terms of competitiveness and private sector activity. The short-term outlook in Tunisia also remains favorable. Economic prospects in the region are affected by developments in the international oil market and by the situation in the Middle East. High international oil prices could boost the economies of Algeria, Libya and Sudan, and in the absence of terrorist attacks, Egypt, Morocco and Tunisia could see a surge in tourism in 2005, as Western travelers seek alternative holiday destinations to South East Asia. In Mauritania, oil production is due to commence in 2006 but the non-oil sector will suffer from the lingering impact of the locust attack that devastated cereal production in 2004.

Southern Africa

Ten countries make up Southern Africa — Angola, Botswana, Lesotho, Malawi, Mozambique, Namibia, South Africa, Swaziland, Zambia and Zimbabwe. The sub-region is heavily reliant on exports of non-oil minerals (gold, diamonds, copper, platinum) and agricultural products (including tobacco, cotton, horticulture and fruit). All countries except Angola are net crude oil importers. The more developed economies in the sub-region also export labor-intensive manufactured products. In 2004, Southern Africa contributed 34.3 percent of Africa's GDP, making it the second-largest sub-regional wealth contributor on the continent after North Africa. South Africa accounts for 79.1 percent of the sub-region's total GDP.

The population in Southern Africa totaled 121.4 million in 2004, or 14.1 percent of the continent's total. Per capita income stood at $2,232 in 2004. But this average hides considerable disparities between middle income countries — Botswana, Namibia, South Africa and Swaziland — where per capita GDP ranges from $2,106 to $4,816, and some of the world's poorest Mozambique, Malawi, and Zambia, and more recently, Zimbabwe — where per capita incomes range from $154 to $446.

The year 2004 was marked by elections in Southern Africa. In Botswana, the incumbent President, Festus Magae, was reelected for a second term in office in October 2004. In Malawi, the Ruling Party candidate, Bingu wa Mutharika, succeeded President Bakili Muluzi following general

elections in May 2004. In Mozambique, there were delays in vote counting after general elections took place in early December 2004. President Joaquim Chissano, who stepped down after 18 years in power, was replaced by ruling party candidate Armando Guebuzo. In Namibia general elections gave victory to the ruling party and its candidate, Hifikepunye Pohamba, succeeding President Sam Nujoma. In South Africa, the ruling party won a landslide victory in general elections in April 2004, with President Thabo Mbeki sworn in for a second term.

Recent Trends in the Domestic Economy

Economic Growth

GDP growth in Southern Africa increased slightly from an annual average of 3.1 percent during 2000–03 to 4.0 percent in 2004 (see Table 2.11 and Figure 2.4). This was 1.1 percentage point below the continental average. The higher rate of regional growth mostly reflected improved performance in South Africa, which benefited from strong domestic and overseas demand for its products, despite the continued strength of the South African rand. Strong growth was also recorded in Angola and Mozambique. Meanwhile, a tight food situation and the spread of HIV/AIDS continued to take its toll on other countries, and Zimbabwe's economic crisis deepened further.

In **Angola**, real GDP growth accelerated to 10.9 percent in 2004, on account of rising oil production. Nonetheless, poverty remains widespread. Over 279,000

Table 2.11: Southern Africa: GDP and Export Performances

Country	Real GDP Growth Rate (%)		GDP Per Capita (US$)		Real Exports[c/] Growth (%)		Exports[b/] Per Capita (US$)	
	Average 2000–2003	2004[a/]	Average 2000–2003	2004[a/]	Average 2000–2003	2004[a/]	Average 2000–2003	2004[a/]
ANGOLA	6.0	10.9	818	1,439	4.9	14.4	637	983
BOTSWANA	5.4	4.4	3,496	4,816	3.4	1.5	1693	2056
LESOTHO	3.7	2.3	493	799	28.9	3.4	221	330
MALAWI	0.7	4.3	149	154	–3.0	7.2	40	42
MOZAMBIQUE	7.3	7.8	205	290	35.2	41.4	55	84
NAMIBIA	3.0	4.4	1,785	2,703	1.5	9.1	749	846
SOUTH AFRICA	3.3	3.8	2,958	4,737	2.6	1.2	865	1067
SWAZILAND	2.2	2.1	1,330	2,106	8.4	–0.8	1151	1512
ZAMBIA	4.2	5.1	350	490	10.3	4.9	102	147
ZIMBABWE	–6.5	–4.8	635	446	–11.5	–11.3	144	100
SOUTHERN AFRICA	**3.1**	**4.0**	**1,459**	**2,232**	**2.9**	**3.3**	**487**	**616**

Notes: a/ Preliminary estimates
   b/ Exports of goods and non–factor services
   c/ Real exports of goods growth
Source: ADB Statistics Division, 2004

refugees have returned since the end of the civil war in 2002. Delays in post-war reconstruction largely explained the lackluster growth outside the oil sector. Increased areas under cultivation, favorable weather, and the return of farmers contributed to an estimated 9 percent rise in the 2004 cereal harvest to 713,000 tons — equivalent to 46 percent of domestic consumption requirements.

Growth in **Botswana** decelerated to 4.4 percent in 2004, down from the yearly average of 5.4 percent during 2000–03. The drop in export earnings, due to the

depreciation of the dollar, has been a contributory factor to the slowdown in GDP. Similarly, the high oil prices and the scourge of the HIV/AIDS pandemic have combined to impact adversely on economic activity.

GDP in **Lesotho** increased by a low 2.3 percent in 2004, as strong performance in textile production and exports only partly compensated for a drought-related fall in agricultural production and lower activity in construction.

Growth in **Malawi** rose substantially to 4.3 percent in 2004, up from an average 0.7

Figure 2.4: Southern Africa: Selected Economic Indicators, 2000–2004

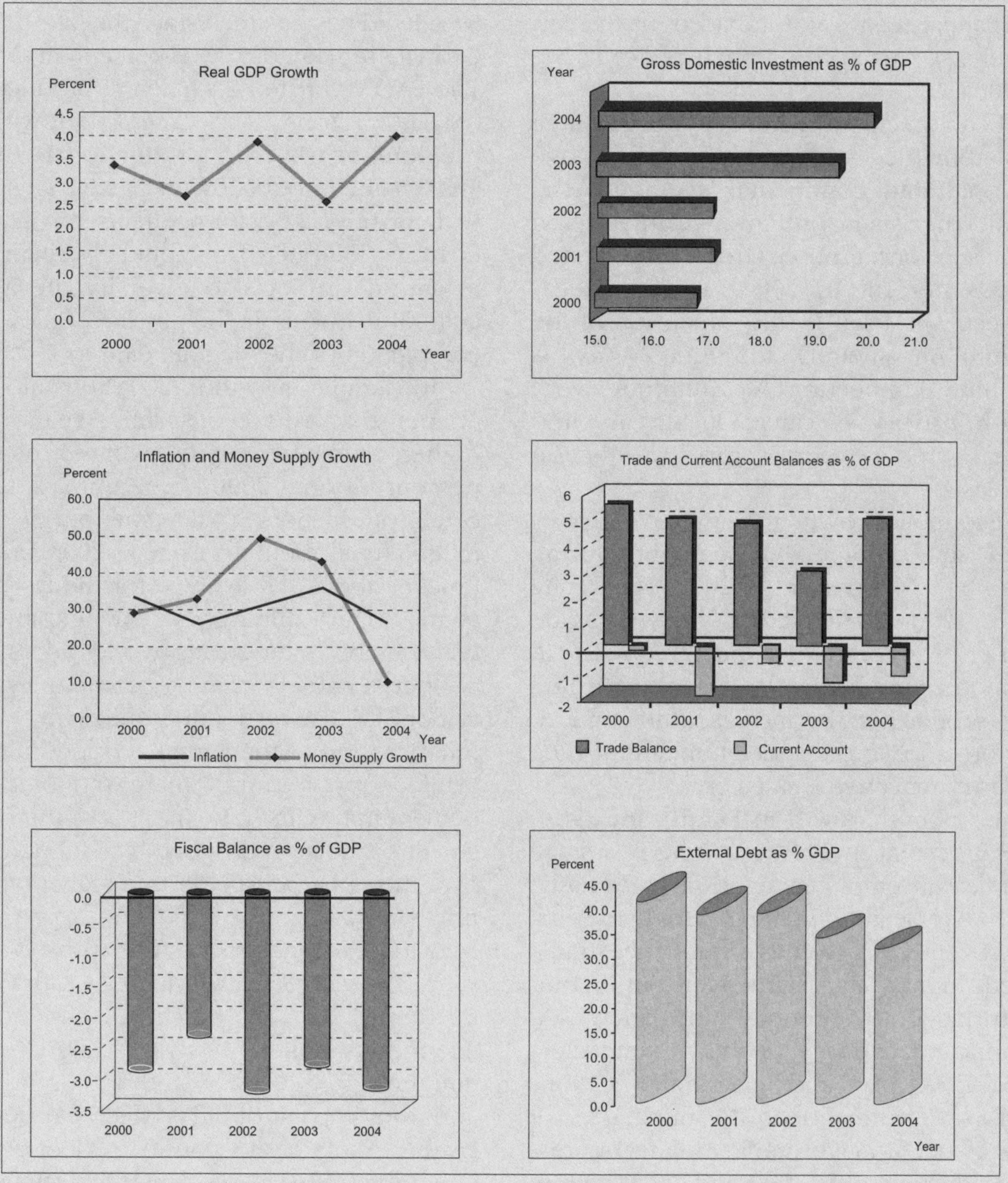
Real GDP Growth
Percent
4.5
4.0
3.5
3.0
2.5
2.0
1.5
1.0
0.5
0.0
2000
2001
2002
2003
2004
Year
Gross Domestic Investment as % of GDP
Year
2004
2003
2002
2001
2000
15.0
16.0
17.0
18.0
19.0
20.0
21.0
Inflation and Money Supply Growth
Percent
60.0
50.0
40.0
30.0
20.0
10.0
0.0
2000
2001
2002
2003
2004
Year
Inflation
Money Supply Growth
Trade and Current Account Balances as % of GDP
6
5
4
3
2
1
0
-1
-2
2000
2001
2002
2003
2004
Trade Balance
Current Account
Fiscal Balance as % of GDP
0.0
-0.5
-1.0
-1.5
-2.0
-2.5
-3.0
-3.5
2000
2001
2002
2003
2004
External Debt as % GDP
Percent
45.0
40.0
35.0
30.0
25.0
20.0
15.0
10.0
5.0
0.0
2000
2001
2002
2003
2004
Year

Source: ADB Statistics Division, 2004

percent during 2000–03, in spite of the drought-related 14 percent fall in cereal output, according to FAO estimates. A substantial recovery in tobacco production largely explained the growth performance in 2004.

Economic performance in **Mozambique** has remained strong and well above regional and continental average, as a result of rising foreign investment and domestic consumption. Growth accelerated to 7.8 percent in 2004, as two mega-projects — Mozal II (the expansion of the aluminium smelter) and SASOL (a gas pipeline connecting Mozambique with South Africa) — came on stream, and cereal and export crop production increased.

Economic growth in **Namibia** increased from an average 3.0 percent during 2000–03 to 4.4 percent in 2004. The strong demand for diamonds on the worldwide market supported a robust recovery in diamond production in 2004. Copper and zinc production also increased. In contrast, performance in the agricultural and fishing industry remained lackluster.

Economic growth in **South Africa** rose to 3.8 percent in 2004, resulting in a small increase in employment. Higher domestic and overseas demand, alongside an improvement in business confidence, translated into a sturdy recovery in manufacturing and services and increased production capacity in the mining, electricity, transport and telecommunications sectors. Performance in the mining sector was mixed, notwithstanding higher volume of production in the diamond and platinum industries. The level of agricultural and livestock production remained broadly unchanged.

GDP per capita in drought-prone **Swaziland** has declined since the late 1990s. Growth remained at 2.1 percent in 2004. The FAO estimated 2004 cereal production of 64,000 tons, 12 percent below the previous year's crop production figures. Sugar cane production increased slightly, with positive knock-on effects on manufacturing output. New publicly financed irrigations projects to diversify the agricultural sector are in the pipeline, following completion of the Maguga dam in 2002.

In **Zambia** growth in 2004 remained at 5.1 percent for two consecutive years, and higher than the yearly average of 4.2 percent during 2000–03. Zambia's total cereal production in 2004 was put at 1.37 million tons, about the same as 2003, but 23 percent above the average for the last five years. The mining sector expanded considerably after strong world prices for copper enabled mining companies to undertake investment, allowing the rehabilitation of the Monani copper mines. While copper output increased by 18.3 percent in the first nine months of the year, cobalt production dropped by 34.3 percent over the same period, despite higher world prices.

Zimbabwe entered its fifth consecutive year of negative growth in 2004, with GDP declining by 4.8 percent. Inadequate economic policies, capital flight and emigration, adverse weather conditions and the impact of HIV/AIDS pandemic largely explain the country's deepening economic crisis. The FAO estimated Zimbabwe's cereal production at 976,000 tons in 2004, which is 40 percent below the previous five-year average, while the production of export crops (notably tobacco) was also well below average.

Prices and Exchange Rates

Price and exchange rate developments in Southern Africa closely follow that in South Africa, the largest economy of the region. Three countries, Lesotho, Namibia and Swaziland, have their currencies pegged to the South African rand at parity under the Common Monetary Area. The rand is also a currency of reference in Botswana. The external value of the rand strengthened for the second consecutive year in 2004, which helped to contain inflation in the five countries and, in part, compensate for higher fuel prices. Loose fiscal and monetary policy in Angola, Zimbabwe and Malawi caused high inflation in those countries. Overall, the Southern African inflation rate increased to a still high 24.6 percent in 2004, compared with a continental average of 7.7 percent.

Inflation in **Angola** fell from an average 170.8 percent during 2000–03 to 43.5 percent in 2004, indicating some progress in improving economic management. The rate of depreciation of the kwanza also slowed significantly.

Inflation in **Botswana** remained within the target rate of 4-6 per cent in 2004 in spite of the rising oil prices, the broadening of VAT, and the devaluation of the domestic currency, the pula by 7.5 percent in February 2004. The Bank of Botswana maintained a relatively tight monetary policy stance in 2004, although the bank rate was left unchanged at 14.25 percent. In

November 2004, the central bank introduced a 14-day certificate to allow for short-term liquidity adjustment. The 91-day BoB Certificate remains the main instrument of liquidity control.

Despite serious food shortage, inflation in **Lesotho** slowed to 4.7 percent in 2004, reflecting lower inflation in South Africa. The Central Bank of Lesotho lowered its interest rates in line with the South African Reserve Bank's monetary policy stance.

Inflation in **Malawi** fell sharply to 6.0 percent in 2004, from a yearly average of 20.1 percent during 2000–03, due to tighter monetary policy to mop up the excess liquidity arising from government borrowing in the previous year.

The Central Bank of **Mozambique** has operated a *de facto* informal peg to the US dollar since mid-2002. Monetary policy was tight in 2004, with the growth of broad money projected to slow down to 15 percent, from an average 19 percent during 2000–03. Inflation targets were met in 2004, with inflation decreasing to 8.1 percent, as a result of improved food supplies, and lower imported inflationary pressures following the relative stabilization of the metical against the South African rand.

Consumer prices in **Namibia** declined by 0.7 percent in 2004, compared with an average inflation of 9.2 percent during 2000–03 — supported by a strong exchange rate, lower imported inflationary pressures and improved food supplies. Interest rates were kept unchanged until August 2004, when the Bank of Namibia mirrored monetary developments in South Africa by reducing the bank rate by 25 basis points to 7.50 percent.

South Africa recorded a historically low level of inflation in 2004, at 2.6 percent, indicating a successful macroeconomic stabilization policy and the impact of a strong South African rand. The South African Reserve Bank accordingly reduced its repurchase rate in August 2004 to 7.5 percent. The exchange rate was relatively stable in nominal effective terms, rising by 3.5 percent, compared with 25.09 percent in 2003. The continued strength of the rand largely reflected a weak US dollar and an increase in commodity prices.

Monetary policy in **Swaziland** principally consists of supporting the pegged exchange rate system between the lilangeni and the South African rand. In line with the rand, the lilangeni strengthened against the US dollar in 2004. Inflationary pressures followed a declining trend for the second consecutive year, with consumer prices rising by an average 6.7 percent in 2004.

The Bank of **Zambia** tightened its monetary policy in 2004, using monetary market operations and auctions of government securities to restrict money supply growth. Reduced government borrowing on the domestic market also helped to reduce pressures on inflation and interest rates. The inflation target was achieved, with consumer prices rising by an average 17.8 percent in 2004, against a yearly 22.9 percent during 2000–2003, mostly because of higher petroleum products prices and transport costs. The exchange rate, which is market determined, remained relatively stable, following the introduction of an interbank foreign exchange market in 2003.

Inflation in **Zimbabwe** averaged 350 percent in 2004, reflecting acute shortage of fuel and basic goods, a heavily managed foreign exchange system (revised in January 2004) and excessive monetary expansion. Most price controls have now been removed. The Reserve Bank of Zimbabwe has maintained an inconsistent monetary stance, with only occasional tightening. Interest rates were kept negative in real terms and the external value of the Zimbabwe dollar depreciated further against all major traded currencies.

Public Finance and Structural Reforms

Fiscal Developments

Overall, public finances in Southern Africa have strengthened, although much more is needed to strengthen priority spending allocation, including those related to health and HIV/AIDS. The increase in the sub-region's fiscal deficit to 3.2 percent of GDP in 2004 largely reflected South Africa's expansionary policy. With the exceptions of Angola, Swaziland, and Zimbabwe, most countries made significant progress towards fiscal consolidation and public expenditure restraints. New IMF programs were approved in Malawi and Zambia by mid-2004. Table 2.12 shows the macro-economic indicators.

Fiscal deficit in **Angola** declined to 3.5 percent of GDP in 2004, from an average of 6.6 percent during 2000–03, as a result of good progress on transparency in oil revenue tracking and management, reflecting ongoing negotiations with the IMF.

The government of **Botswana** achieved a fiscal deficit of 0.3 percent of GDP in 2004, in contrast with a fiscal surplus of 0.6 percent of GDP during 2000–03. There was a 13.7 percent revenue shortfall in fiscal year 2003/04, following a lower-than budgeted rise in VAT collection and a drop in mineral export revenues (because of the weak US dollar). On the expenditure side, two supplementary budgets were adopted in August and December 2004 to tackle the HIV/AIDS pandemic. Emergency measures included a drawing of dividend payments from profit-making state-owned enterprises, a reduction in capital outlays and

the sale of the public debt service fund loan book.

Budget performance in **Lesotho** was stronger than envisaged, with the fiscal balance changing from a deficit of 1.2 percent of GDP in 2003 to a surplus of 2.4 percent of GDP in 2004. Revenues were higher than budgeted, following the successful introduction of VAT and the establishment of an autonomous revenue authority in 2003. The postponement of local government elections, lower transfers and subsidies, and a lighter debt burden helped to keep total expenditures below the budgeted figure in fiscal year 2003/04.

Table 2.12: Southern Africa: Macroeconomic Management Indicators

Country	Inflation (%)		Fiscal Balance as % of GDP		Gross Domestic Investment		Gross National Savings	
					as % of GDP			
	Average 2000–2003	2004[a]	Average 2000–2003	2004[a]	Average 2000–2003	2004[a]	Average 2000–2003	2004[a]
ANGOLA	170.8	43.5	–6.6	–3.5	34.6	33.4	10.1	20.8
BOTSWANA	8.1	4.5	0.6	–0.3	23.4	27.2	39.9	36.9
LESOTHO	7.7	4.7	–1.2	2.4	38.2	31.4	23.5	25.1
MALAWI	20.1	6.0	–6.5	–12.7	8.0	11.9	–0.4	1.0
MOZAMBIQUE	13.0	8.1	–6.4	–5.2	41.9	44.3	14.8	15.1
NAMIBIA	9.2	–0.7	–2.9	–2.1	20.7	22.6	25.4	28.3
SOUTH AFRICA	6.5	2.6	–1.8	–3.2	16.0	17.1	15.6	14.3
SWAZILAND	9.7	6.7	–3.7	–6.6	20.5	19.2	16.1	13.2
ZAMBIA	22.9	17.8	–4.8	–3.9	22.0	25.4	4.4	11.8
ZIMBABWE	173.1	350.0	–8.2	–9.7	3.2	3.1	–1.1	–4.0
SOUTHERN AFRICA	**22.1**	**26.4**	**–2.8**	**–3.2**	**17.5**	**20.0**	**14.5**	**15.1**

Note: [a] Preliminary estimates
Source: ADB Statistics Division, 2004

Malawi's fiscal performance was mixed in 2003/04. Revenues were higher than expected, thanks to an increase in excise taxes and a widening of the personal income and value added tax bases. Spending overruns (some related to the costs of the elections) were, however, significant. As a result, the overall budget deficit rose to 12.7 percent of GDP in 2003/04, up from an average 6.5 percent of GDP during 2000–03. Additional domestic borrowing financed the deficit, bringing domestic debt stock to 26 percent of GDP. The government has committed to spending restraint under its 2004/05 budget.

In **Mozambique**, the government's fiscal deficit declined slightly from an annual average of 6.4 percent of GDP during 2000–03 to 5.2 percent of GDP in 2004. This reflected further increases in the collection of income and indirect taxes following continued improvement in tax administration and upward adjustment in the fuel taxes. Government expenditures were largely devoted to priority spending and were also used to finance the 2004 general elections. The government exercised stricter control over the wage bill.

In **Namibia**, the budget deficit fell from an annual average of 2.9 percent of GDP during 2000–03 to 2.1 percent of GDP in 2004. There was a fall in revenue from the diamond sector, but further expenditure restraints were also exercised. Part of the budget deficit was financed through issuing new securities, with public domestic debt rising to 24.5 percent of GDP by the end of fiscal year.

The government in **South Africa** maintained a moderately expansionary fiscal stance in 2004, and the budget deficit rose to 3.2 percent of GDP. Social and capital spending increased, with a larger proportion of the budget spent at provincial and local government levels. The impact of lower interest rates on debt service payments helped to finance the expansionary stance. The tax base remained broadly unchanged, although a moderate income tax relief and higher taxes on fuels, tobacco and alcohol were announced for the fiscal year 2004/05.

Fiscal policy has remained loose in **Swaziland**. The budget deficit widened to 6.6 percent of GDP for the fiscal year 2004, up from an average 3.7 percent during 2000–03 owing to an unchecked rise in public expenditures — including capital spending for millennium projects. The government has plans to introduce a value-added tax and curtail public expenditures to compensate for rapidly falling customs revenues from SACU.

The government of **Zambia** has secured a new PRGF with the IMF after large fiscal adjustments were made in the first quarter of 2004. Spending overruns had characterized 2003, with the fiscal deficit rising to 4.8 percent of GDP in that year. Spending restraints (including a freeze on civil service wages) brought the fiscal deficit down to 3.9 percent of GDP in 2004. The 2005 budget allows for increased spending in priority sectors.

Zimbabwe's budget deficit rose to 9.7 percent in 2004, following a 220 percent wage increase in January (followed by another of 50 percent in May) and rising capital spending. Maize purchases by the government's Grain Marketing Board were nonetheless significantly lower than expected. VAT and a new levy on petroleum products were successfully introduced in January 2004 to strengthen revenue. The government has, however, continued to accumulate domestic and external payment arrears.

Structural Reforms

Reforms in Southern Africa have mostly taken the form of fiscal consolidation, as fiscal policy remains loose compared with other sub-regions, while declining revenues under the new SACU agreement are anticipated in some member countries. The new SACU agreement came into force in June 2004. The restructuring of state owned enterprises and their eventual privatization remain high on the agenda, although progress was slow in 2004. In countries like Botswana, South Africa and Mozambique, policy has also focused on creating an enabling environment for the private sector.

The **Angola** government's program of post-war reconstruction and structural reforms has yet to take off. Efforts in 2004 focused on securing a staff monitored program with the IMF by early 2005. Concerns have been expressed about lack of transparency. There was nonetheless an improvement in data reporting and clarification in the transactions between the Treasury, the Banco Nacional de Angola (BNA), and the national oil company (Sonangol) in 2004. Specific sectoral and structural policies are soon to be highlighted in an interim PRSP.

In 2003, the **Botswana** government launched the ninth National Development Plan for 2003/04 — 2008/09, outlining a strategy to diversify the economy away from mining. Major reforms include financial ones (including the privatization of the public pension system), a relaxation of controls on prices, the establishment of an autonomous central statistics office, the adoption of a rural sector development policy, and the privatization of public enterprises. Progress was slow in 2004, and the sale of national air carrier, Air Botswana, has suffered a series of setbacks, after the short-listed candidate withdrew. The government now plans to sell shares of the airline on the stock market.

Recent reforms have helped to improve transparency and accountability in **Lesotho**. Government accounts have been audited and the recently established anti-corruption unit has prosecuted a number of international companies involved in the Lesotho Highlands Water Project scandal. Reforms in the legal system are also being envisaged. The liberalization of the electricity sector, including the sale of a majority stake in the Lesotho Electricity Corporation, ranks high on the country's reform agenda. The PRSP, being finalized, will mostly address structural constraints in the agricultural sector and the fight against HIV/AIDS.

Measures to improve public expenditure management are central to a staff monitored program, which the IMF approved in **Malawi** in July 2004. New acts for public finance management, public audit, and public procurement were passed by parliament in mid-2003 and the anti-corruption bureau was strengthened in early 2004. Little progress was made under the structural reform agenda with regards to the privatization of state-owned utilities and the liberalization of the telecommunication, electricity and water sectors.

The pace of structural reforms has remained satisfactory in **Mozambique**. Measures to strengthen the financial sector were pushed through in 2004. A new financial institutions law was approved by parliament, strengthening the central bank's supervisory function, while a review of major banks by international auditors has started. Preparations for privatization and/or sector liberalization are also underway for the remaining parastatals, including telecommunications, electricity, ports, petroleum and the railroads. The authorities also envisage reforms to enhance the investment climate, by streamlining business regulations, addressing labor rigidities, and revising the land tenure system.

Land reform and the implementation of black economic empowerment programs have dominated **Namibia**'s reform agenda. In practice, little progress has been made and there have also been continuous delays in the restructuring of state-owned enterprises. Meanwhile, steps have been taken with regards to fiscal consolidation, against a backdrop of trade liberalization and projected declining revenue from SACU. These included a review of the tax system and the adoption of a medium-term expenditure framework.

Public policy in **South Africa** has centered on measures to combat unemployment and inequality, amidst continued efforts to strengthen the health system and combat HIV/AIDS. A labor-intensive public work program was launched in 2004. On measures to improve the environment for the private sector, new black economic empowerment charters in the financial sector were completed and the pace of land redistribution picked up in 2004. Progress in privatization has remained slow since the sale of a 28 percent stake in Telkom (electricity) in 2003, although new investment is needed to improve the efficiency of major public enterprises.

Little progress has been made in **Swaziland**'s structural adjustment program. Non-performing state-owned enterprises that need restructuring include Swaziland Railways, the Central Transport Authority, the Swaziland Development and Savings Bank and the National Maize Corporation. Under pressure to strengthen the rule of law, the government amended the Industrial Relations Act in April 2004. The government also plans to revise the investment code.

Reforms in **Zimbabwe** have been uneven. While the fuel market and the trade regime have been partially liberalized and most price controls removed in an effort to improve economic fundamentals, privatization and civil service reforms have fallen low on the policy agenda, and continued uncertainty over property rights and land reforms has continued to discourage investment.

Recent Trends in the External Sector

Current Account Developments

There was an overall improvement in the sub-region's terms of trade, largely

Table 2.13: Southern Africa: The External Sector

Country	Trade Balance as % of GDP		Current Account as % of GDP		Terms of Trade (%)		Total External Debt as % of GDP		Debt Service as % of Exports	
	Average 2000–2003	2004[a]	Average 2000–2003	2004[a]	Average 2000–2003	2004[a]	Average 2000–2003	2004[a]	Average 2000–2003	2004[a]
ANGOLA	40.6	36.9	–3.4	9.2	10.0	31.9	86.1	37.2	25.2	9.2
BOTSWANA	14.7	9.0	11.1	6.4	–4.0	–6.2	21.6	16.1	2.4	2.0
LESOTHO	–52.1	–44.7	–14.9	–6.4	–2.2	–1.0	65.5	43.2	13.8	9.1
MALAWI	–6.6	–7.4	–6.9	–10.0	–2.9	–1.3	159.3	157.5	19.3	19.2
MOZAMBIQUE	–16.1	–3.6	–19.4	–9.3	3.3	0.5	131.8	101.8	27.8	24.4
NAMIBIA	–5.9	–11.4	4.7	5.5	0.9	–7.1	2.5	2.3	1.8	2.0
SOUTH AFRICA	3.7	1.1	–0.1	–2.0	2.1	2.9	27.4	22.6	14.3	13.9
SWAZILAND	–7.5	–9.0	–4.3	–6.0	–1.1	1.1	27.1	26.4	…	…
ZAMBIA	–7.1	–3.2	–16.7	–10.8	–2.0	10.3	155.9	106.3	13.7	23.4
ZIMBABWE	–1.3	–7.3	–2.8	–7.1	–0.8	–0.3	41.8	90.3	7.8	4.1
SOUTHERN AFRICA	**4.6**	**3.5**	**–1.0**	**–1.1**	**2.0**	**7.4**	**37.4**	**29.8**	**15.0**	**12.4**

Note: [a] Preliminary estimates
Source: ADB Statistics Division, 2004

reflecting rising commodity prices, including gold, diamond, platinum and copper, and zinc, and for Angola only, oil (see Table 2.13). The strength of the South African rand against the US dollar, while having a dampening impact on fuel imports, dented export competitiveness in some countries, especially in those that have preferential access to the US market under AGOA. Overall, the sub-region's current account deficit in 2004 virtually remained unchanged at 1.1 percent of GDP.

Angola's trade surplus remained high in 2004, on account of rising oil prices and production, crackdown on diamond smuggling, and low demand for imports owing to delays in reconstruction. The current account deficit turned into a surplus of 9.2 percent in 2004, against an average deficit of 3.4 percent of GDP during 2000–2003, notwithstanding heavy debt service commitments and service outflows paid to international oil companies.

Botswana's current account surplus continued a declining trend in 2004, as the rise in diamond exports (in volume terms) failed to compensate for the weakness of the US dollar and a lower-than-expected rise in world diamond prices. Meanwhile, imports continued to rise — fuelled by an increased demand for medicine (mostly related to HIV/AIDS), food and intermediate goods.

Lesotho's external situation has continued to improve. The external current account deficit declined from an average 14.9 percent of GDP during 2000–03 to 6.4 percent of GDP in 2004, notwithstanding the exchange rate appreciation, lower workers' remittances, and rising food imports. This positive trend is largely explained by Lesotho's vibrant textile export sector, which benefits from the expanded AGOA.

Malawi's external current account deficit rose from 6.9 percent of GDP during 2000–03 to 10.0 percent of GDP in 2004. Export volumes increased in 2004 on account of a strong recovery in tobacco production, while import volumes continued to reflect the country's fragile food situation and rising oil world market prices. Official transfers have fallen in recent years, reflecting frequent policy slippages.

Mozambique's current account deficit continued to be heavily influenced by the pace of execution of the mega-projects. The deficit declined significantly to 9.3 percent of GDP in 2004, mostly reflecting movements in the trade balance. Exports in 2004 grew by over 40 percent as a result of a sharp increase in aluminum and natural gas, while imports associated with the construction of mega-projects declined, following the completion of the construction phase of the gas pipeline. Meanwhile, the services and income account recorded large deficits in 2004, because of significant increase in payments of dividends by the mega-projects.

The current account surplus in Namibia increased from an average 4.7 percent of GDP during 2000–2003 to 5.5 percent of GDP in 2004. There was a recovery in exports, against a backdrop of rising world prices for zinc and copper and resumed exploration activities by diamond companies. The strong Namibian dollar, however, dampened export performance in some sub-sectors, including tourism. The trade deficit remained well above average, at 11.4 percent of GDP, reflecting higher import demand for food and capital goods. This was more than offset by a rise in net transfers, as a result of increased SACU revenues (under the old 1969 agreement), and development assistance.

The current account balance in South Africa remained in deficit for the second consecutive year in 2004, rising to 2.0 percent of GDP. Lower prices for imported products and the improved domestic environment largely explained the rising demand in the import of capital and consumption goods. Export performance was mixed. The mining sector strongly benefited from buoyant world prices for gold and platinum, but the strength of the rand rendered manufacturing exports less competitive on international markets. The country's international reserve position nonetheless continued to strengthen, indicating large foreign exchange inflows in the capital account. The South African Reserve Bank closed its open position in the foreign exchange market in February 2004.

The strengthening of the lilangeni has dented export competitiveness in Swaziland, with the current account deficit increasing to an equivalent 6.0 percent of GDP in 2004. The Swaziland Sugar Association has raised concerns over plans by the EU to reduce guaranteed sugar prices to ACP countries from July 2005, although prospects for clothing exports remained good after preferential access to US market under the AGOA agreement was renewed in 2004.

Zambia's current account deficit declined to a still high 10.8 percent of GDP in 2004, mostly reflecting a favorable external environment. Copper prices continued to increase sharply, with metal export receipts rising by 30 percent, while non-traditional exports (including tobacco) recorded a strong growth for the second consecutive year.

Zimbabwe's external current account deficit rose to 7.1 percent of GDP in 2004, against an average 2.8 percent of GDP during 2000–03, indicating poor export performance (despite new incentives introduced by the government in 2004, including new subsidy schemes for gold and tobacco) and a depressed demand for imports as a result of currency shortage.

External Debt

Southern Africa is the least indebted sub-region in the continent, and the external debt-to-GDP ratio averaged 29.4 percent in 2004, but there are wide disparities across countries. Malawi, Mozambique, and Zambia are all classified as heavily indebted poor countries. By contrast, the stock of external debt in Botswana, Namibia, South Africa and Swaziland stood below the regional average. The debt service ratio declined to 12.4 percent in 2004, against a 2000–03 average of 15 percent, indicating rising exports in goods and services. The strengthening of the

South African rand and other regional currencies against the US dollar also helped to alleviate the external debt burden in that year.

Most countries in Southern Africa have been successful in attracting FDI over the years, because they are richly endowed with mineral resources, and/or because they have actively pursued broad-based reforms.

External debt in **Angola** decreased to an estimated 37.2 percent of GDP in 2004, reflecting strong economic growth. The government, which has relied on expensive oil-backed loans from commercial banks to bridge the financing gap, hopes to organize a donors' roundtable in 2005, with the support of the World Bank. Aid inflows have been slow to come since the end of the war, because of continued allegation of financial mismanagement. The central bank consolidated external debt statistics in 2004, with a compilation of arrears outstanding by source and creditors.

Botswana's external debt burden was estimated at 16.1 percent of GDP in 2004, which is low by Sub-Saharan African standards. As a result, the country's sovereign credit risk rating is the highest in Africa, reflecting a high level of foreign exchange reserves, a stable outlook and a prudent public borrowing policy. Despite strong credentials, the government has stopped short of issuing sovereign bonds on the international market. Government bonds (ranging from 2, 5 and 12 years) were successfully re-introduced on the domestic market in 2003. The country benefits from low but steady inflows of FDI in the mining sector and, more recently, in the textile and retail industries.

Lesotho's external debt-to-GDP ratio continued to decline to a manageable 43.2 percent of GDP in 2004, reflecting the government's prudent external borrowing policy and the weak US dollar. Foreign capital inflows to Lesotho have declined following completion of the first phase of the Lesotho Highland Water Project. FDI in the textiles and clothing industry has also declined.

Malawi reached decision point under the HIPC initiative in 2000, but there have been delays in the implementation of debt relief packages by the Paris Club and multilateral donors. The IMF, which approved the resumption of its interim assistance under HIPC in October 2003, withheld all balance of payments support after program implementation went off track in the first half of 2004. Most donors followed suit. The (mostly public) stock of external debt declined to an estimated 157.5 percent of GDP in 2004, with completion point now unlikely to be reached before 2006.

Mozambique's total external debt fell to 101.8 percent of GDP in 2004. The government has maintained a prudent external borrowing policy since reaching completion point under the enhanced HIPC initiative in September 2001 and signing an agreement with the Paris Club in November 2001 (the authorities have now signed bilateral agreements with nine out of 12 Paris Club creditors). Private capital inflows, especially FDI, have increased significantly in the past five years. According to UNTAD, FDI inward stock totaled $1.8 billion in 2003. The country's

external debt is expected to remain sustainable over the medium-term, on account of the strong international reserve position.

The external debt burden in **Namibia** appears manageable in the medium-run. The debt-to-GDP ratio amounted to 2.3 percent of GDP in 2004, against an average of 2.5 percent during 2000–03.

South Africa's external debt in 2004 increased in US dollar terms, reflecting new long-term government borrowing, but declined to 22.6 percent as a ratio to GDP. In May 2004, the government successfully issued sovereign bonds, worth $1 billion, on the international market to help finance its deficit. In line with exchange control reforms, foreign firms were allowed to raise debt and equity finance on the Johannesburg securities or bond exchanges for the first time in 2004.

Swaziland's external debt reached 26.4 percent of GDP in 2004. Inflows of FDI have declined since the mid-1990s, as the country's advantage as an investment location eroded with the end of South Africa apartheid. According to UNCTAD statistics, FDI inflows totaled $44million in 2003.

Zambia's external debt fell sharply to 106.3 percent of GDP in 2004. The country hopes to reach completion point under the enhanced HIPC initiative by 2005.

Although most bilateral and multilateral creditors have withheld their assistance to **Zimbabwe**, the country's debt burden has continued to increase in local currency terms and as a percentage of GDP. The debt-to-GDP ratio stood at 90.3 percent in 2004, against an average of 41.8 percent during 2000–2003 despite the absence of foreign financing, because of negative growth and the currency depreciation. The Zimbabwean government has continued to fail its external debt payment obligations, with debt service (paid) representing only 4 percent of all exports in 2004.

Outlook

Growth in Southern Africa is forecast to accelerate to 4.6 percent in 2005. Economic projections in South Africa and Angola may largely dictate the regional outlook. South Africa's growth is projected to accelerate to 4.7 percent in 2005, building on recent years' successful macroeconomic stabilization and assuming a relatively robust world economy. The rand is unlikely to strengthen much further, which should help to boost South African exports, while low interest rates and declining inflation will also support rising consumer demand on the domestic market. Business confidence in Southern Africa is at its highest since the end of apartheid in 1994, with value added in all sectors projected to grow in 2005. As a result, employment is set to increase. Growth in Angola is expected to accelerate to 14.7 percent in 2005 due to increased oil production and modest oil prices. Growth in Lesotho is also forecast to accelerate, on the back of strong economic performance in South Africa, its main economic and trading partner. Economic performance will also strengthen in Malawi and Zambia, assuming public sector management is back on track as a result of IMF deals signed in 2004. Mozambique will continue to maintain its growth momentum as one of the best

performers in the region. Much will, however, depend on climatic conditions for the 2004/05 growing season. Botswana, which used to be the best growth performing country in the region, is likely to see its growth decelerate due to constraints imposed by the HIV/AIDS problems.

West Africa

A total of 15 countries make up the West African sub-region. Eight countries — Benin, Burkina Faso, Côte d'Ivoire, Guinea Bissau, Mali, Niger, Senegal and Togo — belong to the CFA zone, while the non-CFA zone consists of Cape Verde, Ghana, Guinea, The Gambia, Nigeria, Liberia and Sierra Leone. The sub-region is dominated by Nigeria, which accounts for some 55.4 percent of its output. Nigeria is also the largest exporter, a reflection of its rich endowment of crude oil and gas. With the exceptions of Côte d'Ivoire and Nigeria, all other countries are net oil importers. In 2004, regional GDP constituted 16.5 percent of the continent's total, a contribution higher than that of Central and East Africa combined.

The sub-region's population totaled 247.6 million, or 28.9 percent of the continent's total, in 2004. Nigeria, which is one of the most densely populated countries in continental Africa, alone accounts for 51.3 percent of the sub-region's total. With a GDP per capita of $527, West Africa ranks far behind the North and Southern sub-regions in terms of living standards, but slightly ahead of the Central and East African sub-regions.

The civil war in Côte d'Ivoire continued to have a negative impact on the West African economy in 2004, on account of the fact that Côte d'Ivoire is the second largest economy, accounting for 11.8 percent of its GDP. After 18 months of a fragile ceasefire under the vigilance of French and UN peace-keeping troops, fighting resumed in the north of the country in November 2004. The UN Security Council voted a 13-month arms embargo and warned of further sanctions if no progress was made towards peace. In effect, the country remains divided between the rebel-held north and the government-controlled south. In Liberia, a national transitional government was installed after its former president, Charles Taylor, took exile in Nigeria. A 15,000 UN peacekeeping force was fully deployed in 2004 and the disarmament process began. Ghana's President John Agyekum Kufuor was re-elected for a second term in December 2004. Presidential elections held in December 2003 in Guinea resulted in the election for another seven-year mandate of President Lansana Conté. In March 2004, Guinea-Bissau held its first legislative elections since the September 2003 military coup, with the Partido Africano da Independencia da Guiné e Cabo Verde winning by a landslide. Although the newly installed government supports the interim president, Henrique Rosa, the situation remains fragile, as revealed by a military mutiny in October 2004. In December 2004, Mamadou Tandja of Niger was re-elected as president for a second five-year term.

Recent Trends in the Domestic Economy

Economic Growth

Growth in West Africa decelerated sharply from a 7.0 percent peak in 2003 to 3.4 percent in 2004, a 1.7 percentage point below the continental average (see Table 2.14 and Figure 2.5). Economic performance varied greatly across individual countries in the sub-region. Growth in The Gambia, Ghana, Senegal and Sierra Leone was above 5 percent, while growth failed to resume in Côte d'Ivoire, as no progress was made towards reconciliation. Growth decelerated sharply in Burkina Faso and Mali — 2003 was a bumper year for agriculture in these two countries — and in Nigeria — despite higher international oil prices.

Benin's economic growth decelerated from 4.8 percent in 2003 to 2.2 percent in 2004. This largely reflected lower performance in cotton — cotton production was expected to fall from 333,400 tons in 2003/04 to 250,000 tons in 2004/05, as a result of continued difficulties and delayed reforms in this sector. Re-exports to neighbouring Nigeria slowed down, following import restrictions in this country and the strengthening of the CFA franc against the naira.

Growth in **Burkina Faso** decelerated from a peak 8 percent in 2003 to 4.8 percent in 2004. Cereal production peaked to 3.6m tonnes in 2003, and although agriculture continued to perform well in 2004, cereal production was much lower, at 3 million tonnes. Cotton production remained higher than average for the

Table 2.14: West Africa: GDP and Export Performances

Country	Real GDP Growth Rate (%)		GDP Per Capita (US$)		Real Exports[c] Growth (%)		Exports[b] Per Capita (US$)	
	Average 2000–2003	2004[a]	Average 2000–2003	2004[a]	Average 2000–2003	2004[a]	Average 2000–2003	2004[a]
BENIN	4.8	2.2	418	590	0.2	–3.8	60	80
BURKINA FASO	5.3	4.0	260	379	4.6	15.8	24	36
CAPE VERDE	6.1	4.0	1,431	2,045	18.6	11.0	433	695
COTE D'IVOIRE	–1.4	–2.0	724	914	0.0	–0.1	319	389
GAMBIA	3.7	7.7	289	284	3.9	42.3	126	130
GHANA	4.4	5.8	296	409	0.1	10.8	130	156
GUINEA	2.8	2.5	391	438	1.6	–3.3	94	99
GUINEA–BISSAU	0.3	1.0	150	175	8.0	5.6	45	49
LIBERIA	..	..	..	..	...	...	...	...
MALI	5.0	2.1	263	381	11.3	0.1	74	101
NIGER	3.5	1.0	190	255	3.7	3.9	32	41
NIGERIA	5.2	3.7	416	569	9.2	–0.5	195	288
SENEGAL	4.7	6.0	520	730	3.0	4.8	160	210
SIERRA LEONE	14.5	7.4	179	201	20.8	19.6	32	46
TOGO	2.3	2.9	314	426	4.7	–4.8	106	163
WEST AFRICA	**4.2**	**3.4**	**392**	**527**	**4.9**	**1.2**	**159**	**221**

Notes: [a] Preliminary estimates
[b] Exports of goods and non-factor services
[c] Real exports of goods growth
Source: ADB Statistics Division, 2004

second consecutive year. Services performed well, but the manufacturing sector continued to suffer from the impact of Côte d'Ivoire crisis.

Growth in **Cape Verde** remained strong in 2004. Although the agricultural output declined significantly in 2004, successful macroeconomic stabilization continued to encourage private sector activity and boost foreign investment. Meanwhile, the government continued to increase capital spending, on the back of continued donors support. The tourism industry also expanded.

Growth in **Côte d'Ivoire** was elusive for the fifth consecutive year with real GDP declining by 2.0 percent in 2004, from the yearly average negative growth of 1.7 percent during 2000–03. Cocoa production remained roughly unchanged, but there

Figure 2.5: West Africa: Selected Economic Indicators, 2000–2004

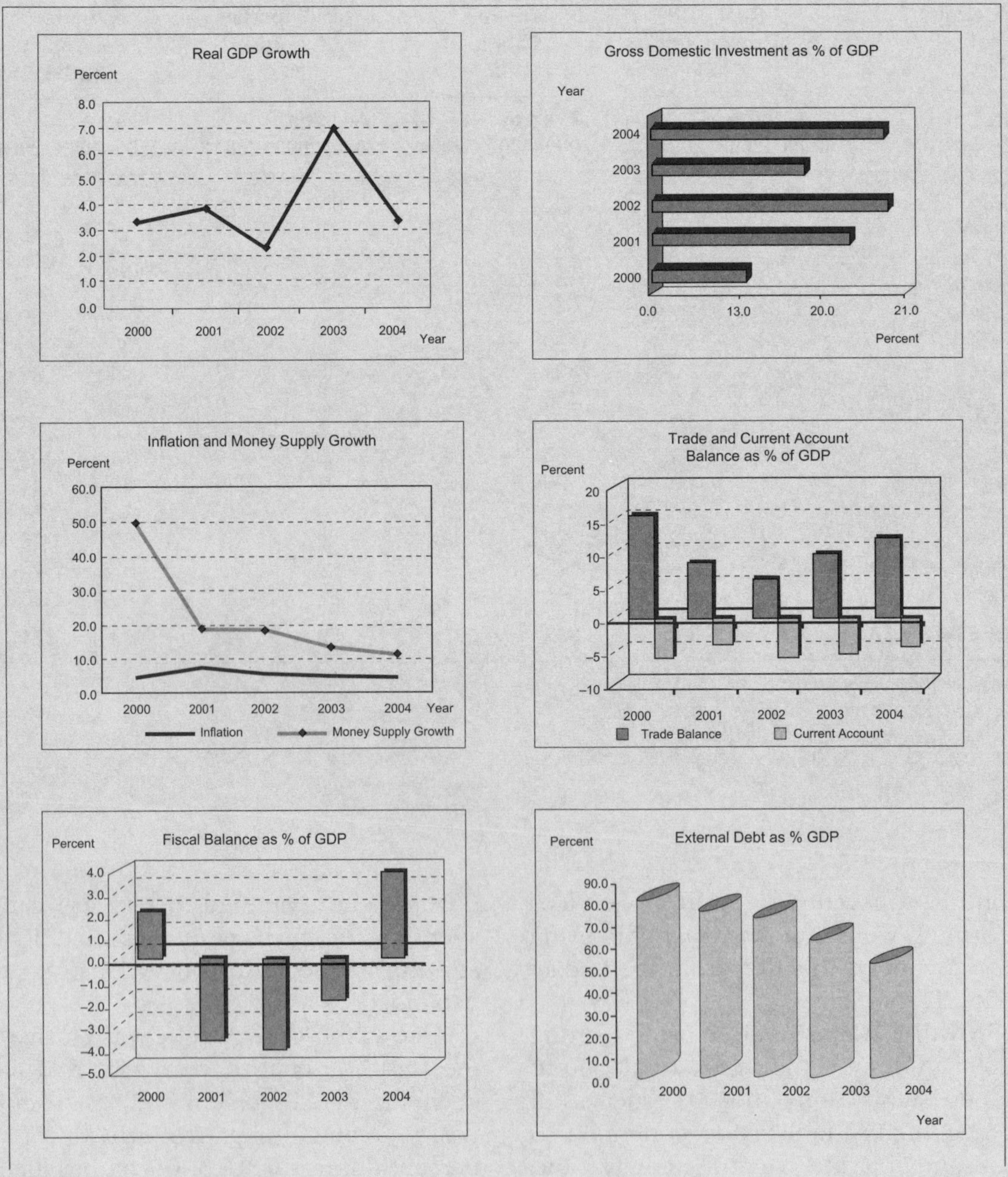

Real GDP Growth

Gross Domestic Investment as % of GDP

Inflation and Money Supply Growth

Trade and Current Account Balance as % of GDP

Fiscal Balance as % of GDP

External Debt as % GDP

Source: ADB Statistics Division, 2004

was a rise in oil production, supported by rising international oil prices. However, GDP in manufacturing and services continued to decline as a result of continued instability and disruptions to relations with its neighbors.

Economic growth in **The Gambia** improved slightly from 6.7 percent in 2003 to 7.7 percent in 2004, in large part owing to rising output in food crops and groundnut, the country's main export, following good weather conditions. Tourism, construction and re-export performances also improved in 2004.

Growth in **Ghana** continued to strengthen in 2004. Real GDP grew by 5.8 percent that year, against a yearly average of 4.4 percent during 2000–03. Rising cocoa output and increased cocoa processing capacity resulted in growth in manufacturing, which, together with the expansion of gold mining, explained the country's continuous strong performance.

Real GDP growth in **Guinea** increased to 2.5 percent in 2004 vis-à-vis 2003, owing to a slight pick up in activity in the secondary sector, following the adoption of an emergency recovery plan by the government in March 2004 and improved agricultural output. Macroeconomic instability and electricity and water shortages, however, continued to have a negative impact on the economy.

There was a slight growth recovery from the impact of the September 2003 coup in **Guinea-Bissau**, although it remained weak, with real GDP increasing by 1 percent. This compared favorably with the yearly growth average of 0.3 percent during 2000–03. Some donor-funded

projects resumed in 2004, while cashew nut production increased slightly. According to FAO estimates, cereal production increased from 121,000 tonnes in 2003 to 165,000 tonnes in 2004.

Although economic performance in **Mali** remains strong, growth declined considerably from 7.4 percent in 2003 to 2.1 percent in 2004. This largely reflected a decline in cereal production, as a result of the locust attack and reduced rains; cotton production also declined from its 2003/04 peak of 617,800 tonnes. Performance in manufacturing and construction strengthened, indicating increased cotton ginning activity, higher industrial activity (a new spinning mill opened in 2004) and continued development in infrastructure projects. Trade and services also performed well in 2004.

Real GDP growth in **Niger** decelerated to 1.0 percent in 2004. The locust attack dented performance in agriculture although weather conditions were favorable, but continued donor support for infrastructure projects and other priority sectors (including roads, water, electricity and rural development) as well as bumper crops the year before, continued to stimulate the economy. Cereal harvests fell from a peak of 3.6 million tons in 2003 to 3.1 million tons in 2004 (as a result of the locust attack and lower rainfall).

Economic performance in **Nigeria** hinges heavily on oil output and prices. Growth peaked at 10.7 percent in 2003, as oil and gas production, agricultural growth, and foreign investment in the oil sector, picked up. But instability in the Delta region and a tight OPEC production quota had a dampening impact on growth performance in 2004, when real GDP increased by only 3.4 percent.

Growth in **Senegal** increased from 4.7 percent during 2000–03 to 6 percent in 2004, activity in construction and public works remained healthy, and the production of phosphate and phosphate derivative products increased substantially, as a result of new investment plans by the Industries Chimiques du Sénégal. Meanwhile, cereal harvests fell slightly from a peak 1.5 million tonnes in 2003 to 1.2 million tonnes in 2004, as a result of the locust attack and lower rainfalls.

Improved security conditions and increased donor support continued to support a strong economic recovery in **Sierra Leone**. Real GDP growth increased by 7.4 percent in 2004, lower than the yearly average growth of 14.5 percent during 2000–03, as agricultural activity increased with the return of refugees to their lands in recent years. The slow resumption in mining activity (notably rutile, diamonds, gold and bauxite) and donor-supported post-war reconstruction programs (roads, electricity and water) boosted growth.

In the absence of external assistance, **Togo**'s economic performance has remained well below its potential since the early 1990s. Real GDP in 2004 increased by 2.9 percent, against a yearly average of 2.3 percent during 2000–03. This largely reflected a slight increase in cotton production and a recovery in the phosphate sector. Port and transport activities continued to benefit from trade diversion from Côte d'Ivoire.

Prices and Exchange Rates

Reflecting generally tight monetary and fiscal rules, inflation in West Africa averaged 4.3 percent, against a continental average of 7.7 percent in 2004. However, there was double-digit inflation in The Gambia, Ghana, Guinea, Liberia and Nigeria. Most non-CFA countries have committed themselves to forming a new West African Monetary Zone, but this has not yet been implemented.

Monetary policy in the West African CFA Zone is conducted at a regional level by the Banque Centrale des Etats de l'Afrique de l'Ouest (BCEAO) which has successfully switched to the use of indirect instruments; the bank's discount rate, reserve requirements ratio and money market auctions are the main regulators of the zone's liquidity. Direct advances by the central bank to governments have been gradually replaced by treasury bills since the late 1990s and were no longer permitted from 2003. The BCEAO's tight monetary policy is geared towards maintaining the fixed exchange rate between the CFA franc and the euro. The regional central bank cut its discount rate to 4.5 percent in March 2004. The strengthening of the regional currency against the US dollar helped to mitigate the inflationary impact of higher world oil prices, but also reduced the value of export earnings in CFA terms. Inflation in the CFA zone remained low, compared with other sub-regions of Africa.

In **Benin** inflation declined from 3.0 percent in 2003 to 0.4 percent in 2004, owing to abundant food supplies. Consumer prices in **Burkina Faso** declined by 0.7 percent in 2004. Inflation in **Côte d'Ivoire** in 2004 averaged 0.2 percent in 2004, in spite of supply bottlenecks and higher transport costs. Tight liquidity conditions kept inflation in **Guinea-Bissau** at 1 percent in 2004. Consumer prices in Mali declined by 4.6 percent in 2004, in sharp contrast with the inflation rate of 0.9 percent during 2000–03. **Niger** too experienced deflationary situations with prices falling by 1.7 percent in 2004. Falling food prices following bumper harvests in 2003/04 helped to compensate for higher fuel prices. In **Senegal**, inflation stayed low at 1.7 percent. In **Togo**, it averaged 2.5 percent.

Inflation in **Cape Verde** decreased marginally from 1.2 percent during 2000–03 to 1.1 percent in 2004, as a result of improved food supply conditions and a tightening in monetary policy. The main objective of the central bank is to support the Cape Verdean escudo which is pegged to the euro at a rate of CVE110.27:Euro1. The rediscount rate has remained unchanged since 1999, at 8.5 percent, while the level of international reserves increased in 2004.

Inflation in **The Gambia** accelerated to 16.7 percent in 2004, due to continued excess liquidity conditions, caused by excessive government borrowing, and the introduction of new taxes. The central bank kept its interest rates unchanged in 2004, with the 91-day treasury bill rate standing at 31 percent. Because of an improvement in the balance of payments, trading in the foreign exchange market increased significantly in 2004.

The Bank of **Ghana** missed its inflation target of 7 percent in 2004, with an observed inflation figure of 12.7 percent, albeit much lower than the 24.8 percent annual average inflation recorded during 2000–03. This was explained by the impact of a 2.5 percentage point increase in VAT, as introduced in August 2004, and increased government spending in the run-up to the elections. While monetary policy remained quite tight, the central bank also pursued its objective of lowering interest rates to encourage private sector borrowing and mirror interest rate developments on the international markets. The prime rate was reduced from 21.5 percent to 20 percent in February 2004, and further to 18.5 percent in May 2004. Despite inflationary pressures, the depreciation of the cedi against main traded currencies slowed down in 2004, indicating a healthy level of foreign exchange reserves and the weakness of the US dollar.

Inflation in **Guinea** rose from 5.3 percent during 2000–03 to 13.3 percent in 2004 due to weak fiscal position, currency depreciation and rising fuel oil prices. Guinea's central bank continued to accommodate the expansionary policies of the government in 2004, by providing finance for up to an equivalent 10 percent of the previous year's fiscal receipts. The bank has plans to eventually switch to T-bills, although their use has remained limited so far. The central bank has pegged the Guinean franc to the US dollar since late 2002. Foreign exchange rationing and rising inflation caused the gap between the official exchange rate and the parallel rate to increase to almost 40 percent in the first six months of 2004. As a result, the central bank announced new exchange rates, in

July 2004, of Gnf2,600:US$1 and Gnf3,200:US$1, to reduce the spread to 25 percent.

In **Liberia**, the slow normalization of the economy and the strengthening of the Liberian dollar resulted in a fall in inflation to 10 percent in 2004. The direction of monetary policy was unclear. The majority of transactions are conducted in US dollars.

Inflation in **Nigeria** declined slightly from to 12.7 percent during 2000–03 to 11.7 percent in 2004 in spite of increased domestic fuel prices, high level of government spending and rapid money supply growth. In January 2004, the Central Bank of Nigeria (CBN) reaffirmed its commitment to use open-market operations and rediscount rates as main policy instruments, while the Dutch auction system, introduced in 2002 would continue to determine the value of the naira. However, the government continued to exert pressure on the CBN to keep interest rates low. Growth in public sector credit slowed down by 38.8 percent (against a target of 23.3 percent) in the first nine months of 2004, while private sector credit growth accelerated to 22.9 percent. After depreciating by an average 7 percent in 2003, the naira remained roughly stable against the US dollar in 2004.

Inflation in **Sierra Leone** averaged 3.5 percent in 2004. Monetary policy in Sierra Leone tried to continue to focus on building foreign reserves and controlling inflation by rising interest rates in 2004. The leone, which strengthened towards the end of the year, depreciated by an average 13 percent against the US dollar in 2004.

Public Finance and Structural Reforms

Fiscal Developments

The fiscal position in West Africa improved in 2004 (see Table 2.15), despite the impact of Côte d'Ivoire's crisis on the CFA zone's fiscal position. By virtue of their membership of the West African Economic and Monetary Union (WAEMU/UEMOA), CFA zone countries aim to converge towards commonly agreed fiscal targets. These benchmarks, combined with the CFA zone rules on government borrowing, mean that fiscal performance has traditionally been better in CFA countries. At the same time, the fiscal situation in Ghana and Nigeria improved in 2004 despite some over-spending, as a result of higher export tax revenues. Nonetheless, West Africa's overall fiscal balance swung from a deficit of 2.0 percent of GDP during 2000–03 to a sizeable surplus of 3.7 percent of GDP in 2004.

Benin's fiscal performance worsened slightly in 2004, with the deficit rising to 2.2 percent of GDP. Spending in the 2004 budget reflected priorities under the PRSP, which was finalized in early 2003. As part of the decentralization process, the 2004 budget also increased spending allocations to local governments. Despite efforts to strengthen tax administration, fiscal revenues fell below target in the first quarter of the year, forcing the government to cut annual spending by a substantial CFA30 billion, as part of its economic recovery plan. Civil service pay reform to replace across-the-board pay rises with a system based on merit has remained stalled.

Table 2.15: West Africa: Macroeconomic Management Indicators

Country	Inflation (%)		Fiscal Balance as % of GDP		Gross Domestic Investment		Gross National Savings	
					as % of GDP			
	Average 2000–2003	2004[a]	Average 2000–2003	2004[a]	Average 2000–2003	2004[a]	Average 2000–2003	2004[a]
BENIN	3.0	0.4	−2.0	−2.2	19.3	18.2	10.5	9.2
BURKINA FASO	2.2	−0.7	−3.9	−3.5	19.6	20.6	8.8	11.8
CAPE VERDE	1.2	1.1	−7.5	−4.6	19.4	17.5	8.7	9.5
COTE D'IVOIRE	3.7	0.2	−1.2	−3.9	10.0	8.5	12.0	9.5
GAMBIA	7.4	16.7	−6.2	−3.6	19.8	24.6	16.3	16.1
GHANA	24.8	12.7	−6.0	−2.7	23.4	24.8	20.5	23.5
GUINEA	5.3	13.3	−4.2	−2.5	15.1	10.7	10.7	7.8
GUINEA–BISSAU	2.9	..	−12.1	−14.7	11.4	15.3	0.2	13.1
LIBERIA	10.1	10.0	..	..	..	..	..	..
MALI	0.9	−4.6	−2.7	−2.9	21.8	27.0	16.1	16.5
NIGER	2.0	−1.7	−3.3	−2.8	13.0	15.4	7.1	8.2
NIGERIA	12.7	11.7	−1.4	7.4	23.1	22.7	22.8	24.2
SENEGAL	1.5	1.7	−0.3	−2.4	18.8	20.2	13.5	14.8
SIERRA LEONE	1.4	3.5	−8.5	−5.9	9.6	19.6	0.2	5.9
TOGO	0.9	2.5	−1.0	0.0	14.4	13.3	2.8	5.0
WEST AFRICA	**5.1**	**4.3**	**−2.0**	**3.7**	**20.0**	**20.7**	**18.0**	**18.0**

Note: [a] Preliminary estimates
Source: ADB Statistics Division, 2004

Public finances in **Burkina Faso** are relatively healthy, allowing for a moderate expansion in the fiscal deficit in 2004. The overall fiscal deficit in Burkina Faso narrowed to 3.5 percent of GDP in 2004, from 3.9 percent of GDP in 2003. In December 2003, the authorities adopted an action plan to strengthen revenue collection and widen the tax base. This, coupled with strong donor commitments, supported a projected 8 percent increase in total revenue and grants in 2004. Meanwhile, total expenditures were projected to rise by 20 percent, largely reflecting increased capital spending (up by 30 percent) and recurrent expenditures in education and health. Concessional lending from donors and grants largely financed the bulk of the budget deficit.

Cape Verde's fiscal deficit declined from 7.5 percent of GDP in 2000–03 to 4.6 percent of GDP in 2004, slightly below the government's projection of 5.6 percent. This reflected improved tax arrears collection, higher dividends from public enterprises, and falling public transfers and subsidies. A 15 percent VAT and higher import tariffs for sensitive, import-substitution, manufacturing products were introduced in January 2004. Recurrent and capital expenditures have grown rapidly with social spending (notably in education). The government has been finalizing its PRSP.

The government in **Côte d'Ivoire** belatedly released its new budget in April 2004. A small budget surplus of 0.8 percent was projected, assuming resumed donor support and a growth recovery to 2.4 percent. This soon proved unrealistic. Government spending remained high, because of war-related expenditure, while revenue collection deteriorated rapidly, as a result of depressed economic activity and forfeited revenues from the rebel-held north. The budget deficit rose from 1.2 percent of GDP during 2000–03 to 3.9 percent of GDP in 2004.

A National Revenue Authority was installed in **The Gambia** in early 2004, while new taxes, custom duties, and licenses, were introduced in a bid to boost government revenues. The government also increased fuel prices. This helped to pay for the government's excessive spending, with the fiscal deficit falling to 3.6 percent of GDP in 2004. In the absence of budgetary support (the last IMF disbursement took place in July 2002), the bulk of the deficit was largely financed through domestic borrowing and an accumulation in external and domestic payment arrears.

The **Ghana** government reduced its fiscal deficit from 6.0 percent of GDP during 2000–03 to 2.7 percent of GDP in 2004, as a result of a freeze on public-sector salaries in real terms and rising tax revenues. Despite increased government spending in the run-up to the elections, improved tax administration and higher revenue from the gold and cocoa sectors resulted in a larger-than-expected fall in the fiscal deficit.

The authorities in **Guinea** took some measures in 2004 to strengthen fiscal management. Despite continued expenditure overruns related to security spending and poor expenditure management, and a freeze in external assistance since 2003, as a result of poor macroeconomic and policy performance, the budget deficit declined from an average 4.2 percent of GDP during 2000–03 to 2.5 percent of GDP in 2004.

The interim government in **Guinea-Bissau** made significant progress in restoring public finances. In December 2003, the government formulated with technical support from multilateral lenders, including the ADB, an emergency budget for 2004 and an Emergency Economic Management Plan, highlighting key commitments. A multi-donor fund was set up, with pledges totaling $18.3 million. Budgetary support helped to pay civil servants wages, and yet the fiscal deficit rose to 14.7 percent of GDP in 2004.

The budget deficit in **Mali** increased marginally from 2.7 percent of GDP during 2000–03 to a still manageable 2.9 percent of GDP in 2004, in large part reflecting the government's accommodating fiscal stance since the PRSP was finalised in 2003. Total revenues (excluding grants) were projected to rise to 17 percent of GDP, as a result of strengthened tax administration, specific tax measures (including an increase in petroleum products taxes), and reduced tax exemptions. Total expenditure was projected to rise to 24.5 percent of GDP, on the back of higher priority spending. Strong budgetary support and concessional lending, coupled with debt relief under the HIPC initiative, largely met the government's financing gap.

The authorities in **Niger** have remained committed to fiscal consolidation and prudent public spending management. The fiscal deficit declined to 2.8 percent of GDP in 2004 despite election-related expenditures, combined with increased spending in priority sectors since the country's PRSP was completed in 2002. The government also postponed a number of tax measures, notably the widening of the VAT base and new excise taxes, in the run-up to the December elections.

The government in **Nigeria** based its 2004 budget on the assumption that world crude oil prices would average $25 per barrel. With crude oil prices rising to an average $38.3 in 2004, public revenues surpassed all expectations, with the budget balance turning into a surplus of 7.4 percent of GDP in 2004. The government created a special holding account for excess oil revenue to keep government spending stable and to use the surplus fund for infrastructure development. Additional measures such as freezing of civil service hiring, tightening the budgets of parastatals and reducing non-essential recurrent expenditures were introduced in order to control government spending.

In **Senegal**, the government remained committed to increase spending allocation to priority sectors since its PRSP was finalized in January 2002, while also pursuing fiscal consolidation, by strengthening tax administration capacity. The fiscal deficit in 2004 increased slightly to 2.4 percent of GDP.

The fiscal deficit in **Sierra Leone** decreased from 8.5 percent of GDP during 2000–03 to 5.9 percent of GDP in 2004 following the government's attempts to strengthening tax administration and expenditure control in 2004. The National Revenue Authority maintained its efforts to reclaim tax arrears, while the government tightened its control over civil servants wages, by tightening its management of the public sector teachers' payroll. Donors continued heavily to support post-war reconstruction efforts and bankroll the government's budget deficit. Grants provided around half of total government revenues in 2004.

The fiscal situation in **Togo** was characterized by a continued freeze in foreign assistance. The budget was roughly in balance in 2004, indicating low spending in capital expenditures, contained recurrent expenditure, and a slight increase in revenue, in part as a result of continued efforts in collecting tax arrears.

Structural Reforms

The sub-region's commitment to structural reforms remained strong in 2004. New bids were launched for majority shares in export crop marketing boards and strategic utilities, although few sales were brought to completion. Other market-based reforms also made some progress, with the adoption of new regulatory frameworks and automatic price adjustment mechanisms.

Public policy in **Benin** has switched away from the stalled process of privatization and civil service reforms to focus on the Economic Recovery Program, which the government launched in May 2004 to tackle the country's structural weaknesses, notably its high dependence on trade with Nigeria. This included measures to strengthen the port's transit trade by revising tariffs and improving customs clearance procedures, remove road blocks on the main corridor to the north of the country, regulate second-hand car re-export trade, provide low cost supply of local raw materials for the domestic industry and reduce energy costs. The government has also showed its continued commitment to privatization, by calling for bids for the privatization of ginneries belonging to the state owned cotton company, Sonapra, in July 2004. Other companies mooted for sale include the electricity utility, the telecommunications company, the Continental Bank and the Autonomous Port of Cotonou.

Burkina Faso's privatization program made some progress in 2004. The sale of two cotton producing zones belonging to the cotton ginning parastatal, Sofitex, was finalized in September, more than a year after the bid was launched in May 2003. In the meantime, following the liberalization of the oil distribution sector, plans for the privatization of the national petroleum company, Sonabhy, have been revised, with the government now only selling a minority stake in the company, while the restructuring of the electricity utility, Sonabel, has also been subject to changes and delays. Another 34 percent stake of the telecommunications company, Sonatel, has meanwhile yet to be sold.

The pace of structural reforms in **Cape Verde** has been satisfactory. Substantial progress has been made in restructuring the state airline, TACV. Unprofitable routes have been dropped, high cost aircrafts replaced, and a redundancy package has been effected. The government has commissioned an external audit to draw up options for the privatization of the airline. Arca Verde (maritime transport services), Interbase (cold storage) and Emprofac (pharmaceutical distribution) have yet to be privatized. The government is also committed to improve the regulatory framework for strategic sectors.

Structural reforms in **Côte d'Ivoire** have been in disarray since the beginning of the civil war in September 2002. Allegations of irregularities in the management of the cocoa and coffee sector have continued. The new privately owned organizations and regulatory agencies that emerged from the liberalization of the cocoa sector in 1999–2000 have been accused of lacking transparency. Although first results have been released, the auditing of the companies' accounts which the government commissioned under international donor pressure in July 2003 has yet to be fully completed. In February 2004, the government cancelled a concession agreement, that the Abidjan Port Authority had awarded to the French group, Bolloré, to manage the Vridi container terminal, after allegations that the sale had not been based on a fair, transparent and open bidding process. Meanwhile, the government resumed plans to privatize the CAA (bank), although details of the sale were not released. Many agro-industrial plants (rubber, textiles, sugar, palm oil) and commercial banks, and some of the key utilities (electricity, telecommunications, water and port) had already been open to private participation before the war.

The Gambia's Privatization Act, adopted in June 2000, has remained stalled, although the government announced that the divestiture of the Gambia Groundnuts Corporation had become a priority. The sale of the Gambia Cotton Company was also back on the agenda, after the government failed to secure a deal with the French company, Dagris. A feasibility study into the privatization of the Social Security and Housing Finance Corporation was reported to be underway.

In February 2004, the **Ghana** government announced that a price adjustment mechanism in the petroleum, water and electricity sectors would be effected to help restore the financial viability of loss making utilities. This measure, together with other politically sensitive reforms, was subsequently postponed until after the elections. The privatization program made some progress — a 30 percent share of Ghana Airways was sold to a US consortium, Ghana International Airline, in the second half of the year, with the government retaining a 70 percent share in the company. An auditing into the cross-debts of the Volta River Authority, Electricity Company of Ghana, the Ghana Water Company Limited, and Tema Oil

Refinery (TOR) was completed in April 2004, in preparations for their divestiture. Long mooted for sale, the Ghana Commercial Bank has yet to be sold, pending the restructuring of TOR debt. Meanwhile, options are being explored with technical assistance from the IMF for the sale of the Volta Aluminium Company.

Guinea's difficult political situation and uncertain business environment have long hindered the government's privatization program, outside the mining sector.

In **Guinea-Bissau**, the new administration has shown renewed commitment to civil service reforms and privatization. In August 2004, a new public-sector salary scale that trims off salaries for top ranking civil servants and military officers, was adopted, freeing up resources for the settlement of months of salary arrears. The government awarded a new ten-year concession to Portugal Telecom Internacional and Guiné Telecom to help develop the telecommunications sector. About 60 state-owned enterprises in the tourism, fisheries, transport and energy sectors could be opened to private participation.

The government in **Liberia** intends to privatize major public utility companies, including telecommunications, water and electricity, although attention has remained focused on post-war reconstruction and macroeconomic stabilization.

Mali's privatization program entails preparation for the sale of the cotton parastatal, CMDT, its cottonseed oil company, Huicoma (a 2002 bid was declared unsuccessful in early 2004) and the telecommunications utility, Sotelma, and Aéroport du Mali. The government agreed to a new restructuring plan for the cotton sector in November 2003. CMDT is now to be split into three or four privately-owned regional companies, with each company enjoying exclusive rights to purchase cotton in its region, while also providing support to producers in the form of supply of seeds, fertilizers, pesticides and technical support. The reform process, which was due for completion in 2006, has been extended to 2008. In July 2004, the government issued a new call for bids, restricted to a few pre-selected enterprises, for a majority stake in Huicoma.

Structural reforms in **Niger** continued to focus on the privatization of the electricity company (Nigelec) and the petroleum distribution company (Sonidep); the strengthening of the financial sector with the restructuring of the National Postal and Savings Office (ONPE) and the privatization of the commercial bank (CDN). No progress was made in 2004, with much of the government's attention focusing on the preparation of the elections. Although the privatization of Nigelec was delayed, discussions between Nigerien and French companies to form a consortium that would take a 51 percent stake in the company were reported to be ongoing.

Nigeria's privatization program has remained slow. Although the second phase of the program has yet to be completed — much of the delay being explained by strong opposition in parliament, red tape and lack of political will — the Bureau of Public Enterprises released in March 2004 details of the country's revised third phase of privatization, involving short-, medium-

and long- term projects. The sale of the National Electric Power Authority (NEPA), which stalled as a result of delays in enacting the power sector reform bill in parliament, was listed in the long-term category, with another 12 companies. The medium-term category relates to the divestiture of 36 enterprises. One of the short-term projects, involving the sale of the Aluminium Smelter Company subsequently failed in July 2004, after the selected buyer, the US-based BFI Group, missed the deadline to pay the required deposit. The government nonetheless managed to sell stakes in six companies in 2004, including Delta Steel and Peugeot Automobile of Nigeria, in 2004.

In **Senegal**, the privatization of the groundnut parastatal, Sonacos, suffered delays in 2003, but was back on track in 2004, after the government finally awarded a 66.9 percent stake of the company to the consortium led by Senegalese firm, Advens, in December 2004. Meanwhile, the IMF has pressed for an improvement in the performance and further private sector participation in the state electricity company, Senelec, but the poor quality of infrastructure and the cost of rehabilitation have kept potential buyers away.

In **Sierra Leone**, the National Commission for Privatization prepared in 2004 a plan for the sale or concessioning of public enterprises, with 24 enterprises selected for privatization.

Togo's privatization program made little progress in 2004. No major sales took place, as the privatization process for the state cotton company, Socoto, Togo Telecoms and UTB (bank) remained

Table 2.16: West Africa: The External Sector

Country	Trade Balance as % of GDP		Current Account as % of GDP		Terms of Trade (%)		Total External Debt as % of GDP		Debt Service as % of Exports	
	Average 2000–2003	2004[a]	Average 2000–2003	2004[a]	Average 2000–2003	2004[a]	Average 2000–2003	2004[a]	Average 2000–2003	2004[a]
BENIN	−11.2	−10.4	−8.0	−8.4	2.3	12.6	68.8	50.7	14.8	13.1
BURKINA FASO	−9.9	−8.5	−9.6	−8.4	−2.3	−0.4	51.4	36.6	24.1	21.9
CAPE VERDE	−35.9	−35.6	−10.7	−8.9	−0.6	−0.4	81.1	72.6	21.5	15.8
COTE D'IVOIRE	18.2	17.7	1.5	−0.2	4.6	−6.1	89.4	74.0	10.9	16.8
GAMBIA	−15.3	−17.0	−3.6	−6.1	3.0	−19.9	141.0	143.6	30.8	34.9
GHANA	−13.9	−10.9	−2.9	0.3	1.0	−7.0	112.7	71.1	15.3	11.1
GUINEA	3.9	4.6	−4.4	−2.9	−0.2	−3.3	99.5	91.4	13.4	13.0
GUINEA-BISSAU	−7.5	−5.5	−12.4	−2.2	−1.9	−3.9	387.4	341.4	6.1	8.3
LIBERIA	...	...	...	...	...	...	...	...	...	...
MALI	1.5	2.4	−6.9	−5.0	−2.1	7.1	63.6	30.2	7.7	6.1
NIGER	−3.6	−5.9	−5.9	−7.9	−0.6	0.3	81.0	51.2	12.8	9.9
NIGERIA	18.4	22.6	−0.3	2.9	11.2	19.7	63.2	46.2	7.2	4.9
SENEGAL	−9.4	−11.3	−5.8	−7.3	0.1	−1.9	65.1	56.9	13.2	17.6
SIERRA LEONE	−12.8	−17.6	−10.9	−12.1	−4.8	−2.0	37.5	52.6	33.7	11.0
TOGO	−15.3	−11.4	−15.1	−8.6	0.9	13.9	112.4	103.6	5.5	15.0
WEST AFRICA	**9.8**	**12.0**	**−5.6**	**−5.2**	**6.8**	**12.0**	**73.1**	**54.4**	**9.2**	**8.0**

Note: [a] Preliminary estimates
Source: ADB Statistics Division, 2004

stalled. The IMF has called for a 'diagnostic study' in the cotton sector as a condition for a new staff monitored program. The Franco-Spanish consortium, SE2M, which has a stake in the Port Autonome de Lomé since 2002, has continued to invest in the development of the container terminal.

Recent Trends in the External Sector

Current Account Developments

West Africa's external position improved in 2004, with the current account deficit slightly declining to 5.2 percent of GDP, against a yearly average 5.6 percent in 2000–2003 (see Table 2.16). This compared unfavorably with the continental average surplus of 0.7 percent of GDP in 2004. The region's export base is poorly diversified.

Nigeria relies exclusively on oil and gas. Other countries rely on agricultural and/or non-oil mineral exports. Côte d'Ivoire is the only country that exports manufactured goods (including petroleum products), mostly to the sub-region.

The sub-region's terms of trade improved in dollar terms in 2004. The main gainers in that year were the oil and gold exporting countries, as prices of those commodities rose strongly. World cocoa prices declined from 175.1 cents/kg in 2003 to a still high 155 cents/kg in 2004. International cotton prices fell moderately by 2.4 percent to 136.6 cents/kg. For CFA countries, the continued strengthening of the CFA franc against the US dollar deflated export earnings in local currency terms, but also reduced the oil import bill.

All 15 West African countries belong to ECOWAS, which is in principle committed to the suppression of customs duties and equivalent taxes within the region and the establishment of a common external tariff. In 2001, all non-CFA ECOWAS countries agreed to adopt WAEMU's common external tariff, but progress under the trade liberalization program has been slow. Of all ECOWAS countries, Nigeria has one of the most complex external tariff structures, with over 15 tariff bands, and custom duties varying from 0 percent to 150 percent.

Comprising all eight West African CFA countries, WAEMU is one of the most integrated economic groupings in Africa. Besides having a common currency, WAEMU has been a customs union since 2000, when all intra-regional tariffs were lifted and a common external tariff structure was adopted. There has also been considerable progress in harmonizing fiscal policies, banking regulations, and business and law procedures.

Benin's current account deficit remained broadly stable at 8.4 percent of GDP in 2004, against 8.0 percent of GDP during 2000–03. High cotton prices helped to compensate for falling cotton export volume, but import growth continued to outpace export growth, with the trade deficit widening in nominal terms as a result. Net service and income outflows as well as private and official transfers remained roughly unchanged.

The current-account deficit in **Burkina Faso** declined to 8.4 percent of GDP in 2004. This largely reflected rising cotton output following the bumper harvest in 2004, still high cotton prices on the international market. Import growth remained strong, driven by a robust domestic demand in fuel, consumer and capital goods. The services deficit rose while the income deficit benefited from lower debt payment outflows, as a result of debt relief under the HIPC initiative. The surplus in transfers indicated lower worker remittances from Côte d'Ivoire, but strong inflows of donor support in the form of official transfers.

The current account deficit in **Cape Verde** fell to 8.9 percent of GDP in 2004. The country's export base is slowly shifting away from traditional products (coffee and fish) as a result of tourism expansion, improved access to US and EU markets, and the development of export-oriented industrial parks. These are early stages, however. The country's trade deficit remains largely structural, with import growth slightly outpacing that of exports in

2004. Increasing tourism receipts, private remittances and rising official transfers, coupled with reasonably low debt service payments, have kept the invisible balance in surplus.

Côte d'Ivoire's external sector has continued to suffer from the political and economic crisis. The current-account balance switched from an average annual surplus of 1.5 percent of GDP during 2000–03 to a deficit of 0.2 percent of GDP in 2004. The trade balance turned to a surplus equivalent to 17.7 percent of GDP, as a result of sturdy cocoa earnings and a rise in oil export revenue, stemming from higher volume and value. The service, income and transfers balance remained firmly in deficit, at 17.8 percent of GDP, on account of private transfer outflows, and the government's efforts to honor some of its external debt obligations, notably with the IMF.

The Gambia's current-account deficit increased to 6.1 percent of GDP in 2004. Export earnings and imports increased in the same proportion (although higher food crops reduced the need for food imports), thus maintaining the trade deficit stable at 17 percent of GDP. A slight increase in tourism receipts, coupled with rising official and private transfers meanwhile helped to compensate for rising debt service.

Ghana's current account balance switched from an annual average deficit of 2.9 percent of GDP during 2000–03 to a surplus of 0.3 percent of GDP in 2004. A rise in gold production, coupled with rising gold prices on the world market, and higher cocoa output boosted export

receipts in 2004. The higher oil import bill pushed up imports significantly, resulting in a trade deficit of 10.9 percent of GDP in 2004. The services and income accounts also remained in deficit, but workers remittances and donor support ensured a healthy surplus on the current transfers account.

Guinea enjoys a robust trade surplus as a consequence of its exports of bauxite, alumina, gold and diamonds. The country's current account balance nonetheless remained in deficit in 2004, at 2.9 percent of GDP. There was moderate export growth but the services account remained in deficit and net current transfers failed to pick up, owing to the continued suspension of budgetary assistance.

Guinea-Bissau's current account deficit improved slightly in 2004 to 2.2 percent of GDP, as a result of higher cashew nut exports.

Mali's current-account deficit decreased to 5 percent of GDP in 2004. Cotton export earnings increased significantly, following the bumper harvest in 2003, while gold export earnings declined, despite rising prices on the international market. Mali is set to see its exports of clothing and textiles increase in the next few years, as new clothing factories open to take advantage of preferential access to the US market AGOA, since December 2003. Despite rising oil import costs, there was a slight rise in the trade surplus to 2.4 percent of GDP in 2004 (from 2.3 percent of GDP in 2003). Meanwhile, the services account remained in deficit, reflecting high transport costs, and workers' remittances remained depressed owing to the crisis in

Côte d'Ivoire, where an estimated 2 million Malians live.

Niger's current account deficit widened to 7.9 percent of GDP in 2004. Lower food imports and the strengthening of the CFA franc against the US dollar failed to compensate for rising world oil prices — the oil import bill accounted for 11.5 percent of the country's imports in 2003. There was a large increase in the imports of capital and intermediate goods resulting from public investment program. Export growth remained sluggish. Increased freight costs pushed up the deficit in the invisibles account, for which debt relief under the HIPC initiative and sustained external assistance failed to compensate.

Nigeria's oil receipts increased with international petroleum product prices in 2004, resulting in a trade surplus equivalent to 22.6 percent of GDP. This, combined with a high level of workers' remittances, helped to compensate for rising services and income outflows, resulting from external debt payments and profit remittances by multinational oil companies. As a result, the current account recorded a surplus of 2.9 percent of GDP in 2004.

The current account deficit in **Senegal** narrowed in 2004 to 7.3 percent of GDP, in large part reflecting movements in the trade deficit. There were increased export earnings from phosphates and phosphate derivative products, but import growth slightly outpaced that of exports in 2004, with the trade deficit rising to 11.3 percent of GDP in 2004. Grant inflows remained strong, which combined with interim debt relief under the HIPC initiative — helped to

keep the invisible balance in small surplus of 4 percent of GDP in 2004.

The current account deficit in **Sierra Leone** rose to 12.1 percent of GDP in 2004. Although increased diamond exports boosted export growth, high imports resulting from continued post-war reconstruction efforts produced a rise in the trade deficit to 17.6 percent of GDP in 2004. Rising official transfers continued to finance a significant part of the current account deficit significantly, the rest being paid by long-term concessional lending.

The current account deficit in **Togo** declined from 11.4 percent during 2000–03 to 8.6 percent in 2004. Cotton and phosphate exports rose while imports growth remained depressed.

External Debt and other capital flows

West Africa's total debt stock is mostly made of concessional, long-term official loans. All countries except Cape Verde, Liberia, Nigeria, and Togo, qualify for debt relief under the enhanced HIPC initiative. Burkina Faso, Benin and Mali had reached completion point in by 2003, followed by Ghana, Niger, Senegal in 2004. West Africa's debt burden eased in 2004, with the debt-GDP ratio declining to 54.4 percent.

West Africa has limited access to international capital markets, although Ghana, Benin, Senegal, and Mali have recently received their first sovereign credit rating. FDI in West Africa is driven by oil developments in Nigeria, and has proved to be erratic elsewhere. According to UNCTAD *World Investment Report 2004*, West Africa received $2.1 billion in FDI inflows in 2003, bringing the total inward stock to $34.1 billion.

Benin reached completion point under the enhanced HIPC initiative in March 2003, paving the way for total relief of $460 million. A debt sustainability update, released in 2004, confirms that Benin's debt as well as the debt service will remain sustainable in the medium to long term. In 2004, the debt-to-GDP ratio fell to 50.7 percent, reflecting both debt relief and prudent borrowing policy.

Burkina Faso has benefited from generous debt reduction deals since reaching completion point under HIPC in 2000 and under the enhanced HIPC initiative in 2002. As a result of unsustainable levels of debt and the vulnerability of the country to external shocks, the IMF and the World Bank agreed, in 2002, to top-up the HIPC initiative, bringing total nominal debt relief to $930 million. In 2004, the debt-to-GDP ratio declined to 36.3 percent of GDP, while the debt service ratio amounted to 21.9 percent.

The government in **Cape Verde** has pursued a prudent borrowing policy since taking office in 2001. Debt payment arrears were cleared with all but two external creditors by mid-2003, while the government remained current on all its external obligations throughout 2004. Most of the country's external debt is owed to multilateral institutions (notably the World Bank and the ADB), and official bilateral creditors (the most important being Portugal). External debt declined to 72.6 percent of GDP in 2004, which remains high by regional standards. Cape Verde is not eligible for debt relief under the enhanced

HIPC initiative, however. The debt service ratio declined to 15.8 percent in 2004.

Côte d'Ivoire's external debt decreased slightly in 2004 to 74 percent of GDP, while the debt service ratio increased to 16.8 percent (against 4.2 percent in 2003). The government has fallen behind its external payment obligations with most bilateral creditors and some multilateral lenders (including the ADB and, since June 2004, the World Bank), as of end-2004, and was honoring only payments owed to the IMF. Financial assistance has remained frozen as a result. Talks with the Fund have not resumed since it last paid a mission to the country in late 2003.

The government in **Ghana** reached completion point under the enhanced HICP initiative in June 2004, paving the way for a debt relief package totaling $3.5 billion ($2.2 billion in net present value terms) over 20 years. As part of the initiative, the Paris Club of bilateral external creditors has agreed to cancel $823 million and reschedule another $737 million. The country's total external debt declined to an equivalent of 71.1 percent of GDP in 2004, while the debt service ratio also fell to 11.1 percent, as a result of rising exports and interim debt relief.

The Gambia, which reached decision point under HIPC initiative in December 2000, has failed to reach completion point. The external debt burden has remained high, as a result, with the external debt stock falling slightly to 143.6 percent of GDP in 2004, while the debt service ratio increased to 34.9 percent.

Guinea's external debt-GDP ratio slightly declined to 91.4 percent in 2004.

The IMF has suspended its disbursement (including HIPC debt relief assistance) to the country since December 2002 following policy slippages, while the deal signed with the Paris Club in May 2001 expired in April 2003. The government has continued to default on its external debt payment obligations as a result. The debt service ratio in 2004 remained broadly stable at 13.0 percent.

Guinea-Bissau is the second most heavily indebted country in Africa, after Sao Tomé & Principe, with the external debt-to-GDP ratio reaching 341.4 percent in 2004. The former government had won approval of a new PRGF with the IMF and reached decision point under the HIPC initiative in December 2000. The government soon fell behind its obligations, however, and the PRGF went off-track in 2001 and expired at end-2003 with no interim debt relief concluded.

Mali reached completion point under the enhanced HIPC initiative in March 2003, paving the way for a debt relief package totaling $675 million. Prudent borrowing policy and implementation of previous debt relief deals with the Paris Club allowed the debt-to-GDP ratio to fall to a low 30.2 percent in 2004, while the debt-service ratio was estimated at 6.1 percent. Bilateral negotiations with the Paris Club over a new Cologne terms agreement in March 2003 have now begun, and full debt relief from multilateral lenders has started.

Niger reached completion point under HIPC in April 2004, making the country eligible for debt relief from all main creditors. As a result, the Paris Club creditors agreed to cancel $250 million of the country's total external debt in May. In 2004, the debt-to-GDP ratio fell to 51.2 percent in 2004, while the debt service ratio stood at 9.9 percent.

The external debt stock of **Nigeria** stood at 46.2 percent of GDP in 2004. The government continued to pursue a debt conversion program as part of its debt management strategy and redeemed part of its external debt under the auction system. A number of bilateral agreements were also signed as a follow-up to the debt rescheduling deal signed with the Paris Club of official bilateral creditors in December 2000. Although debt servicing resumed in 2003 after a short period of moratorium, the government continued to build up arrears.

Senegal is moderately indebted by regional standards. It reached completion point under the HIPC initiative in April 2004, paving the way for debt relief totaling $850 million ($488 million in net present value terms). In June, the Paris Club accordingly announced that a debt cancellation of $463 million (including $127 million being cancelled). In November, the French government agreed to a 100 percent cancellation of Senegal's sovereign debt, totaling $287.9 million. Its debt-to-GDP ratio declined from 65.1 percent during 2000–03 to 56.9 percent in 2004.

Sierra Leone reached decision point under the HIPC initiative six months after the signing of a PRGF with the IMF in September 2001. A deal with the Paris Club was subsequently signed as part of the initiative. Prudent borrowing policy, coupled with a strong grant element in donor financing, have also helped to keep the lid on the country's external debt burden, since post-war reconstruction started. Accordingly, the country's external debt continued to decline to 52.6 percent as a ratio to GDP in 2004. Foreign investment improved in 2003 is expected to increase in the coming years.

The government of **Togo** in 2004 continued to face limited access to lending, because of international sanctions over human rights and elections issues. Significant progress in dealing with these issues is needed for normalising relationship with the EU. Talks with the IMF over a staff monitored program have yet to resume. In 2004, the debt-to-GDP ratio stood at 103.6 percent, while the debt service ratio increased sharply to 15 percent.

Outlook

Growth in West Africa is forecast at 4.9 percent in 2005, compared with the 3.4 percent recorded in 2004, based on better prospects for Nigeria, the biggest economic player in the region. Growth in Nigeria is projected to accelerate to 6.2 percent in 2005 following good progress towards economic reforms. Growth in Benin will remain strong in 2005, assuming continued progress in the cotton-sector reforms and increased public spending in social sectors. Agriculture, livestock, and cotton processing (following good cotton harvests in 2004) will remain the main sources of growth in Burkina Faso. Growth in Cape Verde would increase to around 6.0 percent in 2005, assuming improved export performance and high in private transfers.

Côte d'Ivoire's economic prospects remain uncertain. Continuous instability and delays in the national reconciliation process will further undermine business confidence. A regularization of relations with bilateral creditors is unlikely to make much progress unless the next presidential elections, scheduled in October 2005, are deemed fair and transparent. Talks with the IMF have yet to resume.

The Gambia's growth prospects for 2005 will largely hinge on getting the IMF program back on track. With no progress in structural reforms, the level of activity in agriculture and tourism might not be enough to keep per capita GDP growth positive in 2005. Further developments in Ghana's gold mining sector and good relations with donors following completion point under the enhance HIPC initiative in 2004 will continue to support the country's strong growth performance in the next few years. Guinea's economic prospects will improve; assuming the government successfully negotiates a staff monitored program with the IMF and security conditions ameliorate. The full deployment of the UN Mission in Liberia and the completion of the disarmament process should help boost the economy in 2005. Economic growth will continue in Mali in 2005, reflecting favorable growing conditions for cotton and food crops, rising mining production, and a dynamic manufacturing sector. Increased public investment and rising external support will help support growth in Niger in 2005. Much will depend, however, on agricultural performance in 2005. Growth would remain above 5 percent in Senegal, thanks to a dynamic export sector. Assuming stable security conditions, growth prospects in Sierra Leone will hinge on continued momentum for donor-supported post-war reconstruction. Progress towards democratization and human rights will be needed in Togo to normalize relations with donors and boost economic growth. On the political front, the West African sub-region will remain focused on efforts initiated by the AU to resolve the crisis in Côte d'Ivoire.

PART TWO

PUBLIC SECTOR MANAGEMENT IN AFRICA

CHAPTER 3
The State and Economic Development in Africa: Theory, Policy and Practice

Introduction

The terms 'public sector' and 'the state' are often used synonymously for the reason that there can be no strong state without an efficient public sector. In the past, in many African countries, the clearest evidence of the weakness of states is provided by the poor performance of the public sector. In a previous study (ADR, 2001) and in the context of investigating the issue of Governance in Africa, it was concluded that the public sector in Africa was in large part characterized by poor service, corruption and inefficiency. The legitimacy of governments was seen to be undermined by a lack of openness, transparency and accountability, resulting in public dissatisfaction and lack of confidence in public institutions. At the roots of the malaise affecting the public services in Africa was, at first, the failure to adapt the inherited colonial public administration to African culture and society and, subsequently, the changing perception of what constituted the most appropriate route to development.

In several countries, the military's foray into governance and politics caused public sector management and administration to be further centralized, while local and provincial systems were impoverished. In many of these countries, under a variety of political situations, local governance has remained too weak to make a meaningful impact in the provision of social services.

The ADR 2005 here revisits the issue of public sector and its reform. In this chapter it reviews theoretical issues relating to the role of the state in guiding Africa's development, before discussing the stages, dimensions and difficulties of public sector reforms in Africa (Chapter 4), issues related to public accountability (Chapter 5), and the multilateral development banks' support to public sector reform (Chapter 6).

This chapter begins with a short review of the changing development practice as it relates to the public sector. It then looks at the implications of the emergence of theoretical underpinnings, specifically of New Institutional Economics, Public Choice Theory, New Public Management, and Governance. It also provides a comparison of the African state with the 'developmental state' of some Asian countries.

Changing Development Policy and Practice

Much water has flowed under the bridge since the concept of development was first adapted for use at the international level by development practitioners in the late 1940s and early 1950s. The history of development theory and policy is long and has many twists. What is often overlooked, however, is that the shifts that have taken place are the results of an often unsatisfactory, if not negative, experience with the way the development concept has been operationalized. Development itself, in other words, has always been a moving target, thus constantly generating demands for new approaches. It is possible to identify at least four distinct ways by which the international community has tried to make operational sense of development.

The First Phase: concentration on projects

The initial approach goes back to the days of the Marshall Plan for Western Europe after the Second World War. This was the first major transfer of public capital to enhance the pace of international development. Influenced by the success that this Plan had in generating reconstruction of Western Europe, economic analysts began to turn the same ideas into universal recipes. With these efforts, a new field — development economics — was born. In the perspective of these economists, development in the emerging states of what has since become the Third World or the South would be best achieved through transfers of capital and technical expertise (Rapley, 1996). This philosophy prevailed in the last days of colonial rule and the early years of independence in Africa. It was also applied to Asia and Latin America with few modifications. Being lodged in a modernization paradigm — implying that development is a move from traditional to modern society — this approach was characterized by great confidence and optimism. Although it was not reconstruction but development that was attempted in these instances, the challenge looked easy. Defined largely in techno-cratic terms, development was operational-

ized with little or no attention to context. The principal task was to ensure that institutions and techniques that had proved successful in modernizing the Western world could be replicated.

The intellectual efforts were concentrated on plans and projects. Comprehensive national development plans were produced as guides for what policies should be prioritized. These plans stated the anticipated macroeconomic conditions under which specific program and project activities should and could be developed. Projects also took on a special significance. They constituted the means by which macroeconomic goals could be realized. Good project design was the key to success. It is no exaggeration to suggest that in this first phase of development thinking, which lasted into the latter part of the 1960s, the *project* level was regarded as most important. Project design, however, was the prerogative of technical experts. It was done on behalf of potential bene-ficiaries without their input. Government and other public institutions were identified as responsible for ensuring effective implementation. Private and voluntary sector organizations were ignored. The implication of this development orthodoxy for Africa was that many countries began to lay the foundations for increased state control and centralization of resource allocation in a broad range of economic activities. As a result, national planning became the order of the day, with public enterprises and government parastatals playing a crucial role in plan implementation.

The Second Phase: towards integrated programs

In the latter part of the 1960s, analysts and practitioners had begun to recognize that a singular focus on projects in the context of national plans was inadequate. The critique followed at least two lines. First of all, projects designed with little attention to context typically had more unanticipated than anticipated outcomes. For instance, the assumption that development would 'trickle down' from the well endowed to the poor, thus generating ripple effects, proved to be mistaken. Secondly, projects were inevitably 'enclave' types of inter-vention with little or no positive externalities. For example, evaluations confirmed the absence of meaningful backward or forward linkages in this type of interventions. Analysts concluded that the project approach failed to realize improvements, especially in the conditions of the poorer segments of the population. Convinced that something else had to be done to reduce global poverty the international community decided that a sector-wide approach would be more effective. In operational terms, this meant substituting *programs* for *projects*.

In this second phase of development practice, the important issue was how to design integrated programs that addressed not a single dimension of human needs but a wide range of them. For example, integrated rural development programs became very fashionable instruments of action. As a consequence, governments also engaged in administrative reforms that stressed the value of decentralizing authority to lower levels of government organization in order to enhance co-ordination and management of these new sector-wide programs (Caiden, 1991). Also, there emerged a growing emphasis on education and training of the masses. Human capital mattered. While capacity building in the first phase had been concentrated on the elite, the second focused on such areas as adult education and universal primary education, the assumption being that these measures were integral parts of a poverty-oriented ap-proach to development. The implication of this for Africa was the dominance of large-scale production by public enterprises (mainly import-substitution industries), specific social sector programs, such as health and education, and attempts for a continental wide action plan for economic development of Africa.

The Third Phase: focus on Government

At the end of the 1970s there was another shift, this time of even greater consequence than the first. It was becoming increasingly clear that governments typically could not administer the heavy development burden that had been placed on their shoulders. This was most apparent in Sub-Saharan Africa, where the state lacked the technical capacity, but it was acknowledged also elsewhere because of bureaucratic short-comings. Government agencies simply did not work very efficiently in the develop-ment field. Placing all 'development' eggs in one basket, therefore, was being increasingly questioned as the most useful strategy, as was the role of the state, by comparison with the market, as an allocating mechanism of public resources. As analysts went back to the drawing board, the challenge was no longer how to manage or administer development as much as it was to identify the incentives that may facilitate it. The strategic focus was shifted to the level of *policy*.

The World Bank took the lead on this issue and, with reference to Sub-Saharan Africa, the most critical region, it produced the so-called 'Berg Report' (*Accelerating Development in Sub-Saharan Africa: An Agenda for Action*, World Bank, 1981), which came to serve as the principal guide for structural adjustment in Africa in the 1980s, although the strategy was also applied in other regions of the world. These reforms, in combination with parallel financial stabilization measures imposed by the IMF, were deemed necessary to 'get the prices right' and to free up resources controlled by the state that could potentially be better used and managed by other institutions in society — particularly the private sector. However, this period also witnessed an increase in voluntary organizations around the world and preliminary efforts to bring such organizations into the development process. With more responsibilities delegated to the market, private and voluntary organizations could play a more significant role in working with people to realize their aspirations, whether individual or communal (Korten and Klauss, 1985).

The Fourth Phase: focus on politics

By the 1990s there was a growing recognition that development is not only about projects, programs and policies, but also about *politics*. For a long time, politics and development were seen as two entirely separate and distinct areas of human activity. Development analysts, and especially economists, preferred to treat 'development' as apolitical. Out of respect for national sovereignty, donors and governments upheld this notion, despite its inherent weakness, for a long time. It is only in the last ten years that it has been challenged. Although it can be controversial in government circles in the Third World, there is a growing recognition that 'getting politics right' is, if not a *precondition*, at least a *requisite* of development. The implication is that conventional notions of state sovereignty are being challenged by the actions taken by the international community, notably the international finance institutions and the bilateral donors.

UN agencies also find themselves caught up in this process. For example, human rights violations, including those that limit freedom of expression and association, are being invoked as reasons for not only criticizing governments of other countries but also withholding aid if no commitment to cease such violations and improvement is made. Underlying this shift towards creating a politically-enabling environment is the assumption that development, after all, is the product of what people decide to do to improve their livelihoods. People, not governments, constitute the principal force of development. They must be given the right incentives and opportunities not only in the economic but also the political arena. They must have a chance to create institutions that respond to their needs and priorities.

Development, therefore, is no longer a benevolent top-down exercise, not even a charitable act by non-governmental organizations, but a bottom-up process. The role of the state is seen as being an effective regulator and facilitator.

Recent experiences in parts of Africa, and in other countries in transition, have shown that weak states cannot support sophisticated market economies and that the failure of the government to play its essential role could result in political and economic failure. This is recognized by NEPAD, which accepts that the state has a major role to play in promoting economic growth and development, and in implementing poverty reduction programs. However, many countries lack the capacity to do this, and they also lack the necessary policy and regulatory frameworks for private sector-led growth. They have difficulty implementing programs, even when funding is available. They recognize increasingly that targeted 'capacity building' should be given priority. The government thus needs to establish the regulatory institutions which set the platform for private competition, and the rules protecting consumers. It is the government that should also design plans and programs to solicit concessional assistance for infrastructure development and for the social sector, especially in low-income and war-affected countries.

The discussion above highlights the shifting nature of public sector reforms in Africa. In the 1960s, the strategic focus was on the role of the state and projects in the development process. In the 1970s and 1980s, however, more emphasis was laid on policy, with the primary objective of 'getting the prices right'. In other words, the key issue, particularly in the 1980s, was 'fixing the system' by policies and governance measures. A further shift in focus was introduced in the 1990s, with additional emphasis on politics. Thus 'getting the politics right' became a precondition for development agenda. As a result, there was a growing recognition that the underlying basis for sustainable growth and development lies in markets and good governance.

Theoretical Approaches and their Relevance for Africa

The changing pattern of public sector reforms in Africa was largely a reflection of new thinking, grounded in a number of theories that have emerged over the years. These theories include the New Institutional Economics (NIE), Public Choice Theory (PCT), New Public Management (NPM) and Governance issues. These theories, and their relevance to public sector management in Africa, are discussed below.

New Institutional Economics

New Institutional Economics (NIE) has been an important mode of thought within the discipline of economics and among economic policy advisors for the past two decades. Its significance has been recognized internationally in the form of at least two Nobel Prizes[1]. Its message is

---

[1] Both Ronald H. Coase and Douglas North received the Nobel Prize in Economics in 1991 and 1993, respectively, for their work on New Institutional Economics and related fields.

[handwritten annotations at top of page: "Public Finances Know preferences", "Property Rights contracts rules"]

rather simple, but one that was initially overlooked as the neo-classical approach to economics was rehabilitated in the 1980s. Thus, the initial policy prescriptions issued by the international finance institutions under the 'structural adjustment' label ignored institutions and preached the message of perfect market rationality. This more radical edict may be understood as a way of pinpointing as explicitly as possible how dramatic a change was required in countries where the economy had been extensively regulated and managed by the state, as the case was in Africa in the 1960s and 1970s. The problem with the initial phase of structural adjustment — largely through the 1980s — was twofold. By virtue of its strong words in support of market liberalization, it generated a lot of political opposition. The second part of the problem was that structural adjustment made simplistic operational assumptions. Especially in Africa where markets were little developed and the prospects for market perfection were dim, the neglect of institutions led to important critiques of the advocates of structural adjustment.

From a purely operational point of view, therefore, the NIE must be viewed as a step forward because it begins from the assumption that institutional structure exerts an important influence on human behavior and choice. It transcends the microeconomics of the more orthodox model, which assumes economic efficiency under ideal-type conditions of perfect information and foresight. As such, NIE helped extend the range of applicability of neo-classical theory.

The basic assumptions of the NIE are as follows:

- People have different tastes and preferences; hence, the state, firm, or political party cannot be treated as if they are all alike.
- Individuals are assumed to seek their own interests as they perceive them and maximize utility, subject to the constraints established by the existing institutional structure.
- Preferences of decision-makers are recognized as incomplete and subject to change over time; hence the notion of '"bounded rationality"', originally attributed to Herbert Simon (whose Nobel Prize award may also qualify as recognition of NIE).
- In addition to rationality being bounded, human behavior may be dishonest in the sense that people may disguise their preferences, distort data, or deliberately confuse issues; hence, what Williamson (1975) calls '"self-seeking with guile"' and the need for contracts to be regarded as incomplete.
- A country is able to develop economically only if property rights exist and contracts are being respected; society, therefore, must be concerned with the social arrangements that regulate the transfer of property rights in a reliable manner.
- The property -rights configuration existing in an economy is determined and guaranteed by a system of rules and the instruments that serve to enforce these rules; hence, the

transactions

concern with governance structures that secure such rights.

- The NIE concept refers to a set of working rules that are actually used, monitored, and enforced when individuals make choices about the actions they will take; these rules may arise spontaneously on the basis of the self-interest of individuals or come about as when a public authority, e.g. parliament, tries to introduce an institutional structure it deems appropriate.
- Institutions, together with people taking advantage of them, are called organizations and they require real resources to operate; hence, the notion of transaction costs associated with using the market and securing adequate coordination within an organization, as well as between organizations.

The NIE approach, as it has evolved in the practice of international finance institutions in recent years, also has a number of problems. First, NIE is good at offering diagnostic steps, but is much less effective when it comes to providing solutions. Thus, it helps to recognize market failures in new ways, but, as Bates (1995) suggests, when it comes to solutions, the recipe is much less clear. Second, NIE is too functionalist — making the assumption that institutional solutions arise in response to failures occurring in the way the '"perfect"' market operates. It assumes that institutions, like the World Bank, with more comprehensive knowledge than individual actors in the market place, possess the necessary information to solve the problem.

Third, because it is functionalist in its mode of application, NIE legitimizes top-down interventions at the systems level that typically lack the support of key political actors. Thus, because the proposed reforms are sweeping, they tend to become politicized. The result is that reforms are being ignored or resisted.

Fourth, because NIE is part of a larger effort at economic liberalization on the global level, it tends to give priority to failures occurring in the market without paying enough attention to other issues that are critical for national development. Economic analysis gives scant attention to technology and to Africa's rudimentary modes of production. Earlier efforts at industrialization in Africa, justified in the context of Old Institutional Economics, have been reversed and the many countries have suffered 'de-industrialization' since the 1980s. The domestic economic base of African countries, therefore, has deteriorated. The opportunities for investment are seized by foreigners or immigrant minorities with ties to the global economy, like the (e.g. Indians in East Africa and the Lebanese in West Africa). From a political perspective, this trend carries social and political risks.

Fifth, the rudimentary technology and modes of production that prevail in Africa means that the assumptions of NIE rarely hold that the principal issue in need of resolution is the social dilemma arising from an infinite number of individuals autonomously pursuing their own interest. NIE assumes that this conflict between private interests and public solutions can be resolved satisfactorily through specific institutional measures, assuming the prevalence of a policy orientation that is rarely there in African contexts, because rational individuals find other ways of resolving disagreements between themselves.

Sixth, NIE assumes the notion of common goals that individuals can only obtain by agreeing upon a sub-optimal solution within the context of some form of institutional arrangement that encourages collective action. In Africa, however, where division of labor has not yet brought people together into functional inter-dependencies, people negotiate informal solutions based on the notion of shared expectations, not a common public goal. The typical approach to problem solution is more like a 'deal', i.e. where the two parties agree that if A gives something to B, the latter can expect something in return, even if it is not specified in contractual terms.

Public Choice Theory

The Public Choice Theory (PCT) is a variant of the 'rational choice theory'. It is concerned with the provision of public goods, goods that are delivered by government rather than by the market, because, as with clean air, their benefit cannot be withheld from individuals who choose not to contribute to their provision. It assumes that political society is composed of self-interested individuals who coalesce into organized interests. Interest groups, which tend to form around relatively narrow issues of special importance to their members, are created

by individuals seeking specific self-interested goals. Individuals join with other self-seeking individuals to acquire access to public resources (Grindle and Thomas, 1991). At the heart of PCT is the 'self interest maximization' hypothesis.

Four principles underline PCT: (i) public sector actors or officials behave as if they maximize their own interests; (ii) all social entities are fundamentally sets of individual actors; (iii) political interaction is to be based on voluntary exchange; (iv) politics as voluntary exchange requires the making of an economic constitution that is to guide the relationship between the state and the individual; (v) citizens provide rulers or the state with resources and power for which they expect a return of goods and services as well as laws regulating society that matches what they are giving up (Buchanan et al, 1978; Buchanan, 1987; Lane, 1993).

The public choice model is important for a number of reasons. First, it offers a coherent explanation for seemingly non-rational decision making by governments. Why should governments adopt public policies and programs that are harmful to society? The solution to the problem is to limit the activities to fall under the regulatory power of the state. Secondly, it explains why 'the public interest' is not achieved. Thirdly, by focusing on the power of vested interests, it demonstrates the barriers to reform that are created by pre-existing policies and by the political relationships that they engender. In so doing it explains why existing public policy could result in rent-seeking (Lane, 1993; Grindle and Thomas, 1991). It provides an explanation for the willingness of public officials to respond to the pressures and imprecations of lobby groups and other types of special interests. It also provides an explanation for policy choices that are detrimental to society as a whole, over both the shorter and the longer terms and offers a way of understanding the constraints on policy change that develop over time.

In spite of its relevance, PCT is limited for two reasons. First, it is much less able to explain how policy changes or how policy itself can lead to broadly beneficial outcomes. There is little room for public officials who adhere to particular ideologies, whose professional training provides them with independent judgment in the analysis of policy issues, or who may adopt goals that transcend the interests of any particular group or coalition groups. Policy elites are creatures of vested societal interests, however much they seek to work these to their individual rent-seeking advantage, and their actions — devoid of ideological or technical content — can be explained by motivations to maximize political support. Secondly, PCT is not able to explain how, why, or when, reform occurs, except through events or appearance of wise statesmen or technocrats who, for unexplained reasons, exhibit behavior that is politically irrational. Though it indicates the importance of the power-seeking motivations of decision makers, it tells us little about how their motivations are developed or altered over time (Grindle and Thomas, 1991; Lane, 1993; Turner and Hulme, 1997).

New Public Management

New Public Management (NPM) may be viewed as an outgrowth of NIE in that it shares many of its underlying premises about the need to treat institutions from the perspective of enhancing efficiency in public transactions. It certainly complements the NIE. Its origin lies in the calls for administrative reform in Western countries that reflected neo-liberal concerns about making public services more efficient and service-oriented. Governments, as monopoly providers operating under the auspices of the Keynesian welfare state, had become very inefficient. Offering citizens more choice would stimulate competition and thus efficiency. Faced with what in the 1970s became a financial crisis, governments in many countries, e.g. Australia, New Zealand, Sweden and the UK, initiated measures not only to cut but also to control public expenditures. This quest for efficiency and effectiveness in government operations led to a surge of effort to reorganize and modernize public bureaucracies and to move public sector management reforms to the top of the political agenda in these countries. Economic liberals like Hayek (1973) and notable public choice theorists like Niskanen (1971) and Buchanan (1975) provided the theoretical justification for these public sector management reforms.

NPM, then, is a short-hand for a range of administrative reforms that were initiated in the OECD countries from the late 1970s onwards (Larbi, 1999). A review of the publications by some notable analysts and advocates of NPM, e.g. Hood (1991), Pollitt

Box 3.1: NPM and its Core Measures

Variable	Managerialist measures	Enabling Factors
Professional Management	Delegating management authority within public services	Breaking up existing bureaucracies into separate agencies
Output Control	Results orientation and funding of outputs, not inputs	Encouraging greater public awareness by adopting 'citizens' charters'
Operational Efficiency	Greater discipline and parsimony in resource use	Greater competition in the public sector and fees for services rendered
Terms of Service	Flexibility in hiring and firing employees	Downsizing the public service and limiting union influence
Budgeting	Making budgets more transparent in accounting terms	Encouraging governments to become more enterprising by earning, not spending

(1993), and Ferlie et al (1996), suggests that the concept is not homogenous. Many different components are typically subsumed under its label. These may be conveniently organized into two major clusters: (i) making the public sector more managerially oriented, and (ii) creating an economic and political environment in which this managerialism can flourish. Box 3.1 shows the recommendations of these two broad components of reforms in more detail. By stressing these largely private sector management practices, the objective of the NPM movement has been a move away from the classical model of public administration, which is rules-oriented and rigid, towards a smaller, flexible service-

delivery organization that would have to be user-responsive and outcome-oriented to survive. In the NPM model, the private sector is seen as not just setting an example for the public sector, but also serve as its extended arm in providing services to the public.

In the specific African context, the emergence of NPM is best understood in the light of reforms carried out under the Structural Adjustment banner. Recovery and adjustment were not possible without an approach to reform that went beyond the parameters of the first public sector reforms in the late 1960s and 1970s (Wamalwa 1991; Balogun and Mutahaba, 1991). This first generation of reforms had been carried out in the context of

Africanizing and professionalizing the system of public administration that had been inherited from the colonial powers. The predominance of this system for delivery of goods and services were never called into question. The level of ambition of the second generation of reforms, and notably NPM, is much higher and thus more complex and difficult, especially in countries like those in Africa, where the private sector is relatively weak and politics tends to permeate the way the public service operates.

The relevance of the NPM to public sector management can be found in many African countries, through the creation of autonomous executive agencies, decentralized management, subsidiarity, accrual accounting, and commericialization. For example, in Ghana and Uganda, the customs and Excise and Internal Revenue Departments were hived-off from the civil service to form separate agencies in the 1980s. However, the fervor with which NPM was being pursued by the international donor community has since been tempered by experience, as a uniform template for reform rarely works across the board. The key lessons from implementing NPM measures in Africa (see Box 3.2) may

---

Box 3.2: Key Lessons from Implementing NPM Measures in Africa

1. Whereas the downsizing of the public sector in African countries has been significant, by up to 40 percent in some instances like Ghana and Uganda, the cost savings have been much less, in most cases by a mere 6-7 per cent, largely due to high compensation costs in a context of previous low salaries (Larbi, 1995). Retrenchment is a costly exercise, as evidence from North Africa also confirms (Bulmer, 2000).

2. The creation of independent executive agencies has moved ahead in many African countries and, while those like revenue authorities have helped increase government income, they have also incurred high managerial costs stemming from the need to pay top executives salaries competitive with those of the private sector. In specific cases of decentralization to sub-national units, serious problems have arisen in monitoring the use of funds, thus increasing rather than lowering transaction costs (Ayee, 1997).

3. More countries than in any other region have adopted user fees for health care services in Africa. In the mid-1990s only three countries — Angola, Botswana, and Sao Tome and Principe — had no user fees in the government sector (Adams and Hartnett, 1996). The problem in most countries that have adopted this system is that management and accounting capabilities have been inadequate to support cost recovery programs. The gains, therefore, have remained modest, if any at all (Larbi, 1999).

4. Performance standards have been introduced in many African countries and have in some instances contributed to improving public services. Such reforms in the Tanzanian public sector are a case in point. At the same time, there is evidence that many employees feel that their remuneration is not commensurate with what they are expected to do (ECA, 2004).

Source: ADB, Development Research Division, 2004).

have contributed to the realization that market-inspired reforms of government 'failures' do not really work very well in conditions where the state remains weak and subject to informal influences.

The NPM has not succeeded in eliminating the 'clientelistic' tendencies that tend to permeate African governments. While in such a context the creation of independent agencies is a step in the right direction — the manner in which NPM has been introduced as a 'technocratic' fix —, its full effectiveness is still to be harvested.

African public services are being subjected to the influence of at least three models. These are: the NPM, the classical model of public administration, and the more informal practices associated with 'neo-patrimonialism' (Olowu, 2003).

The way that African public services operate reflects cross-cutting influences from all three models. They sometimes contradict each other and make work very hard. In other more fortunate instances, they may complement each other. In any case, because of these cross-cutting influences, implementing the objectives of NPM is continuously an uphill battle.

Governance

Governance is the third of key concepts that have been applied to public sector reform efforts in Africa in recent years. It is part of the international development vocabulary and often used rather indiscriminately to cover a wide range of reform packages from economics on to administration and politics (Kjaer, 2004). It is possible, however, to distinguish between at least two different uses of the term: (i) as

a way of managing complex organizational arrangements in a disaggregated system (cf. NPM above); and (ii) as a reference to how well formal rules are adhered to by actors in the public realm. The first is rather practical and managerial, and is closely related to NPM and the two are sometimes treated as part and parcel of the same reform effort. The second is more normative and focused on measuring performance with regard to key reform objectives, such as transparency, public accountability, and respect for human rights. The international discourse on 'good governance' centers primarily on this second usage of the term, and is discussed in greater detail in chapter 5. The discussion here therefore focuses on the former dimension of governance.

Governance, however, has a separate rationale in that it relates to the overarching coordination of policy implementation in an increasingly disaggregated and more complicated system of organizational relationships. In a public sector managed along the lines of NPM there are a number of operationally independent actors whose decisions and actions must be harmonized. Management consultants tend to believe that such coordination can be achieved by non-political means, e.g. by creating crosscutting networks of mutually interdependent entities. In this perspective, governance is a rather apolitical term, in fact one that is meant to neutralize politics.

Experience from African countries, however, demonstrates that not only are NPM reforms in themselves political, but are also the operations of such a system. Disagreements among agencies or between a ministry and an executive agency are easily politicized. The result is often that implementation is blocked or side-tracked. For instance, agencies are not ready to share the necessary information with others concerned in order to have a problem solved in an effective manner (ECA, 2004.). Governance, therefore, is essentially a recognition that following NPM reforms, not only have the boundaries between public and private sector activities been blurred, but so has the line between politics and administration. In fact, many of the political responsibilities have inadvertently fallen into the hands of managers. Their professional responsibilities are being compromised by having to take on matters that embroil them in political controversies.

The second usage of the Governance concept transcends the managerial issues that arise under NPM. It applies to the overall quality of not just the public sector but the 'system' at large, including the relationship between state and society, public and private sector, and government and citizen. With some over-simplification, one might say that the normative purpose of governance is to promote the rule of law.

The World Bank and other agencies compile data on Governance, specifically to how it relates to such issues as rule of law, the extent to which governments are transparent and publicly accountable, and how far citizens have an undisputed opportunity to participate in politics (Kaufmann, 2004). None of these approaches to dealing with Governance is free from controversy. For example, questions arise over whether Governance

should be measured primarily in relation to corruption, as Transparency International does, and over how relevant the aggregate measures of Governance that the World Bank Institute uses actually are. According to Hyden et al (2004), the first seems too narrow and the second seems to be 'mixing apples and oranges'.

Comparative Experience of East Asian Developmental States

In addition to the above development paradigms and theoretical perspectives, there was the influence of the East Asian development experiences, where the State had played a complementary role to, and sometimes corrective influence on, the market. Indeed, the success story of most East Asian countries in promoting rapid growth had been invigorated through a mixture of complementary institutional reforms, notably the creation of a sound technocratic bureaucracy, good governance, prudent macroeconomic management and effective industrial and manpower policies. Clearly, some African countries, particularly Botswana and Mauritius, had tried to consider the East Asian model in pursuit of their own development strategies and policies.

The idea of the developmental state is associated with Johnson (1981) who analyzed Japan's very rapid, highly successful post-war reconstruction and (re)industrialization. Johnson's argument was that Japan's remarkable industrial renaissance was a result of the efforts of a 'plan rational state' (Beeson, 2003). A 'plan rational' or developmental state is one that is determined to influence the direction and

pace of development by directly inter-
vening in the development process, rather
than relying on the uncoordinated
influence of market forces to allocate
economic resources. The developmental
state took upon itself the task of
establishing economic and social goals,
which guided the process of development.
In the case of Japan, its goal was the
reconstruction of its industrial capacity.
Essentially, such a state is one whose
underpinning is 'developmentalist' in the
sense that it conceives its 'mission' as
that of ensuring economic development,
usually interpreted to mean high rates
of accumulation and industrialization
(Mkandawire, 2001). The most successful
imitators of Japan were Taiwan and South
Korea.

A distinguishing feature of the developmental state, as reflected in the East Asian
success story, is a highly competent
bureaucracy dedicated to devising and
implementing a planned process of
economic development. An essential
prerequisite for managing the development
process is the existence of a pilot agency,
which directs the course of development.
In Japan, the Ministry of International Trade
and Industry (MITI) fulfilled this role. Many
East Asian states also had efficient
bureaucracies, staffed by bright and
competent staff, among the nation's best.
The pilot agencies enjoyed a high degree of
legitimacy and prestige, which allowed
them to recruit outstanding personnel. This
pattern of state-led intervention was
adopted by other states in the region with
varying degrees of success. Japan's North
East Asian acolytes were the first to copy

the Japanese model. They were more
successful than the South East Asian
countries that followed later (Beeson,
2003). In any case, the developmental state
has been central to East Asia's development
process and the countries experienced
substantial sustained increases in per capita
incomes.

In the early 1960s, many expected rapid
growth in Africa and stagnation in Asia
(Court and Yanagihara, 1998). In Gunnar
Myrdal's three celebrated volumes of *Asian
Drama,* he saw Asia, with its vast
population and limited land resources,
doomed to stagnation. Africa was, in
contrast, viewed as poised to grow steadily
along a path of relative prosperity. Many
African countries were better off than their
Asian counterparts, their strong natural
resource bases augured well for future
trade, growth and development. For
example, in 1965, incomes and exports per
capita were higher in Ghana than in South
Korea (World Bank, 2000d). However,
while Asian countries have grown rapidly,
the majority of African countries have
stagnated. Although the East Asian financial
crisis of the 1990s dented the image of the
region, there are some lessons of
experience for African countries, which
tried state-led development with very
limited success.

The East Asian experience demonstrates that the following elements were
essential for success (Beeson, 2003):

- A key to an effective development
  state is state capacity, or the ability to
  formulate and implement developmental policies. Key bureaucratic
  agencies should have the staff and

policy tools to guide the development process.

- A competent bureaucracy is essential.
- An effective relationship between the bureaucracy and the domestic business class lies at the center of any successful developmental initiatives. The bureaucracy should be close enough to the business class so it can nurture it, but not so close as to risk capture by particular interests which prevent it from acting in the national interest.
- Institutionalization of the developmental state is essential for its initial success. Care should be taken to guard against the dangers of collusion, corruption and non-transparency if the relationship between the bureaucracy and private interests become too cosy.

Experiences of the South East Asian countries, whose achievements were less spectacular than their North East Asian counterparts, showed that institutions for general effective performance should be in place. These institutions include a reliable judiciary, secure property rights, the rule of law, and competent core economic agencies (see Box 3.3). A high level of political commitment is essential, implying the willingness to risk political capital in the interest of growth. A high degree of political stability is also important. Regimes in South East Asia were willing to shield top economic planning agencies from political pressure and to follow their policy advice. In Africa, by contrast, governments have tended not to be able to put long-term

> **Box 3.3: Broad Policy Message of the South East Asian Experience for Africa**
>
> The main message from the Southeast Asian experience for African countries trying to integrate into the global economy and promote economic growth are:
> - *Sound 'general' economic policies are important:* These include investment in human and physical capital, a stable macroeconomic environment, and greater outward orientation.
> - *Improving 'general' institutional foundations is important:* Rather than technical capacity building, reform should aim at improving general institutional foundations. Key institutional foundations include: political commitment and credibility; an efficient and non-corrupt bureaucracy; a degree of bureaucratic insulation from political pressures; a positive relationship between government/bureaucracy and the private sector; ensure basic property and contractual rights.
> - *Policy choices should be matched with institutional capacity:* Scarce institutional capacity should be concentrated on the most important development priorities.
>
> *Source*: Court and Yanagihara, 1998

national development priorities over their more immediate political or personal ones (Court and Yanagihara, 1998). Furthermore, while clientelistic and rent-seeking behavior existed in both regions, East Asian countries appeared to have been able to keep them within bounds, or to grow in spite of such behavior.

Merit-based recruitment and promotion practices in the bureaucracy helped to foster a capable and highly motivated civil service. Adequate compensation was used to attract and retain competent staff, while merit-based promotion ensured relatively efficient performance. Many African countries, on the other hand, were more preoccupied with securing public employment than with promoting the quality of the civil service. Key positions in public sector institutions were rendered ineffective because of political appointments and politically controlled funding. Transparency and accountability of public institutions was consequently minimal. Inadequate economic management capacity and cumbersome administrative structures of some African bureaucracies limited successful formulation and implementation of economic policies. It is therefore important to improve capacity of state institutions, if African states are to be able to assume the roles of developmental states. However, it should be noted that the international environment may pose several hurdles to African countries wanting to follow the East Asian model.

Firstly, the global economy is at this stage characterized by increased competition, because of the large number of countries attempting 'export-oriented' strategies. Secondly, the levels of debt in Africa are much higher than they were in South East Asia. Thirdly, many policies undertaken by the South East Asian countries would no longer be permitted in the new global trading environment as represented by the WTO.

The experiences of two African countries (Mauritius and Botswana) that adopted the roles of developmental states, however, demonstrate that it is possible for African states to achieve successful state-led development if the political will exists. Mauritius followed the East Asian model in terms of adopting an export-led growth based on manufacturing, complemented by generous tax incentives. Mauritius currently enjoys a high GDP per capita and relatively low unemployment level. According to Osei (2001), its success is attributable to the following factors:

- Mauritius has implemented policies providing a conducive environment for the private sector to propel the economy. In this respect, the government in the 1980s implemented structural adjustment that put in place the conditions for sustainable growth.
- An exchange rate regime helped to make exports internationally competitive.
- Favorable terms of trade for Mauritian exports in developed countries were a major factor. For example, Mauritian exports benefited from the Lome Convention.
- Availability of cheap labor facilitated the export-oriented strategy.

Botswana, initially a very poor country, has one of the world's best rates of growth, surpassing that of Mauritius, Korea, and other East Asian countries. In the 1980s, it had the fastest economic growth rate in the world, averaging 10 percent per annum, despite a six-year drought that hit the cattle industry (Osei, 2001). Several factors contributed to Botswana's success. First, mineral resources, especially diamonds, have propelled economic growth. Second, Botswana has invested its earnings in social and infrastructural services, with rapid expansion of education and health facilities, housing and roads, in both urban and rural areas. Third, the political and bureaucratic elite pursued realistic foreign exchange, fiscal, monetary and wage policies, attractive to private foreign investment and conducive to national development. An effective partnership allowed politicians to seek and accept economic advice from technocrats, especially concerning national development plans and budgets. Fourth, an efficient, politically neutral and stable bureaucracy has meant proper utilization and allocation of resources. The bureaucracy is characterized by relatively low levels of corruption among the senior bureaucratic and political elite. Botswana has continually been one of the highest-rated African countries by the Corruption Perception Index, as well as indices of economic freedom and governance (see Chapter 5).

Analysts tend to attribute Botswana's development performance more to effective state management than to her 'diamond fortune' because of the sharp contrast with several oil-rich countries in Africa that have remained poor. However, its story of good governance and sustained development has not translated itself into a significant degree of socio-economic transformation, as reflected in the country's continued dependence on one mineral — diamonds — as well as high unemployment and poverty levels. To overcome this problem, the government has embarked on

new generation public sector reforms aimed at changing its development strategy from state-led to private sector-led development.

Conclusion

When African countries gained independence in the 1960s, the state was the institution of choice for nationalist politicians and international donors alike. For approximately two decades, the assumption in these circles was that the state is the sole engine of growth and development. The political emphasis was on accelerating the indigenization of public institutions so that they better reflected the values and priorities of the new nations. Virtually all energy was devoted to capacity-building aimed at strengthening the role of the state in development. Institutions in the private and voluntary sectors were largely ignored in the early planning of development.

Because of the poor performance of the public sector, it eventually became apparent that the state could not deliver on its promise. The watershed took place in the early 1980s with the publication of the Berg Report. Since then, a series of reform measures have been carried out under the overall rubric of 'structural adjustment', to reduce the role of the state in the economy and enhance the position of both market and civil society as contributors to national development. A second generation of public sector reforms in the 1980s and 1990s, focused on a broader set of issues, involving changes not only in the internal structure of the public service but also the relationship between state and market, government and citizen. Thus the shifting emphasis of development agenda in Africa was grounded in the principle of 'getting the politics right' and in the growing recognition that the basis for sustainable growth and development lies in markets and good governance.

The changing nature of public sector reforms in Africa also reflected the subsequent developments associated with the emergence of a wide range of theories, such as the new institutional economies, public choice theory and new public management. In principle, key reform measures in Africa, encapsulated in the banner of the structural adjustment programs, creation of autonomous executive agencies, decentralization of public management, commercialization and privatization schemes all have their roots in these theories. Although good progress has been made in recent years with respect to public sector management in many African countries, the limited success of such reforms owe much to the limitations and constraints of these theoretical approaches. The assumptions of some of these models were based on structural characteristics of developed countries and implemented in Africa and other developing countries with little regard to the institutional constraints of these countries. As a result, too many reform programs were externally (supply) driven and were based on 'quick fixes' rather than on sustainable results.

Lessons from the East Asian development experiences, however, suggest that the success of public sector reforms depends on an effective development State that can influence the direction and pace of development through selective interventions. The key to an effective development state is state capacity, grounded in a competent bureaucracy dedicated to devising and implementing a planned process of economic development. It also requires a strong political will. It is argued that the success stories of a few African countries, such as Botswana and Mauritius, in the development process were largely attributable to an effective state management. To a large extent, these countries followed the Asian model of State-led development with reforms being home-grown, demand-driven, internally consistent and nationally coordinated.

CHAPTER 4

Public Sector Reforms in Africa: Past, Present, Future

Introduction

The demands of development require the state, amongst its other responsibilities and functions, to be an effective regulator, facilitator and provider, as discussed in Chapter 3. A development-oriented state therefore needs a strong administrative capacity, comprising an efficient, open and accountable civil service, one that is competent to design and implement appropriate policies and to manage the public sector. Without an effective public sector and civil service, it is difficult for governments to formulate or implement sound economic strategies and policies, to create an enabling legal and regulatory framework, or to provide social services, such as education and health, efficiently. Effective implementation of development policies requires strong administrative capacity, not only in central government, but also at the regional, provincial, and local levels. While the central administration can concentrate on national strategies and policies, the local and provincial administrations can assist with implementation and monitoring, and to some degree even set local policies, following the principle of 'subsidiarity'.

This chapter examines the process of public sector reform in Africa, reviewing the reforms undertaken in the past and present, and pointing out what needs to be done in the future. Public sector reform is concerned with improving the capacity of institutions to make policy and deliver services in an efficient, effective, and accountable manner. This also implies the need to strengthen the way the public sector is managed. Public sector reforms usually include a range of reform measures dealing with core government functions such as civil service reform, financial and fiscal reform, decentralization, enhancing accountability, legal and judicial reform, and improving corporate regulatory frameworks. Democratization, decentralization, devolution of responsibility, improvement in service delivery, and local government reform have all been major components of public sector reforms in Africa. The chapter discusses these issues and difficulties encountered. It concludes with a forward-looking analysis.

Phases of Public Sector Reforms in Africa

Three Waves of Reform

Since the early 1980s, three distinct waves of public sector reforms in Africa have been identified (Mutahaba and Kiragu, 2002). The first wave covered the decade of the mid-1980s to the mid-1990s. The impetus for this phase emerged from the macro-economic and fiscal reforms embedded in structural adjustment programs. The primary focus of public service reform was on fiscal consolidation by way of reducing fiscal deficit and achieving macro-stability. This resulted in cost reduction and containment measures, including rationalizing the machinery of government through divesting it of non-core operations, downsizing the civil service and adopting measures to control the wage bill. The second wave was dominant in the late 1990s with the emphasis on capacity building. The third wave started around 2000, with the focus on improving service delivery. African countries achieved varying levels of success with these reforms.

Today, it is widely recognized that public sector reform is about strengthening the way the public sector is managed. The public sector is generally synonymous with government. It includes not only the executive arm of government, but also the legislature and the judiciary. The executive arm implements government policies. It consists of the political leadership — the president and/or prime minister, cabinet ministers, and a set of public departments or ministries, and/or agencies whose staffs are on the public payroll and which report, ultimately, to a cabinet minister. Central agencies are specialized around various government functions. Yet, there has been an increasing tendency in recent years for government to take some defined functions of government outside line ministries and place them in specialized agencies, for example, customs and revenue collection. The public sector also comprises state-owned enterprises that undertake commercial, industrial or financial activities.

Public Sector Management Reforms

At independence, most countries in sub-Saharan Africa (SSA) inherited public administration (PA) systems that performed two key functions of a modern state fairly satisfactorily: assuring the continuity of the state and maintaining law and order within each country's territorial boundaries. Most countries moved quickly to recruit and train nationals to replace the departing colonial officials and to assure the steady supply of trained personnel for their expanding public services. There was also a re-orientation of the service delivery function of the PA from the interests of the colonial countries to those of the new states. In many cases, this meant more rapid expansion of the provision of services in agriculture, the social sector, and infrastructure than was the case during the preceding decades of colonial rule. The functions of the public services were further expanded through the establishment of many public enterprises that were operated with varying degrees of autonomy from the civil services that were at the heart of the machinery of government in each country.

Another significant re-orientation was making the PA accountable to national political leaders and the public instead of the erstwhile accountability to colonial masters. In general, the momentum for nurturing a development-oriented PA was maintained up to the mid-1970s in most countries. At different times from the late 1970s through the 1980s, the decline of the PA system in many SSA countries became noticeable. At the onset, the deterioration in the PA system coincided with a steady decline of commodity prices and the weakening of the economies of many countries, widespread political instability, and the accession to power of new political leaders (many of them military officers) who undermined rather than nurtured PA institutions. By the late 1980s, there was widespread acknowledgment of a development crisis in SSA and the decline of the PA in the majority of the countries.

During the early 1990s, events in SSA evolved in two diametrically opposed directions. On the one hand, the governance crisis deepened in a few states, culminating in the phenomenon of failed states or failing states, suffering from civil strife or civil wars of varying magnitude. On the other hand, many states were joining the worldwide waves of democratization and economic liberalization. Significantly, the two waves broadly relate to the interlinked problems of bad governance and poor economic performance. Given the critical functions that a PA system performs in the modern state, it is not surprising that reversing its decline was one of the priority actions of the countries that embraced both democratization and economic liberalization. This section reviews the public management reforms (widely used expression to refer to efforts aimed at rehabilitating PA systems) that were embarked upon in many SSA countries since the early 1990s.

Civil Service Reforms

The most critical public administration institution at the central government level is the civil service and it was logical that it was a major focus of attention in the public management reforms launched in the 1990s in most SSA countries. In general, each country with a public management reform program sought to rehabilitate its civil service system. Regardless of whether the reform program was home grown or introduced within the context of structural adjustment programs financed by multilateral and bilateral donors, they had two common goals. First, there was the influence of some elements of the "Weberian model" of career civil service inherited by the countries at independence that still had relevance within the new political and economic contexts. The idea of a body of permanent officials appointed to assist successive political executive teams in formulating and implementing governmental policies is a good example. Other elements of the model that have had continued relevance are the concept of political neutrality, the principle of recruitment on merit and an emphasis on efficiency in the conduct of government business. The problems that needed to be addressed in these areas were the significant failures that took place in the 1970s and 1980s (decades of crises in public administration systems) in many SSA countries: meritocracy was diluted in varying degrees and politicization was rampant (in the name of one party ideology or patronage politics under civilian and military rulers).

The second, and more recently, public sector reform had also been influenced by NPM (see chapter 3). The NPM, which had originated from reforms in some OECD countries, seeks to apply market principles to governmental administration, with an emphasis on competition, contracting, and customer orientation. It also emphasizes merit-based recruitment and promotion and increased autonomy for managers with corresponding responsibility, performance-related pay, continuous skills development and upgrading. There is also an emphasis on performance measurement, with particular attention to the delivery of services to the public.

By 2004, drawing on three existing assessments of civil service rehabilitation efforts in SSA, the countries can be classified into four groups: advanced reformers, committed reformers, hesitant reformers, and beginners/non-starters.

The first group (advanced reformers) comprises a few countries that did not experience significant public administration decline because the inherited tradition of merit-based and politically neutral civil service system was maintained and nurtured (e.g. Botswana and Mauritius).[1] The same countries made reasonable progress in socio-economic development and were, therefore, able to finance the cost of nurturing their civil service systems — providing decent pay levels for officials; funding educational institutions at fairly

---

[1] Up to 1990, Namibia and South Africa were one country under the infamous apartheid system. Because of its racial exclusion policy, the similarities in institutional capacity, socio-economic development between it and Botswana and Mauritius cannot be described as virtuous. However, post-independent Namibia and post-apartheid South Africa qualify to be in the same category as Botswana and Mauritius.

adequate levels to assure supply of trained manpower; and progressively consolidating democratic political culture, including respect for the rule of law. In a sense, these developments constitute a *virtuous cycle*. In Botswana and South Africa, for example, the nurturing of a career civil service remains a priority of the governments despite the introduction of NPM-style appointments in the late 1990s. The governments reacted to a new reality in which the fairly decent pay for qualified and experienced senior administrative and professional staffs in the civil service was lagging behind pay levels for comparable staffs in the private sector. The Botswana experience is discussed in Box 4.1.

The second group of SSA reformers comprises countries that experienced a decline of their PA system but were seriously committed to rehabilitating their civil service systems. They also embraced the democratization wave of the 1990s but with significantly varying speeds towards establishment of democratic institutions and respect for the rule of law. Benin, Burkina Faso, Ethiopia, Ghana, Kenya, Mali, Malawi, Mauritania, Senegal, Rwanda, Tanzania, Uganda and Zambia belong to this group. Because of the strong commitment to reform in these countries, both bilateral and multilateral donor agencies accepted to provide assistance. Such external support, tied to the implementation of structural adjustment programs, was largely aimed at reducing the civil service wage bill. In practical terms, attention was focused on civil service staff reduction, freezing of new recruitments, and removal of 'ghost' workers. Only modest results

Box 4.1. Botswana: Role of a competent administration in public sector management

Botswana is well known for its good institutions, prudent macroeconomic management, political stability and efficient civil service. Enforcing market discipline and promoting efficient allocation and use of economic resources, through the encouragement of private sector activity in economic development has been one of the key aspects of public policy and public sector reform agenda in Botswana. Recent reforms include the adoption of the Performance Management System (PMS), Work Improvement Teams (WITS), Computerized Personnel Management System (CPMS), Organization and Methods (O&M) Reviews, Performance Based Reward System (PBRS), and Decentralization. The Government has also reorganized and restructured some of the Ministries and Departments in order to improve efficiency and effectiveness in service delivery. Part of the reform has led to the establishment of autonomous authorities or boards, working largely on commercial principles. All these reforms have been driven largely by a succession of competent leadership and dedicated workforce who are committed to continuous administrative reform. As Ayeni (1992) points out:

The [Botswana] public service has been generally well respected, and it enjoys the confidence of the political elites for its

professionalism ... Botswana's record of performance has been made possible, to a large extent, by the quality of its public administration, the caliber of people employed in it, and the appropriateness of the institutions and processes put in place (pp.192–212).

Indeed, public management reform features prominently in the country's successive Development Plans and in its 'Vision 2016'. The following lessons can be learned from Botswana's public sector management:

1. Institution building, development-oriented leadership, and committed workforce play an important role in nurturing a well functioning PA system.
2. Administrative reform is a continuous exercise and it tends to develop its own momentum that successive political and administrative leadership teams would deepen, depending on prevailing circumstances within and outside the country.
3. Sound economic policies and a vibrant public service are key ingredients for keeping a country in a 'virtuous' cycle zone of governance/public administration continuum.

Source: ADB, Development Research Department, 2004

were, however, achieved as some retrenched workers returned through revolving doors, some new appointments had to be made in the social sector, and the largest numbers of retrenched staff came from the lower level cadres.

While none of the 'committed reformers' has fully rehabilitated its civil service system by 2004, several of them

have implemented key reforms that resulted in varying degrees of improved efficiency and effectiveness of the civil service. Some of the reform measures include the enclaving of tax administration, creation of executive agencies out of government's ministries or departments, and salary enhancement for some groups of civil servants. Enclaving implies the transfer of tax administration function from the civil service to new structures (called tax administration or revenue authorities) run at arms-length from the civil service and enjoying significant autonomy in staff recruitment and compensation, linked to a clearly articulated performance regime. In Kenya, for instance, tax revenues as percentage of GDP has been consistently over 25 percent since the revenue authority was created, compared to an average of about 16 percent in the majority of SSA countries. Results in some other countries that have adopted the approach have yet to produce similar outstanding results (Zambia and Uganda).

In the case of executive agencies, they have responsibilities for discreet service delivery or development programs for which they are accountable. The staffs in the executive agencies are regarded as civil servants but they can be hired or fired depending on performance. Ghana was the first SSA country to create an executive agency in 1994, but Tanzania has gone furtherest with 12 executive agencies by 2001 and 50 more in the pipeline. Assessments of the Tanzania experience suggests that the executive agencies have impacted positively on service delivery: "better roads maintenance, higher quality airport services, faster business registration, improved counter services and a more efficient and effective National Statistics Office."[2] In addition, there is what is called a selective accelerated salary enhancement

(SASE) scheme, aimed at raising the salaries of key technical and professional staff in line with (if not better than) those of the private sector. By 2003, only Tanzania was implementing the SASE scheme and was receiving donor support in financing the significant salary increases involved. Donor support is provided over a five-year period during which Tanzania would progressively assume full responsibility for the scheme, pending the time that a competitive salary regime can be introduced for the entire civil service.[3]

The third category of countries consists of 'hesitant reformers'. These countries have introduced some of the reform initiatives undertaken by the 'committed reformers' but without any noteworthy successes (see Box 4.2).

The fourth group of SSA countries consists of 'beginners' of reforms. These countries appear to have been caught up in a *vicious cycle* of heightened conflicts and weak economies, with decaying PAs. Liberia, Sierra Leone, and Somalia belong to this group. Nonetheless, Sierra Leone, in particular, has been vigorously pursuing reform initiatives. It has identified the enclaving of tax administration (through the establishment of a national revenue authority) as an "entry point" to public management reform.

Downsizing the civil service

Civil service reforms in Africa generally, implemented as part of structural adjustment reforms, have taken the form of civil service downsizing, compensation

---

[2] Tanzania Government's Public Service Reform Annual Report, 2000/2001, cited in Mutahaba and Kiragu (2002).

[3] See Stevens and Teggermann (2004).

Box 4.2. Togo: Limited Progress in Civil Service Reform

During an interview survey conducted in 2001/2002, senior public officials in Togo (a minister and several senior civil servants) stated that the main thrusts of the government's proposed civil service modernization efforts were:

(i) revision of the statute of the civil service with a view to incorporating new ideas such as emphasis on neutrality of civil servants, transparency, honesty and efficiency (the statute adopted in 1968 has never been revised);

(ii) human resources management (including staff reduction and functional review);

(iii) professional training, including the strengthening of the National School of Administration; and

(iv) decentralization.

An Inter-Ministerial Commission was to be appointed to develop a modernization strategy, including an implementation plan. More than a year after the decision was announced, the chair of the Commission who was the Director of the Civil Service was still unable to convene the first meeting because the members to be nominated from the coordinating ministries (Finance and Planning) and the Office of the Prime Minister had not been designated.

Another illustration of inadequate attention to civil service modernization is the failure of the government to implement the guidelines of the sub-regional organization, West Africa Economic and Monetary Union, regarding wage bill control (wage bill not to exceed 40% of government revenue in the late 1990s, with 35% as the target for 2002). A joint team of officials from the Civil Service Department and the Military organized a manpower audit in 1997. The objective was not achieved as the wage bill remained at over 50% of total revenues. Two subsequent audits undertaken in 2000 and 2001 made no difference. Significantly, the desirable administrative reform (modernization) issues identified by participants involved in three Focus Group Discussion sessions organized in 2002 are broadly similar to those in the government's outline agenda for modernizing the civil service. The participants in the Focus Group Discussion sessions were drawn from the government, civil society, academia, and the private sector. In other words, there is broad consensus among all the key stakeholders on what needs to be done; it is government's willingness to act that is lacking. The Focus Group Discussion participants not only linked the decline in the capacity of the civil service to the poor performance of the economy in the last decade or so, but they were also of the view that turning the situation around would require faithful implementation of the reform measures they recommended. Two key lessons can be learned from Togo's experience.

1. Lack of champions of reform at the level of the strategic leadership groups (political and administrative) in the government can slow down reform efforts. In such situations, reform measures would be abandoned along the way.

2. With a declining public administration and a poor performing economy, both linked to problems in the governance environment (political uncertainties, absence of oversight institutions, and corruption) there is little incentive for the design and implementation of meaningful public sector management reforms.

Source: ADB, Development Research Department, 2004

schemes and wage policy reforms. Governments sought to reduce the civil service to bring it in line with the new, scaled down role for the state in economic activities. The reforms also aimed to provide civil servants with appropriate incentives, skills, and motivation as well as to enhance management and accountability (Lienert, 1998).

Much of the initial reduction in size of the civil service in most African countries was achieved through removal of 'ghost' and temporary workers. More recent downsizing has been achieved through early retirements and voluntary retrenchments with generous severance payments. In several countries, ministry-by-ministry audits of civil servants have been carried out. In francophone countries, governments have used imaginative methods such as removal of employment guarantees to new graduates (Benin, Côte d'Ivoire and Niger), compulsory retirement at legal age (Burkina Faso and Senegal) or reduction of statutory retirement age (Togo). These measures have been preceded by censuses of public employees to remove 'ghost' workers, elimination of vacant posts and limits on hiring. Some countries have tried to use 'one-to-one' recruitment policies (Côte d'Ivoire, Senegal) while others have used 'three-out-one-in' as the basis of limiting employment in the civil service (Benin).

Ghana was a pioneer in the World Bank and IMF-sponsored structural reforms in Africa, and so it is one of the early starters of the downsizing policy. The number of central government employees was reduced from 301,000 in 1986 to 260,000 in 1990. By 1990, government's wage bill had been reduced to 4.5 percent of GDP. Uganda embarked on similar reforms in the 1990s. Between 1990 and 1997, the number on the government's payroll was reduced by more than half, from about 320,000 to 147,000. The number of ministries was also reduced from 39 to 17. Tanzania also followed suit. It reduced its work force by about 30 percent between 1992 and 1997 from 355,000 to 270,000. Tanzania and Uganda were, however, successful in monetizing some in-kind pay benefits and consolidating these with non-salary allowances. The objective of lowering the wage bill was not achieved because the reduction in staff numbers was offset by rises in pay levels to reverse erosion of civil service wages in the previous decade (Mutahaba and Kiragu, 2002).

The pace of implementing the downsizing policy was much less far-reaching in other SSA countries, such as Kenya and Zambia. In Kenya, the retrenchment of public servants through a voluntary early retirement scheme between 1994 and 1996 was reversed through the hiring of teachers during the same period. In Zambia, the downsizing of the public service only started in earnest in 1997. Between 1997 and 2000, total numbers of government employees declined from 139,000 to 102,000 (Mutahaba and Kiragu, 2002).

In some countries, such as Malawi, public service employment increased rather than decreased in the early 1990s. Since 1995, however, about 20,000 temporary employees have been retrenched and 'ghost' workers eliminated. In spite of this, at the beginning of the 21st century, the number of civil servants had again increased from 127,000 to 130,000 (Durevall, 2003).

In the WAEMU zone, several countries have taken significant steps towards trimming the size of their civil services. In many countries, reductions in the civil service have been through elimination of ghost workers, voluntary retirement and retrenchment. But some countries have experienced difficulties. Niger has implemented four freezes on hiring since 1987 and it has reduced nominal wages in the public sector twice. Countries such as Burkina Faso and Mali have been able to contain labor costs in the civil service; this has not been the case in majority of WAEMU countries. In Senegal, the wage bill increased while it remained constant in Côte d'Ivoire and Togo in the 1990s.

Civil service reforms have also been slow in the countries of North Africa, where the public sector accounts for about 20 percent of total employment and about one-third of non-agricultural employment (see Table 4.1). The public sector, which includes central government, local governments, and state-owned enterprises, has served as an employer of last resort, inflating wage bills. In most North African countries, the wage bill accounted for 30 percent of government spending in the early 1980s, and 35 percent in the late 1980s, before leveling off by the late 1990s (Abed and Davoodi, 2003).

Problems of downsizing

There is no 'ideal' size for a country's civil service; the actual or optimal size is likely to be dictated by a country's macro-economic realities, such as the need for fiscal adjustments, the amount of tax revenue available to pay civil servants, and the balance between governments' wage and non-wage spending. Without taking these factors into account, downsizing policy could weaken the civil service. Downsizing must be done in such a way that it ensures a sufficient, motivated and competent workforce in the civil service. The experience of many African countries suggests that such a policy was missing, and this led to reform reversals even in successful countries such as Uganda and Ghana where the size of the civil service has recently risen again (Mutahaba and Kiragu, 2002).

Overall, excessive or inappropriate downsizing in several African countries has constrained the capacity of the state to perform and deliver services effectively. Staff reduction and employment freezes have created shortages of skilled professionals and technicians throughout the services, and of front-line workers needed to sustain, improve quality and expand public services in key areas such as education, health and agricultural extension. Even the reduction of semi-skilled support staff, such as drivers, significantly constrained the performance of the public service managers. (Mutahaba and Kiragu, 2002). Often, retrenchment has concentrated on labor in the lower echelons — drivers, messengers, and daily-paid workers. Wages saved from such retrenchments are substantially insufficient to achieve desired targets. Freezing of employment also contributes to the ageing

Table 4.1: Government and Public Sector Employment in North Africa, 1996–2000

Country	General government employment		Public sector employment	
	% of total employment	% of non-agricultural employment	% of total employment	% of non-agricultural employment
Algeria	25.7	32.0	31.3	39.0
Egypt	28.2	56.6	34.9	70.3
Morocco	8.5	18.6	9.5	20.7
Tunisia	14.9	19.1	21.9	28.2

Source: Gardner, 2003

of the civil service, with implications for pensions payments as the older civil servants retire.

In some countries, governments found it difficult to meet the retirement or severance packages of retrenched and compulsorily retired workers. In the WAEMU countries, for instance, in addition to an average of three months' pay in lieu of notice, average severance package was 12 monthly salaries in Guinea-Bissau, 48 in Mali, and up to 60 monthly salaries in Senegal. (Danielson, 2001). During the 1990s, however, donors became more willing to help finance severance packages. The World Bank decided to provide soft loans, and the IMF endorsed the treatment of severance packages as investment rather than as recurrent expenditures. Several bilateral donors also acknowledged that aid to assist retrenched workers may speed up civil service reforms. This approach substantially eased the situation and made it possible for governments to reduce

public sector employment at a faster rate (Danielson, 2001).

Pay and incentive systems

Public sector reforms in Africa would be incomplete and will not succeed without addressing pay policy and incentives in the civil service. The need for an efficient and effective civil service requires reforms that go beyond containment and retrenchment to address the crisis of incentives that confront African countries. An important issue that needs to be addressed is the public-private salary differential. If public sector wages continue to be eroded relative to private sector salaries, skilled personnel will leave the public service. Those who remain in the civil service would become demoralized and engaged in absenteeism, moonlighting and corruption. Often, the civil service is unable to attract and retain highly skilled officials due to the relatively poor wage structure. To overcome this problem, the public sector has to offer competitive remuneration. The salary structure within the public sector also needs to be reformed. Pay and promotion systems are often not performance-based; years of service, rather than performance, determine upward mobility. The public service cannot be improved until professional and technical staffs are given the necessary incentives to perform.

Many African countries have realized these problems, and have recently started addressing them, by striking a balance between 'quantitative' and 'qualitative' adjustments. 'Second-generation' reforms which address quality issues include: restructuring remuneration so as to narrow differentials between the public and private

sectors, as well as changing promotion and personnel management policies so that merit and initiative are rewarded. For example, Senegal launched a reform of civil service promotions based on both seniority and merit (Danielson, 2001). Uganda made efforts to increase real wages from low levels and improve incentives for higher-paid staff. In countries such as Ethiopia and Mozambique, which had socialist 'wage equalization' policies, the salary structure was extremely compressed and decompression was part of initial civil service reforms. Figure 4.1 shows changes in real wages for the administrative and professional cadres in the Mozambique civil service. The decline in real wages

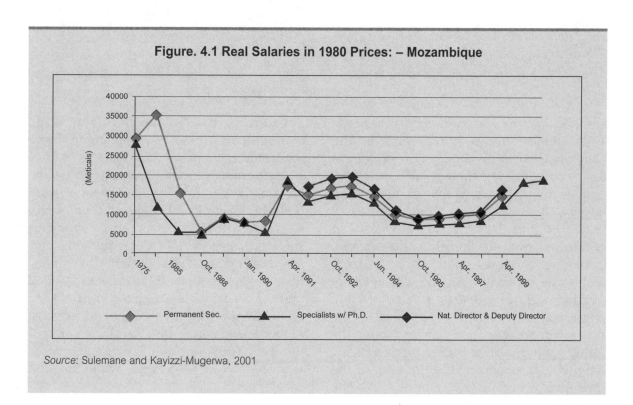

Figure. 4.1 Real Salaries in 1980 Prices: – Mozambique

Source: Sulemane and Kayizzi-Mugerwa, 2001

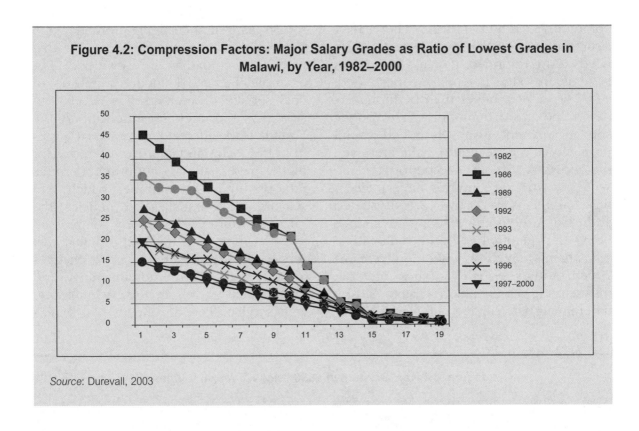

Figure 4.2: Compression Factors: Major Salary Grades as Ratio of Lowest Grades in Malawi, by Year, 1982–2000

Source: Durevall, 2003

stopped with the adoption of reforms in the 1990s. Reforming countries such as the Gambia, Ghana and Guinea also set targets for decompressing their salary structures and, in general, were able to meet their targets. Real wages per employee also increased. In some Southern African countries, such as Lesotho and Malawi, governments were unable to resist large real wage increases, and they made little headway in restructuring salaries and employment (Lienert, 1998). In Malawi, the wage compression that resulted from the indigenization of the civil service after independence remained at the core of the incentive problem (see Figure 4.2). The

government had to resort to non-wage complements to keep its labor force motivated.

Although African countries have implemented reforms aimed at improving both the level of real wages and the salary structure, in many of these countries success has generally been limited. Very few countries achieved their objectives. Real wages continued to decline by 2 percent a year on average during 1990–96. Francophone countries accounted for most of the decline; after the 1994 devaluation of the CFA franc, nominal wage increases were limited to 10 percent, while inflation accelerated.

In Cameroon, there was no nominal wage increase at all, following a decline of about 40 percent in salaries in late 1993. In Congo, following a wage freeze in 1994, nominal wages were reduced by 15 percent in 1995. In the countries experiencing decline in real wages, evidence suggests that there was further compression of upper-wage salaries (see Table 4.2). In Cameroon, for example, the highest civil service wage was six times the lowest salary in 1994, and ten times as large during 1984–92 (Lienert, 1998). At the beginning of the 1980s, top government employees in Malawi were earning up to 45 times more than the lowest paid messenger and the gap was reduced to between 12 and 18 times in the following decade. The compression was more for those in the middle cadres, with some ratios falling from around 20 to only about 5. Government tried to reverse the effects of wage compression by inventing a variety of employment benefits such as housing and transportation allowances to keep its workers motivated.

Progress in reducing differentials between civil service and private sector salaries has been limited. Evidence from seven francophone countries showed that, on average, civil service remuneration at the beginning of the 1990s, including both cash and in-kind benefits, was higher than average private sector remuneration, due mainly to the higher skill levels of civil servants. However, there are indications

Table 4.2: Real Wage per Civil Servant in CFA Franc Countries (1990 = 100)

Country	1986	1988	1993	1994	1996
Benin	n.a	100[c]	120	108	120
Burkina Faso	76	97	85	73	66
Guinea-Bissau	91[a]	104	81	70	65
Mali	121[b]	121	140	133	126
Niger	68	87	116	97	59
Senegal	81	96	105	89	87
Togo	80	97	94	82	79
Non-CFA, averaged	n.a.	n.a.	93	88	85

Note: Data for Côte d'Ivoire unavailable
n.a. not available
[a] 1987
[b] 1988
[c] 1989
[d] unweighted average for Burundi, Ethiopia, The Gambia, Ghana, Kenya, Lesotho, Madagascar, Malawi, Mauritania, Rwanda, Sierra Leone, Tanzania, Uganda, Zambia and Zimbabwe
Source: Lienert and Modi, 1997

that the situation has changed since the devaluation-induced declines in civil service real wages.

Salaries still need to be restructured comprehensively to enhance transparency and improve the ability of government to recruit and retain skilled staff. There is a need to replace automatic 'in-grade' salary increases and promotions based solely on seniority with policies that reward the most competent staff and penalize poor performers. Public-private sector wage differentials in jobs that require the same skills and experience should be monitored so that wage gaps for comparable jobs are eventually eliminated. Thus for countries that have achieved a relatively low wage bill/revenue ratio, the focus should move towards increasing salaries for skilled professionals, especially where these salaries are much lower than in the private sector.

To attract and retain highly-skilled civil servants it may be necessary to create a cadre of senior civil service into which entry will be competitive and based on merit. The senior cadre should be given better professional opportunities and rewarded with higher pay, close to or even higher than levels in the private sector. This will require African governments to accept widening differentials between low and highly skilled civil servants (ADR, 2001). In several countries, there is an urgent need to increase the remunerations for professional, technical and managerial positions. This measure, it is hoped, will not only reduce the brain drain from the civil service to the private sector, but it will also reduce corruption as low salaries are highly correlated with civil service corruption.

Reform should also address other factors that encourage corruption such as lack of explicit performance standards, highly subjective recruitment and promotion procedures, and failure to apply administrative sanctions on erring workers.

Public Enterprise Reforms[4]

Besides the civil service, the other public organizations that have been affected by public management reform efforts are the public enterprises (PEs), also referred to as state-owned enterprises (SOEs) or parastatals[5]. Addressing the failures of PEs has been at the center of economic structural reform programs all over the world. Many of such enterprises have constituted a burden on the budget through payment of subsidies. Others have engaged in activities that could have been performed better by private economic operators. In both cases, the objective of reform is to free states from these commercial activities in order to better

---

[4] See Laleye (1999).

[5] The term "parastatal" is used in a broader sense than PE to refer to all government-sponsored bodies that are outside the framework of the civil service. In addition to PEs, they include autonomous or independent agencies, advisory governmental bodies and administrative tribunals. They are sometimes considered as part of the public service in the broadest sense. In France and francophone Africa, the term *fonction publique* is used to refer to this broader definition and it is commonly translated as the synonym of both civil service and public service. The French-inspired usage is also common in continental European countries and some other countries in Asia and Latin America. PE is used in this report as synonymous with parastatal.

focus on core state functions. The main responses to the problems of PEs in both developed and developing countries were privatization, market liberalization and changes in incentives and control, often through changed ownership. For changes in incentives and control, the options ranged from commercialization, through alternative forms of management such as public private partnerships (PPPs), to partial or full privatization (Commission for the European Communities, 2003).

Privatization

Privatization of public enterprises is one of the preferred approaches to rationalization of public sector activities in Africa. By 2002, the majority of SSA countries have been involved in some form of privatization exercises. These countries can be divided into two broad groups, first according to their degree of privatization — whether 'major', 'modest' or 'minimal' privatizers — and secondly according to when countries embarked on privatization programs — whether 'early' starters, 'not-so-early' and 'late' starters. 'Major' privatizers, where the majority of state enterprises were divested, include: Benin, Guinea and Mali. 'Modest' privatizers are those countries where less than 10 percent of total value of assets were divested, and these include Burkina Faso, Côte d'Ivoire, Gambia, Ghana, Kenya, Madagascar, Mozambique, Niger, Nigeria, Senegal, Tanzania, Togo, Uganda and Zambia. Other countries in Sub-Saharan Africa are 'minimal' privatizers. 'Early' privatizers, from the late 1970s to the mid1980s, included Benin, Guinea, Niger, Senegal and Togo. This group was

followed by the 'not-so-early' countries whose privatization programs took effect from the late 1980s, including Côte d'Ivoire, Ghana, Kenya, Madagascar, Malawi, Mali, Mozambique, Nigeria and Uganda. 'Late' starters, which did not privatize until the 1990s, include Burkina Faso, Cameroon, Ethiopia, Sierra Leone, Tanzania and Zambia (Etukudo, 2000).

Outcomes of privatization have varied widely between countries and sectors. While many countries have moved vigorously with privatization, some countries remain sluggish. Countries that have recently accelerated the process of privatization include Ethiopia, Ghana, Guinea, Madagascar, Mali, Mozambique, Tanzania, Uganda and Zambia. Notable positive results from privatization have been recorded in the telecommunication sector (for example, South Africa and several francophone countries) and in air transportation (for example, Kenya and Tanzania). Box 4.3 illustrates cases of privatisation with positive outcomes in SSA.

North African countries have also engaged in privatization exercises. In addition to outright sale of government assets, privatization attempts took other forms such as financial contracts and PPP agreements. A successful use of the PPP was the Moroccan telecommunications business. In 1999, Morocco awarded a $1.1 billion mobile phone concession for 15 years to Medi Telecom, a consortium of Spanish Telefonica, Portugal Telecom and Moroccan investors. The government used the proceeds, which represented half of its total annual capital inflows, to repay some 6 percent of the country's debts as well as

---

Box 4.3: Examples of Privatization with a Positive Impact

Privatization can have a positive impact on firms' financial performance. In Kenya, profits of the Housing Finance Company, privatized in 1992, rose by more than 100 percent between 1992 and 1993. Privatization also enabled firms to diversify product lines, upgrade and rehabilitate facilities. In Uganda, Shell International reported that privatization allowed the firm to concentrate on core activities and to contract out more non-core activities. Investment far exceeded requirement under the privatization deal to invest $10 million over three years; in just two years $13 million was invested in new and rehabilitated filling stations.

Management changes and new investments associated with privatization have resulted in improvements in performance. In Ghana, the acquisition of a majority stake by Lever International in Unilever Ghana Limited, which increased its shareholding from 45 percent to 70 percent brought about significant changes in the company. It gave the investor the necessary flexibility on matters relating to strategic direction, capital investment, mergers and acquisitions. The capital investment made has enabled the company to reduce unit costs and to report a 50 percent increase in production without increasing energy consumption.

Source: Commission of the European Communities, 2003

---

to make fresh investments in the public sector (Commission of the European Communities, 2003). In Egypt, some government holdings were divested by the use of domestic stock exchange floatations and employee buyouts. Morocco raised an estimated $1.2 billion by awarding a

second global systems license for mobile communications in 1999, and $2.1 billion with the sale of Morocco Telecom in 2000 (Abed and Davoodi, 2003).

However, there are cases of flawed privatisation in Africa. The most common criticism of the privatization processes was the lack of transparency. Often, public assets were transferred to private hands by non-competitive methods, fuelling the system of political patronage and corruption. Lack of transparency also reduced proceeds. The privatization of the Zambian copper mining is an example of how lack of transparency and adverse market trends can lead to shortfalls in divestiture proceeds (see Box 4.4). Sales revenue can also be reduced because of lack of real competition in the bidding process or lack of bargaining power on the part of government.

Commercialization

For some SSA countries, the preferred choice of public enterprise reform was commercialization, which involves reforms aimed at making PEs more efficient. — subjecting PEs to market-related management disciplines while retaining state ownership. There is partial commercialization as well as full commercialization. Fully commercialized PEs are expected to become entirely self-sufficient, with capacity to contribute a proportion of its profits to the state treasury. They are supposed to raise their capital and operating expenses from the capital markets. Partly commercialized PEs are expected to at least cover their operating costs. However, where the operations of a

Box 4.4: Zambia Consolidated Copper Mines (ZCCM): A Flawed Reform Process

ZCCM, with its own farms, schools and hospitals, was more than a mining company, accounting for over 10 percent of Zambia's GDP and at one stage 90 percent of total foreign currency earnings. After nationalization in 1972, lack of maintenance and capital re-investment, and widespread mismanagement, reduced ZCCM's copper output from a peak of 720,000 tonnes in 1969, to just over 286,000 tonnes in 1999. At the time of its privatization, it was losing $1–1.5 million a day (9 percent of GDP in 2000) and had a total indebtedness of US$1 billion.

The Privatization Act entrusted the Zambian Privatization Agency with the responsibility for all divestiture, a task it had been performing in transparency and honesty in most other instances. However, the divestiture of ZCCM was carried out in an opaque manner by a special negotiating committee appointed by the President, amid widespread allegations of corruption and asset stripping. Attractive bids were declined and the process became stalled for several years. The Asian financial crisis led to a sharp fall in copper prices. Potential buyers either lost interest or sought to renegotiate their deals.

Finally in 2000, after the World Bank withheld a $530 million credit until ZCCM was sold, the divestiture process was completed. Many analysts contended that the deal compared very unfavorably with the June 1997 bid by the Kafue consortium, especially when incentives to Anglo American Corporation, such as a cut in corporation tax, a 20-year exemption from profit tax and a reduced power tariff, are taken into account. This rather generous treatment did not, however, prevent Anglo American from deciding to halt its operations in 2002 after it had spent over $350 million, leaving the government with the daunting task of finding another operator.

Source: Commission of the European Communities, 2003

partly commercialized enterprise require a high level of capital investment, the government might have to intervene.

In many cases, commercialization involves the change of the relationship between the management of the PE and the government through performance contracts or management contracts. A commonly cited example of successful commercialization is the case of Ethiopian Airlines. The restructuring of PEs that remain in the public domain and are not commercialized most often involve the introduction of reform measures that include greater clarity in the definition of PEs' objectives, increased managerial autonomy, explicit performance agreements, introduction of new oversight bodies, and emphasis on profitability.

Burkina Faso provides a good example of the commercialization method for the reform of its water sector (see Box 4.5). The range of management options within the public sector include price liberalization, removal of barriers to entry of private competitors, the introduction of performance contracts, and greater autonomy to managers of state-owned enterprises to determine prices, hire and fire employees and make investment decisions.

Administrative Decentralization

In an era of persistent economic problems and adjustments, many national governments in Africa have been forced by circumstances to withdraw from certain activities and reduce the services they provide. Justification for government withdrawal from providing certain goods and services include resource constraints,

---

Box 4.5: Reform of Water Sector in Burkina Faso: Successful Commercialization

During the 1990s the national Burkinabe water provider, ONEA, underwent extensive technical and management restructuring, including the separation of rural and urban water supply. The aim was to make the public utility commercially viable and to extend both water and sanitation access to low-income areas at an affordable price. The government identified its objectives clearly through a series of policy documents setting time-bound targets for reform. At the end of the process in 1999, ONEA had achieved 95 percent cost recovery and 80-85 percent of the population was served with clean water, regardless of their income, a better achievement than in most of Africa.

Sustainability of service provision and affordability were secured through higher tariffs for large consumers in order to cross-subsidize social

tariffs, allowing tariff revenue to cover operational and capital costs. Improvements in access to water were mainly obtained by connecting existing small-scale systems to the network and placing commercially-operated kiosks in informal settlements. This allowed for a minimum service affordable to all, and tacked the problem of unregulated mobile vendors. Quality was improved through government investment programs and subsidies for installing sanitation.

There was heavy pressure for privatization, but the strong political commitment of the Burkina Faso government and the support of some EU member states, plus the provision of technical and financial assistance by the whole donor community, made reform within the public sector a success.

Source: Commission of the European Communities, 2003

---

the need for adjustment, and the fact that development experience has shown that highly centralized top-down approach to service delivery is expensive, cumbersome, inflexible and prone to abuse (Wunsch, 2000). Although the private sector can and should provide some of these services, the problem is that some of these services are non-profitable public goods. In these cases, the most logical step is for the services to be provided by sub-national or local governments, that is service provision should be decentralized (see Table 4.3).

Beyond delivering public services, building effective and efficient local governance is increasingly seen as a crucial component of the democratic project in Africa and as a way to establish a well-

functioning economic and political system. The relevance of local governance for socio-economic progress stems from the need for local economic development, improved service delivery, increased popular participation in governance, and the desire to bring governments closer to the people. Good governance must be rooted in the effective participation of the people in decision-making, and functioning local self-governance institutions.

Experiences of Decentralization

While decentralization had been the practice in many African countries since the colonial era (for example through the 'indirect rule' system in British colonies), some countries have introduced reforms to

Table 4.3: Key Political, Fiscal and Administrative Features of Decentralization for Service Delivery

Degree of decentralization	Political features	Fiscal features	Administrative features
Deconcentration (minimal change)	• No elected government • Local leadership vested in elected officials, such as a governor or mayor, but appointed by and accountable to the center. • Voice relationships are remote and possibly weak.	• Local government is a service delivery arm of the center and has little or no discretion over how or where services are provided. • Funds come from the centre through individual central ministry or department budgets. • No independent revenue sources.	• Provider staff working at local level are employees of center, and are accountable to center, usually through their ministries; weak local capacity is compensated by central employees. • Accountability remains distant; the short route to of accountability may be weak and citizens may have to rely on a weak long route stretching to politicians at the center; a strong compact between policy-makers and providers can compensate to some extent.
Delegation (intermediate stage)	• Local governments may be led by locally elected politicians, but it is still accountable, fully or partially, to the center. • Voice relationships are more to local and proximate, but can be overruled by center.	• Spending priorities are set centrally, as well as program norms and standards; local government has some management authority over allocation of resources to meet local circumstances.	• Providers could be employees of central or local government, but pay and employment conditions are typically set by the center. • Local government has some authority over hiring and location of staff, but less likely to have authority over firing. • Both long and short routes of accountability potentially stronger; greater local knowledge

Table 4.3: Cont.

Degree of decentralization	Political features	Fiscal features	Administrative features
		• Funding is provided by the center through transfers, usually a combination of block and conditional grants. • No independent revenue sources.	can allow better matching and monitoring of supply with local preferences, strengthening both the compact and client power.
Devolution (substantial change)	• Local government is led by locally-elected politicians expected to be accountable to the local electorate. • Voice relationships can be very strong, but also subject to capture by elite, social polarization, uninformed voting, and clientelism.	• Subject to meeting nationally set minimum standards, local government can set spending priorities and determine how best to meet service obligations. • Funding can come from local revenues and revenue-sharing arrangements and transfers from center. • A hard budget constraint is imperative for creating incentives for account-able service delivery.	• Providers are employees of local government. • Local government has full discretion over salary levels, staffing numbers and allocation, and authority to hire and fire. • Standards and procedures for hiring and managing staff may still be established within an overarching civil service framework covering local governments generally. • Potentially strongest long and short routes of accountability, but now also more influenced by local social norms and vulnerable to local capacity constraints and politics.

Source: World Bank, *World Development Report,* 2004a

decentralize their administrative and political processes as part of on-going adjustment and reform programs. An important aim of the revolution in public sector governance is to move decision-making for services closer to the people. For many countries, the creation of effective local institutions for decentralization has only just begun. Reforms have been introduced partly because decentralization is seen as a key element in the process of democratization generally, and of participatory approaches to development. It is also seen as helping to slim down ineffective central administrations by shedding some functions and transferring the costs of others to their users. Decentralization to democratic local government units was expected to improve governance through increased government responsiveness and greater accountability (Ayee and Tay, 1998). African countries have recorded mixed experiences with decentralization.

Broadly, the Anglophone countries have moved faster in implementing decentralization policies than the Francophone countries.[6] The progress of implementing decentralization in Ghana, South Africa, Tanzania, and Uganda is far superior to the slow progress in Benin and Senegal. Togo is an example of hesitant decentralization implementation. It is noteworthy that Sierra Leone, a 'beginner' in public management reform, has

identified decentralization, including elected local governments, as an 'entry point' to public management reform; local government elections were held in the country in July 2004 and the on-going implementation of a decentralization project is supported by a World Bank credit.

By the end of 2003, there were elected local governments or municipal governments in many SSA countries, including Benin, Botswana, Burkina Faso, Cameroon, Ethiopia, Ghana, Madagascar, Mali, Nigeria, Senegal, South Africa, Tanzania, Uganda, Zambia, and Zimbabwe. In some of these countries, the tradition of self-governing local governments predated the new wave of democratization of the early 1990s. But in a majority of countries, local governments were extensions of central governments and instruments of control under one party or military regimes.[7] An example of good practice in respect of fiscal decentralization is that for Kenya (see Box 4.6).

On a broader level, the commonly cited examples of good practice in achieving improved development performance through elected sub-national governments in SSA are Ghana and Uganda.

In 1988/89, Ghana adopted a package of reforms aimed at decentralizing its

---

[6] This difference is a carry over from the former colonial rulers: Britain's decentralized "indirect rule" system in Africa and the extension of France's centralized national administration to its colonies in Africa.

[7] With the exception of Botswana that has maintained elected local governments without interruption since independence, elected local governments have appeared and disappeared at intervals in some Anglophone countries before 1990. Examples include Ghana, Kenya, Nigeria and Tanzania.

Box 4.6: Limited fiscal decentralization yields results in Kenya

In Kenya, where a clear-cut decentralization policy is not yet in place, the public service reform program has a component of local government reform that reflects the need for institutional pluralism in service delivery. In this context, Government has introduced a Local Authority Transfer Fund to which it disburses 5 percent of all its revenues to the local government councils. However, the release of funds to a council is tied to the submission of service delivery improvement plans, and a plan to achieve a 5 percent reduction in spending on staff each successive year in the medium term. This simple fiscal decentralization measure appears to be effective. Accountability by the councils has vastly improved, with 100 percent return of proposals and accounts. There is also ample anecdotal evidence of significant improvements in service delivery in many local government councils.

Source: Mutahaba and Kiragu (2002:61).

---

political and administrative system. The structure of decentralization is a mixed type of authority where institutions extending from the central government combine with locally based institutions (district assemblies) that are linked into one organizational structure. The ultimate aim was to abolish the distinction between local government and central government field agencies. The objectives of decentralization in Ghana included empowerment, participation, accountability, effectiveness, efficiency, responsiveness, decongestion of the national capital and checking of rural-urban drift. Decentralization increased

access of people living in previously neglected areas to resources and institutions of the central government and created opportunities for young people to aspire to politics. The process failed, however, to achieve the stated objectives of empowerment, accountability and efficiency. Mechanisms for transparency and accountability have proved difficult to implement. The provision of basic amenities (education and health facilities, water, electricity, etc) to rural areas, and their accessibility to a wider majority of the population — the most important functions of decentralized units — were not achieved (Ayee and Tay, 1998). Studies showed that the district assemblies generally ignored the preferences of the communities.

In Uganda, the post-independence constitution provided for decentralization based on regional governments. These were abolished in 1966 when the constitution was abrogated and all executive powers were vested in the presidency. Central government centralized all powers until 1993 when Parliament enacted the Local Government (Resistance Councils) Statute and functions, powers and services were gradually transferred from the central government to the local government. Objectives of decentralization were to: transfer power (devolution) to local governments, thereby reducing the workload on central government officials; ensure citizens' participation and democratic control in decision-making; and achieve good governance. Other goals included: bringing political and administrative control over services to the point where they are actually delivered, thereby improving accountability and effectiveness;

promoting people's feeling of ownership of programs and projects executed in their areas; and improving capacities of councils to plan, finance and manage delivery of services to their constituents. To enhance accountability, grants to local governments are categorized into conditional and unconditional grants. Conditional grants are disbursed when the local government has met approved targets. Allocations to local councils are also published in local newspapers as a deterrent to financial abuse. Results have been mixed, but success has been achieved for some objectives. Limited success has been achieved in service delivery because of limited financial and human resources. Given that conditional grants account for up to 80 percent of local government revenue in some cases, their discretionary powers to allocate funds to their priority areas have been curtailed.

Overall, the experience of decentralization in Africa reveals local governance to be highly inadequate with regard to development planning, financing, administration, and accountability. In some cases there are no clear guidelines on the interface between central line ministries (such as education and health) and local governments. In some countries, decentralization has been used by ruling parties at the central level to renew or consolidate their influence at the grassroots level. Others have, however, adopted a decentralization scheme that deliberately fragmented potential local power bases into smaller, weaker, and politically insignificant units.

Inadequate finance is a major constraint to local government performance. Local governments are heavily dependent on national and regional governments for funds. The tendency in many SSA countries is for central governments to assign or transfer functions to local governments without due regard to the financial and human resources required to carry them out. For instance, Nigeria has a constitutional arrangement that provides for the allocation of a fixed proportion of national revenue to local governments to perform functions that are clearly spelled out in the country's constitution. In practice, the discretion of the local governments to use the funds is constrained by spending decisions imposed by state and federal governments. Another factor that has affected the functioning of local governments in some countries is the challenge of accommodating traditional chiefs who remain influential, especially in rural areas. In a few countries such as Botswana and Senegal, there is also a need for accommodating them at the national level.

Decentralization should not be used by the central government as a way to reduce its responsibilities. It must be part of a national strategy to create more responsive and equitable governance and service delivery. Effective communication must be maintained between central and local governments. Resources should be 'appropriately' shared between all levels of government and mechanisms should be put in place to promote accountability and to reduce corruption. Local institutions will have to be strengthened and capacity of local authorities built to manage the development process.

The central government has an important role to play in facilitating the decentralization process through establishing financial guidelines, capacity building (for policy-making and fiscal management), enabling legislation, and setting up advisory or regulating bodies. Lack of human resources limits the ability of local governments to perform effectively. Poor salaries and working conditions, lack of training opportunities, and unwillingness to work in rural areas make it difficult to attract competent staff at the local level. Fostering capacity is best done in partnership between the center and the local governments. In the partnership, the functions of central staff should change from line management to policy formulation, technical advice and monitoring (World Bank, 2004a). Civil service reforms should be extended to all levels of government and not targeted only at central government staff.

Sustained long-term development in Africa will require viable local governance. The consolidation of local governance is necessary to create a democratic developmental state. This requires not just decentralization, but also a genuine devolution of authority to local governments and building a viable local political process that can mobilize people and demand accountability from local officials. Effective local governance, which will facilitate long-term growth and development, will require real decentralization.

Fiscal Management Reforms

Fiscal management (that is, the mobilization, allocation and utilization of resources) is at the core of public sector management. Its key objectives can be summarized as follows: (i) proper planning and budgeting for public expenditures; (ii) effective and efficient administration of government revenues; (iii) proper use of budget resources; (iv) effective control of public expenditure; (v) accounting and reporting on public finance; and (vi) full accountability for all public spending.[8]

Broadly, fiscal policy management, which comprises tax administration and expenditure management, is crucial to economic outcomes. Tax policies have significant implications for investment decisions and could be used to enhance national competitiveness and economic performance. Similarly, expenditure management has important ramifications for the performance of government functions and for the economy.

Tax/Revenue Reforms

In principle, the reform of the tax regime should be guided by three axioms. First, the tax system should promote economic efficiency by limiting its interference with labor, investment and consumption decisions. It should consider the extent to which the tax code introduces distortions in economic decision-making and the impact of the tax structure on economic outcomes. Second, the tax system should involve a strong notion of fairness and strive to ensure that the overall tax burden is fairly distributed among members of society. Fair distribution of burdens is frequently called tax equity, which has two directions: horizontal equity and vertical equity. Horizontal equity involves imposing similar

---

[8] See Kiragu (1999).

burdens on people in similar circumstance, i.e. ensuring that individuals with equivalent incomes pay equivalent tax. Vertical equity involves creating an appropriate differential in burdens for people in unlike circumstances. The desire to instill vertical equity is the rationale for a 'progressive' tax system, which imposes higher tax rates for individuals with higher incomes. Third, the enforceability of the tax regime should be ensured. What may appear as an ideal tax policy on paper may fail to achieve its objectives on the ground due to the difficulty of enforcing it or a lack of adequate information and education among taxpayers.

In the 1980s, large fiscal deficits in most African countries were a result of growing expenditures and a weak revenue base. Government revenues were about 18 percent of GDP, with variation between countries. A review of 30 countries showed that one-third of them had revenue-to-GDP ratios of less than 12 percent for the period 1988-93, which was barely enough to cover interest payments and salaries. One of the factors contributing to this was that limited efforts were made by governments to improve tax and non-tax revenues. The revenue base was weak and the tax structure was heavily weighted in favor of levying taxes on international trade, leading to instability in tax revenues. Resource mobilization was also hampered by the existence of large informal sectors.

Another factor contributing to weak revenue performance was lack of indexation of taxes to domestic prices to offset losses in revenue due to collection lags, especially in countries with high rates of domestic inflation. A further major constraint in domestic resource mobilization was the weak administration of existing tax systems. Real wage reductions in the public sector had affected public sector efficiency, especially in tax administration and the enforcement of tax regulations.

With respect to non-tax revenues, African countries make little use of user fees as in other developing countries. The share of non-tax revenue in current revenue was only 12 percent, compared to 21 percent for other developing countries. There is considerable scope for revenue mobilization through user charges for services such as electricity, water, roads and communications. However, issues of equity and impact on vulnerable sectors have to be borne in mind if user fees are to be charged for such services (Ramakrishnan, 1998). Thus improvements in tax administrations and tax compliance are important fiscal reforms necessary to improve the efficiency of the tax systems.

A key priority in developing a capable fiscal administration regime is to build a revenue department made up of competent and committed professionals, and a fair integrated tax assessment and collection mechanism. In addition to the infrastructure for assessing and collecting revenues, it is important to design and formulate appropriate tax policies. This will help to overcome the problem of tax compliance. Tax evasion, in which both the taxpayer and tax collector can escape legal censure, is all too common in African countries as a result of corruption and ineffective state institutions. Private gain from tax evasion, in Africa, is quite high, while the risk of punishment is low because of corruption and the lack of enforcement.

Tax reforms in African countries have been targeted at strengthening the tax administration system as well as extending the tax bases. Reforms sought to broaden direct and indirect tax bases and to lower the marginal income tax rates in order to make the tax systems simpler, more efficient, and easier to administer. To overcome the problem associated with tax administration in Africa, some countries such as Ghana, Kenya, Uganda, Zambia and Tanzania had set up independent and 'autonomous' tax authorities outside the

normal civil service with better terms and conditions of service for its employees. Tax revenues from such schemes rose considerably. For instance, in Ghana, the growth in tax revenues almost doubled since the introduction of the economic reform program (ERP) in 1983. The component of tax revenues had also changed. Trade taxes which had been the major source of revenues for Ghana, declined from an average of 40 percent in the pre-ERP period to about 28 percent in 1998 (Addison and Osei, 2001). As a result, there has been a closure of the revenue-expenditure gap over time (see Figure 4.3).

In North Africa, faced with persistent fiscal deficits since the 1970s, some

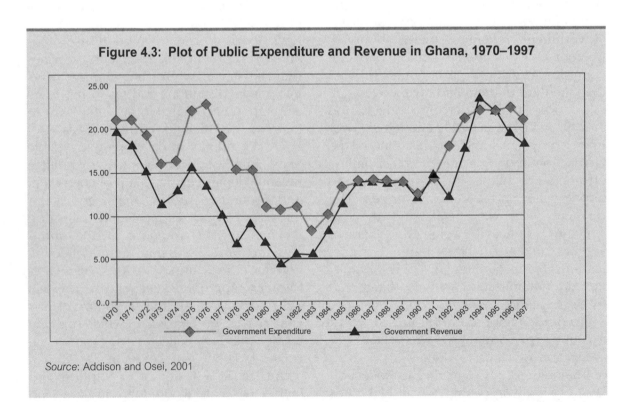

Figure 4.3: Plot of Public Expenditure and Revenue in Ghana, 1970–1997

Source: Addison and Osei, 2001

countries in the region introduced tax reforms from the mid-1980s to improve fiscal balances. IMF policy advice and technical assistance have contributed to improving fiscal management in these countries. Notable successes included the introduction of VAT in some countries. Some fiscal reforms were also aimed at reducing the cost of domestic resource mobilization by improving the administration of the tax system. Adoption of VAT and its associated tax administration improvements, helped to enhance the efficiency of the entire tax system. Other fiscal reforms were targeted at broadening the tax base through reduction or elimination of tax exemptions; the modernization of procedures, including computerization; and the reforms of customs administration in countries such as Egypt and Morocco (Abed and Davvodi, 2003).

Public Expenditure Reforms

A distinguishing feature of many African countries was their tendency to rely heavily on trade taxes and donor support to meet their ever-increasing public expenditure programs. Yet governments in these countries have generally found it difficult to control the rate of growth of public expenditure, even under very restrictive fiscal conditions. Expansion in government payrolls and subsidies for public enterprises financed by short-term revenues, create future commitments that are difficult to cut back when resources are no longer available.

Public expenditure reforms in Africa have largely focused on reducing capital expenditures, subsidies, and wage bill. In recent years, several countries have approached these reforms through medium term expenditure frameworks (MTEFs). An MTEF is a whole-of-government strategic framework for ensuring effective linking of policy, planning and the budget. The objectives of MTEF are to: improve macroeconomic balance by developing a consistent and realistic resource framework; improve the allocation of resources to strategic priorities between and within sectors; increase commitment to predictability of both policy and funds so that ministries can plan ahead and programs can be sustained; and provide line agencies with a hard budget constraint and increased autonomy, thereby increasing incentives for efficient and effective use of funds (World Bank, 2004a).

However, before a country introduces an MTEF, there is a need to get the basics of budgeting right. The following "basics" of public financial management can be highlighted:[9] a realistic budget that is faithfully implemented; high transparency in public finance; public funds spent for authorized public purposes; reported expenditure corresponds to actual expenditure; reliable external and/or internal controls; and spending units have reasonable certainty as to the funds that will be available.

Against this backdrop, public financial management reform efforts in most SSA countries have sought to combine getting the basics right with the introduction of MTEF. Predictably, this has proved difficult to achieve. Of 19 SSA countries that have

---

[9] See Schick (1998).

adopted the MTEF process during the last decade, only five have successfully integrated it with their budget processes (Namibia, Rwanda, South Africa, Tanzania, and Uganda). Many of the other countries are only piloting an MTEF. In reality, this means that the process is unlikely to have a beneficial effect on the budget process. In the countries with functioning MTEF processes, a key feature is the involvement of stakeholders in the budget process in its preparation. The stakeholders include cabinet members, parliamentarians and civil society. South Africa, Tanzania, and Uganda are arguably the leaders in this field.[10]

The obvious lesson from existing experiences is a reconfirmation of the counsel that getting the basics of budget right should precede the introduction of an MTEF that should be government-wide when the relevant prior conditions are met.

Procurement and Financial Accountability

Almost at the same time as MTEF was being introduced, many countries, in partnership with some donors, began to implement two initiatives aimed at improving two critical aspects of public financial management: one is focused on procurement reform and the other is focused on financial account-ability. The diagnostic tool used for the former is called a country procurement assessment report (CPAR) while the diagnostic tool used for the latter is called a country financial accountability assessment

(CFAA). One of the main points raised in CFAAs is the widespread inadequacy of qualified accounting staff. This is the major explanatory factor for the small number of accounting staff in public services (those that are available prefer the "greener pastures" of the private sector), resulting in delayed audits. This means that technical auditing is usually delayed in such countries and there are no prospects of moving towards value for money auditing. However, there are a few exceptions (for example, Botswana, Kenya, and South Africa). Botswana has moved further to introduce and implement accrual accounting — a practice that is at the cutting edge of accounting practice (see Box 4.7).

In the CFAAs that have been completed the reform measures that are usually recommended focus on the improvement of systems and procedures with emphasis on the prevention of fraud, waste and mismanagement. Although the technical quality of these assessments is high, the pace of implementation and the extent to which they enhance financial accountability is yet to be systematically carried out.

Regarding CPARs, the important point to emphasize is that over 60 percent of the average SSA country's public spending (at both the national and subnational levels) involves procurement. Again, the CPARs are usually of high technical quality, covering all the issues of transparency, competition and regular public reporting. However, implementation in most countries leaves much to be desired. In some countrie, it is a case of long delays or total inaction until donors decide to undertake another round

---

[10] On the good practice in South Africa, see Garnett and Plowden (2004).

Box 4.7. Accrual Accounting in Botswana

Government accounting is maintained on a cash basis plus a system of modified cash and accruals for special funds and trading accounts. The data for the computerized system, which was first introduced in 1977, is processed in batches and budgets. There are 27 local council authorities in Botswana: 6 urban councils, 9 district councils and 12 land boards. All councils are required to produce annual accounts within three months of the year-end and to have them audited by an auditor appointed by the Office of the Auditor-General. Accrual basis of accounting is used and the training of professional accountants is provided by the Botswana Accountancy College (BAC). BAC is a private sector college largely subsidized by the Botswana Government and the Debswana Diamond Company. There appears to be a strong recognition by Government of the importance of establishing a supply of qualified and trained accountants for the public and private sectors.

Source: East and Southern Association of Accountants General (ESAAG), cited in ECA, *Public sector management reforms in Africa: lessons learned*, 2004, page 21.

of CPARs. Even in the countries described as 'committed reformers', implementation of procurement reforms is largely sluggish. The poor implementation of procurement reforms in so many countries may be linked to the problem of corruption that some countries are now addressing seriously (see Chapter 5).

Effective Delivery of Social Services

A key developmental function of government is to provide social services or public goods. Despite the emerging consensus on the need to rely more on the private sector, there is certainly a case for governments to continue to participate in the provision of certain services. The questions of what the government should provide in terms of services will necessarily depend on a country's circumstances and its stage of development. However, the general consensus is that from the point of view of citizens' rights, governments ought to be active in such basic services as education and health. Also, from the point of view of market failure, they ought to be active in the provision of infrastructure and other public goods in areas where the private sector initiatives are not forthcoming.

In the period immediately following independence, from the late 1950s to the 1980s, most African countries invested significantly in the provision of education, health and infrastructure and there was remarkable progress in these areas. In education, the proportion of children in primary school doubled between 1960 and 1980, while the proportion in secondary school increased by a factor of four (ADR, 1998). Life expectancy increased significantly while mortality declined by more than a quarter. In infrastructure, the average main telephone lines per 100 inhabitants in 1980 was 0.74 — a 64 percent increase compared to 0.45 main telephone lines per 100 inhabitants in 1965, and by 1986 that figure had increased again by 43 percent to 1.06 mainlines. In the same way, electricity production increased from a per capita of 43 kilowatts in 1965 to 87 kilowatts in 1986, a 100 percent increase, only to remain virtually stagnant since then (ADR, 2001).

The economic crisis of the late 1970s and 1980s, however, slowed down these gains. In education, primary enrolment ratios stagnated while secondary enrolment ratios increased, but at a much slower rate (ADR, 1998). Higher education, which experienced a notable expansion in the earlier two decades, encountered difficult problems, particularly with regard to finance, the quality of education, and its relevance to employment opportunities. In health, HIV and its associated diseases emerged as one of the greatest threats. Malaria remained one of the most important causes of mortality and morbidity. In infrastructure, the explosion of urban populations and subsequent shrinking of resources in the wake of economic crisis after the mid-1980s have rendered public provision incapable of meeting the needs of economy and society. This is evidenced in the combination of poor management, inadequate capital structures, bad investment decisions and the bureaucratization of decision-making, which characterized public providers.

In response to these growing challenges and as part of donor-supported reform programs, African countries have endeavored to find alternative modalities of delivery, taking into account resource constraints as well as the limitations of the public sector model. Tanzania launched a "quick-wins" service delivery improvement program, the model is technically simple, fast, and low cost to implement, and it has demonstrated that tangible results can be achieved rapidly (see Box 4.8).

Ghana pioneered the recourse to the 'agency model' in the search for options for

---

Box 4.8: Tanzania's 'Quick-Wins' Services Improvement Scheme

Tanzania's 'quick-wins' program for services delivery improvements is a deliberate initiative to demonstrate that public sector reform programs are not all about sacrifices and pains inflicted by such measures as retrenchment, employment freeze and other cost containment measures. The first phase of the initiative focuses on 11 service areas concentrated in key domains of public concerns. The outputs and outcomes relate to timeliness, quality of service/customer care and responsiveness to the public. In order to ensure ownership, it is based on leadership and implementation by the ministry themselves. It uses simple business process reengineering supported with local technical assistance (Eastern and Southern Africa Management Institute — ESAMI). The early results are promising with a clear indication that time has been drastically reduced to process passports, work permits and licenses in several areas. Land titles are processed much faster. Investment certificates are also issued faster (ten days instead of 270). There is also marked improvement in the administration of small loans to women groups and students.

Source: Mutahaba and Kiragu, 2002

---

improved public service delivery, by transforming its Rural Water and Sanitation Department to an agency in 1994. The agency is considered to be a model for comparatively efficient and effective delivery of rural water and sanitation services in Sub-Saharan Africa. Tanzania also introduced a comprehensive and active agency program that is judged to have significantly improved service delivery (Mutahaba and Kiragu, 2002).

ICT and Public Service Delivery

The adoption of information and communications technology (ICT) has been recognized as a key strategy for improving public service delivery (see Box 4.9). It is regarded as an essential facilitator of service improvement, especially as governments worldwide are facing an increasing trend towards knowledge-based production and communications revolution. ICT can play an important role in improving service delivery in African countries. In the education sector for example, more efforts are needed to redirect public resources toward primary education, while relying more on private funding at secondary and higher levels in order to promote efficient and equitable public spending on education. Information technology is a delivery mechanism, which can be employed by government to provide some services cheaply and more efficiently. It can be used to provide education and health care to many more people while keeping costs down (see Box 4.10).

Box 4.9: Realizing the Potential for Enhancing Procurement

E-government is the use of ICT to enhance the efficiency, transparency, and accountability of government. These tools, particularly the Internet, are increasingly used in developing and developed countries alike to provide public services that for years were delivered only in person or by mail (if at all). These information technologies can:

- meet citizen's demands more efficiently, saving time and money for both service providers and their clients;
- cut through red tape and associated opportunities for corruption, discrimination and harassment;
- enhance access to public information and services, leading to greater transparency and equity.

According to a recent survey carried out by Andersen Consulting, E-government is expanding in many countries (with the US and Singapore being among the leaders), although even in those settings, only a small part of the Internet's potentials has been tapped to date. Developing country governments are adapting them to their particular needs and constraints. One area that has witnessed remarkable changes in recent years is government procurement. The Chilean and Mexican governments have implemented new Internet-based systems for public procurement. In Chile, for example, all companies that wish to be considered for a public contract register themselves according to their business activity (for example, construction, IT consulting, office furniture, etc.). When a public agency needs to purchase goods or services, it files a request in the new electronic system. An e-mail message soliciting for bids is then sent automatically to all companies registered in the relevant business area. Once a decision is made, all information concerning the companies, their bids, and the results of the decision-making process are posted electronically. E-government solutions like this can generate cost savings for government and reduce opportunities for corruption, leading to increased public confidence in government.

Source: World Bank, 2000a

Box 4.10: ICT and Education Delivery

Education is crucial to entrench democracy and improve governance, increase productivity, diversify the product base, raise exports, reduce population growth, improve the health status of the population and reduce poverty. Development will remain sluggish unless Africa is able to invest in its people. After four decades of development experience, it is quite clear that education is essential for socio-economic and industrial development. ICT can help Africa educate its citizens and facilitate life-long learning.

ICT offers African countries effective tools to educate citizens, build the capacity of its labor force and improve the quality of life. ICT can help reduce the cost of education and make education accessible to a much wider audience. The Internet and Web can facilitate distance education, provide new methods of learning, while also improving educational productivity. New technologies are increasing the opportunities for life-long learning for those wanting to update their knowledge or skills in order to remain competitive.

From the Africa Virtual University — initiated by the World Bank — to much smaller programs, efforts are being made in the continent to employ ICT to educate the people and build capacity for socio-economic development. The African Virtual University was set up to remedy the shortfall in education particularly in science and technical education. In Uganda, a new Satellite University has been launched under the auspices of Makerere University in Kampala. Twenty sites will be established when it is fully operational and students in the sites can participate in courses and programs offered by Makerere. The effect of this will be expansion of educational opportunities in Uganda and a lowering of the costs of education.

In 1997, UNESCO launched the Learning Networks for African Teachers (LNAT) to help teachers 'become better learners and teachers'. Pilot projects are being implemented in Namibia, Senegal and Zimbabwe, with proposals for other pilot projects.

Another ICT project to promote education within the continent is Global Education Network for Africa (GENA). GENA is a regional project to share national programming for distance education. The project will allow broadcasters to share the cost of accessing educational programming. The initial participating countries in GENA are Kenya, Namibia, Swaziland, Uganda and Tanzania. Ghana has recently developed special programs to network schools to provide distance learning and telemedicine applications.

Source: ADR, 2001

The systems of primary and secondary education in many African countries suffer from serious shortcomings, including low teacher-student ratios, limited availability of instructional materials and poor quality of education. In higher education there are few libraries, most of them lacking access to international journals and being generally deprived of educational materials, while research facilities are limited. Most of these educational problems are related to inadequate funding and inefficient use of available resources. Here too, ICT offers a wide range of low-cost solutions. One of the most important applications is distance education in Africa, which could be extensively used to pursue entirely conventional educational ends.

The main advantages of distance education are economy, flexibility, and suitability for widely scattered student bodies.

Information technology can not only help Africa to attain universal primary education, but it could also turn some of its disadvantages in this field into advantages. It is well known that Africa's population has the youngest age structure where children below the age of 15 years constitute about 45 percent of population, compared with 30 percent for the rest of the world. Children take quickly to computer knowledge the way they do to languages. Hence, introducing computer education, could turn Africa's high dependency ratio, which has always been viewed as a retarding load, into a powerful source of growth and socio-economic development. In addition, ICT has the potential to connect African educational institutions continent-wide, and link them with international universities, hence, facilitating research and the exchange of ideas. Access to data and educational materials would also be simplified (Oshikoya and Hussain, 1998).

In the health sector, African countries are presently encountering serious problems. Information technology can help control and sometimes eradicate some of the health problems plaguing the continent. It has brought about the innovations of 'virtual medicine' and 'telemedicine', by which patients located in rural areas can have access to medical experts located thousands of miles away. Information technology can facilitate the development of computer-aided diagnosis of diseases for the rural areas where highly specialized

physicians are not available. Isolated medical institutions and practitioners can treat people better by communicating with colleagues and researchers worldwide.

E-Government and Service Delivery

As noted above, E-Government refers to the use of information technology application to perform government functions with maximum efficiency and at minimum cost. It enables governments to deliver information and in some cases, services, to citizens, businesses and other government agencies. The goals of E-government are: better service delivery to citizens, improved services for business, transparency and empowerment of the citizens through information, and efficient government purchasing. E-government enables citizens to interact and receive services from government 24 hours a day, seven days a week. Some see the primary goal of e-government as the facilitation of citizen interaction with government. It can help to attenuate the process-laden and bureaucratic nature of many government services, which make them time-consuming. It is suggested that one of the goals of implementing e-government initiatives is to create a 'one-stop shopping' site where citizens can carry out a variety of tasks, especially those that involve multiple agencies, without requiring the citizen to initiate contacts with each agency individually (Seifert, et al. 2003).

African countries are beginning to use the web to enhance service delivery (see Box 4.11). Many African countries, however, need to enhance their capacity in this regard. Information systems — which

Box 4.11: E-Government in Selected African Countries

With an initial investment of $1 million, Mauritania implemented an ICT-based trade management system. The system reduced transactions costs associated with external trade as customs processing time was cut from 48 hours to 30 minutes, and the time it takes to clear goods from 5-20 days to between one and two days.

Morocco applied ICT to achieve a better administration of its tax system. In 1989, under the Public Administration Support Project, Morocco began to use ICTs to enhance the capacity of its Ministries of Finance and Planning. The project focuses on increasing the efficiency of the ministries in tax administration, auditing, planning public investment and monitoring. It is estimated that time required for preparation of its budget has been halved since 1989.

In Tanzania, the Muhimbili Medical Center in Dar-es-Salaam is effectively using the Internet to reduce the high rate of mortality among its paediatric patients. Using the Net, the Muhimbili Medical Center is able to consult experts worldwide and also source outside support.

HealthNet, a major health care network is providing support to African countries to improve their health interventions. The network is facilitating collaboration among medical staff in countries such as Mozambique, Tanzania and Uganda. HealthNet is also providing a system for data collection and sharing in the Gambia, which is saving time and money. The HealthNet system is being used to disseminate information in DRC, to facilitate various research studies on malaria in Ghana, the London School of Hygiene and the Tropical Research Center in Geneva, and to provide early warning on the outbreak of epidemics.

In Egypt, to reduce red tape and petty corruption and streamline government trans-actions, the ministry of administrative development created citizen service centres where citizens and investors can do their government business without going to the relevant ministries. The ministry publishes a guide of the 450 most requested services (out of a total of 728) and posts it on the Internet, specifying the documents and official fees associated with each.

Sources: Adesida, 2001; TI (2004).

can help governments design, implement, and assess the effectiveness of economic measures — are an essential aid to public policy, with the potential to provide powerful catalysts to confront Africa's complex mix of development challenges. Such information systems could increase the speed, volume, quality, transparency, and accountability of government transactions, yielding large productivity increases in government services.

It must be emphasized, however, that information technology is not a panacea in itself. It is rather a means to an end and a powerful tool that can bear results only if it is put into effective use. And to do this, African countries would have to overcome, as a matter of priority, numerous obstacles including the inadequate state of telecom-munications services and the high cost of computers and software. Efforts will have to be made to bridge the digital divide between those who have access to the Internet and those who do not, as well as take special steps to include those who are not literate.

The Private Sector and Service Delivery

Governments in Africa are increasingly turning to the private sector to provide health, education and infrastructure. Private participation in infrastructure has been pursued through various approaches, including divestiture, leases, management contracts, and concessional arrangements, such as build-operate-transfer (BOT) and build-own-operate (BOO). Although the private sector invested in virtually all infrastructure sectors, its early beginnings were in telecommunications, which provided learning experiences for engagement in other sectors. In telecommunications, private sector participation has been predominantly in the form of concessions and de-monopolization followed by divestiture and management contracts (ADR, 2001).

Three main drivers may be expected to push the African infrastructure market forward. An important factor is the renewed interest within Africa in revitalizing regional groupings, which is expected to expand markets and increase regional infrastructure projects, which would attract more private investment. A second factor that should enhance private sector participation is the increased realization, on the part of private investors, that risk perceptions in Africa are often overstated and that building relationships in the region is necessary to take advantage of the emerging investment opportunities. This is particularly true in view of the potential market growth in the continent and its rich but under-utilised resources. A third positive element is the catalytic role played by regional and international financial institutions and financiers such as the ADB.

The private sector is now an important partner in the health care sector of many countries. While the contribution of the private sector to health care is significant, there are concerns that their services are usually priced beyond the accessibility of average-income citizens. Governments may need to work closely with private providers to address such concerns. There should be more collaboration on training, improved co-ordination on price setting, and potential for contracting arrangements. All governments need considerable capacity to plan and co-ordinate diverging interests and to ensure that private sector providers are accountable. These goals require fundamental changes in health policy to achieve institutional, organizational, managerial and financial reforms. They also place some burden on the administrative or political capacities of the administration. For the contribution of the private sector to be fully harnessed, there is a need for clear legal frameworks for national policy and for strengthening supervisory capacity of the public sector. However, regulatory issues concerning private sector participation have to be addressed.

The Politics and Administration Nexus[11]

The politics and administration nexus in the conduct of government business is a

---

[11] The contents of this Part include material drawn freely from Adamolekun (1983) and Adamolekun (2000a).

special focus in Public Administration literature because it determines, to a great extent, the quality of a public administration system. And the reason is simple, even if it is trite: leadership matters. Strong leadership at the top of the machinery of government, provided jointly by the political leadership team and the leadership of the career civil service is essential for both policy formulation and implementation which sum up what governmental administration is about. A diagrammatic representation of a conceptual framework that summarizes the respective roles of politicians and administrators in the conduct of government business is provided in Figure 4.4.

The basic assumption of this framework is that there exists a distinction between the

political judgment content and the technical expertise content of major issues with which politicians and administrators deal. It is postulated (a) that politicians dominate the issues which have a high content of political judgment and a low content of technical expertise (e.g. decentralization policy); (b) that administrators dominate the issues with a high content of technical expertise and a low content of political judgment (e.g. science and technology policy); (c) and that in regard to issues with both a high content of political judgment and technical expertise, politicians and administrators take decisions by cooperative effort, as partners in a joint enterprise (e.g. the budget process). Each postulate is represented in Figure 4.4.

Although the above illustrations relate to policy formulation, they can be extended to policy implementation. The implementation stage of the policy process can be described as highly technical, with little room for political judgment (notwithstanding the intrusion of political considerations), until the monitoring and evaluation stage when politicians in both the executive and legislative arms of government do become involved. This point confirms the salience of the cyclical nature of the policy process: ideas about new directions for existing policies or totally new policies could emerge at the implementation and evaluation/monitoring stages (see Figure 4.5).

Although SSA countries inherited politics-administration relationships that reflected, in varying degrees, the features of the framework summarized in Figure

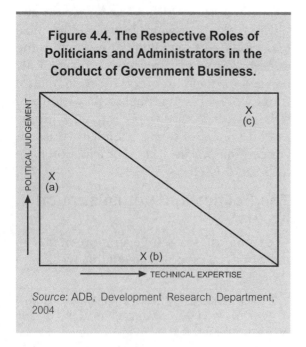

Figure 4.4. The Respective Roles of Politicians and Administrators in the Conduct of Government Business.

Source: ADB, Development Research Department, 2004

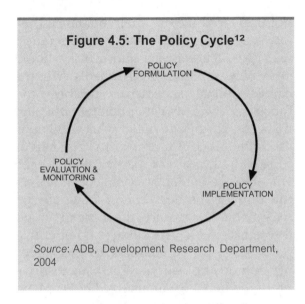

Figure 4.5: The Policy Cycle[12]

POLICY
FORMULATION

POLICY
IMPLEMENTATION

POLICY
EVALUATION &
MONITORING

Source: ADB, Development Research Department,
2004

4.4, the dominant trend in most countries before the public management reforms of the 1990s was the progressive politicization of administration and the bureaucratization of politics. The same trend was noticeable in all the regime types that emerged in the majority of SSA countries from the late 1960s to the advent of the new wave of democratization of the early 1990s. The differences in politics-administration relationships were essentially in the details, depending on whether it was a one-party state regime (for example Guinea and Tanzania), a military regime (for example, Benin and Nigeria), or a state that maintained constitutionalism (for example, Senegal). In almost every case, there was

---

[12] The Policy cycle begins at the policy formulation or policy-making stage; it continues to the implementation and the evaluation and monitoring stages; and then returns to the formulation stage.

failure to nurture technical competence and bureaucratic domination of the policy process resulted in weakness in both policy formulation and implementation. There were only a few examples where politics-administration relationships approximated our framework (for example, Botswana and Mauritius).

One aspect of the politics-administration relationship problem that has been addressed in many of the public sector reform programs in SSA countries is how to assure a quality administrative leadership that is also loyal to an incumbent political leadership team. This is linked to a broader issue of how best to separate political from career appointments. There is need to acknowledge and accept that under a democratic order where political executive teams could change after periodic elections, newly elected leadership team members would want to appoint a few staff whose loyalty includes personal confidence and who are totally committed to the achievement of their programs. This category of public officials constitutes a distinct group within the leadership of governmental administration in many of the old democracies. They are known variously as special advisers in the United Kingdom, political administrators in Germany, political appointees in the USA and members of Ministerial Cabinets in France. They are responsible for policy advocacy and are not bound by the norms of anonymity and political neutrality. They are able to speak out in public in defense of policies being pursued by the political leadership. This enhances open and accountable government, as those responsible for government policies can be identified and named for praise or blame.[13]

In the SSA contexts, it would be sensible to specify the number of such appointments and prescribe some minimum technical professional qualifications. A good practice is the arrangement in South Africa that allows each minister to have two or three special advisers with a slightly larger number for the president and his deputy. In the Francophone African countries, they constitute the Ministerial Cabinets.[14] In all cases, the tenure of political appointees should be coterminous with that of the appointing political executive. What is required in every case is total transparency in all matters relating to

political appointees: their qualifications, job descriptions and remuneration packages. The relevant information should be widely published in the media. When a career official accepts to perform the functions of a political appointee, it would be necessary to state under what conditions the official could return to the career service. In the case of a political appointee who seeks a career or contract position at the end of his/her tenure, it would be reasonable to require the official to go through the prevailing competitive procedures for recruitment to the career or contract position. The suggestions proffered here are summarized in Box 4.12.

As shown in Box 4.12, the group of officials next to the political appointees (i.e. the chief administrative heads of ministries/ departments or agencies) can be appointed on contract. Such contract appointments are already the practice in some SSA countries, including Botswana, Ghana, Malawi, South Africa and Uganda. The salary factor in contract appointments at this level has already been mentioned. Another factor that has been invoked, in varying degrees, is the need to open the most senior civil service positions to talents from both within and outside the service. Although not explicitly acknowledged, the incumbent political team would like this category of officials to be loyal to them. In particular, they would like them to be sympathetic to their policy thrusts and priorities without the concern for partisan loyalty they require of political appointees.

While all these justifications for the use of contract appointments at the immediate level below political appointees are

---

[13] Of course, career higher civil servants would also contribute to policy advice. The career higher civil servants have, as their primary responsibility, the leadership of the programmatic activities of their ministries, departments and agencies. They would also be responsible for providing leadership for the civil service as an institution. However, in countries that have adopted the executive agency arrangement, the smaller number of higher civil servants in ministries, departments and agencies would focus on regulatory management and the management of the contracts for the agencies, especially the monitoring and evaluation of performance

[14] The establishment of Ministerial Cabinets in Francophone African countries is an imitation of an institution by the same name in France. Although the emphasis is on the political responsiveness of members of French Ministerial Cabinets, they are mostly drawn from the higher civil service, which also happens to produce the majority of Cabinet Ministers most of the time. In the Francophone African countries, partisan political considerations predominate, and this means a loss in technical and professional competence in many cases.

Box 4.12: Proposed composition of staff in the civil service in SSA

A. Political appointees: Temporary tenure, coterminous with that of the appointing political executive. Key criteria for selection are loyalty and policy compatibility. Minimum professional qualifications to be specified for different types. Number must be small at all times.

B. Contract appointments: Transitional arrangement to be phased out as an element of strategy as "C" below becomes adequately strong. Total number of top managers and top-notch professionals to be appointed on contracts to be determined by the needs of each country, especially the initial capacity condition at level "C". (The occasional contract appointments that are found in most state bureaucracies would remain a permanent feature in the SSA countries).

C. Small but strong career civil service: Could have a small corps of senior executives — a Senior Executive Service (SES). Rest of the career civil service to be recruited on merit with appropriate measures introduced to ensure some degree of representativeness — notably race, gender and ethnicity. Overall size would vary from one country to another. Civil Service Commissions whose independence is enshrined in national constitutions would be needed to provide overall direction for the career civil service, including the protection of the merit system. If necessary, there should also be provision for judicial protection of the security of tenure of career officials.

D. Non-career officials: Messengers, cleaners, lift attendants, food caterers and so on should not be included in the career service. They should be hired under the prevailing labor market laws. And their pay, allowances and separation terms would be in accordance with these laws.

Source: ADB, Development Research Department, 2004

sensible, it must be acknowledged that it is a temporary 'solution' that would eventually be replaced by a more robust and sustainable arrangement that is integrated with the career system. To derive satisfactory results from the contract appointments, the procedures need to be transparent and competitive and there should be credible arrangements for monitoring and evaluation. This is not likely to be an easy task because the limited information available on the working of contracts for senior managers in the public services of the few SSA countries that have adopted the reform measure highlights the following main problems: inadequate transparency in the contracting process; ineffective monitoring and evaluation of the performance of the hired managers and technical professionals (fear of political manipulation) and weak enforcement of the contracts in some cases.[15] It might be useful to fix most contract terms longer than each country's political cycle with provisions for the removal of non-performers whenever adequate evidence is available. The merit of the contract

---

[15] Given the evidence that these contracting problems also exist, in varying degrees, in older states with stronger contract cultures, the learning curve for effective implementation of contracts could take many years in most SSA countries. It is noteworthy that some of these contracting problems were mentioned to a team of World Bank Public Sector Management Specialists who visited New Zealand in January/February 1997. New Zealand is widely acknowledged as the pioneer country that introduced contract appointments on a large scale at the senior levels of its public service, beginning in the late 1980s.

'solution' is that it would help ensure that the hired staff could be held responsible to deliver the results spelled out in their contracts. The results of a better performing civil service could produce additional resources that would enable government to progressively increase the pay levels of its career civil service staff. An interesting variation on the contract theme was the short-lived experiment of a team of national experts brought from outside to inject new life into the lethargic civil service of Kenya in July 1999 (see Box 4.13).

The third group of officials involved in the politics-administration nexus relationships consists of senior career civil servants. The failure of most SSA countries to fully re-introduce merit-based recruitment in

---

Box 4.13: The Kenyan 'Change Team' Experiment (July 1999–March 2001)

The 'Change Team' (also referred to as the 'Dream Team') comprised six top rate Kenyan professionals drawn from the parastatal and private sectors inside Kenya and from international organizations in July 1999. They were recruited through a 'search' procedure for a two-year stint on salaries and allowances equivalent to what they were earning at the time of their recruitment. The Government of Kenya also successfully arranged a re-entry guarantee for each member of the team. The team was specifically mandated to clean the civil service of its inefficiency and corruption and to develop and begin to implement an economic recovery program.

By August 2000, the 'Change Team' had succeeded in bringing about the resumption of development assistance to Kenya by the IMF, the World Bank and several other donors, notably the European Union and the UK DFID. This achievement was made possible by several improvements made by the Team in national economic management. By December 2000, the highlights of the Team's achievements included the production of an Interim Poverty Reduction Strategy Paper (I-PRSP); adoption and progressive implementation of transparent and competitive procurement reform measures; removal of poor performers from some key civil service and parastatal positions and their replacement with competent and honest professionals; strong support for the serious anticorruption measures of the Kenya Anti-Corruption Authority (KACA) that included the catching and prosecution of many corrupt public officials, including a few 'big fishes'.

However, the work of the 'Change Team' came to an abrupt end in March 2001 when its leader and two other members were removed. One other top rate Kenyan professional recruited to join the team in June 2000 to serve as the privatization 'czar' was also removed. Reports in newspapers in the immediate weeks after the dismantling of the Team suggest that some key persons in the incumbent regime had become uncomfortable with the overall thrust of the Team's work, especially in respect of anticorruption and privatization. KACA was declared illegal in December 2000 and the privatization effort lost steam. The obvious question to pose is whether the experiment was worthwhile since the sustainability of the Team's achievements was highly unlikely.

Note: On immediate reactions to the demise of the 'Change Team', see, for example, *Daily Nation* (Nairobi) for March, April, May and June 2001. The newspaper's archive can be found on the Internet: *http://www.nationaudio.com*

Source: ADB, Development Research Department, 2004

their civil services means that those who occupy the topmost positions in the career civil service are indistinguishable in many respects from the two groups of political appointees and chief administrative heads of ministries/ departments. Some Anglophone countries (e.g. Kenya and Uganda), are considering the creation of an elite corps of higher civil servants, similar to the Senior Executive Service (SES) that was first established in the USA in 1978 and has already spread to several OECD countries (e.g. Australia, New Zealand, and theUnited Kingdom).

In the francophone countries, a rather inappropriate imitation of French-style ministerial cabinets (*cabinets ministeriels*) is the major cause of the muddle between political appointees and senior career civil servants. Normally, members of ministerial cabinets are temporary political appointees who are to assist the members of the political executive through the combination of their technical expertise and un-conditional political loyalty. In a majority of the francophone countries, the political appointees are strong on the political loyalty criterion and weak on the technical competence criterion. In some of the countries, the problem is exacerbated by a confused arrangement in which the political appointees also constitute the leadership group of the state administration.

International experience shows clearly that the depth of political appointments in government ministries and departments is inversely related to public administration capability. It is important to stress that the ultimate objective of getting the political

leadership team and the appointed officials (both permanent and temporary) to work well together is to ensure that the policy process, which is at the heart of their interactions, is managed in a manner that assures the formulation of sound policies as well as their faithful implementation, resulting in the delivery of desired goods and services to the public. Persistent underdevelopment in SSA region shows that the majority of these countries are experiencing serious problems in respect of their policy processes. By the logic of democratic politics, prescribing educational qualification for elected politicians has to be strictly limited, for example, exclusion of persons who cannot read or write in a country's official language.

However, given the explosion in knowledge and the advance in technology (especially ICT), and the reality of globaliza-tion, there is a strong argument in favor of developing appropriate programs to raise the level of understanding of politicians in SSA countries (both in the executive and legislative branches). Failure to do this would result in a much wider ability gap between politicians and permanent officials, resulting in virtual domination of the policy process by the latter. One possible solution would be to expose political appointees and some political leaders to aspects of the managerial training and leadership development programs offered to top public managers and professionals. Programs that could be adapted and integrated into the education and training programs for top managers and professionals in public services in SSA is provided in Table 4.4.

Table 4.4: Executive Core Qualifications

Leading Change	Leading People	Results Driven	Business Acumen	Building Coalitions and Communications
Continual learning; Creativity and innovation; Strategic thinking; Vision	Conflict management; Cultural awareness; Integrity and honesty; Team building	Accountability; Customer service; Problem solving; Technical credibility	Financial management; Human resources management; Technology management	Influencing and negotiating; Interpersonal skills; Oral and written communication; Political savvy

Source: Adapted from OECD, 2001:97–99.

The Future for Africa's Public Sector Reforms

Essential lessons for the future can be extracted from Africa's difficult experiences with public sector reform. Under their adjustment programs, many African countries responded to the need for budget stringency, not by reducing the scope of their activities, but by reducing public service pay, especially at higher levels. This led to an exodus of the most skilled personnel from the public sector, and a consequent crisis of capacity within the civil service. Experience with public sector management reforms has also been uneven, with only 29 percent of completed interventions and 45 percent of ongoing ones rated as 'satisfactory' (Adamolekun, 2004).

African governments have also learned lessons in the aftermath of their countries' weak economic performances of the 1980s and the first half of the 1990s. Most have now embarked on a development path comprising a set of strategic choices that place poverty reduction at the center of the development process. These strategic choices, also championed by NEPAD, recognize the pivotal role of the private sector in economic growth, the importance of strong public institutions to facilitate and regulate private activities, and the importance of an outward orientation and open regionalism to enable countries to compete in the new global economy. Recent improvements in the policy environment and in economic performance provide some optimism.

To sustain and improve the current positive momentum, African countries still have to deepen their public sector reforms and capacity building with a view to developing a high quality public sector capable of formulating and implementing good policies and ensuring effective service delivery to citizens. They need to appreciate that reforms are matters of policy, and that policies are no more effective than the bureaucracies trying to implement them. Reform process could not proceed effectively without sustained and palpable political and administrative commitment, the enforcement of agreed proposals, and provision of adequate resources. Future efforts must aim at reforming and strengthening the politics-administration nexus in the conduct of government business.

In earlier phases of reforms, the focus was on the executive branch of the public sector which designs and implements policies and programs to fulfill the government's broad economic and social policies. Traditionally, public sector management is seen as a sector focused somewhat narrowly on the workings of core areas of government. Recently, however, the approach has gone beyond a compartmentalized approach to public service management. Emphasis must now be placed on the links between core public institutions, including not only the executive arm, but also the legislature and judiciary and sectoral institutions (World Bank, 2000a). Key institutions of accountability, including auditors general, public ombudsmen, the judiciary, the legislature and human rights commissions, must play an active role in the conduct of governance (Schacter, 2000).

African governments need to recognize that public institutions have to work together and support each other. Sometimes, some weaknesses affect all arms of government. Attempting to improve one institution when others need

equal attention is not likely to generate the desired results in the long run. Institutional externalities also need to be addressed by public sector reforms. For example, if the judiciary does not work well, other institutions are likely to suffer. A holistic approach that addresses problems in different institutions at the same time is necessary, because adopting a piece-meal approach will not yield the desired objectives. Public sector reforms should fulfill the state's objectives with the minimum degree of distortion of the market, with the lowest burden of taxation on taxpayers, with the smallest number of public employees, and with the lowest absorption of economic resources by the public sector (Tanzi, 1999).

In terms of civil service reforms, early efforts in many African countries focused on quantitative issues — wage and hiring freezes, down sizing, and retrenchments. They paid little attention to the more subtle and challenging issues of bureaucratic quality, and that the reforms faced severe political and administrative constraints. Even so, quantitative measures, such as retrenchments, should be targeted towards 'ghost' workers and non-performing staff. However, this requires mechanisms for objective assessment of employee performance. Reform efforts should be guided by a holistic vision, shared by all key stakeholders, as public service reforms require champions and political commitment from the highest levels of government and society.

The process of reforming the public enterprises sector is still ongoing, and progress has been made in many African countries, but the process of rationalizing the role of the state and adapting it to the requirements of a modern competitive economy remains incomplete. Many African economies are still dominated by their large public sectors. They should intensify the process of privatization of public enterprises and strengthening of regulatory frameworks with a view to creating a better environment for private sector participation and for attracting foreign direct investment. Governments need to define their objectives clearly and in ways that can be monitored transparently.

Fiscal management reform is an important policy instrument area that requires particular attention. To improve tax regimes, increased adherence must be made to the three principles of efficiency, fairness and 'administrability' of tax regimes. An efficient tax system must consider the impact of the tax structure on economic outcomes. It should maintain horizontal equity and vertical equity in the distribution of the tax burden and it should be easy to enforce. An important component of the fiscal reforms involves the introduction of strong checks and balances to minimize corruption and tax evasion. Tax compliance should, at the same time, be better motivated by improvements in the state's ability to deliver basic services in the areas of education, health care and infrastructure. The promotion of local and provincial governments should be instrumental in attaining these goals, as they can help monitor expenditures, generate taxes, spread information and assist with rolling investment plans in key areas of government expenditure programs.

Conclusion

One of the main lessons from the review of Africa's public sector reforms is that public sector management reform is a continuous process; it takes a long time to achieve fundamental reform of the public sector. African countries, like others in the developing world, are trying to achieve in the space of a few decades what took hundreds of years in the developed world. It is not therefore surprising that the record appears to be one of disappointments and failures. A key challenge for African countries in the years ahead is that they should view their reform experiences as learning opportunities, and stay focused and committed so that they can achieve the objective of building a high-quality public sector. Critical success factors in reform process include strong political support, well trained and profession administrators, clarity of vision and effective collaboration with all relevant stakeholders in the reform process.

Often, African countries have been accused of not being committed to the reform process, of lacking the 'political will' to implement reforms, and of succumbing to what has been referred to as a 'partial equilibrium' syndrome — i.e., they undertake initial reforms but, when strong resistance is encountered, the reforms are subsequently abandoned (Addison, 2001). Public sector management in Africa needs to adapt to the changing economic and political contexts. New approaches and orientation are required. There is a need to put in place mechanisms that will enhance and guarantee the quality of public services. Credible reforms that galvanize broad-based support should address critical problems affecting the lives of millions of Africans. Greater accountability should be promoted. Systems are required that can strengthen mechanisms for expenditure control, as well as the exposure of and sanctions against misspending and corruption. Professionalism and merit-ocracy should be established and promoted to ensure effective and efficient delivery of public services and to combat bureaucratic corruption.

Against a background of mixed results of past reform efforts, there is a need for the introduction of a broader and long-term approach relating it to the role of the state in the economy. There is also a need to link civil service reforms to such components as financial management, decentralization, and sector-wide approaches. A long term,

system-wide approach to civil service and public sector reform should be adopted. A selective introduction of New Public Management ideas and practices should be adapted.

To perform the state's role more effectively, African governments need to build a vibrant public service capable of understanding the challenges of develop-ment, analyzing development policy proposals and designing and implementing effective policies in a changing domestic and global environment. An efficient and effective public service requires not only cost containment and staff retrenchment but also incentives to attract and retain highly skilled administrative officials. When the incentive structures in the public civil service remain poor, its efficiency as well as ability to effect policies will remain very low.

CHAPTER 5

Public Accountability and Political and Economic Governance

Introduction

While governance is not a new topic in the area of economic development, it is an issue that has become pertinent for Africa in recent times for several reasons: (i) the development failure of the African continent in the 1980s; (ii) the rise of pro-democracy movements across the continent, advocating democracy and good governance; (iii) concern about widespread corruption in many African countries; (iv) the renewed calls for sound macroeconomic management to address some of the risks and challenges posed by globalization. Indeed, in an era of globalization, governments everywhere must necessarily play a critical role in promoting competitiveness, economic growth, and sustainable development. This role can best be served in the presence of good political and economic governance.

The promotion of good governance has been an important focus of development efforts for African governments and donor agencies since the early 1990s. The first and second generations of economic reforms emphasized structural adjustment and stabilization in order to reduce the role of government and expand the role of markets. Recently, however, emphasis has shifted towards the role of domestic institutions in achieving policy reform outcomes. The renewed focus on reforms in Africa was premised on lessons from the continent's widespread failure to attain rapid growth in spite of a decade or so of structural adjustment programs. Weak institutions, civil strife, and lack of accountability and transparency have contributed to the pervasiveness of weak governance in several countries. Together, they served to undermine economic growth and development.

This chapter discusses the nature and extent of political and economic governance in Africa, and it also examines the extent and pattern of corruption in Africa, its causes and possible strategies for curbing the phenomenon in different contexts, having a good understanding of corruption is pertinent in addressing a range of governance challenges in Africa.

Promoting Political Governance and Accountability

The NEPAD Approach

In recent years, African leaders have recognized that the process of achieving good economic and corporate governance in their countries is influenced largely by political considerations. Good political governance is a prerequisite for good economic and corporate governance. This is captured in the NEPAD framework document (see Box 5.1). The establishment of NEPAD's African Peer Review Mechanism (APRM) aims to encourage governments to provide policy certainty, effective law enforcement, and efficient delivery of public goods and services. The overall objective of the APRM is to ensure that the policies and practices of participating states conform to agreed NEPAD political, economic, and corporate governance values, codes, and standards. The results of the APRM assessments on governance and development issues will be published and used for mutual learning and cooperation amongst countries. It is hoped that the transparency of the APRM process will encourage compliance with good governance standards by all stakeholders in each country.

The interface between political and governance outcomes calls for a strong institutional framework to support good governance. For African institutions to function effectively, reforms must focus on the administrative and civil services, the strengthening of parliamentary oversight, the promotion of participatory decision-making, the adoption of effective measures to combat corruption and embezzlement and the undertaking of judicial reforms.

What is Accountability?

Accountability is generally defined as holding responsible elected or appointed individuals and organizations charged with a public mandate to account for specific actions, activities or decisions to the public from which they derive their authority. Accountability focuses on the ability to account for the allocation, use and control

---

Box 5.1: NEPAD's Political Governance Initiative

In the NEPAD framework document, African leaders pledged to promote good political governance in Africa. They affirmed this in the following paragraphs of the NEPAD document:

81) The states involved in NEPAD adopted a political governance initiative which consists of a number of elements as follows:
   • A series of commitments by partici-pating countries to create or consolidate basic governance processes and practices;
   • An undertaking by participating countries to take the lead in supporting initiatives that foster good governance.
   • The institutionalization of commitments through the leadership of the New

Partnership for Africa's Development to ensure that the core values of the initiative are abided by.

83) In order to strengthen political govern-ance and build capacity to meet these commitments, the leadership of the New Partnership for Africa's Development undertake a process of targeted capacity building initiatives. These institutional reforms will focus on:
   • Administrative and civil services;
   • Strengthening political oversight;
   • Promoting participatory decision-making;
   • Adopting effective measures to combat corruption and embezzlement;
   • Undertaking judicial reforms.

Source: NEPAD, Abuja, October 2001

of public spending and resources in accordance with legally accepted standards, that is budgeting, accounting, and auditing (ADB, 1999). Political accountability, in particular, refers to the constraints placed on the behavior of public officials by organizations and constituencies which have the power to apply sanctions to them. It limits the use of, and sanctions the abuse of power. Actors and institutions that promote political accountability attempt to bind the exercise of power to specific benchmark standards. As political accountability increases, the costs to public officials of taking decisions that benefit their private interests at the expense of the broader public interest also increase, thus working as a deterrent to corrupt practices.

Political accountability is best promoted through political institutions, both state and non-state institutions. Democracies, parliamentary systems, political plurality and freedom of the press are associated with greater accountability and lower corruption. Numerous reforms are needed in African countries to promote political accountability. These include the reform of political and legal structures of account-ability, such as: political competition; separation of powers/checks and balances (horizontal accountability); external oversight by civic groups and the media (vertical accountability); and ensuring integrity in the public sector through appropriate incentives and controls.

Electoral Pluralism and Competitive Politics

Sanctions on politicians can be enhanced most effectively through a meaningful degree of political competition in the electoral process. Such competition increases the likelihood that alternative candidates and parties will try to expose corruption in government or hold politicians accountable for poor perform-ance associated with high levels of corruption. Historically, anti-corruption and accountability measures were by-products of such political struggles (World Bank, 2002). Political competition is most effective in promoting political account-ability when it is channeled through organizations that provide broad constituencies with political parties and interest groups to express collective demands to political leaders.

Africa has made significant progress in achieving electoral plurality in the last decade. In the 1990s, and most notably following the end of the Cold War, the political environment in Africa began to change dramatically. The period was characterized by popular demand for democracy and the subsequent collapse of most military and autocratic regimes on the continent. After years of military rule, as well as one-party states and authoritarian regimes, there was a resurgence of democracy and popular participation in governance.

Africa's record in politics is documented in a study by the Economic Commission for Africa (ECA, 2002). According to that study, political regimes in Africa fall into 11 different types, of which five are noteworthy: (i) 'dominant party rule', which is practiced by 22 countries, covering a population of 325 million and accounting for 41.8 percent of Africa's population; (ii) the 'presidential-parliamentary' system, which applies to 12 countries with a population of 200 million, accounting for 25.7 percent of Africa's population; (iii) 'presidential-legislative democracy', relevant to six countries, covering a population of 81 million, and accounting for 10.5 percent of the population of Africa; (iv) 'military-backed dictatorship', in place in three countries with a population of 58 million, accounting for 7.5 percent of the population of Africa; (v) the 'civilian-military' system, applying to three countries with a population of 65 million, accounting for 8.4 percent of the population of Africa.

About 42 countries covered in the ECA study have held multiparty presidential or parliamentary elections since the early 1990s. A detailed analysis by Ali (2001) further confirms improvements in Africa's political environment. The study shows that for the period 1998–1999 about 68 percent of the population of Sub-Saharan Africa was living under 'partly free' conditions compared with the 1980s where about 88 percent of the population was living under 'not free' conditions.

Since the path-breaking national conference and multiparty elections in Benin (1989), most African states have undergone some form of competitive multiparty elections. Even though the results are at best mixed, there are political success stories that have widened the scope of good economic governance (Chege, 1999). These cases include Botswana, Ghana, Malawi, Mauritius, Nigeria, Senegal and South Africa. In other cases, competitive party politics has resulted in sharpening ethnic and regional cleavages, even inducing warfare between winners and losers when the gains are obviously confined to one ethnic group. In some cases, it is feared that the phenomenon of one-party rule might give way to one-party ethnic groups or cultural coalitions. This fear is instigated by the mismatch between the ethnic expression of voters and the failure of constitutional structures to cater for such ethnic expressions. There are, however, some cases where ethnic expressions were reflected in the construction of the constitution.

Overall, African countries have made significant progress towards democracy, but much remains to be done to improve citizens' influence and oversight over the conduct of the government, to elect responsive and responsible leadership and to promote social reciprocities. In many parts of Africa there needs to be greater adherence to the axioms of good politics including basic political order, political legitimacy and rule of law. There are still cases where democracy is superficially based on ethnic elections that do not reflect the judgment of the people on the performance of the government. There have been only limited achievements in turning electoral democracy into a tool for political liberalism and efficient economic governance. More needs to be done to improve the degree of political equality, inter-group tolerance, inclusiveness, and popular participation. There is still insufficient respect for human rights, especially in those countries experiencing instability and conflict (ADR, 2001).

Political pluralism is desirable, but excessive political competition can become a destabilizing factor if it leads to fragmentation of the political system.

Other measures needed to promote political accountability include public disclosure of votes in parliament, repeal of unconditional parliamentary immunity, public disclosure of sources and amounts of political party financing, and public disclosure of assets of senior public officials (and their key dependents). Regulations are needed against conflict of interest for officials, and protection of personal employment security for public officials who disclose abuse of public office by others, that is 'whistle blowers' (Thomas et al, 2000).

There is also a need to improve governance within political parties, with good ethical standards, training, discipline and financial management. Parties should professionalize their management. Africa's electoral systems also need to be more transparent. The distorting influence of money in politics has to be addressed through reform of political finance with limits on spending and contributions in order to improve transparency (Aringo, 2004). African leaders made certain commitments to democracy in the Lome Declaration of 2000 and should endeavor to adhere to these principles in the interest of good governance, peace and stability in Africa (see Box 5.2).

Box 5.2: The Lomé Declaration's Principles of Democracy

In their Lomé Declaration of 2000, African leaders spelt out the principles underlying their common concept of democracy by stating the following:

'We have agreed on the following principles as a basis for the articulation of common values and principles for democratic governance in our countries:

i. Adoption of a democratic constitution: its preparation, content and method of revision should be in conformity with generally acceptable standards of democracy;

ii. Respect for the constitution and adherence to the provisions of law and other legislative enactments adopted by Parliament;

iii. Separation of powers and independence of the judiciary:

iv. Promotion of political pluralism or any other form of participatory democracy and the role of the African civil society, including enhancing and ensuring gender balance in the political process;

v. The principle of democratic change and recognition of a role for the opposition;

vi. Organization of free and regular elections, in conformity with existing texts;

vii. Guarantee of freedom of expression and freedom of the press, including guaranteeing access to the media for all political stakeholders;

viii. Constitutional recognition of fundamental rights and freedoms in conformity with the Universal Declaration of Human Rights of 1948 and the African Charter on Human and Peoples' Rights of 1981;

ix. Guarantee and promotion of human rights.

Source: African Human Security Initiative, 2004

Checks and Balances

Along with political competition, the existence of checks and balances mechanisms across different branches of government, as well as external checks by civil society, can help promote political accountability. Accountability depends largely on the effectiveness of the sanctions and the capacity of accountability institutions to monitor the actions, decisions, and private interests of public officials. Accountability institutions can promote either vertical or horizontal accountability. Vertical accountability refers to the relationship between the people and their elected representatives in parliament. Institutions for achieving vertical accountability are the electoral channels (elections, political parties, the legislature, the mass media and civil society organizations). In several African countries, vertical accountability is often minimal as elected representatives who form the branch of government to which popular complaints should be addressed rarely relate with their constituents once the election is over. Constituents have little access to their representatives. Furthermore, parties for which they voted and which should be a vehicle for the people to express their desires and influence the government agenda do not function in favor of the citizens. In some African and other developing countries, opposition parties disappear soon after the elections and, within Parliament itself, parties behave as if they operate under a single party. With patronage flowing from the ruling party, members of opposition parties may 'cross the aisle' and join the ruling party. In some countries, even sitting members of opposition parties have 'defected' to the ruling party without a by-election (Aringo, 2004). With inadequate public funding, parties depend on a few wealthy individuals (in some cases, from illicit wealth), to finance their campaign activities, in return for patronage after elections. As a result, there is little room for vertical accountability in some African countries, despite multi party elections. There is a need for African countries to strengthen their democratic institutions to make them more accountable to the people.

In the absence or ineffectiveness of vertical accountability institutions, horizontal accountability mechanisms exist in most modern democracies (Gloppen, Rakner and Tostensen, 2003). These include: the constitution, which defines the rules of the political game; the legislative branch, which has an important role to play through its oversight functions; the judicial branch which is to ensure that power holders operate within the laws of the land and their mandates; and accountability agencies. In modern democracies, special institutions have been established to prevent the political leadership from abusing power. They include human rights commissions, ombudsmen/public protectors, auditors-general, electoral commissions, independent central banks, independent revenue agencies, and anticorruption agencies (see the example of Mauritius in this regard, Box 5.3).

Box 5.3: Accountability Mechanisms in Mauritius

Mauritius has a track record of governments being legitimately established through regular multi-party elections. The country has long enjoyed basic freedoms, individual rights, rule of law and regular competitive elections. Elections are organized in a transparent manner and are judged to be free and fair by winners and losers alike. Elections are managed by the Electoral Commission, under the direction of an Electoral Commissioner. The position of the Electoral Commissioner is recognized in the Constitution, and he/she is appointed by the Judicial and Legal Service Commission. The Commissioner is not subject to the authority of any person or institution. At independence, the Constitution provided for the position of Leader of Opposition. The President has to consult the Leader of Opposition on some matters, such as the appointment of members of the Public Service Commission.

Mauritius follows the principle of separation of powers between the legislature, the executive and the judiciary. Constitutional provisions relating to the Chief Justice, Senior Puisne Judge and other judges are 'entrenched'. The Chief Justice cannot be removed from office unless so recommended by the Judicial Committee.

The Constitution provides for the creation of a Director of Audit who is independent of the executive and is answerable only to Parliament. The Department of the Director of Audit scrutinizes the accounts of government, and the Director gives his report, more often critical of government than not, to Parliament. The report is laid in Parliament, and given wide publicity by the press.

Parliament has two avenues to force transparency and accountability. The first one is through 'Question Time', as practiced in the British Parliament, and the second is through the Public Accounts Committee. The Public Accounts Committee is set up by Parliament where the opposition party has the majority of members. The committee is empowered to call civil servants on all matters of public accounts, generally using the Director of Audit's report as a basis for such actions.

Source: Darga, 1998

Role of the Legislature

The separation of powers with the different branches of government (executive, legislative and judicial) disciplining each other in the citizen's favor is expected to promote accountability. This implies that the legislature performs oversight functions, while the judiciary guards the constitution and ensures that the actions of other branches of government comply with the constitution.

As long as it is not in the interest of one of the branches of government to collude with the other branches, separation of powers creates a mechanism to punish public officials who misbehave. Legislatures have three important roles: law making, oversight, and representation. These functions depend on the structure of the legislature (whether presidential, parliamentary or other wise) as well as a country's own historical, political and economic contexts. Enhancing the capacities of legislatures in African countries to perform these functions has been a component of development assistance in recent years. The legislature's oversight function involves monitoring the executive arm of government for efficiency, probity and fidelity. In many democracies, effective oversight has been difficult to exercise because it requires information about the executive arm, legislative capacity to process the information, the legislative's will to act, and the power to back up demands for improvements.

Oversight functions, however, tend to place the legislature in an adversarial relationship with the executive. The oversight powers of effective legislatures include the capacity to remove the executive (through votes of no confidence, impeachment, etc.), the power to extract information from the executive (compel testimony, for example at public hearings or committee meetings), the effective use of the power of the purse, and a functioning committee system capable of monitoring and assessing the executive branch's activities (Johnson and Nakamura, 1999).

Performing oversight functions tends to be easier in a presidential system than in a parliamentary setting, especially if competing parties control significant proportions of the legislature. In several African countries, while the apparatus of legislatures exist, the legislatures have been very weak in performing their oversight functions. Many of the legislatures in Africa in the 1990s were virtually powerless and insignificant, as the executive branch often takes decisions without involving the legislature. For example, in many countries, the legislatures had little say in the preparation of Poverty Reduction Strategy Papers (PRSPs), which seek to reflect the

results of broad consultation. Recently, however, legislatures in some African countries have started to assert their oversight powers, which often brought them into conflict with the executive arm of government.

In several African countries, legislators may only recommend and it is up to the executive to reject or accept such recommendations. Executive control of patronages and appointments to positions such as ministers, diplomats, and board members as well as control of resources and party machinery inhibit the exercise of parliamentary oversight functions in Africa. Weak parliamentary research and information services in many countries mean that legislators are not well informed about the activities of the executive branch. In addition, constituency pressure by citizens who are more interested in their representatives securing access to social services for their people, instead of engaging in struggles with the executive, is another constraint. In some countries, corruption among legislators has inhibited legislative effectiveness. In some countries, legislators are divided fractionally or along ethnic or religious lines and are generally pursuing local, ethnic and personal interests, rather than national interests.

The budget formulation process is usually dominated by the executive, with little meaningful debate of the budget by many legislatures. Budgets in some African countries tend to be unrealistic exercises in political rhetoric. Budgets are also often revised during the year in several countries in response to political demands or economic factors. Actual spending often depends on availability of cash rather than on some pre-set plan. Under these circumstances, it is difficult for parliaments to have the required information to monitor the executive effectively.

There is a need to develop the capacities of African legislatures so that they can become independent of the executive as spelt out in their constitutions; conduct oversight of the executive branch and successfully hold it accountable for poor performance. Parliamentary committees, especially finance and budget committees, offer scope for oversight functions. However, legislatures need to attain full autonomy from the executive and must exercise professionalism to actualize their constitutional mandates of representation, legislation and oversight functions (Aringo, 2004). Autonomy should be complemented by provision of infrastructure to support research, well-trained staff (research assistants), and modern technology (for example, computers and the Internet) to enhance their performance. Greater transparency on the part of legislators will increase their ability to discharge their mandate effectively. Measures such as codes of conduct, declaration of assets, transparent pay levels and allowances, conflict of interest guidelines, and building of alliances with civil society, will increase legislative accountability and effectiveness (ECA, 2002). Successful parliamentary oversight leads to better law making and political accountability. Recently, many African countries have received assistance for capacity building to strengthen their parliaments to perform their oversight role more effectively (see Box 5.4).

Role of the Judiciary

Over the years, several African countries have witnessed serious declines in key institutions such as the police, the judiciary, the prisons, and other security agencies. A well-functioning judicial system is crucial to the improvement of governance, the fight against corruption, and the consolidation of the democratic order thereby promoting sustainable development (World Bank, 2002a). Sound legal frameworks are critical for economic growth and social development. The judiciary is expected to provide a primary accountability mechanism through its review of government actions. As guardians of the public trust, judges should make decisions with independence and impartiality. An independent, impartial and informed judiciary has a central role to play in a just, open and accountable government. Effective judicial systems should be an important objective of government.

Some African countries are characterized by inadequate application and enforcement of laws. Powerful politicians, elite interests and other interest groups influence the operations of the judiciary and law enforcement institutions, including the police. All this makes it difficult for the ordinary citizen to have easy access to the judiciary. Thus the judicial systems in some African countries need to address the issue of inefficiency and external interference (see Box 5.5). While causes of inefficiency vary between countries, they include inadequate numbers of courts and judges; corruption in the police forces; poor working environment; corruption among

Box 5.4: Parliamentary Strengthening in Ghana

In late 1996, the Parliament of Ghana requested support for members of its Public Accounts Committee (PAC) and Finance Committee. It was thought that the elections of December 1996 would result in an effective opposition, and that new members of parliament (MPs) would benefit from understanding the 'what', 'why' and 'how' of financial management reforms.

Collaborating initially with Ghana's Institute of Economic Affairs, the World Bank Institute (WBI) and the Parliamentary Centre of Canada planned a series of workshops, whose objective was to provide practical advice to MPs on the budget process and relate it to the wider economic reform programs to modernize and streamline Ghana's public sector.

Although the WBI's program focused primarily on enhancing capacity at the organizational level, namely on building the capacity of the PAC and the Finance Committee, this necessarily involved working at the level of the individual MPs (by increasing their ability to understand governance and budgetary issues) and at the institutional level (by enhancing the interaction of Parliament with both the Executive and civil society).

Ghanaian MPs reported that the capacity enhancement enabled them to participate more effectively in parliamentary deliberations. At the organizational level, within the committees, partisan considerations began to play a lesser role. The Ghanaian economic committees were better able

to understand the basic insights on the budget process, the audit role of Parliament, and the ways the committees can exercise their powers. Also, each committee began to see itself as a unit, with members acting as part of a committee, rather than as party representatives. The committees also learned how to improve financial reporting transparency and detailed monitoring of expenditures to prevent abuse, and to increase cooperation between the PAC and the Serious Fraud Office. The PAC began to use field-based reviews of projects by sub-committees to provide assessments of government spending, thereby initiating a process partially compensating for late release of the Auditor General's reports. The Finance Committee also developed a detailed checklist of points for consideration in approving foreign loans.

In addition, MPs also began to appreciate the need to involve the civil society in committee processes (e.g. through public hearings and meetings in various parts of the country), and the usefulness of developing closer links with the Executive. Interactions with civil society have helped to ensure that individual MPs look at national development issues from a broader perspective. Linkages with the Auditor General's office were also strengthened, and the Auditor General established a parliamentary liaison office to foster greater interaction between his staff and PAC members.

Source: Stapenhurst, 2004

lawyers; political interference in the appointment of judges; and corruption among judges. In some countries, governments ignore court rulings that are not in their favor, while some executives/legislatures amend the constitution at will.

Judicial institutions need to be independent of the executive and legislatures as demanded by the constitution. An independent judiciary can make and issue judgments which are respected and enforced by the executive

Box 5.5: Indicators for Assessing the Judiciary

Questions to which answers should be sought when assessing a country's judicial system include the following:

- Do judges have the jurisdiction to review the lawfulness of government decisions? If so, are these powers used? Are decisions respected and complied with by government? Is there a perception that the Executive gets special treatment, be it hostile or preferential?
- Have judges adequate access to legal developments in comparable legal systems elsewhere?
- Are members of the legal profession making sufficient use of the courts to protect their clients and to promote just and honest government under the law? If not, is access to the courts as simple as it can be? Are legal requirements unnecessarily complicated?
- Are appointments to the senior Judiciary made independently of other arms of government? Are they seen as being influenced by political considerations?
- Are judges free to enter judgments against the government without risking retaliation, such as the loss of their posts, the loss of their benefits, transfer to obscure and unattractive parts of the country?
- Are cases brought to trial without unreasonable delay? If not, are the delays increasing or decreasing? Are judgments given reasonably quickly after court hearings? Are there delays in implementing/ executing orders of the court, e.g., issue of summons, service, grant of bail, listing for hearing? Are there delays in delivering judgments?
- Are court filing systems reliable?
- Are the public able to complain effectively about judicial misconduct (other than appeal through the court system)?

Source: TI, *An Independent Judicial System*, 2000

and legislative branches of government. However, judges themselves have to be accountable. They should operate within the rules and in accordance with their oaths of office. Holding judges accountable undoubtedly increases the integrity of the judicial process. Since corruption within the judiciary leads to distrust by the citizens and it damages judicial integrity, judges have to be persons of high personal integrity. Thus a code of conduct for judges can be useful in reducing judicial corruption and maintaining judicial integrity. Maintaining proper balance between judicial accountability, integrity and independence is critical if the judiciary is to be able to perform its role of holding governments accountable (see Box 5.6). To reduce judicial corruption, governments have to ensure adequate funding for the judicial system. Adequate pay and other incentives should be provided as well as guaranteeing personal security of judges. Funding and adequate remuneration are important for reducing corruption in the judiciary and other legal institutions (Islam, 2003). Terms of appointment and removal are also crucial, especially tenure of appointment. Furthermore, citizens should be able to challenge government actions through the court system.

In their Lomé Declaration, African leaders recognized the need for the separation of powers and independence of the judiciary and the need for judicial reforms. Judicial reforms are ongoing in several countries, sometimes as part of donor-assisted programs. These often encompasses modernizing the legal frameworks, establishing and strengthening

---

Box 5.6: Profile of an Independent Judge

Judges in Colombia were asked to indicate what the profile of a modern Colombian judge should look like. The following attributes of an independent judge were suggested:

- **Independence:** As supreme authority within the judicial process, judges should always be in a position to ensure the precedence of the public interest above the interests of the parties in conflict and their legal counsels, in accordance with due process principles; they should also be protected against the interference of other members of the judiciary, officials of the executive branch or any outside interest.
- **Autonomy:** This refers to the judge's ability to make decisions free from pressures from litigants, support staff, other judicial or state authorities, or political and economic interests, and relieved from fear of persecution or retaliation. Where there is such pressure, the judge should be in a position to neutralize any attempt to bias his or her decisions.
- **Stability:** Judges are entitled to minimal assurances about career development (subject to periodic evaluation and satisfactory performance), remuneration consistent with their responsibilities and special recognition for outstanding achievements.
- **Impartiality:** Judges should remain detached from personal or intellectual preferences that may bias their decisions during a judicial process.
- **Mission:** Judges have a mission to adjudicate conflict among members of the society on behalf of the state. In their private and public demeanor, they should embody the strictest ethical principles.
- **Learning:** Judges should be ready to cope with changes — in economic conditions and amendments of statutory laws by the legislative branch — through regular training programs that include not only legal subjects, but also topics in other sciences that may assist them in the exercise of a function that requires interdisciplinary tools and approaches.
- **Flexibility:** A judge should develop intellectual openness through regular interaction with various shades of opinions. Intellectual dogmatism is unacceptable in a judge since it closes the door to innovation and progress.
- **Teamwork:** The complexity of the modern world makes it impossible for a judge to accomplish the difficult task of administering justice without the active cooperation of other judges and support staff. A team contributes to the delivery of a justice service, with different inputs, all are important for the prompt resolution of conflicts.

Source: Adapted from Said and Varela, 2002

judicial sector institutions, restructuring ancillary institutions, improving legal education, and modernizing court administration practices. An important component of judicial reforms should be judicial training. In some African countries, judges are personally responsible for upgrading their own knowledge and skills with attendance at a few occasional seminars. Training, however, has to be systematic and continuous. African countries can borrow from other regions with more efficient legal systems. Some African countries are making efforts to promote the integrity of the judiciary (see Box 5.7).

Role of Civil Society Organizations

Civil society organizations (CSOs) can play an important role in promoting accountability and good governance. Such organizations include community-based societies, NGOs, labor unions, students and youth organizations, charitable organizations, religious organizations, professional associations and the media (African Human Security Initiative, 2004b). At both domestic and international levels, CSOs can spearhead the fight against corruption, as they can publicize information about the patterns and severity of corruption and can build coalitions against corruption and poor governance. They can also monitor government actions and attempt to promote or influence anti-corruption legislation and advocate for judicial reforms and freedom of information (World Bank, 2002). However, for civil society to be effective it requires an appropriate legal

Box 5.7: Strengthening Judicial Integrity in Nigeria

Worried by the rising incidence of corruption in the judiciary, the Chief Justice of Nigeria, in conjunction with the UN Center for International Crime Prevention and the Independent Corrupt Practices Commission (ICPC), initiated a project in 2001 to strengthen judicial integrity. Four key concerns were identified:

- The quality and timeliness of the trial process;
- Access to courts;
- Public confidence in the judiciary;
- Efficiency in dealing with public complaints.

The Nigerian Institute of Advanced Legal Studies was contracted to conduct a comprehensive assessment of judicial integrity and capacity in three states — Lagos, Delta, and Borno. During 2002–03, efforts were made to improve judicial integrity in the three pilot states through ICPC monitoring of judges and court staff, ethics training for judges and court staff, the creation of transparent complaints systems involving 'court user committees', and increased coordination within the criminal justice system.

These measures point to a determined effort by the National Judicial Council and the Chief Justice to strengthen Nigeria's justice system. Judges have stalled corruption trials in Nigeria by granting *ex parte* applications despite repeated warnings by the Chief Justice. Since 1999, however, several cases of corrupt practices involving judges have been resolved, and the National Judicial Council has forcibly retired more than 20 judges.

Source: TI, *Global Corruption Report*, 2004, Country Report on Nigeria

and regulatory framework, opportunity to mobilize funding, and access to information about government activities.

Empowering citizens entails their active participation in governance through the right to select their leaders in competitive elections and fair electoral systems. Additionally, governments must be close to the people through decentralization of government functions and devolution of power to local communities. Effective participation also requires that citizens be able to form their own associations and pressure groups to facilitate political activism. Good political governance needs a civil society that is able to articulate popular interests, facilitate participation in governance and monitor government performance. Citizens must be educated and endowed with the necessary civic knowledge in order to be able to effectively participate in the political process (ADR, 2001).

African Heads of State have long recognized the role of civil society as reflected in the 1980 Lagos Plan of Action. Provision for this is also made in the recent AU Convention on Preventing and Combating Corruption. There is a need to have the political will to implement these provisions in the Convention and other declarations by encouraging effective involvement of civil society organizations in policy making and monitoring. Civil societies on their part should be transparent and coordinated.

Particular attention should be given to raising the political status of women, who represent about half of the voters in Africa, through general awareness and civic education. Until recently, efforts to raise gender equality in the political process were mainly restricted to electoral participation. The introduction of multi-party politics has provided the opportunity to enhance women's civic knowledge and to increase their participation in governance. Current endeavors by national governments, the UNDP and NGOs concentrate on training women candidates who wish to run for elective positions in parliament or other governance bodies. Within its overall commitment to foster sustainable human development, the UNDP has a mandate to ensure a greater role for women as contributors to, and participants in, the development process.

The media also has a role to play in promoting good governance and combating corruption by exposing cases of corruption. This is impossible in a repressive environment where government has imposed strict censorship on the media. In Africa, the ability of the media is constrained by state ownership of media houses, conflicts of ownership interest, and weakened capacity within the media itself.

The involvement of stakeholders helps to build a sense of ownership for reforms and will generate sustainability. It is important for African governments to promote civil society and popular participation in governance activities. CSOs played critical roles in the economic and political lives of many pre-independent African countries. Many of them, mainly ethnic groups, were interested in advancing the interests of their members. They were used by the middle class to exert pressure on colonial administrators, and subsequently, gave birth to the independence struggle. In the last two decades, there has been a rebirth and proliferation of CSOs all over Africa. In countries such as Ghana, Senegal, South Africa and Uganda, civil societies currently operate freely. Other countries are beginning to tolerate them. In Kenya and Nigeria, CSOs in the past had to fight against repressive regimes (especially dictatorship and a military junta). In Botswana, popular participation is institutionalized, as constitutional amendments cannot be made by parliament alone (ECA, 2002).

A recent study of seven African countries revealed that African countries, where press freedom is guaranteed, showed features of tolerance, political and social inclusion, and elements of good governance. Countries such as Ghana, Senegal and South Africa, where CSOs operate relatively freely with limited government interference, are experiencing stability, democratic development and improvements in governance. African governments should encourage CSOs to be involved in the monitoring of government activities as a means of promoting good governance and combating corruption.

Promoting Economic Governance

The importance of economic good governance is widely recognized. Factors which promote good governance include transparency, accountability, an enabling environment for private sector growth, and effective institutions. Good economic governance promotes sound macro-economic policies and establishes an appropriate monitoring and regulatory framework for efficient coordination of economic activities. First, African countries that promote good economic governance can enhance their ability to implement development and poverty reduction policies with their scarce resources more effectively. Secondly, good economic governance creates a credible policy environment in which domestic and foreign investors have confidence. Thirdly, it can strengthen the absorptive capacity of states to attract and mobilize development assistance. Overall, it can help African countries to create a more stable, predictable macroeconomic environment and to enable them maximize the gains from globalization. Key components of economic governance reviewed here include fiscal policy management, regulatory capacity, and monetary and financial systems.

Fiscal Policy Management
Public Expenditure

Fiscal policy management, which comprises tax administration and expenditure management, is crucial to economic outcomes. The main focus here is on public expenditure management as most African countries have serious weaknesses in budget preparation and execution. Factors responsible for poor budget performance include: basing budgeted expenditures on optimistic projections of revenues that do not materialize; under-estimating the costs of some items in the budget; poor expenditure controls; and general lack of financial discipline (ECA, 2002). If African countries are to achieve good economic governance, they need to reform their public expenditure management systems and institutions, leading to management efficiency gains and accountability (see Box 5.8).

Some African countries in the past decade fell short of the standards of good public expenditure management. On average, government deficits in SSA countries have exceeded 4 percent of GDP. A good progress was, however, made in

2004 with the continent recording, for the first time in history, an average balanced fiscal outcome. African countries need to continue to maintain such budget discipline, ensure more equitable resource use, engage in revenue mobilization through tax reforms, and generally improve fiscal transparency. Several African countries have embarked on improving fiscal performance and introducing new tax regimes (see Chapter 4). In Tanzania, the government was able to achieve significant improvements in budget outcomes since

---

Box 5.8: Sound Public Expenditure Management Systems

The fundamental objectives of a sound Public Expenditure Management System include:
- Securing aggregate fiscal discipline, especially ensuring that budget deficits and aggregate expenditures are fairly close to the budget projections;
- Allocating resources to sectoral programs;
- Efficient use of resources in line with the expenditure program.

A sound Public Expenditure Management system will be characterized by satisfactory institutional arrangements and should comprise:
- A clear legislative basis for budgeting with rules that can be adhered to;
- A sustainable macroeconomic and budget framework;
- A comprehensive budget that excludes extra-budgetary activity;
- A powerful ministry of finance, or some ministry, to ensure budget discipline, including appropriate costing of expenditure items; formal constraints on budget deficits and expenditures;

- Adequate technical capacity and conscientiousness in responsible parliamentary committees, ministries and other government agencies;
- An effective accounting system that produces timely and quality fiscal reports;
- Functioning audit arrangements to ensure compliance with financial regulations and effective accountability by ministries and agencies;
- Mechanisms for handling uncertainty and shocks such as severe shortfalls or pressure for spending increases;
- Adequate civil service pay and benefits to attract and retained skilled staff (economists, accountants, budget analysts, etc.;
- Appropriate mechanisms to demonstrate full system transparency and accountability, particularly with respect to availability of budget information, participation in the budget preparation process by interested stakeholders, and open methods of execution and reporting to allow for independent assessments.

Source: ECA, 2002

the mid-1990s, by bringing aggregate expenditures in line with resource availability; reduce variance between appropriations and outcomes, and increase share of resources allocated to poverty reduction (ECA, 2002).

Debt Management

The accumulation of foreign indebtedness in many African countries is related, partly, to the structure of their economies and, partly, to the manner in which the borrowed funds were contracted and utilized. The production structure and pattern of trade in many African countries is such that these countries consistently import more than they export, and hence they borrow from abroad to bridge the gap. The persistence of this pattern led to accumulation of debt and debt repayment problems. Such an outcome indicates that the borrowed funds to bridge the external financing gap were either mismanaged or used to finance consumption, or invested in activities that did not alter the pattern of trade to generate sufficient foreign exchange earnings for debt repayment (Hussain, 2000). It is difficult to ascertain the magnitude of each of these contributory factors, but the result is evidenced in the heavy debt burden shouldered by African countries. The essence of good debt management practice is to ensure that borrowed funds are fully and efficiently utilized as well as the country has the capacity to repay.

For many African countries, the debt overhang places severe constraints on economic recovery and achievement of sustained growth. It further threatens to undermine the recent improvements in economic performance as the gains in income and output are absorbed by unsustainable debt service payments. Past empirical research has shown that a significant accumulation of external debt could stifle investment, slow down economic growth and induce macroeconomic instability through a series of complex price and disincentive effects.

Since the onset of the debt crisis, a number of international initiatives and debt relief mechanisms have been implemented to assist the indebted developing countries cope with external financial obligations. These include actions undertaken under the Baker Plan (1985), the Toronto Terms (October 1988), the Brady Plan (1989), the London Terms (December 1991), the Naples Terms (January 1995) and the Lyons Terms (1996). In 1996 the World Bank, IMF, the ADB and other multilateral creditors launched the Heavily Indebted Poor Countries (HIPC) initiative. More recently, at their Gleneagles, UK, summit (July 2005), the G8 Heads of State and Government agreed to provide 100 percent debt relief on the multilateral debt of countries that have reached their HIPC Completion Point.

Debt reduction is not an end in itself, but a means to prevent the recurrence of the debt problem. Thus, international efforts to reduce foreign debt must be accompanied by the promotion of internal debt management policies, which aim at optimizing the contribution of foreign borrowing to economic growth and avoiding the emergence of an indebtedness crisis. Proper debt management is important to prevent further deterioration and ensure that financial resources are used prudently. This necessitates making external borrowings consistent with a country's macroeconomic objectives.

Debt management cannot be seen in isolation from good fiscal and monetary policies and general macroeconomic management. Debt has strong linkages with other macroeconomic variables and interacts closely with aid, trade, net factor income from abroad and investment flows *inter alia*. Sound debt management means that a country must have coherent and integrated policies addressing all these areas (Maruping, 1993). Debt management functions must be linked to the government's development and economic management program, particularly to the budgetary process and the balance of payments. Effective debt management system involves many coordinated, interrelated and interdependent functions performed by a number of government agencies. While the organizational arrangements can vary greatly between countries, it needs to be co-ordinated by a central policy unit with authority on all debt matters, together with the involvement of top officials responsible for the financial management of the country (see Box 5.9).

The executive debt management functions need to be situated at the appropriate level of government. The representations should be, preferably, at the ministerial level. At the operational level, there should be an allocation of responsibilities and tasks among government agencies, with a clear definition of their relationships in the process. It would be most appropriate for an autonomous and separate debt office to co-ordinate a country's debt management functions, reporting to the ministry or government agency that has the statutory responsibility for the government domestic and external debts. To be effective, the debt management unit should possess the necessary administrative and political clout to decide on its budget and staffing needs.

The main functions of a debt management unit involve the regulation of activities of units of government involved in raising and administering external debt and monitoring sources of funds and approaching them with appropriate borrowing techniques. These techniques include capacity for skilful loan negotiation and operating schemes for withdrawing loan funds and paying debt service. The debt management unit must also create and co-ordinate statistical and analytical capacity on debt to underpin management decisions. The purpose of these activities is to assure smooth flow of relevant information to and among debt managers, and from them to decision-makers, creditors and the public. The debt management unit must have adequate staff resources, office space and equipment, and communications systems. Capacity building for debt management should thus be a priority for African countries.

Regulatory Capacity

An essential foundation for good economic and corporate governance is the regulatory capacity of the state. This refers to the ability of the state to establish and enforce rules that guide or regulate behavior of agents, such as ability to enforce the rule of

Box 5.9: Nigeria's Debt Management Office

The establishment of the Debt Management Office (DMO) is one of the steps taken to improve Nigeria's debt management capabilities. It commenced operations in October 2000. It was set up by the Federal Government to centralize and professionalize the management of Nigeria's public debt. Before then, the responsibility for managing debt was split between several agencies, including:

- The Federal Ministry of Finance (External Finance Department; the Multilateral Institutions Department/African and Bilateral Economic Relations Department, and the Home Finance Department);
- The Treasury Department of the Office of the Accountant General;
- The Central Bank (Debt Management Department, Debt Conversion Committee Secretariat and Public Debt Office).

This duplication of activities led to: inefficiencies and coordination problems; inadequate debt data recording system and poor information flows between agencies resulting in inaccurate and incomplete loan records; complicated and inefficient debt service arrangements which created protracted payment procedure; and lack of a coherent and well defined debt strategy.

The main objective of creating the DMO was to ensure proper coordination. The DMO centralizes and coordinates the country's debt recording and

management activities, including debt service forecasts, debt service payments and advising on debt negotiations as well as new borrowing. The DMO's specific functions include:

- Maintaining a comprehensive inventory of loans together with forecasts of debt service;
- Provision of timely and accurate information on the country's debt to assist policy makers and improve transparency in debt management;
- Effecting debt service payments accurately and on time;
- Managing the country's debt portfolio so as to minimize returns with an acceptable risk profile;
- Advising government on borrowing policy;
- Assisting in formulating and implementing the country's debt management strategy, ensuring appropriate linkages to fiscal and monetary policies as well as overall macroeconomic management;
- Negotiating with, and securing debt relief from the Paris Club and other creditors.

The Supervisory Board of the DMO is the National Council on Debt Management. The Office of the Vice-President, the Minister of Finance, and the Chief Economic Adviser to the President, provide oversight functions to the DMO. Direct responsibility for day-to-day running rests with the Director General.

Source: ADB, Development Research Department, 2004

law relating to contracts and property rights. African countries are faced with major challenges in their reorientation towards private sector-led growth and the development of private sector participation in the provision of services. To harness the

full potential of private sector initiatives, the state would need to address the challenges of establishing effective regulatory rules and ensuring their enforcement. The state also needs to create proper incentive regimes to encourage and sustain private sector participation. The regulatory functions of the state can be grouped into those pertaining to the participation of the private sector in the provision of services and those related to the functioning of the financial system.

Private Participation

Regulation is a difficult and costly business and, wherever possible, competition should be used instead. However, where necessary, the proper design of the regulatory rules and institutions is critical to the objective of increasing private participation in the provision of infrastructure and other services. The regulatory process consists of three closely interrelated components — setting the rules or standards; monitoring for compliance; and enforcement. The regulatory framework needs to be both simple and yet sophisticated enough to address the fundamental objective of regulation, which is mainly to correct for market failure. The regulatory framework typically includes rules governing entry, exit, scope of participation, and cost recovery. The framework should also provide performance criteria against which the operation of the franchise can be assessed. To be effective, it should be one that strikes the right balance between removing restrictions on private participation, on the one hand, and protecting consumers and safeguarding the country's socio-economic objectives, on the other.

The quality of regulatory rules is closely related to the state of political governance, as the latter provides the institutional framework within which regulatory agencies operate. A sound legal framework

requires enforcement to be credible. Without effective enforcement, the legal framework and government lose credibility. From the perspective of the private operators, failure to comply with the rules and regulations leads to wrong impressions and may damage a country's reputation. Both government and the private sector must have a mutual interest in the transparent and consistent application of enforcement procedures. In some countries, to avoid abuse due to over-concentration of power, efforts are made to separate the roles of adjudication and enforcement. Country differences, diversity of experience and the complexities of enforcement indicate the need for African countries to adopt a prudent, common-sense approach that best suits their situations.

New challenges emanating from globalization mean that African countries must be equipped with the information on global and regional conventions *vis-à-vis* national rules. African countries have to comply with laws or norms set at the global level to guide corporate governance while also participating in enacting these regulations. The approach used in formulating some of these international rules or norms poses a challenge. In many cases, rules are harmonized or standardized without Africa's participation. In cases when they are present, African countries are not adequately represented. African countries have to address these problems by becoming more active and getting involved in developing international regulations.

It is mainly for cost-recovery reasons that investors in an uncertain regulatory environment prefer the pricing system to be determined and authorized by regulatory statute. Price cap regulations provide incentives to reduce costs through efficiency gains and promote efficient use of resources. However, they have the drawback of increasing regulatory risk, with the possible capping of investment as a consequence, because of the pressure to keep profits within reasonable limits. But the limitations of price cap regulation can largely be overcome by a carefully designed system of regulatory review (ADR, 2001).

An important issue concerns the nature of the institutions responsible for implementing regulatory rules. The choice between multi-industry and single-industry regulatory institutions has been posed as an issue for African countries for several reasons. These include the absence of the required technical skills, the small size nature of the industry, and the cost of regulation.

The single-industry approach to regulation provides for specialist experience and expertise in issues of investment, tariffs rates, licensing abuses, performance standards, and customer services on a daily basis. Where the primary function of the regulatory institution in Africa is to address issues of income distribution, empowerment, quality of service and cost recovery, the need for consistency and universality in regulatory approaches and decisions is paramount. Moreover, the regulatory decisions from a single source provide investors with a better reading on the government's position on issues of concern (ADR, 2001).

Economic reforms being implemented by several African countries have included efforts to improve the regulatory environment. Trends in the annual Index of Economic Freedom produced by the Heritage Foundation and *Wall Street Journal* suggest that the regulatory environment in many African countries is improving (see Box 5.10).

Monetary and Financial Systems

An important aspect of good economic governance relates to transparency of monetary and financial policies. This requires central banks and financial agencies to be accountable, especially if they are given a high degree of autonomy. Transparency in mandates, and clear rules and procedures in the operation of agencies strengthen governance and facilitate policy consistency (ECA, 2002). Transparency by financial agencies, especially in clarifying objectives, contributes to policy effectiveness by reducing uncertainties in decision-making by financial markets participants. Furthermore, by enabling financial market participants and the general public to understand and evaluate financial and monetary policies, transparency is conducive to policy making. A positive attitude towards transparency and accountability of central banks and financial agencies is evolving in many African countries as part of global trends of economic and financial reforms.

In recent years, the global trend has been to give central banks a stronger role in the design and implementation of monetary policy measures to promote economic growth. In major industrialized

Box 5.10: Economic Freedom and Growth.

The Index of Economic Freedom measures how well countries score on a list of 50 independent variables divided into ten broad factors of economic freedom. They are: trade policy; fiscal burden of government; government intervention in the economy; monetary policy; capital flows and foreign investment; banking and finance; wages and prices; property rights; regulation; and informal market activity. Analyses show that countries with the highest levels of economic freedom also have the highest living standards. In order to grow, countries need to implement policies that attract investors and encourage entrepreneurs.

The 2004 index shows that North African countries made little improvement over the preceding year. In Sub-Saharan Africa, 21 countries' economic freedom scores improved over the figures for 2003, while scores for 15 countries declined. Government intervention showed the greatest net improvement. Five countries in SSA are among the world's ten 'most improved'

economies — Rwanda, Ethiopia, Cape Verde, Senegal and Mauritius.

Rwanda showed improved trade policy, government intervention, monetary policy, and regulation scores. Ethiopia enhanced its score in trade policy, capital flows and foreign investment, fiscal burden of government, and government intervention.

Three SSA countries are among the 11 which have made the greatest improvement since the Index was first published in 1995: Rwanda (1.24), Mozambique (1.11) and Mauritania (0.99). Rwanda was first included in 1997. Among the 11 countries which showed the greatest declines since the Index was first published are: Nigeria (0.53), Zimbabwe (0.45), and Zambia (0.33).

The categorization of countries is based on the following cut-off scores: 0–1.99 (free); 2–2.99 (mostly free); 3-3.99 (mostly unfree), and 4+ (repressed).

Source: Heritage Foundation, 2004, *Index of Economic Freedom*

countries, it is generally acknowledged that central bank policies have significantly contributed to the achievement of low rates of inflation and a long period of sustained growth. To pursue their key objective of price stability, many industrialized countries have granted their central banks autonomy from political decision-making processes. This has been justified on the grounds that an independent central bank will be less susceptible to short-term political pressure, and hence, better able to implement long-term policies to promote price stability.

In the SSA region, however, emphasis in the post-independence years was on promoting the real sectors of the economy. Up to the mid 1980s, most African countries supported development through selective allocation of credit. Government was directly involved in the operations of the financial sector through the establishment of commercial and development banks. Bank funds were used to finance budget deficits and to provide liquidity to government owned enterprises. All these weakened the ability of central banks to pursue standard monetary policy objectives such as price stability. By the mid-1980s, the financial systems of most African countries were showing signs of weakness and vulnerability. In the face of rising fiscal deficits, governments resorted to borrowing from their central banks, contributing to high rates of inflation. Abuse of preferential lending, over-valued exchange rates and general lack of financial discipline led to distortions in the financial sector, which culminated in financial distress in the banking systems in several African countries. Reforms in the financial sector became imperative.

Central banks in Africa are state-owned and have a powerful role in economic policy-making. They help to determine the structure of interest rates and, through their intervention, they also influence the volume and allocation of credit. In addition, they supervise the banks for economic prudence. In spite of the powers entrusted by legislation establishing central banks in African countries, it has proved difficult in many countries to carry out their regulatory duties adequately. Inadequate personnel, both in terms of quantity and quality, can limit the ability to supervise the banking system. In some cases the actual enforcement of regulations is lax for political and other reasons. Politics sometimes enters into the licensing process itself through the rent-seeking activities of politicians and bureaucrats. In some countries, licenses have been granted by political entities that were not subsequently responsible for the supervision of the institutions after the licenses were issued. In other countries, government interference in banking operations in favor of

public sector enterprises, or state-supported projects, has made it difficult for the central bank to conduct strict banking supervision and monetary control (ADR, 2001).

Central bank independence means, first, that it has broad latitude to decide what to do in pursuit of its basic goals of macroeconomic stability and employment creation. Secondly, it means that once the monetary policy decisions are made, no governmental organ can reverse them, except under circumstances stipulated by the legislature. A third condition for central bank autonomy is to have independence of personnel. This includes the selection and appointment of board members with a high professional competence and without an obligation to yield to political and other pressures. Finally, it must have instrumental independence, which means control over the instruments that affect the inflation process, including, in particular, the prevention of any direct financing of government deficits.

Empirical studies have established that there is strong correlation between central bank independence and low inflation rates. They have also found that countries with independent central banks tend to have smaller budget deficits than those with government-controlled central banks (ADR, 2001). A crucial aspect of financial sector reforms was that governments should grant central banks greater autonomy to conduct monetary policy. Governments were to withdraw from active participation in and control of financial sector operations, while central banks were to play a greater role in supervision and regulation of the financial sector. To do this effectively, financial sector reforms included measures to strengthen central banks' regulatory and supervisory functions (AFRACA, 1999).

Central banks in Africa should encourage and facilitate the establishment of other financial institutions, especially those providing long-term loan finance for development. The financial sector is an integral component of private sector development and the development of the financial sector should be among the first priorities of a development strategy. Where no functioning financial system exists, it will be difficult to promote a strong private sector. Financial sector reforms already undertaken in many African countries constitute the first steps towards making the financial systems responsive to the needs of the private sector. There is, however, a need to deepen these reforms particularly in the areas of addressing the problems of distressed banks, supporting micro-finance, and developing non-bank financial instruments (ADR, 2001).

Considerable progress has been made in strengthening banking supervision functions. However, one of the remaining problems for most central banks in Africa is lack of autonomy in the conduct of monetary policy. Only a few countries are considered to have central banks with considerable autonomy; these include South Africa, Kenya and Botswana (AFRACA, 1999). In recognition of the many benefits of independent central banking, several African countries have introduced legislation that grants statutory autonomy to the central banks in the

management of monetary policies and other related activities. Although not all countries have granted full autonomy to their central banks, many have adopted or are adopting prudential regulations that are basically in line with the Basle Committee's Core Principles (AFRACA, 1999).

Corruption — Symptom and Outcome of Poor Governance?

Definitions

Corruption is sometimes categorized into 'high-level', 'grand', or 'political' corruption, and 'petty', 'administrative', or 'bureaucratic' corruption. Grand corruption describes corrupt acts that involve senior government officials, senior judges, legislators, cabinet ministers, the police, the military, and even heads of governments and states (Moody-Stuart, 1997, Tanzi, 1998). Corrupt behavior taking place during the budget preparation phase, when political decisions are made, reflects political corruption (Tanzi, 1998; Collier, 1999). Grand corruption is also associated with international business transactions and usually involves politicians as well as bureaucrats. Transparency International describes political corruption as the abuse of entrusted power by political leaders for private gain, with the objective of increasing power or wealth. It need not involve money changing hands; it may take the form of 'trading in influence' or granting of favors that poison politics and threaten democracy. It involves a wide range of crimes and illicit acts committed by political leaders, before, during, and after leaving office (TI, 2004).

By contrast, petty or administrative or bureaucratic corruption involves individuals and lower-level officials such as agency bureaucrats, immigration officials, customs clerks, and policemen. Corruption during the execution phase reflects mainly bureaucratic corruption. Incentives for political and bureaucratic corruption differ. Petty corruption may be pervasive throughout the public sector if firms and individuals regularly experience it when they seek a service from the government (Collier, 1999). Bribes may be retained by one person or pooled in an elaborate sharing arrangement (World Bank, 1997a). Political corruption levels soar very high when the state becomes so involved in economic management 'that in the absence of adequate alternatives, the state apparatus becomes the main vehicle of economic advancement and capital accumulation for those in power' (Theobald, 1990). From the viewpoint of Transparency International, political corruption is distinct from bureaucratic corruption in so far as it is perpetrated by political leaders or elected officials who have been vested with public authority and who bear responsibility of representing the public interest (TI, 2004). Corruption is said to be isolated when non-corrupt behavior is the norm. It is systemic (pervasive or entrenched) when bribery, on a large or small scale, is the routine way of dealing with the public (World Bank, 1997a). In any case, corruption undermines development, as it weakens the ability of government to carry out its functions effectively.

Patterns of corruption in Africa

Corruption is commonplace. It occurs in poor and rich countries alike, regardless of the level of social and economic development. It also occurs in countries with diverse forms of government, ranging from dictatorships to established democracies. However, a defining distinction between countries can be made when corruption becomes the rule rather than the exception, that is, whether it is isolated or systemic corruption (see Table 5.1). Corruption is isolated when it is rare, and therefore easy to locate. In such a case, non-corrupt behavior is the norm. Corruption is systemic when it is widespread and institutionalized, and bribery on a large or small scale is the routine when dealing with public officials. It is noteworthy that the corrosive effects of corruption are much more problematic for developing countries, as it comes at a high cost for those that are poor (Rose-Ackerman, 1998).

Corruption in Africa has many faces. It comes through a number of channels. Administrative corruption comes in the form of arbitrary application and implementation of existing rules, laws and regulations for illicit private gain by a public office holder. Public procurement corruption occurs when bribes are paid to secure contracts. There is also issue of 'state capture', which refers to the actions of economic agents or firms in both the public and private sectors to influence the formulation of laws, regulations, decrees, and other government policies to their own advantage, as a result of illegal payments (Thomas et al, 2000).

Table 5.1: A Simplified Typology of Corruption

Type	Main actors	Mode
Incidental	Petty officials, interested officials, opportunistic individuals	Small-scale embezzlement and misappropriation; bribes, favoritism and discrimination.
Systematic	Public officials; politicians; representatives of donor and recipient countries; bureaucratic elites; businessmen and middlemen	Bribery and kickbacks; collusion to defraud the public; large-scale embezzlement and misappropriation through public tender and disposal of public property; economic privileges accorded to special interests; large political donations and bribes.
Systemic	Bureaucratic elites; politicians and businessmen; white-collar workers.	Large-scale embezzlement through 'ghost workers' on government payroll; embezzling government funds through false procurement – payment for non-existent goods; large-scale disbursement of public property to special and privileged interests under the pretext of 'national interest'; favoritism and discrimination exercised in favor of ruling parties in exchange for political contributions.

Source: Kpundeh, 1997

In Africa, lack of accountability and corruption have become pervasive in many public services. Outright bribery, patronage, embezzlement, influence peddling, use of one's position for self-enrichment, bestowing favors on relatives and friends (nepotism), moonlighting, partiality, absenteeism, late-coming to work, abuse/theft of public property, leaking of government information, are all manifestations of corruption in many Africa's public services (Rasheed, 1995). In some African countries, bribes are paid to obtain services or shorten processing time, or to secure contracts. Corruption can occur at all levels, from major pay-offs at the top of the system, to petty bribes to local officials for the delivery of services and evasion of regulations.

A widespread form of bureaucratic corruption in Africa is appointment and promotion on the basis of connections, as opposed to merit. This creates inefficiencies and undermines professionalism in the public service. Bureaucratic corruption over time becomes self-reinforcing and corrupt practices become institutionalized. Many people benefit from bureaucratic corruption, and people may choose to enter the public service despite low salaries because it offers opportunities for rent seeking.

In some countries, much of the corruption in society occurs at the nexus between the public and private sectors, with actors in the private sector interacting with holders of trust in the public sector. Corruption in this regard manifests itself when private sector officials bribe government officials to make decisions that are favorable to their interests. Another aspect is fraudulent misappropriation of assets or funds. Depending on the circumstances, this phenomenon can occur entirely within the private or public sectors.

In some countries, corruption has become so pervasive that it is difficult to demand routine services from officials, especially in the public sector, without paying a bribe. Similarly procurement corruption is very common, whereby companies bribe officials in order to be favored during contract awards. In such countries, it has greatly distorted government actions and undermined the effectiveness of public interventions. In these countries, corruption has grown into a major problem that hampers development efforts. In other societies, corruption is not pervasive enough to affect resource allocation decisions in any significant manner, even if graft amongst government officials is quite high.

A measure of the extent to which corruption is prevalent in African countries can be obtained from the Corruption Index of Transparency International (CITI). The CITI measures the perception of corruption as seen by business people, risk analysts and the general public. The CITI ranges from ten (highly clean) to zero (highly corrupt). For 2004, the 36 African countries covered by the CITI scored an average of 2.93, indicating widespread corruption in

African countries. For individual countries in Africa, only two countries (Botswana and Tunisia) passed the half-way mark on the road towards a highly corruption-free environment. Botswana, with the best score among African countries (6 points), ranks 31st among the 146 countries covered. Botswana's score is only marginally comparable to one European country — Portugal with a score of 6.3 points.

While a few countries have improved their ratings, some have become worse during that period. In 2000, average score for the 22 African countries included in the CPI was 3.4, but the average score declined to 2.93 in 2004, indicating that corruption levels have worsened in Africa. This is in spite of the fact that many African countries have taken some initiatives to combat corruption. More committed efforts and greater political will are needed to address the problem of corruption in Africa.

The sectors most prone to corruption in African economies include: public works contracts and construction; arms and defense, power, including petroleum and energy; industry, healthcare and education, customs. Corruption is also highly prevalent in Africa's police forces, tax administration, customs, immigration, etc., in different order of prevalence.. Corruption is also rampant in the customs department of several countries.

Studies in some African countries showed that customs fraud took the forms of under-declaration of the value of the goods, misclassification and underpayment of taxes due, resulting in loss of revenue (Doig and Riley, 1997).

In some African countries, corruption is also widespread in the legal system. Access to courts depends on the power of the purse. The poor are left to languish in jail 'awaiting trial' while the rich are granted bail for criminal offences.

An important dimension of corruption in Africa is political corruption, which is essentially linked to access to, and control of, power and the way in which such power is exercised. Thriving areas for political corruption include award of government contracts, use of political positions to leverage kickbacks or illicit payments and appointments to high offices, use of public resources to fund election campaigns, and donations to political parties in the expectations of undeserved benefits. Political corruption has also involved looting of state funds, which are often siphoned out of the country into foreign accounts. Vote buying and other fraudulent acts characterize the electioneering and voting processes in several African countries. Electoral corruption erodes one of the fundamental pillars of good governance — ethical leadership. As long as politicians are allowed to bribe their way to victory, leaders will be elected for no other reason than the quantity of gifts or cash they can give to the voters. Once elected, they would want to recoup their electoral expenses from the state's treasury, and so the vicious cycle of corruption perpetuates itself. Over time, widespread political corruption erodes confidence in the institutions of government.

Causes of Corruption

Causes of corruption are many and are contextual, they tend to be rooted in a country's policies, bureaucratic traditions, political development and social history. Available research suggests that corruption is a symptom of weak institutions. According to the World Bank (1997a), the opportunity for corruption is a function of the size of the rents under a public official's control, the discretion the official has in allocating those rents, and the accountability that official faces for his/her decision. A workshop on governance and corruption in Africa emphasized that corruption is a symptom of 'sick' institutions (USAID/IRIS, 1996). Sick institutions can be defined as those where:

- a substantial number of employees do not come to work or do other work or nothing at all while there;
- corruption and favoritism are not isolated instances but the norm;
- pay scales in real terms have collapsed and low and middle level employees cannot feed and their families on official pay;
- employees seek other forms of compensation, including travel, study allowances, non-wage benefits (which have imploded in many African countries in recent years), as well as illicit payments for doing their official duties.

Many of Africa's public institutions are characterized by these features. Factors identified as encouraging corruption in African public administrations include over-centralization of power, lack of freedom by the media to expose scandals, the impunity of well-connected officials, absence of transparency in public fund management, clientelism, and low salaries. In authoritarian regimes, control systems and counter powers are precarious because there is no culture allowing the use of expertise or freedom of expression (Cartier-Bresson, 1999). Political rights, which include democratic elections, a legislature and opposition parties, and civil liberties, which include rights to free and independent media and freedom of assembly and speech, are negatively correlated with corruption. Available evidence suggests that these are yet to be entrenched in African countries. In addition, many newspapers, radio and television media remain state-owned (see Box 5.11).

The share of national wealth derived from a single natural resource, especially mineral resources such as petroleum, gold, and diamonds is also correlated with high levels of corruption. In Africa, as stated

---

Box. 5.11: Access to Information in West Africa

Constitutions guarantee the right to information and freedom of expression in almost every country in West Africa, even the less open ones, but not a single country has passed legislation to put freedom of information into practice. Ghana and Nigeria have drafted the freedom of information laws, but progress has been slow. Nigeria's bill is pending before the Federal House of Representatives, and Ghana's bill, developed by the civil society organizations, is being redrafted by the attorney general's office.

The legislative constraints on access to information — particularly information on grand corruption — are exacerbated in many West African countries by laws that prohibit insulting the head of state or other senior members of government. In July 2001, however, the Ghanaian Parliament repealed the criminal libel and section under which many journalists had previously been jailed. The NGO Article 19 declared that 'the repeal of criminal libel law puts Ghana at the forefront of African countries when it come to meeting the international standards on free expression'.

In a report released in July 2002, Article 19 condemned the 'culture of secrecy' in Burkina Faso. The report argued that civil society and the media are routinely denied access to official information and called for a freedom of information access legislation conforming to international norms.

In Guinea, where the government has a monopoly on the broadcast media and owns the only daily newspaper, criticism is limited to a small number of weeklies, all subject to restrictive laws. In Guinea-Bissau, two journalists from thee newspaper Diario were arrested in June 2001 for articles alleging corruption in the government.

There is little independent journalism in Togo and the opposition press is frequently subjected to intimidation. A 2001 report by the Committee to Protect Journalists found that 'reporting on Togo's rampant official corruption landed several journalists in jail and resulted in more newspaper seizures.

Source: TI, 2003, *Global Corruption Report*

earlier, perceived corruption levels are high in petroleum-rich economies. Corrupt trade partners who are willing to offer bribes to win contracts, mining and other concessions, have also contributed to corruption.

Excessive government regulations as a result of over-centralization of activities also encourage corruption. Public officials have considerable discretion in accumulating wealth through exploiting their monopolistic, low and irregularly paid positions, often in collusion with politicians and indigenous or foreign businessmen. Corruption is widespread where there is considerable discretion for public officials, limited accountability and little trans-

parency in government operations (see Box 5.12).

Corruption thrives in emerging and transitional economies where the political system is immature. The complexity, overregulation, and lack of predictability serve as incubators for corruption in emerging economies. Too many controls and too much political and administrative discretion encourage the creation of rent-seeking 'colonies', as do inappropriate pricing policies, which encourage the development of parallel markets. In general, the government imposes regulations, levies taxes and enforces criminal laws, but when the underlying legal

---

Box 5.12: Determinants of Corruption

1. **Wage incentives**
   a) inadequate pay
   b) fringe benefits and other financial incentives

2. **Inefficient internal control**
   b) inadequate supervision and control systems
   c) lack of explicit standard of performance for employees and organizations
   d) poor recruitment and selection procedures for personnel
   d) too few or too many (non-transparent) rules and procedures (red tape).

3. **Insufficient external control**
   e) lack of information to the public and freedom of the press
   f) mechanisms for citizens' participation and complaint
   g) difficulty of proving cases in court
   d) high social acceptance of corruption

4. **Statutory penalty rate**
   h) amount of fine, prison sentence
   i) administrative sanctions
   j) prohibition of being ever re-employed in the public sector
   d) penalties for relatives

5. **Amount of distortions**
   k) pervasive government regulations
   l) High statutory tax rates, non-transparent tax regulations
   c) Provision of government services short of demand (government monopolies) .

6. **Other factors**
   m) cultural factors
   n) culture of bureaucratic elitism and education of civil servants
   o) leadership
   p) ethnic diversity

Source: Salisu, 2003

framework is inefficient, and individuals and firms are emboldened to pay for relief from these costs. For example, individuals and firms may collude with tax authorities to perpetuate fraud and reduce their taxation by bribing tax collectors.

Reducing excessive economic control will not eliminate corruption, as there are other opportunities, especially in government procurement. Ironically, the transition from a controlled to a liberalized economy has increased opportunities for corruption. As economies liberalize, the liberalization process itself, at least in the initial phase, provides new areas for corruption to flourish. A case in point, here, is the process of privatization — where the selling of government assets provided opportunities for government officials to receive bribes from potential buyers. This phenomenon of rising corruption during liberalization is closely related to the lack of transparency in the liberalization process.

Low salaries of public sector officials in many African countries also encourage corruption.. In Madagascar, perceived levels of petty corruption declined between 1995 and 2001 as real wages increased. Experience of petty corruption declined by 42 percent, while real wages increased by 50 percent. Over the last three decades the real incomes for many public service employees have declined significantly (see Chapter 4). Low pay forces highly skilled people to depart to the private sector or emigrate to developed countries, leaving behind weak institutions and administrative systems. Those that stay behind may be tempted to engage in corrupt practices to supplement their incomes. In some cases,

government employees actually believe that corruption is the only rational behavior available to earn enough income to satisfy the needs of their families. In some cases civil servants continue to go to 'work' whereas they claim that their salaries are not enough to cover their transport cost to the office (Hussain, 1992).

International factors which encourage political corruption include bribery by foreign business concerns, the negative sovereignty factor (non-interference in affairs of states) which was the prevailing attitude during the Cold War era, and asylum granting to ousted corrupt leaders by other countries (Collier, 1999). Widespread bribery of foreign businesses offering bribes to receive contracts or other commercial favors in host states is a major factor in grand corruption.

Cultural factors also play an important role in promoting corruption in Africa. Corruption levels are higher where the interests of the family and clan predominate. The survival of the extended family in Africa, whereby 'successful' family members are expected to bear the costs of several expenditures in the family — marriages, burials, school fees, health, etc., — which are often several multiples of theofficial salaries of public officers, also encourage corruption. Other factors are the lack or enforcement of codes of conduct for public officers, lack of punishment for corruption offenders, and poor working conditions in addition to low salaries in the public sector.

Consequences and Costs of Corruption

Corruption has been identified as one of the major obstacles to economic and social development. It undermines development by distorting the rule of law, the allocation and efficient use of scarce resources and weakening the institutional foundation on which economic growth depends (World Bank, 2000a). Corruption saps the resources available for development, distorts access to social services, and undermines public confidence in government. The harmful effects of corruption are very severe on the poor who are most reliant on public services, and are least capable of paying the extra costs associated with bribery, fraud and the misappropriation of economic privileges. Thus corruption impairs growth with serious consequences for poverty reduction.

Corruption retards growth by discouraging domestic and foreign investment, which depend on the quality of the business environment in a country. Corruption increases the uncertainty of doing business because it erodes the rule of law and is associated with high levels of bureaucratic red tape. Some regard corruption as a tax, which adds to the cost of doing business (World Bank, 2002). Corruption also biases infrastructure investment against projects that aid the poor and impairs the use of small-scale entrepreneurial means to escape poverty (see Table 5.2). Corrupt regimes also tend to prefer defense contracts to rural health clinics and schools (Thomas et al, 2000).

Table 5.2: A Synthesis Matrix: Corruption and Poverty

'Immediate' causes of poverty	How corruption affects immediate causes of poverty
Lower investment and growth	• Unsound economic/institutional policies due to vested interests • Distorted allocation of public expenditures/investments • Elite corporate interests capture laws and distort policymaking • Absence of rule of law and property rights • Governance obstacles to private sector development
Poor have smaller share in growth	• State capture by elite of government policies and resource allocation • Regressiveness of bribery 'tax' on small firms and the poor • Regressiveness in public expenditures and investments • Unequal income distribution
Impaired access to public services	• Bribery imposes regressive "tax" and impairs access and quality of basic services for health, education and justice • Political capture by elites of access to particular services
Lack of health and education	• Low human capital accumulation • Lower quality of education and health care

Source: Thomas et al, 2000

Similarly, corrupt procurement leads to contracts being awarded to high-cost bidders without competitive tendering. It decreases state funds since it leads to inflated spending on projects, sometimes of inferior quality. The intention of the state to provide all citizens access to education, health and the legal system will be thwarted if bribery determines the allocation of these resources and services. For instance, in a corrupt regime, public officials may shun health programs because there is less opportunity for rent seeking (Thomas et al, 2000). As a result, the negative impact of corruption falls mostly on the poor since it increases the prices for public services and lowers quality. The poor also suffer when officials embezzle state funds, which are meant to provide social services. The burden of corruption on the poor is worsened by the fact that the poor are more dependent on public services and are the least capable of paying the extra costs associated with corruption than the rich who can afford private services. They are therefore more vulnerable to the demands for 'grease money'.

Widespread corruption reinforces existing economic and social inequalities, and it undermines the credibility of government and public institutions. Consequently, it distorts their relationships with and trust for public officials, the police, and all those in authority who extort bribes from them (World Bank, 2002).

Corruption leads to decay in physical infrastructure because it skews public investment away from needed operations and maintenance spending and directs it to new equipment purchases, thereby reduc-ing the productivity of public investment, especially infrastructure. Corruption distorts the social fabric of the society. When corruption becomes systemic and bribing becomes a habit, people become indolent in trying to follow correct procedures, as too many things are solved by bribery — i.e. bribing becomes the way of getting things done.

Corruption in the use of development assistance has not only undermined the utility of such funds, but it has also served to erode support for aid, in both the donor and recipient countries. Foreign direct investment is also undermined by corruption, as it affects the confidence of foreign investors. As a result, needed capital that could lead to sustained growth is directed to other places, undermining economic development. The costs of corruption are, therefore, particularly high for poor African countries in great need of inflows of productive foreign capital (Common-wealth, 2000). Corruption leads to loss of revenue for the government through foregone taxation as higher levels of bureaucratic corruption drive firms out of the formal sector and provide moral justification for widespread tax evasion. Businesses in the informal sector also do not report revenue and therefore do not pay taxes. Revenue is also forgone through corruption in the customs, involving senior officials as well as low-level customs officials (World Bank, 2002).

Corruption hinders the development of small and medium-sized businesses, which are the engine of job creation and economic growth in emerging economies (Eizenstat, 1999). Newer and small firms tend to bear the brunt of the bribery 'tax'. Studies show that small enterprises pay a larger proportion of their revenues as bribes than do large firms. Corruption in the private sector can cause as much harm to the health of the economy as corruption in the public sector. The distinction between the two sectors is becoming increasingly blurred. Within the private sector, weak corporate governance can engender corrupt practices (Iskander and Chamlou, 2000).

The potential impact of corruption on the economy is summarized in Box 5.13. Once corruption becomes entrenched, its negative effects multiply. It induces cynicism, because people begin to regard it as the norm. It undermines social values because people find it easier and more lucrative to engage in corruption than to seek legitimate employment. It erodes governmental legitimacy because it hampers the effective delivery of public goods and services.

It is difficult to quantify the costs of corruption to Africa, but isolated examples give some indication of the dimension of the problem. In Tanzania, investigation of road construction contracts revealed cost increases of between 101 and 353 percent, which could not be accounted for. In the Gambia, in the early 1990s, it was estimated that customs and tax revenues amounting to 8–9 percent of GDP were forgone, largely as a result of corruption (GCA, 1997).

The cost of corruption is not only monetary. Between 1970 and 1985, Uganda's wildlife was decimated, partly as aresult of collusion between corrupt officials, military personnel, poachers and international dealers. A similar situation

Box 5.13: Costs of Corruption

Many studies have shown the pernicious effects of corruption on development. It is negatively correlated with levels of political rights, civil liberties and economic freedom. It is also negatively correlated with crucial economic variables. It deters investment and hinders growth. It promotes inequality and erodes macroeconomic and fiscal stability. It reduces the impact of development assistance and provides an incentive to exploit resources, further depleting environmental assets.

Corruption reduces the effectiveness of public administration and distorts public expenditure decisions, channels urgently needed resources away from sectors such as health and education into corruption-prone sectors or personal enrichment. It erodes the rule of law and harms the reputation of and trust in the state.

The impact of corruption on socio-economic development may be summarized as follows:

- Misallocation of talent, including underutilization of key segments of the society, such as women;
- Lower levels of domestic and foreign investment;
- Distorted enterprise development and growth of the unofficial economy;
- Distorted public expenditures and investments and deteriorated physical infrastructure;
- Lower public revenues and less provision of the rule of law as a public good;
- Overly-centralized government;
- State capture by corporate elite of the laws and policies of the state, thereby undermining growth of output and investment of the enterprise sector.

Sources: World Bank, 2002; Thomas et al, 2000

occurred in DRC, and Nigeria has also admitted that corruption has encouraged trade in endangered species. The environmental impact of corruption has also to be taken into account. Granting of concessions for logging, or sale of land for tourism, when accompanied by kickbacks and favoritism is unlikely to take environmental factors into account. Corruption can also endanger health and well-being. In Cameroon, adulteration of official supplies of drugs and vaccines came to light. While adulterated supplies passed into the official health system, the real drugs went into the black market (GCA, 1997). In Nigeria, in the last two years, the National Agency for Food and Drugs Administration has been waging a battle against importers of fake drugs.

The negative impact of corruption is demonstrated by the fact that oil-rich economies, which have earned considerable revenues from the exploitation of their resources, have not translated this into broad-based growth. In these countries, the standard of living of the citizens has declined over the years, and although investment is higher than in other countries, it is highly concentrated in the mining industry.

Improving Governance

Combating Corruption

Given that corruption and poor governance are intertwined, measures to combat corruption are nearly synonymous with measures to promoting good governance. Improving governance requires several measures and actions. It requires a system of checks and balances that restrain

arbitrary action and bureaucratic harassment by politicians and bureaucrats. Measures to promote voice and participation by the populace are needed. Incentives for the corporate elite to engage in 'state capture' need to be reduced while the rule of law should be fostered. A 'meritocratic' and service-oriented public administration should be put in place.

A multifaceted strategy that addresses various concerns — political accountability, institutional restraints, citizen voice, public disclosure laws, competition, and good public sector performance — is required to fight corruption and promote good governance (see Figure 5.1). Analysis of corruption in individual societies can shed light on the patterns and root causes of corruption, and thus help to determine priorities and suggest appropriate entry points for combating corruption. Where administrative corruption is high but state capture is not, strengthening accountability within administration, use of expenditure tracking surveys and other tools for financial accountability can be a good entry point. Where state capture at the center is high, political accountability and decentralization may be a better entry point (World Bank, 2004a).

Recently, several African countries have begun to make efforts to combat corruption. Many countries have enacted appropriate legislation to curb corrupt practices. Some of the stringent measures include blacklisting, seizure of assets, mandatory dismissal from public office, and legal action. Others have enacted codes of conduct for public officers, while some have created specialized agencies for

Figure 5.1: Multi-Pronged Strategies for Combating Corruption and Improving Governance

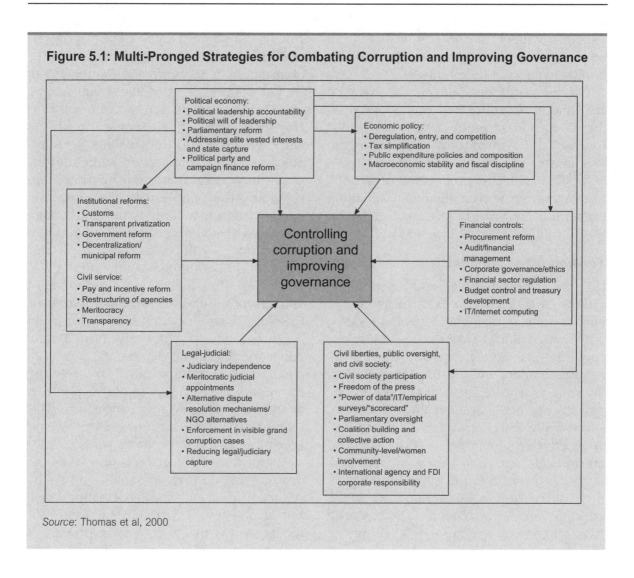

Source: Thomas et al, 2000

combating corruption. Implementation of most existing laws, however, has been ineffective. Most of these anti-corruption agencies have made little progress in fighting corruption because they do not have the powers to become effective. In some countries, Parliament has been the stumbling block, while in other countries anti-corruption laws have not been invoked or important personalities were exempted. In some other countries, however, the anti-corruption institutions have been used to 'witch hunt' political opponents. This has served to undermine anti corruption efforts and erode public support for them. Furthermore, anti-corruption institutions are often under-funded, and in some cases, they are just a veneer to meet donor conditions in a region where many countries depend on donors to support their budgets.

At the continental level, the NEPAD Declaration on corruption was adopted at the AU in Durban in July 2002, which calls for the establishment of a coordinated mechanism to combat corruption effectively. This led to the preparation of the AU Convention on Preventing and Combating Corruption, adopted African Heads of States in July 2003 (see Box 5.14).

Further actions needed

Unless comprehensive and systematic actions are taken to combat corruption, the vicious circle of rising poverty, poor governance and corruption is likely to continue unabated. Corruption transcends national borders and must be combated at the national, sub-regional and global levels. Actions are needed at all three levels to successfully curb corruption. The basis of any effective national action against corruption is a clear sense of national purpose, ownership and strategy. Without this, the efforts are not likely to yield effective long-term solutions. The sense of national purpose requires the development of a new culture with zero tolerance for corruption. There must be a new dispensation that abhors corruption both in public and private life.

None of these, however, can take place without a strong political champion. The political leaders and others with the power to act must be committed to the fight and must lead the efforts. The first step is to secure a strong commitment at the highest political level. When corruption is widespread and involves the political establishment, fighting it will involve political risks (Heilbrum and Keefer, 1999).

Government actions alone will not be effective. To sustain a new culture that is corruption-free, the people must be empowered by making leaders accountable to them and other stakeholders, providing access to information and providing the people with the education needed to understand issues and make informed decisions. A strong and independent press will be indispensable to this effort as is the supremacy of the rule of law. Public opinion has to be supportive of anticorruption efforts as public opinion is the major force in creating an environment of zero tolerance for corruption. Public education about the detrimental effects of corruption is important in creating awareness and an active public response in support of anti-corruption measures. This requires a free and professional press and accessible channels of information.

Opportunities for decision-makers to engage in corrupt practices must be reduced. This will involve creating small but strong and effective state establishments, where the discretionary powers of government officials are reduced while keeping the public administration effective and efficient. An effective civil service with well-paid civil servants, and democratic processes in political parties are important factors that could help to promote good governance and reduce corruption. The tendency to focus only on the symptoms of corruption must be avoided. This means that the actions taken should focus not only on corrupt activities but should also

Box 5.14: AU Convention on Preventing and Combating Corruption

Since the return of multi-party system to African countries in the 1990s, pressure from civil society, media and political parties pushed corruption and governance issues to the fore. International financial institutions also adopted good governance agenda as part of their reform programs. Against this backdrop, African countries decided to seek a continental approach to the problem of corruption. In 1998, the heads of state passed a resolution calling on the OAU Secretary General to call a meeting of experts to consider ways to remove obstacles to the enjoyment of economic, social and cultural rights — such as through the fight against corruption and impunity and propose appropriate legislative and other measures for reform.

Civil society groups, including Transparency International, participated in the writing of the first draft of the AU convention at an experts meeting in Addis Ababa in November 2001 and September 2002. The 28-article document started out as the Convention on Preventing and Combating Corruption, but the drafting committee had included 'and related offences'. The document was designed to be easily applied as a framework for any national anti-corruption strategy.

The Convention was adopted in July 2003 at the AU Summit in Maputo, Mozambique, and awaits 15 ratifications before it comes into force. Countries that have adopted the document, can decide to enact on their own selected provisions of the convention into national law, instead of proceeding with the ratification process (whereby the entire treaty becomes applicable as a national law).

The objectives of the Convention are to:
* Promote and strengthen the development in Africa by each state party, of mechanisms required to prevent, detect, punish and eradicate corruption and related offences in the public and private sectors;
* Promote, facilitate and regulate cooperation among the state parties to ensure the effectiveness of measures and actions to prevent, detect, punish and eradicate corruption and related offences in Africa;
* Coordinate and harmonize the policies and legislation between state parties for the purposes of prevention, detection, punishment and eradication of corruption on the continent;
* Promote socio-economic development by removing obstacles to the enjoyment of economic, social and cultural rights as well as civil and political rights;
* Establish the necessary conditions to foster transparency and accountability in the management of public affairs.

The Convention concentrates on four main approaches to combating corruption: prevention, punishment, cooperation and education. Also the Convention: lists offences that should be punishable by domestic legislation; outlines measures to be undertaken to enable the detection and investigation of corruption offences; indicates mechanisms for the confiscation and forfeiture of the proceeds of corruption and related offences; encourages the education and promotion of public awareness on the evils of corruption; and establishes a framework for the monitoring and supervision of the enforcement of the convention. The civil society is to be involved in the monitoring process. The Convention focuses on both public and private sector corruption and calls for specific anti-corruption laws in both sectors.

The Convention also makes reference to political funding, each signatory is to 'adopt legislative and other measures to proscribe the use of funds acquired through illegal and corrupt practices to finance political parties', and to 'incorporate the principle of transparency into funding of political parties'.

Sources: TI, 2004, *Global Corruption Report*

address their underlying causes. Since these factors are likely to differ amongst countries, each national situation must inform a nation's strategy to combat corruption. It is crucial for national policy-makers to uncover the underlying causes of corruption in order to develop appropriate national responses.

A piecemeal approach will not work. An all-out approach should be adopted from the outset, demonstrating a serious political commitment to fight corruption within all segments of society. The fight to eliminate corruption must permeate national policies and legislative frame-works. The judiciary must also be geared up to participate in this fight. The ultimate goal must be the development of value systems that have zero tolerance for all types of corruption, including corruption at the highest levels. The fight against corruption should go hand-in-hand with general efforts to improve economic and corporate governance. Corruption is essentially a governance issue and reforms in various sectors are needed. Increased governmental accountability and trans-parency, enhanced public participation in decision making, strengthened public sector and civil society institutions and greater adherence to the rule of law will not only help governance, they will also help to reduce corruption. As part of efforts to improve the governance environment, sustained action has to be directed at the root causes of corruption by targeting the underlying weaknesses in economic policy, public administration and politics and to reduce rent-seeking opportunities. Other areas of action may include reform to

improve the effectiveness and probity of the public service, reforms in tax policy and administration, and tightening of controls over public expenditure.

Prevention efforts must focus on the holders of offices of trust and also those who offer bribes. A code of conduct for private business should spell out what corruption practice and what is legitimate business promotion. Similarly, a public code of ethics should be developed to address the issue of corruption. A good prevention strategy requires strong enforcement to provide effective deter-rence. Laws against corrupt behavior at all levels must be enforced without favor. Laws and regulations should be reviewed to remove any ambiguities that create incentives for corrupt behavior.

To create a new culture there is a need for massive mobilization of popular support for the involvement of civil society (Johnston, 1997). This is important in changing public values. It also exerts pressure on governments to take the necessary actions to formulate and implement anti-corruption programs. Public resentment of corruption and the burdens it places on citizens are perhaps the greatest potential capital for reforms to combat corruption. This can provide an important basis of political support for anti-corruption actions and challenging vested interests.

Combating corruption requires a sustained effort over a long-term period. The national efforts should generally involve both a long-term strategy and a series of short-term programs with some decisive time-bound actions. Because of the nature of corruption, there is a need to move on a number of fronts simultaneously, but at varying speeds, as some reforms are easier to implement than others and also, because resources will be limited. The sequencing will be crucial and must depend on a thorough analysis of the national situation. For example, in Egypt, to reduce red tape and petty corruption and streamline government transactions, the ministry of administrative development created citizen service centers where citizens and investors can do their government business without going to the relevant ministries. The ministry published a guide of the 450 most requested services (out of a total of 728) and posted it on the Internet, specifying the documents and official fees associated with each (TI, 2004).

National anti-corruption strategies should encompass both the public and private sectors. Corruption in the private sector can be as corrosive to economic performance as public sector corruption. Public sector corruption often involves actors from the private sector. A national culture opposed to corruption requires high standards of behavior from all sections of society, but especially from political leaders. In addition, national efforts should be reinforced with appropriate support at the international level.

Corruption originating within national boundaries and that resulting from international transactions must be tackled with the same vigor. The international community has a crucial role to play in eliminating corruption in Africa, especially in aid administration and procurement. Along these lines, many African countries have already embarked on creating special-

ized agencies for combating corruption with donor support.

In sum, without political leadership and political will, anti-corruption strategies will fail. Political leadership is required to lead by example and to demonstrate that no one is above the law. Heads of state in particular have to show great commitment and interest and make combating corruption a major public issue. A high profile focus on specific actions can be useful in sending a strong signal that corruption will not be tolerated. This was demonstrated in Singapore, when the prime minister strongly and publicly supported the anticorruption campaign it helped to give it credibility. In some African countries, political leaders have already started taking a strong stance against corruption, but prompt and visible actions must be seen to be taken against corrupt officials if significant progress was to be made on combating corruption.

Conclusion

Despite progress by many African countries in institutionalizing democracy, much remains to be done to improve the conduct of governance. There are still many parts of Africa where progress needs to be made towards greater adherence to the axioms of good governance, including basic political order, political legitimacy, rule of law, and popular participation. This may explain why the practice of electoral democracy is yet to be translated into tangible benefits, in terms of improvements in the livelihoods of the African peoples.

Improved political governance is an imperative for avoiding conflicts, reducing corruption and promoting social cohesion and socio-economic development. African countries must focus on building effective participatory forms of governance. They must make efforts to build the capacity of the legislatures in order to empower them to perform their parliamentary oversight functions more effectively. Their role in sanctioning annual budgets and expenditures must not be merely ceremonial. They must undertake critical reviews, as dictated by the constitution and by their responsibility to taxpayers. Greater parliamentary awareness of the wider economic and political consequences of tax policies and expenditure issues will be required. The legislature will have to use its legislative oversight and rely on independent auditors who report directly to parliament. This will require strengthening the human resource capability of national audit bureaus and judiciaries. The legislature must be willing and able to act under the law to prosecute errant government functionaries on both the revenue and expenditure sides.

Judicial reforms are also required to promote accountability by government, the rule of law, as well as enhanced access to justice for all citizens. African countries must empower their citizens through effective participation and decentralization, to enable them hold governments accountable for their actions and to ensure greater transparency. Systems should be put in place to hold public officials accountable for their behavior, actions and decisions.

Effective regulatory institutions are also crucial for fostering private sector participation and good corporate governance. Key among the institutions and instruments are the legal framework for competition, the legal machinery for enforcing shareholders' rights, and systems for accounting and auditing. Strengthening the regulatory capacity of the state is vital to ensure good economic governance. A sound regulatory framework must create the platform for private competition and the conditions that promote fiscal and financial discipline. African countries should make efforts to strengthen financial controls within the sector to reduce abuse and corruption and to promote greater transparency, predictability and accountability. Technical capacities for budgeting and financial analysis in the public sector have to be raised. Central banks should be granted autonomy in the conduct of monetary policy. With the changing role of the state, the main tasks of the public sector will be increasingly to enforce policies, to ensure that markets function properly and to undertake necessary regulatory measures.

Corrupt practices in Africa are partly responsible for the high incidence of poverty in the continent because it exacts heavy economic costs by distorting the operation of free markets, hampering economic development and destroying the ability of institutions and bureaucracies to deliver services to the public. In some cases, it distorts decision-making processes. African countries must develop specific policies and programs to prevent corruption, enforce laws against it and mobilize public support. The fight against corruption should go hand in hand with efforts to improve Africa's image in the world, for there is an inherent tendency on the part of foreign investors to overstate risk perceptions in Africa.

CHAPTER 6

Public Sector Reforms in Africa: The Role of the ADB

Introduction

The importance of external financing to public sector reform in Africa cannot be overemphasized. In particular, overseas development assistance plays an important part in determining the strategies that are seeking to reduce the continent's poverty, inequality, intolerance, weak civil society and bad governance. Although there was a major downturn in the flow of aid to Africa in the 1990s it has since increased again. This is partly in light of Africa's needs and partly in response to the greater confidence that donors have in the commitment of African governments in bringing about policy reforms and thus accelerate the process of development out of poverty. The adoption of the Millennium Development Goals (MDGs) for 2015 has already encouraged development assistance to continue, and the recent G8 declaration would see the doubling of aid over the next five years. Even though foreign aid has become an integral part of the African development scene, its role and character has changed over the years. The focus of aid has moved away from project support to holistic approaches, including budget support, civil service reform and good governance, with the aim of creating overall conditions for development.

As discussed in Chapter 3, the changing emphases in overseas development assistance to Africa reflected the changes that took place in the development arena, which in the past decade and half focused largely on 'getting the politics' right. Since then, the international financial institutions, especially the Bretton Woods Institutions (The World Bank and the IMF) have increasingly begun to support governance-related public sector reforms in Africa. Indeed, the World Bank and the IMF have provided considerable resources at helping African countries with public sector reforms.

Since the year 2000, the World Bank has been implementing a number of measures towards building public institutions in African countries. In North Africa, for instance, the strategy was aimed at encouraging countries to address governance and public sector issues, and to lay a foundation for a move towards more countrywide programmatic financial support. Countrywide approaches dealing with cross-cutting issues are also adopted. These include, for example, public expenditure management in Morocco, and budget management technical assistance in Algeria. A wide range of sector-specific work aimed at increasing the effectiveness and efficiency of public services and regulations has also been included — for example, the social sector public expenditure review in Algeria, support to activities that empower rural communities in Tunisia, and water user associations in Egypt (World Bank, 2000a). In Sub-Saharan Africa, the World Bank governance and public sector work covers a wide array of activities including poverty reduction (and governance), community driven development and public sector reform, and strengthening expenditure and accountability systems.

The IMF, on the other hand, concentrates on those aspects of governance that are closely related to macroeconomic policies, including the transparency of government accounts, the effectiveness of resource management, and the stability and transparency of the economic and regulatory environment for private sector activity (IMF, 1997). The contribution the IMF makes to good governance through policy advice and, where relevant, technical assistance, is in two principal spheres: improving the management of public resources through reforms covering public sector institutions; and supporting the development and maintenance of a transparent and stable economic and regulatory environment conducive to efficient private sector participation.

In spite of their individual roles, the World Bank and the IMF work together when interests overlap. For example, one such area is the analysis of Public Expenditure Management (PEM) systems in HIPCs and their ability to track poverty-reducing spending. A second area is the World Bank-EU Public Expenditure and Financial Accountability program, of whose Steering Committee the Fund is a member. A third area is civil service reforms, where the implementation of medium-term

structural reforms may at times create a challenge for maintaining macro-fiscal balance. A fourth activity has been the joint effort of the World bank, the IMF, and the OECD to establish an International Tax Dialogue (ITD) with several country-specific pilots to provide a means to share information and lessons of experience among tax administrators worldwide.

In addition, both the World Bank and the IMF collaborate with other multilateral institutions on issues of governance. For instance, the World Bank cofinances many public sector projects jointly with other Multilateral Development Banks, including the ADB. They have established working groups to harmonize various operational policies and procedures, which can impact on effectiveness of implementation of programs and projects at country levels. One such Group is the Working Group on Governance and Anti-Corruption.

Along with the multilateral development institutions, the African Development Bank (ADB) has also increasingly supported public sector reform in its Regional Member Countries (RMCs). The rest of this chapter discusses the role of the ADB in public sector reforms in Africa.

The Role of the ADB

The African Development Bank (ADB) has over the past five years sharpened its focus on governance issues in its RMCs. The Bank has adopted a new governance policy, which emphasizes the critical importance of incorporating good governance into the Bank's activities, and during the past four years, the Board of Directors have approved several policy guidelines on good governance and related issues. The include:

- Operational Guidelines for Bank Group Policy on Good Governance (2001)
- Guidelines for Financial Management Review of Bank Projects (2002)
- Enhanced Performance Based Allocation Framework (2002)
- Guidelines for Country Governance Profiles (2003)
- Guidelines for Preventing and Combating Corruption and Fraud in Bank Group Operations (2003)
- Guidelines for Development Budget Support Lending (2004)
- Guidelines for Using Sector-Wide Approaches (2004)
- Guidelines for Policy-Based Lending on Governance (2004)[1]

The Bank's Strategic Plan 2003–2007 also links governance issues to development effectiveness and results, measured by progress towards achieving the MDGs in the Bank's RMCs.

Issues of governance that are of concern to the Bank include:

- Ensuring accountability of public agencies and officials through formal transparent processes for monitoring and reporting;
- Fostering transparency at all levels of government and public administration, including budgetary transparency;
- Combating corruption;
- Fostering greater participation, and freedom of speech and association, to enable the beneficiaries of government programs to participate effectively in determining and meeting their needs;
- Nurturing an objective and efficient judiciary;
- Enhancing efficiency within public and private institutions by building technical and management capacities.

Good Governance in Bank Group Activities

In operationalizing its agenda for good governance, the Bank is guided by the following:

- The RMC's institutional capacity, social and political situation. The objective in each case is to help in the development of an enabling environment, taking on board all the necessary economic and non-economic factors;
- The need to take into consideration the effects of bad governance on development performance;
- The ownership of development programs and policies by RMCs;

[1] It is noteworthy that the Bank Group became involved in implementing Policy-Based Lending (PBL) in 1986 and this was maintained throughout the 1990s. While great attention was given to the strengthening of institutional and human capacity in the earlier PBLs, it was not until the 1999-2002 cohort of PBLs that explicitly focused on good governance issues, such as public expenditure reforms and legal and judicial reforms. The current Guidelines for Policy-Based Lending on Governance (PBLG) are to increase governance focus by systematically linking policy reforms to capacity building, governance, and development effectiveness.

- The concern for effective partnership among government, private sector, civil society and the international development community in the implementation of governance initiatives/activities.

The ADB Policy Paper on Good Governance and its Implementation Guidelines, adopted by the Board in 1999 and 2001 respectively, provide the basis for addressing governance issues facing RMCs in the Bank's programs. It acknowledges the complexity of the governance concept and the interrelated nature of its different components. Against this background, the Bank also recognizes the need for a more differentiated approach between countries. Issues of good governance continue to be a key criterion in the performance-based allocation of ADF resources. The criterion favors RMCs that achieve high governance ratings with higher ADF allocations.

To operationalize its Governance Policy, a new Governance Division was created in 2002 in the Operations Policies and Review Department. Its mandate is to lend tangible support to governance issues and to mainstream governance concerns into the Bank Group operations. In the same year, the ADB signed an agreement with Norway, Denmark, Finland, and Sweden, establishing the Nordic Trust Fund on Governance, to support good governance activities. Since 2002, the Governance Division has launched a number of programs, diagnostic tools and instruments to incorporate governance issues into the Bank operations (see Box 6.1 for the Bank's policy guidelines on governance).

Country Governance Profiles

To assist in the implementation of its Governance Policy, the ADB prepares Country Governance Profiles (CGPs), which serve as diagnostic tools to identify key governance issues and develop a common understanding of the strengths and weaknesses of governance systems in RMCs (see Box 6.2). CGPs have already been completed for fourteen countries: Benin, Burkina-Faso, Cameroon, Chad, Gabon, Ghana, Kenya, Malawi, Mauritania, Nigeria, Senegal, Swaziland, Tanzania, and Zambia. Five more CGPs are scheduled for completion by December 2005.

Guidelines for Policy-Based Loans (PBLs)

In response to the need to harmonize Bank lending approaches to governance, the ADB developed an instrument to drive policy changes and reforms in this area. The 'Guidelines for Policy-Based Loans on Governance' are an essential tool to improve the efficiency of activities to promote governance and enhance the contribution of the ADB to efforts to reduce poverty in RMCs. The Guidelines provide information for consideration at each stage of the project cycle, and serve as a checklist of actions required to assess governance risk and impact, required policy changes and recommended actions, as well as relevant indicators to measure progress. In line with this, the Bank also collaborated with the World Bank in 2003 to prepare Country Financial Accountability Assessments (CFAAs) in some countries. These include: The Gambia, Madagascar, Senegal

Box 6.1: The Bank Group Policy on Good Governance

Good governance is an essential requisite for sustainable development. The Bank Group's interest in governance arises from its mandate to ensure the effectiveness of the development efforts it supports. It is also in line with the Bank's Vision for sustained African development into the 21st Century. For the Bank Group the key elements of good governance include accountability, transparency, combating corruption, participatory governance and an enabling legal/judicial framework.

In operationalizing its agenda for good governance, the Bank will be guided by the following:

- The country's institutional capacity, social and political situation. The objective in each case is to help in the development of an enabling environment, taking on board all the necessary economic and non-economic factors;
- The need to take into consideration the effects of bad governance on development performance;
- The ownership of development programs and policies by RMCs; and
- The concern for effective partnership among government, private sector, civil society and the international development community in the implementation of governance initiatives/activities.

The Bank acknowledges the complexity of the governance concept, and recognizes the need for a more differentiated approach between countries. Therefore, the Bank's interventions related to governance will be chosen selectively from the range of activities described below, depending upon country circumstances and needs, the state of dialogue with the country and budgetary and staff constraints.

A. Accountability:
- Public Sector Management
- Public Enterprise Management and Reform
- Public Financial Management
- Corporate Governance
- Civil Service Reform

B. Transparency
- Information Disclosure
- Public Expenditure Reviews (PERs)
- Capacity in Public Policy Analysis and Dissemination

C. Combating Corruption
- Support for Research on Corruption
- Prevention and Control of Corruption in Bank-financed Operations
- Sensitization and Provision of Assistance

D. Participation
- Participation of Beneficiaries and Affected Groups
- Co-operation with NGOs, CBOs, and CSOs
- Economic Cooperation and Regional Integration
- Support Decentralization At Various Sub-National Levels
- Public Sector/Private Sector Interface

E. Legal and Judicial Reform
- Law Reform
- Judicial Reform
- Legal Framework for Private Sector Development

These interventions will be pursued in collaboration with the Bretton Woods Institutions, regional and specialized organizations, and bilateral agencies through economic and sector work; policy dialogue; and lending and non-lending activities.

Source: ADB, Operational Guidelines for Bank Group Policy on Good Governance (2001)

Box 6.2: Country Governance Profile (CGP)

The Country Governance Profile (CGP) is a Bank instrument designed to assess the governance situation in a regional member country. Based on discussions with the government, private sector and civil society, and other stakeholders, the CGP:
- Outlines the major governance issues in a country;
- Identifies the key priority areas;
- Performs an activity-mapping of government and donor interventions in the areas;
- Recommends possible areas of intervention.

In particular, the CGP presents the major problems of governance facing the country in terms of transparency, accountability, participation, combating corruption, and legal and judicial reform. It highlights the governance concerns of the government, and the views of other stakeholders on the governance agenda. It is designed to pinpoint government policy actions to redress the manifestations of bad governance that are deemed harmful to the economic and social development of the country. In addition, it provides some indications of the interventions of donors on governance in the country to help the Bank in identifying issues and sectors where the Bank could take the lead, including as coordinator of donor's interventions. Based on the major needs identified, the CGP determines a list of possible actions that could be financed by the Bank, in collaboration with the government and the other stakeholders.

In reviewing the governance situation, the CGP also takes into account relevant country economic and sector work and the results from projects on the ground. Integrated into the CGP process, the CGP findings provide a framework for effective dialogue with RMCs on sustainable governance programming.

Source: ADB, Guidelines for Country Governance Profile (2003)

and Tanzania. The CFAAs are to assess the extent to which RMCs' financial management practices comply with international standards.

Support to Public Sector Reforms

Over the last two decades, the ADB has played an important role in the reform efforts of RMCs. It has provided resources and technical assistance for bank operations for reform of public enterprises, private sector development, decentralization, institutional support, promotion of participation of civil society organizations, and the fight against corruption. Policy-based loans were supported by technical assistance for capacity building and the promotion of good governance in countries such as Burkina Faso, Ghana, Guinea, The Democratic Republic of Congo, Mali, and Mauritania (see Table 6.1). The Bank has also taken steps to promote good governance and more efficient use of resources lent to RMCs. Some of the measures in this regard relate to procurement, financial management, audit diagnostic work, expanded interventions during the project cycle, application of remedies for violations of legal controls, reporting requirements and targeted capacity building (ADB,

Table 6.1: Selected Governance-Related ADB Group Operations, 2002–2004

Country	Project	Description
2002		
Cape Verde	Economic Reform Support Program II	Create conditions for strong growth; upgrade the privatization ofi publc enterprises; help reduce poverty; reinforce governance.
Côte d'Ivoire	National Good Governance and Capacity Building Program	Contribute to the improvement of the legal system; strengthen structures and institutions involved in the decentralization process; and bolster the capacity for public resources management.
Djibouti	Structural Adjustment Loan	Create conditions conducive to strong growth likely to reduce poverty.
Mali	The Good Governance Support Project	Strengthen the human and institutional capacities to effectively support efforts of government, the private sector, and decentralized communes in the implementation of governance activities in concert with the Poverty Reduction Strategy Framework.
Morocco	Financial sector support program	To strengthen regulatory framework of financial sector, sanitize public financial institutions, strengthen competition and effectiveness of services and financial products, and motivate capital markets.
2003		
Chad	Economic Management Support Project	Build capacity in management of development projects, public debt management; and production and dissemination of statistics and socio-economic studies.
Congo	Economic Management Support Project	Develop and consolidate skills in the field of debt management and public investment planning.
Congo Dem. Rep.	Economic Recovery and Reunification Program	Consolidate macroeconomic stability and improve the efficiency of public financial management, promote good governance, boost private sector participation, and contribute to poverty alleviation.
Madagascar	Structural Adjustment Program (SAP-IV)	Support necessary reforms aimed at increasing fiscal receipts, institution good governance in public finance management, and controlling corruption.
Niger	Structural Adjustment Program IV	Promote good governance, increase coverage of essential social services, and reorganize the financial sector.
Senegal	Private Sector Adjustment Support	Enhance the business climate, step up private sector development and job promotion, and consolidate strong and continuous growth.

Table 6.1: *Cont.*

Country	Project	Description
Sierra Leone	Second Economic Rehabilitation and Recovery Loan	Support reforms in governance, provide support to weak balance of payments, and contribute to imports of essential commodities.
2004		
Burkina Faso	Supplementary Poverty Reduction Strategy Support Program II	Reforms hinge on three themes; acceleration of growth by consolidating macroeconomic stability and strengthening economic competitiveness; improving the access to basic social services for the poor; and promotion of good governance.
Cape Verde	Economic Reforms Support Program III	Program comprises of four elements: consolidation of public finances; strengthening of governance; intensification of poverty reduction actions; and elimination of structural constraints on growth and private sector development.
Ethiopia	Institutional Support Project of the Women's Affairs Office	Support for training, procurement of equipment, rehabilitation of women's training centers, and the provision of technical assistance to support the Women's Affairs Office in developing training manuals, gender mainstreaming guidelines and gender monitoring indicators.
Gabon	Structural Adjustment Program III	Program is to help the state to break the culture of impunity, enhance the budgetary process and restore transparency in the management of public resources. Reduce corruption by streamlining budget processes; enhancing control procedures; observing public procurement rules; applying the anti-corruption law; and implementing the public service code of ethics.
Lesotho	Institutional Support to the Ministry of Finance and Development Planning and the Ministry of Works and transport	Training of staff in Ministry of Finance in areas of project analysis, monitoring and evaluation, project appraisal and capital budgeting; and Ministry of Works staff in areas of policy formulation, project management, environmental management, budgeting and financial management.
Niger	Gender Equity Reinforcement Project	Enhancement of capacities of state agencies for design, planning and management of gender activities and the creation of a social environment that is more conducive to gender equity.

Source: ADB *Annual Report*, 2003

Annual Report, 2002). In addition to projects targeted directly at reforms, most of the other loans to social and other sectors contribute to improved services delivery in RMCs.

Monitoring Bank Operations

In 2003, the ADB developed 'Guidelines for Preventing and Combating Corruption in Bank Operations'. It was recommended that an Oversight Committee for Corruption and Fraud be created. Procedures for a 'whistle blower' protection program were also suggested. Also in 2003, in response to the need to strengthen financial management arrangements of projects in the public sector, the Bank developed 'Guidelines to Assist Financial Analysts' when conducting the assessment of the financial management arrangements of entities responsible for the implementation of the Bank Group-financed projects during preparation, appraisal, implementation, and supervision. The Guidelines are to assist task managers to identify and take appropriate actions in order to resolve financial management issues, thereby improving the effectiveness of Bank-financed operations (ADB, *Annual Report*, 2003).

Partnerships and Cooperation with Other Organizations

In accordance with its latest five-year Strategic Plan (2003–07), the ADB has taken steps to strengthen its collaborative efforts with bilateral and multilateral development partners in order to harmonize selectivity in operations and optimize the use of scarce ODA resources. With respect to public sector management

operations, the Bank Group has collaborated with these partners in various ways to maximize effectiveness of its governance-related activities.

Cooperation with Regional Bodies: In partnership with the AU, the Bank helped to finalize the AU Convention on Combating Corruption, which was ratified by the African Heads of State at their meeting in Maputo, Mozambique, in 2003. The Bank also led a multi-institutional partnership with the AU, Transparency International, the World Bank Institute, and the Global Coalition for Africa, to organize regional workshops on combating corruption. The workshops were held in January 2003 in Addis Ababa, Ethiopia, and in October 2003, in Yaounde, Cameroon.

The ADB also works closely with the ECA to harmonize their activities in the area of promoting good governance in Africa. The two institutions have collaborated on a regional initiative on 'Measuring Progress Towards Good Governance'. They cosponsored the African Development Forum IV on the theme "Governance for a Progressing Africa". The Bank also collaborated with the ECA on poverty reduction by supporting the Africa PRSP Learning group, established by the ECA to increase African representation at all stages of the PRSP process. The Bank has also supported capacity building for National Audit Institutions (NAIs) and the restructuring of the African Organization of Supreme Audit Institutions (AFROSAI) in order to enhance its capacity to assume its leadership role and capacity building for African NAIs (ADB, *Annual Report*, 2003). At the request of NEPAD Heads of States and Governments Implementation Committee, the ADB provided technical expertise for benchmarks and indicators of governance.

Partnership with Bretton Woods Institutions: In the realm of policy-based lending, the World Bank (along with the IMF), largely determines the broad parameters of macroeconomic policy, while RDBs support economic reform programs by providing co-financing or parallel financing with the World Bank. The ADB cooperates with the Bretton Woods Institutions in several ways.

Co-financing of Projects and Programs: One aspect of cooperation between the World Bank and the African Development Bank is through co-financing of projects, especially projects aimed at promoting policy reforms. The level of co-financing has increased over the years. In the year 2002, the ADB Group and the World Bank (and other partners) co-financed a total of nine projects and programs in RMCs. These included: three structural adjustment programs in Chad, Djibouti and Mali; two economic recovery/reform support programs in Cape Verde and Cote d'Ivoire; one poverty reduction loan in Uganda; and one multinational project to reform the payment system in WAEMU countries. In 2003, the ADB Group and the World Bank co-financed projects in Benin, Burkina Faso, Democratic Republic of Congo, Ghana, Madagascar, Mozambique, Niger, Senegal and Sierra Leone. The IMF has also co-financed Bank Group projects. In 2002, the ADB Group cofinanced five economic reform programs with the IMF and other partners. These included three structural

adjustment programs and two economic recovery/reform support programs. In 2003, the ADB and the IMF co-financed multi-sector projects and programs in Burkina Faso, Democratic Republic of Congo, Ghana, Madagascar, Senegal and Sierra Leone.

Strategic Partnership: The ADB Group signed a Strategic Partnership Memorandum of Understanding (MOU) with the World Bank in March 2000, allowing the ADB/World Bank Consultations to be held regularly twice a year. In the 2003 consultation meetings, they agreed to collaborate on two levels: on selected countries and on selected themes/sectors. Action plans for monitoring and evaluation of agreed areas were to be developed.

Support for Poverty Reduction: The ADB Group collaborates with the World Bank and other development partners to support work on the Poverty Reduction Strategy Papers (PRSPs) at the country level. At the biannual meetings with the World Bank in 2002, discussions were held on joint support of PRSPs at the country level, including cofinancing of poverty reduction support credits. The ADB Group participates as a member of the PRSP process Task Team under the Strategic Partnership with Africa (SPA). In this regard, the ADB circulated its draft Poverty Policy, which mainstreams poverty reduction into Bank's operations through the Country Policy Institutional Assessment (CPIA) framework. The instrument is used to allocate concessional African Development Fund (ADF) resources to countries on the basis of the quality of their socio-economic policies towards sustainable economic growth as well as their demonstrated commitment to poverty reduction, gender equity and good governance. Furthermore, the Bank supports the activities of the MDBs' Informal Working Group on Poverty. One of the objectives of the group is to harmonize work on poverty reduction and to share experiences and best practices related to the preparation, implementation, and evaluation of poverty reduction programs.

Conclusion

The analysis in this chapter underlies the importance of external aid for public sector management in Africa. Clearly, the nature of aid has changed over the years, with the focus now being on fiscal reform (including civil service reform), decentralization, and governance reforms. The changing emphases in external aid, however, reflected the shifting nature of programs of the major donors, particularly the multi-lateral financial institutions. These institutions have undoubtedly played a key role in aid flows to developing countries, including Africa, and they have been the catalysts behind the numerous reform initiatives in most aid-recipient countries. On its part, the ADB has made significant strides in assisting its regional member countries with reforms in governance-

related arena. In addition, it has provided financial and technical assistance for reform in public enterprises, private sector development, decentralization, institutional support, and capacity building of civil society organizations. Indeed, the progress that many African countries have made in the recent past in public sector management can be linked to external support. These countries should be encouraged to continue to consolidate and deepen their reforms with the view to creating conducive environment for sustainable growth and development. It is noteworthy that the distance that African countries have covered in the reform process is considerable in many instances, but development is, however, a long-term process. African countries have just begun. A longer distance remains to be covered, some of it even more challenging than what has already been completed. Building on recent reforms is a good start for those that are needed in the next phase. It would be inappropriate to suggest that these steps can be identified along the lines of a single model. They have to be taken with the practical experience of individual African countries as the most suitable way forward. Furthermore, donor agencies need to focus more on long-term reform and strengthen their partnerships towards making aid more effective for public sector management reform.

BIBLIOGRAPHICAL NOTES

Introduction

The background papers prepared specifically for the Report are listed below, along with the selected bibliography used in the Report. These papers synthesize relevant literature. The Report has drawn on a wide range of African Development Bank reports, including ongoing research as well as countries' economic, sector and project work. It has also drawn on outside sources, including published and unpublished works of institutions such as the IMF, the World Bank, IFC, OECD, WTO, the United Nations and its agencies such as the ECA, FAO, ILO IFAD, UNAIDS, UNCTAD, UNIDO, UNDP, and WHO. Other sources include publications from various national economic and statistics agencies, African Economic Digest, Africa Financing Review, Africa Research Bulletin, Business Africa, The Economist, Economist Intelligence Unit, Financial Times, International Capital Markets, Middle East Economic Digest, and Southern Africa Monitor.

Background papers

(i)   Goran Hyden (2004), "Making Public Sector Management Work for Africa".

(ii) Ladipo Adamolekun (2004), "Re-Orienting Public Management in Africa: Selected Issues and Some Country Experiences".

(iii) Joseph Ayee (2004), "Public Sector Management in Africa".

(iv) Janine Aron (2004), "The African Economy in 2004".

(v) Charlotte Vaillant (2004), "Regional Economic Profiles".

Selected Bibliography

Abed, G. T. and Davoodi, H.R. (2003). *Challenges of Growth and Globalization in the Middle East and North Africa.* Washington DC: International Monetary Fund. September.

Adamolekun, L. (1983). *Public Administration. A Nigerian and Comparative Perspective.* London: Longman.

Adamolekun, L. (ed.) (1999). *Public Administration in Africa: main issues and selected country studies.* Colorado: Westview Press.

——— . **(2002).** "Special Issues on New Public Management in Africa", *Africa Development*, vol. XXVII, nos.3/4.

——— . **(2002a).** "Africa's evolving career civil service systems: three challenges—state continuity, efficient service delivery and accountability". *International Review of Administrative Sciences.* vol.68, no.3, pp.373–387.

ADB (2002). *Annual Report 2002.* Abidjan: African Development Bank.

ADB (2003). *Annual Report 2003.* Abidjan: African Development Bank.

Addison, T. (2001). "Do Donors Matter for Institutional Reform in Africa? *WIDER Discussion Paper No. 2001/141*, December.

Addison, T., and Osei, R. (2001). "Taxation and Fiscal Reform in Ghana". *WIDER Discussion Paper No. 2001/97*, September.

Adesida, O. (2001). "Governance in Africa: The Role for Information and Communication Technologies". *African Development Bank Economic Research Papers, No. 65.*

ADR (1998). *Human Capital Development in Africa.* Abidjan: African Development Bank.

ADR (2001). *Fostering Good Governance in Africa.* Abidjan: African Development Bank.

AFRACA (1999). *After the Reforms: Which Way Forward for Central Banks in Rural Finance.* Zimbabwe: African Rural and Agricultural Credit Association.

African Human Security Initiative (2004a). "African Commitment to Democracy in Theory and Practice: A Review of Eight NEPAD Countries", *AHSI Paper 1*, June.

African Human Security Initiative (2004b). "African Commitments to Civil Society Engagement: A Review of Eight NEPAD Countries". *AHSI Paper 6*, August.

Aringo, P. O. (2004). "Political Parties in the Context of Legislative Effectiveness". Introductory Remarks at the ADF IV — Governance for a Progressing Africa, 11–15 October, Addis Ababa.

Ayee, J.R.A. (1997). "Local Government Reform and Bureaucratic Accountability in Ghana". *Regional Development Dialogue*, vol.18, no.2, pp.86–104.

Ayee, R.A. and Tay, F. (1998). "A Decade of Decentralisation Reforms in Ghana, 1988–1998". Paper presented at the Project Workshop on *Policies and Practices Supporting Sustainable Development in Sub-Saharan Africa,* organized by the Scandinavian Seminar College. Golf Hotel, Abidjan. November 9–11.

Balogun, M.J. and Mutahaba, G. (eds.) (1991). *Economic Restructuuring and African Public Administration: Issues, Action, and Future Choices.* West Hartford CT: Kumarian Press.

Beeson, M. (2003). "The Rise and Fall of the Developmental State: the Vicissitudes and Implications of East Asian Interventionism", in Low, L. (ed.). *Developmental States: Relevant, Redundant or Disfigured?* New York: Nova Science Publishers.

Buchanan, J.M. (1975). *The Limits of Liberty: Between Anarchy and Leviathan.* Chicago: Chicago University Press.

Buchanan, J.M. (1987). *The Constitution of Economic Policy.* Stockholm: Nobel Foundation.

Buchanan, J.M. et al. (1978). *The Economics of Politics.* London: Institute of Economics Affairs.

Bulmer, E. R. (2000). "Rationalizing Public Sector Employment in the MENA Region",

Middle East and North Africa Region Working Paper Series, no.19. Washington DC: The World Bank.

Caiden, G.E. (1991). *Administrative Reform Comes of Age*. New York: Walter de Gruyter.

Campbell, B.K. and Loxley, J. (eds.) (1989). *Structural Adjustment in Africa*. New York: St. Martins.

Cartier-Bresson, J. (1999). "Les analyses economiques des causes de la corruption". *Courier International*, no.177. October–November.

Chege, M. (1999). "Politics of Development Institutions and Governance", Paper presented at the Second Research Workshop, Abidjan: African Development Bank.

Clapham, C. (1996). *Africa and the International System: The Politics of State Survival*. Cambridge: Cambridge University Press.

Collier, M.W. (1999). "Explaining Political Corruption: An Institutional-Choice Approach". Paper Presented at the 40th Annual Convention of the International Studies Association. Washington DC, February, 16–20.

Commins, S.K. (ed.) (1988). *Africa's Development Challenges and the World Bank: Hard Questions, Costly Choices*. Boulder, CO.: Lynne Rienner.

Commission of the European Communities (2003). *The Reform of State-Owned Enterprises in Developing Countries with a focus on Public Utilities*. Communication from the Commission to the Council and the European Parliament. Brussels, COM (2003) 326 final.

Commonwealth (2000). *Commonwealth Principles on Promoting Good Governance and Combating Corruption*. Durban: Commonwealth Heads of Government Meeting.

Court, J., and Yanagihara, T. (1998). "Asia and Africa into the Global Economy: Background and Introduction". Paper Presented at the UNU/AERC Conference on *Asia and Africa in the Global Economy*. Tokyo, 3–4 August.

Danielson, A. (2001). "Economic and Institutional Reforms in French-Speaking West Africa — Impact on Efficiency and Growth". *WIDER Discussion Paper No. 2001/28*, July.

Darga, A. L, (1998). "Mauritius — Governance Challenges in Sustained Democracy in a Plural Society". *Development Policy Management Forum Conference Proceedings*. Addis Ababa: DPMF.

DeLancey, V. (2001). "The Economies of Africa". In Gordon, A.A. and Gordon, D.L. (eds.). *Understanding Contemporary Africa*. Boulder/London: Lynne Rienner.

Doig, A. and Riley, S. (1997). "Corruption and Anti-Corruption Strategies: Issues and Case Studies from Developing Countries". Paper Presented at a Workshop on Corruption and Integrity Improvement Initiatives in Developing Countries. UNDP.

DPSA (2003). "Analysis of Donor Support to Public Sector Reform in Africa: Analysis of Interim Findings". South Africa: Department of Public Service Administration and NEPAD Secretariat.

Durevall, D. (2003). "Reform of the Malawian Public Sector — Incentives, Governance and Accountability". In Kayizzi-Mugerwa, S. (ed.). *Reforming Africa's Institutions: Ownership, Incentives, and Capabilities.* Oxford: Oxford University Press.

ECA (2002). *Guidelines for Enhancing Good Economic and Corporate Governance in Africa.* Addis Ababa: UNECA.

ECA (2004). *Public Sector Management Reforms in Africa: Lessons Learned.* Addis Ababa: UNECA.

Eizenstat, E. S. (1999). "An Anti-Corruption and Good Governance Strategy for the 21st Century". Washington DC: Global Forum on Fighting Corruption.

Elbadawi, I.A. and Gelb, A. (2003). "Financing Africa's Development Toward a Business Plan", in van de Walle, N., Ball, N. and Ramachandram, V. (eds.). *Beyond Structural Adjustment: The Institutional Context of African Development.* New York: Palgrave Macmillan.

Erubami, M. and Young, I. (2003). "Nigeria's Corruption and Related Economic Behaviour in Their Global Context". *Center for Human Rights Research and Development Research Review* No. 1.

Etukudo, A. (2000). "Issues in Privatisation, Restructuring and Economic Democracy, *Working Paper IPPRED — 5.* Geneva: ILO.

Ferlie, E., Pettigrew, A., Ashburner, L. and Fitzgerald, L. (1996). *The New Public Management in Action.* Oxford: Oxford University Press.

Gardner, E. (2003). *Creating Employment in the Middle East and North Africa.* Washington DC: IMF.

Garnett, H. and Plowden, W. (2004). "Cabinets, Budgets and Poverty: Political Commitment to Poverty Reduction". In Levy, B. and Kpundeh, S. (eds.) (2004). *Building State Capacity for Good Governance in Africa Requires a Paradigm Shift.* Washington DC: The World Bank.

GCA (1997). "Corruption and Development in Africa", *Policy Forum*, no.2. Maputo: Global Coalition for Africa.

Gloppen, S., Rakner, L. and Tostensen, A. (2003). "Responsiveness to the Concerns of the Poor and Accountability to the Commitment of Poverty Reduction". *Chr. Michelsen Institute, Development Studies and Human Rights, Working Paper 2003:3.*

Grindle, M.S. and Thomas, J.W. (1991). *Public Choices and Policy Change: The Political Economy of Reform in Developing Countries.* Baltimore/London: The Johns Hopkins Press.

Harlow, C. (2000). "Public Administration and Globalization: International and Supra-national Administration". Paper prepared at the First Regional International Conference, International Institute of Administrative Sciences, Bologna, June.

Hayek, F.A. von (1973). *Law, Legislation, and Liberty*, vol. 1. Chicago: Chicago University Press.

Heilbrum, J. and Keefer, P. (1999). "Assessing Political Commitment to Fighting Corruption". *PREM Notes, Newsletter Series*, no.29. Washington DC: The World Bank.

Heritage Foundation (2004). *Index of Economic Freedom*. Washington DC: The Heritage Foundation.

Hood, C. (1991). "A Public Management for all Seasons", *Public Administration*, vol.69, no.1, pp.3-19.

Human Rights Watch (2003). *Human Rights Watch World Report 2003: Africa*.

Hussain, M. N. (1992). "Food Security and Adjustment Programmes: The Conflict". In Maxwell, S. (ed.), *To Cure Hunger: Food Policy and Food Security in Sudan*. Intermediate Technology Publications.

Hussain, M. N. (2000). "Exorcism of the Ghost: An Alternative Growth Model for Measuring the Financing Gap". *Economic Research Papers No.57*. Abidjan: African Development Bank.

Hyden, G. (1998). "Reforming Foreign Aid to African Development: The Politically Autonomous Development Fund Model". *African Studies Quarterly*, vol.2, no.2.

Hyden, G., Court, J. and Mease, K. (2004). *Making Sense of Governance*. Boulder CO: Lynne Rienner Publishers.

IMF (1997). *Good governance: The IMF's Role*. Washington DC: The International Monetary Fund.

IMF (2004). *World Economic Outlook*. Washington DC: International Monetary Fund, September.

Iskander, M. and Chamlou, N. (2000). "International Panel of Eminent Personalities to Investigate the 1994 Genocide in Rwanda and Surrounding Events". *Background of the Eminent Personalities and the Secretariat*, July.

Islam, R. (2003). "Institutional Reforms and the Judiciary, Which Way Forward?" *The World Bank Policy Research Working Paper 3134*, September.

Johnson, C. (1981). "Introduction: The Taiwanese Model", in J.H. Hsiung (ed.). *Contemporary Republic of China: The Taiwanese Experience"*. New York: Praeger.

Johnson, J. K., and Nakamura, R.T. (1999). "Legislators and Good Governance". A Concept Paper prepared for the UNDP, July.

Johnston, M. (1997). *What Can Be Done About Entrenched Corruption?* Washington DC: The World Bank.

Kaufmann, D. (2004). "Governance Redux: The Empirical Challenge". In *Global Competitiveness Report 2003–2004*. New York: Oxford University Press.

Kaufmann, D., Kraay, A. and Mastruzzi, M. (2003). "Governance Matters III: Governance Indicators for 1996–2002". *The World Bank Policy Research Working Paper 3106.* August.

Kiragu, K. (1999). "Public Financial Management", in Adamolekun, L. (ed.) (1999). *Public Administration in Africa: main issues and selected country studies.* Colorado: Westview Press.

Kjaer, M. A. (2004). *Governance.* Cambridge UK: Polity Press.

Korten, D. and Klauss, R. (1985). *People-Centred Development: Contributions Toward Theory and Planning Frameworks.* West Hartford CT: Kumarian Press.

Kpundeh, S. J. (1997). "Political Will in Fighting Corruption". In *Corruption and Integrity Improvement Initiatives in Developing Countries.* New York: UNDP.

Lane, Jan-Erik (1993). *The Public Sector: Concepts, Models and Approaches.* London: Sage.

Larbi, G. A. (1995). "Implications and Impact of Structural Adjustment on the Civil Service: The Case of Ghana". *The Role of Government in Adjusting Economies Paper, no. 2,* Development Administration Group, University of Birmingham.

Larbi, G. A. (1999). "The New Public Management Approach and Crisis States", *UNRISD Discussion Paper, no. 112.* Geneva: U.N. Research Institute for Social Development.

Layele, M. (1999). "Public Enterprises", in Adamolekun, L. (ed.) (1999). *Public Administration in Africa: main issues and selected country studies.* Colorado: Westview Press.

Levy, B. and Kpundeh, S. (eds.) (2004). *Building State Capacity for Good Governance in Africa Requires a Paradigm Shift.* Washington DC: The World Bank.

Lienert, I. (1998). "Civil Service Reform in Africa: Mixed Results After 10 Years". *Finance and Development,* vol.38, no.2, June.

Lienert, I. and Modi, J. (1997). "A Decade of Civil Service Reform in Sub-Saharan Africa". *IMF Working Paper, 97/179.* Washington DC: IMF.

Maruping, A. (1993). "Keynote Address" by Governor, Reserve Bank of Lesotho, at the Needs Assessment Workshop on Capacity Building in Debt and Reserve Management for Eastern and Southern Africa, February.

Mkandawire, T. (2001). "Thinking About Developmental States in Africa". *Cambridge Journal of Economics,* vol. 25, no. 3, pp.289–314.

Moody-Stuart, G. (1997). *The Costs of Grand Corruption.* Washington DC: Center for International Private Enterprise.

Moore, M. (1997). "Death Without Taxes: Democracy, State Capacity, and Aid Dependence in the Fourth World" in White, G. and Robinson, M. (eds.). *Towards a Democratic Developmental State.* Oxford: Oxford University Press.

Mutahaba, G., and Kiragu, K. (2002). "Lessons of International and African Perspectives on Public Service Reform: Examples from Five African Countries". *Africa Development*, vol. XXVII, nos. 3/4, pp. 48–75.

NEPAD (2001). *The New Partnership for Africa's Development Framework Document.* Abuja. October.

NEPAD (2004). *Annual Report 2003/04.* Addis Ababa: New Partnership for Africa's Development.

Ngethe, N., Katumanga, M. and Williams, G. (2004). "Strengthening the Incentives for Pro-Poor Change: An Analysis of the Drivers of Change in Kenya". DFID, May.

Niskanen, W.A. (1971). *Bureaucracy and Representative Government.* Chicago: Aldine-Atherton.

Olowu, D. (2003). "African Governance and Civil Service Reforms", in van de Walle, N., Ball, N. and Ramachandram, V. (eds.) *Beyond Structural Adjustment: The Institutional Context of African Development.* New York: Palgrave Macmillan.

Osei, H. (2001). "The State and Development in Southern Africa: A Comparative analysis of Botswana and Mauritius with Angola, Malawi and Zambia". *African Studies Quarterly*, vol. 5, Issue 1.

Oshikoya T.W. and Hussain, M.N. (1998). "Information Technology and the Challenge of Economic Development in Africa". *African Development Review*, vol.10, no.1. Abidjan: African Development Bank.

Pollitt, C. (1993). *Managerialism and the Public Services: The Anglo-American Experience.* Oxford: Blackwell.

Ramakrishnan, S. (1998). "Budgeting and financial Management in Sub-Saharan Africa: Key Policy and Institutional Issues". *Harvard Institute for International Development Discussion Paper No. 622.*

Rapley, J. (1996). *Understanding Development: Theory and Practice in the Third World.* Boulder CO: Lynne Rienner Publishers.

Rasheed, S. (1995). "Ethics and Accountability in the African Civil Service", *DPMN Bulletin*, vol.3, no.1, pp.12–14.

Rose-Ackerman, S. (1998). "Corruption and Development", in Pleskovic, B. and Stiglitz, J. (eds.) (1998). *Annual World Bank Conference on Development Economics 1997.* Washington DC: World Bank.

Said, J. and Varela, D.F. (2002). *Colombia, Modernization of the Itagui Court System — A Management Leadership Case Study.* Washington DC: The World Bank.

Salisu, M. (2003). "Incentive Structure, Civil Service Efficiency and the Hidden Economy in Nigeria". In Kayizzi-Mugerwa, S. (ed.). *Reforming Africa's Institutions: Ownership, Incentives, and Capabilities.* Oxford: Oxford University Press.

SARB (2004). *Monetary Policy Review*, May. Pretoria: South African Reserve Bank.

Schacter, M. (2000). "Public Sector Reform in Developing Countries — Issues, Lessons and

Future Directions", Prepared for the *Canadian International Development Agency*, December.

Schick, A. (1998). "Why Most Developing Countries Should Not Try New Zealand's Reforms", *The World Bank Research Observer*, vol.13, no.1, pp.123-131.

Sebudde, R. and Mutambi, B. (2004). "The Governance Environment of Monetary Policy and Monetary Policy Transmission in Uganda". *Centre for Study of African Economies Working Paper. University of Oxford.* September.

Seifert, J.W., Bouham, G. M. and Thorson, S.J. (2003). "The Transformative Potential of E-Government: The Role of Political Leadership", Paper Presented at Pan-European International Relations Conference, University of Kent, Canterbury, UK (Revised, January 2003).

Stapenhurst, F. (2004). "Parliamentary Strengthening: The Case of Ghana". *Capacity Enhancement Briefs, June.* World Bank Institute.

Stevens, M. and Teggermann, S. (2004) "Comparative experience with public service reform in Ghana, Tanzania, and Zambia," in Levy, B. and Kpundeh, S. (eds.) (2004). *Building State Capacity for Good Governance in Africa Requires a Paradigm Shift.* Washington DC: The World Bank.

Sulemane, J. A. and Kayizzi-Mugerwa, S. (2001). "The Mozambican Civil Service — Incentives, Reforms and Performance". *WIDER Discussion Paper No. 2001/85.*

Tanzi, V. (1998). "Corruption and the Budget: {Problems and Solutions". In Jain, K.A. (ed.). *Economics of Corruption.* London: Kluwer Academic Publishers.

Tanzi, V. (1999). "The Quality of the Public Sector" Paper delivered at the IMF Conference on Second Generation Reforms. November. Washington DC: The World Bank.

Theobald, R.(1990). *Corruption, Development and Underdevelopment.* Durham, NC: Duke University Press.

Thomas, V., et al. (2000). *The Quality of Growth.* Washington DC: The World Bank.

TI (2000). *An Independent Judicial System.* Berlin: Transparency International.

TI (2003). *Global Corruption Report 2003.* Berlin: Transparency International.

TI (2004). *Global Corruption Report 2004.* Berlin: Transparency International.

Turner, M. and Hulme, D. (1997). *Governance, Administration and Development: Making the State Work.* New York: Palgrave.

UN (2001). *The World Public Sector Report 2001: Globalization and the State.* New York: United Nations.

UN (2004). *Global Plan to Achieve the Millennium Development Goals.* New York: United Nations.

UN (2005). *World Economic Situation and Prospects.* New York: United Nations.

UNCTAD (2004). *World Investment Report 2004: A Shift Towards Services*. New York: United Nations.

UNIDO (2004). *Industrialization, Environment and the Millennium Development Goals in Sub-Saharan Africa, Industrial Report Series*. Vienna/New York: United Nations.

USAID/IRIS (1996). *Governance and the Economy in Africa: Tools for Analysis and Reform of Corruption*. USAID Senegal and Center for Institutional Reform and the Informal Sector (IRIS), University of Maryland.

Van de Walle, N. and Johnston, T.A. (1996). *Improving Aid to Africa*. Washington DC: Overseas Development Council.

Wamalwa, W. N. (1991). "An Address by the President of AAPAM", in Mutahaba, G. and Balogun, M.J. (eds.). *Enhancing Policy Management Capacity in Africa*. West Hartford CT: Kumarian Press.

World Bank (1981). *Accelerating Development in Sub-Saharan Africa: An Agenda for Action*. Washington DC: The World Bank.

World Bank (1997). *World Development Report 1997: The State in a Changing World*. Washington DC: The World Bank.

World Bank (1997a). *Helping Countries Combat Corruption: The Role of the World Bank. Poverty Reduction and Economic Management*. Washington DC: The World Bank.

World Bank (1999). *The Drive to Partnership: Aid Coordination and the World Bank*. Washington DC: The World Bank.

World Bank (2000). *Can African Claim the 21st Century?* Washington DC: The World Bank.

World Bank (2000a). *Reforming Public Institutions and Strengthening Governance: A World Bank Strategy*. Washington DC: The World Bank.

World Bank (2000b). *Comprehensive Development Framework — Questions and Answers Update*. Washington DC: The World Bank.

World Bank (2002). "Anti-Corruption". http://www.worldbank.org/publicsector/

World Bank (2002a), "Legal and Judicial Reform". http://www.worldbank.org/legal/leglr

World Bank (2004). *World Development Report 2004 — Making Services Work for Poor People*. Washington DC: The World Bank.

World Bank (2005). *Commodity Price Statistics (Pink Sheets)*, January. Washington DC: The World Bank.

Wunsch, J. (2000). "Refounding the African State and Local Governance: The Neglected Foundation". *The Journal of Modern African Studies*, vol.38, no.3, pp.487–509.

PART THREE

ECONOMIC AND SOCIAL STATISTICS ON AFRICA

Contents

Preface

The main purpose of this part of the Report is to present basic data that enable the monitoring of economic and social progress in regional member countries of the African Development Bank (ADB), and provide benchmark data for analysts of African development. The data cover the Bank's 53 regional member countries, with statistics on Basic Indicators, National Accounts, External Sector, Money Supply and Exchange Rates, Government Finance, External Debt and Financial Flows, Labor Force, and Social Indicators.

Throughout this part of the Report, statistical tables are arranged in sections and according to indicators. The tables contain historical data from 1980 to 2004. Period averages are provided for 1980–1990, and 1991–2004.

The data are obtained from various international sources and supplemented, to the extent possible, with data directly obtained from ADB regional member countries, and estimates by the ADB Statistics Division. Statistical practices vary from one regional member country to another with regard to data coverage, concepts, definitions, and classifications used. Although considerable efforts have been made to standardize the data, full comparability cannot be assured. Care should be exercised in their interpretation. They provide only indications on trend or structure that allow for the identification of significant differences between countries.

Technical information on these data is provided in the explanatory notes to facilitate appropriate interpretation. However, users are advised to refer to technical notes of the specialized publications of the main sources for more details.

The designations employed and the presentation of data therein do not imply any opinions whatsoever on the part of the African Development Bank concerning the legal status of any country or of its authorities. They were adopted solely for convenience of statistical presentation.

Symbols used

...   not available

0   zero or insignificant value

| break in the comparability of Data

TABLE 1.1
BASIC INDICATORS

COUNTRY	AREA ('000 Sq. Km)	POPULATION ('000) 2004	GNI PER CAPITA (US $) 2003	CONSUMER PRICE INFLATION (%) 2004	LIFE EXPECTANCY AT BIRTH (Years) 2004	INFANT MORTALITY RATE (per 1000) 2004	ADULT ILLITERACY RATE (%) 2004
ALGERIA	2,382	32,339	1,930	4.0	70	41	29
ANGOLA	1,247	14,078	740	43.5	40	136	...
BENIN	113	6,918	440	0.4	51	89	58
BOTSWANA	600	1,795	3,530	4.5	37	54	19
BURKINA FASO	274	13,393	300	-0.7	47	90	72
BURUNDI	28	7,068	90	7.0	42	104	47
CAMEROON	475	16,296	640	0.2	45	85	24
CAPE VERDE	4	473	1,440	1.1	71	28	23
CENT. AFR. REP.	623	3,912	260	-2.1	40	99	48
CHAD	1,284	8,854	240	-8.7	45	112	51
COMOROS	2	790	440	5.0	62	63	43
CONGO	342	3,818	650	3.3	49	80	15
CONGO (DRC)	2,345	54,417	100	7.9	43	118	33
COTE D'IVOIRE	322	16,897	650	0.2	42	98	47
DJIBOUTI	23	712	910	2.0	46	99	31
EGYPT	1,001	73,390	1,390	9.7	69	38	42
EQUAT. GUINEA	28	507	9301/	4.0	49	98	14
ERITREA	118	4,297	190	9.0	53	70	40
ETHIOPIA	1,104	72,420	90	7.5	46	97	56
GABON	268	1,351	3,400	-0.7	57	54	...
GAMBIA	11	1,462	280	16.7	55	77	59
GHANA	239	21,377	320	12.7	59	55	24
GUINEA	246	8,620	140	13.3	50	98	...
GUINEA BISSAU	36	1,538	430	0.0	46	116	56
KENYA	580	32,420	400	11.6	44	66	14
LESOTHO	30	1,800	610	4.7	34	89	15
LIBERIA	111	3,487	130	10.0	41	143	42
LIBYA	1,760	5,659	...	2.2	73	20	17
MADAGASCAR	587	17,901	290	5.0	54	88	30
MALAWI	118	12,337	160	6.0	38	111	37
MALI	1,240	13,409	420	-4.6	49	115	71
MAURITANIA	1,026	2,980	420	-6.7	53	93	58
MAURITIUS	2	1,233	4,090	3.4	72	15	14
MOROCCO	447	31,064	1,330	1.5	69	39	47
MOZAMBIQUE	802	19,182	210	8.1	38	118	51
NAMIBIA	824	2,011	1,930	-0.7	42	57	15
NIGER	1,267	12,415	200	-1.7	47	122	82
NIGERIA	924	127,117	350	11.7	51	76	31
RWANDA	26	8,481	220	8.2	40	107	28
SAO T. & PRINC.	1	165	300	14.0	70	30	...
SENEGAL	197	10,339	550	1.7	54	59	59
SEYCHELLES	0.5	85	7,480	4.2	...	...	...
SIERRA LEONE	72	5,168	150	3.5	34	172	...
SOMALIA	638	10,312	...		49	112	...
SOUTH AFRICA	1,221	45,214	2,880	2.6	45	46	13
SUDAN	2,506	34,333	460	5.0	56	74	38
SWAZILAND	17	1,083	1,350	6.7	33	75	18
TANZANIA	945	37,671	300	5.7	44	100	21
TOGO	57	5,017	310	2.5	50	78	38
TUNISIA	164	9,937	2,240	3.6	73	22	25
UGANDA	241	26,699	250	1.9	48	83	29
ZAMBIA	753	10,924	380	17.8	33	101	19
ZIMBABWE	391	12,932	4802/	350.0	32	56	9
AFRICA	30,061	868,097	704	7.7	51	79	36

TABLE 2.1
GROSS DOMESTIC PRODUCT, REAL
(MILLIONS US DOLLARS, CONSTANT 1995 PRICES)

COUNTRY	1980	1990	2000	2003	2004	Av. Ann. Real Growth Rate (%) 1981–1990	1991–2004
ALGERIA	31,660	41,595	48,935	55,819	58,818	2.8	2.5
ANGOLA	5,103	6,402	6,905	8,428	9,347	2.4	3.2
BENIN	1,256	1,635	2,552	2,940	3,006	2.8	4.4
BOTSWANA	1,523	4,267	7,041	7,995	8,346	10.9	4.9
BURKINA FASO	1,449	2,008	3,139	3,766	3,918	3.4	4.9
BURUNDI	728	1,126	946	998	1,052	4.5	−0.4
CAMEROON	6,310	8,752	10,118	11,480	11,950	3.6	2.3
CAPE VERDE	171	381	717	841	875	8.7	6.1
CENT. AFR. REP.	964	1,069	1,269	1,176	1,187	1.2	0.8
CHAD	788	1,311	1,638	2,205	2,895	5.6	6.3
COMOROS	167	223	252	269	274	3.0	1.5
CONGO	1,281	2,050	2,388	2,628	2,733	5.2	2.1
CONGO (DRC)	7,531	8,222	4,624	4,953	5,289	0.9	−2.9
COTE D'IVOIRE	9,513	10,215	12,930	12,519	12,268	0.7	1.4
DJIBOUTI	507	544	492	533	549	0.8	0.1
EGYPT	32,281	54,977	78,579	86,618	90,342	5.5	3.6
EQUAT. GUINEA	94	117	725	1,377	2,200	2.3	25.2
ERITREA	...	...	572	647	658	...	4.8
ETHIOPIA	4,541	5,495	7,376	7,756	8,648	2.1	3.5
GABON	3,633	4,345	5,022	5,266	5,350	2.1	1.6
GAMBIA	241	344	489	535	576	3.7	3.8
GHANA	4,236	5,243	7,983	9,141	9,669	2.3	4.5
GUINEA	2,265	3,075	4,530	4,968	5,092	3.1	3.7
GUINEA BISSAU	172	218	238	223	225	2.4	0.7
KENYA	5,612	8,360	9,884	10,296	10,615	4.1	1.7
LESOTHO	500	768	1,062	1,206	1,234	4.5	3.5
LIBERIA	...	...	...	...	...	...	...
LIBYA	39,789	27,016	33,542	37,688	38,028	−3.5	2.5
MADAGASCAR	3,048	3,212	3,814	3,877	4,084	0.6	1.9
MALAWI	992	1,234	1,724	1,754	1,829	2.2	3.1
MALI	2,267	2,406	3,459	4,319	4,410	0.8	4.5
MAURITANIA	757	891	1,334	1,546	1,626	1.7	4.4
MAURITIUS	1,810	3,193	5,336	5,973	6,221	5.9	4.9
MOROCCO	21,590	31,506	39,309	45,480	47,072	4.0	3.0
MOZAMBIQUE	1,938	1,967	3,381	4,395	4,737	0.5	6.6
NAMIBIA	2,434	2,751	4,161	4,519	4,717	1.2	4.0
NIGER	1,833	1,813	2,163	2,513	2,538	0.1	2.5
NIGERIA	22,357	24,864	33,178	38,446	39,849	1.3	3.5
RWANDA	1,645	2,011	2,046	2,409	2,506	2.1	3.6
SAO T. & PRINC.	48	42	50	58	62	−1.1	2.8
SENEGAL	3,063	4,158	5,790	6,584	6,979	3.2	3.8
SEYCHELLES	326	442	754	700	686	3.2	3.3
SIERRA LEONE	1,052	1,149	720	1,178	1,265	1.0	1.4
SOMALIA	...	...	...	...	...	...	...
SOUTH AFRICA	123,804	144,763	173,382	189,646	196,852	1.6	2.2
SUDAN	4,460	5,701	10,190	12,147	13,034	2.7	6.1
SWAZILAND	641	1,184	1,605	1,719	1,755	6.4	2.9
TANZANIA	3,474	4,808	6,418	7,832	8,413	3.3	4.1
TOGO	1,175	1,304	1,470	1,613	1,660	1.1	2.0
TUNISIA	10,509	14,915	23,699	26,671	28,132	3.6	4.7
UGANDA	2,899	4,102	7,833	9,188	9,730	3.6	6.4
ZAMBIA	3,366	3,733	3,992	4,544	4,776	1.1	1.9
ZIMBABWE	4,376	6,734	7,118	5,858	5,577	4.5	−1.2
AFRICA	384,625	470,636	599,437	668,140	696,686	2.0	3.1

TABLE 2.2
GROSS DOMESTIC PRODUCT, NOMINAL
(MILLIONS US DOLLARS AT CURRENT MARKET PRICES)

COUNTRY	1980	1990	2000	2003	2004	Av. Ann. Nonimal Change (%) 1981–1990	1991–2004
ALGERIA	42,318	66,127	54,462	66,530	82,416	4.9	2.3
ANGOLA	5,400	10,260	9,130	13,825	20,265	7.0	8.9
BENIN	1,405	1,845	2,255	3,557	4,080	3.6	7.2
BOTSWANA	1,152	3,899	5,240	7,925	8,646	14.7	6.1
BURKINA FASO	1,929	3,120	2,601	4,264	5,082	5.7	4.7
BURUNDI	920	1,132	709	595	675	2.3	−3.2
CAMEROON	6,741	11,152	9,213	13,806	16,002	5.7	3.8
CAPE VERDE	107	339	549	831	967	15.0	8.2
CENT. AFR. REP.	797	1,488	953	1,197	1,379	7.5	0.6
CHAD	1,033	1,739	1,392	2,637	4,261	6.0	8.7
COMOROS	124	263	200	308	359	9.0	3.4
CONGO	1,706	2,799	3,220	3,564	4,384	5.7	5.1
CONGO (DRC)	14,869	9,348	4,303	5,681	6,572	−3.5	−1.0
COTE D'IVOIRE	10,175	10,796	10,599	14,045	15,444	1.4	3.5
DJIBOUTI	296	418	553	625	664	3.5	3.4
EGYPT	22,913	43,094	99,049	80,189	75,537	6.8	4.6
EQUAT. GUINEA	61	132	1,263	2,977	4,431	9.7	32.3
ERITREA	...	...	634	751	925	...	6.5
ETHIOPIA	5,024	6,854	6,473	6,637	8,075	3.5	1.9
GABON	4,279	5,952	5,065	6,068	6,839	4.3	1.8
GAMBIA	241	317	421	368	415	3.9	2.1
GHANA	4,446	5,887	4,978	7,624	8,734	3.3	4.0
GUINEA	6,684	2,818	3,112	3,632	3,779	4.8	2.3
GUINEA BISSAU	139	262	215	239	270	8.8	0.7
KENYA	7,265	8,531	10,454	14,376	14,424	1.9	4.8
LESOTHO	431	615	884	1,128	1,439	4.7	7.4
LIBERIA	...	...	...	...	...	...	...
LIBYA	36,273	28,905	34,265	24,129	30,357	−1.8	1.7
MADAGASCAR	4,042	3,081	3,878	5,474	4,273	−1.9	3.3
MALAWI	1,238	1,881	1,707	1,718	1,896	4.6	3.2
MALI	1,787	2,730	2,668	4,218	5,106	5.4	5.6
MAURITANIA	709	1,062	960	1,129	1,257	4.4	1.6
MAURITIUS	1,153	2,667	4,552	5,651	6,360	9.6	6.6
MOROCCO	18,805	25,821	33,335	43,727	50,171	4.2	5.2
MOZAMBIQUE	3,526	2,463	3,738	4,321	5,570	−0.3	6.9
NAMIBIA	2,166	2,350	3,458	4,271	5,435	1.6	6.9
NIGER	2,509	2,481	1,798	2,731	3,163	0.9	2.8
NIGERIA	64,202	28,472	45,984	58,390	72,327	−6.4	8.4
RWANDA	1,163	2,584	1,794	1,684	1,755	8.4	1.7
SAO T. & PRINC.	47	58	46	60	70	2.9	1.9
SENEGAL	2,987	5,715	4,374	6,417	7,550	8.1	3.2
SEYCHELLES	147	368	618	695	709	9.9	4.9
SIERRA LEONE	1,100	650	636	984	1,038	−0.9	4.3
SOMALIA	...	...	..	..	...	...	...
SOUTH AFRICA	80,423	112,014	132,878	165,434	214,168	4.5	5.8
SUDAN	7,617	13,167	12,191	17,792	20,541	7.5	5.1
SWAZILAND	544	859	1,389	1,812	2,281	6.2	8.3
TANZANIA	4,771	4,259	9,081	10,297	10,851	2.0	7.3
TOGO	1,136	1,628	1,329	1,839	2,137	4.9	3.2
TUNISIA	8,743	12,314	19,444	25,000	28,186	3.7	6.4
UGANDA	1,245	4,304	5,414	6,319	7,315	16.9	5.1
ZAMBIA	3,878	3,288	3,238	4,335	5,352	1.4	4.1
ZIMBABWE	6,679	8,773	7,204	7,904	5,763	3.5	−1.5
AFRICA	399,063	472,383	576,443	672,434	792,625	1.8	4.0

TABLE 2.3
GROSS NATIONAL SAVINGS
(PERCENTAGE OF GDP)

COUNTRY	1980	1990	2000	2003	2004	Annual Average 1980–1990	1991–2004
ALGERIA	30.4	31.6	41.4	38.3	42.4	26.9	32.1
ANGOLA	20.8	1.7	44.4	26.5	26.0	12.1	20.9
BENIN	29.3	12.0	10.9	9.8	11.4	9.9	11.4
BOTSWANA	30.7	37.8	33.8	33.4	31.6	31.5	30.3
BURKINA FASO	12.2	15.0	16.4	7.9	10.2	15.2	14.6
BURUNDI	4.8	...	−4.0	3.0	4.6	6.7	1.5
CAMEROON	20.4	16.2	14.7	12.4	11.9	20.0	13.6
CAPE VERDE	−108.0	19.0	10.0	10.4	10.5	13.0	18.4
CENT. AFR. REP.	−2.9	8.5	7.4	5.2	4.0	3.2	5.6
CHAD	11.3	0.4	3.3	6.1	7.0	2.6	4.1
COMOROS	14.7	18.3	10.5	12.1	10.0	17.1	10.8
CONGO	30.5	6.9	29.0	25.5	21.0	25.4	12.4
CONGO (DRC)	6.4	5.2	−1.2	6.3	11.4	6.2	7.9
COTE D'IVOIRE	22.1	−2.1	7.8	19.8	17.7	10.3	9.2
DJIBOUTI	25.3	11.8	5.1	4.0	6.7	8.1	6.9
EGYPT	16.5	19.1	17.2	16.3	...	16.0	18.7
EQUAT. GUINEA	−29.4	−9.0	14.3	21.3	25.1	−12.3	16.9
ERITREA	...	...	2.1	13.3	11.5	...	16.7
ETHIOPIA	7.3	10.5	10.0	14.5	15.1	9.8	13.1
GABON	54.5	24.2	28.0	24.9	25.2	37.5	25.5
GAMBIA	...	17.8	12.7	10.3	8.9	18.4	13.3
GHANA	5.8	23.4	15.6	20.3	22.2	8.4	17.5
GUINEA	9.0	2.7	14.7	16.2	14.1	7.1	14.0
GUINEA BISSAU	9.5	14.2	2.8	2.2	4.3	9.3	5.3
KENYA	7.5	19.9	12.7	14.1	12.1	18.1	15.4
LESOTHO	43.1	46.4	23.4	24.7	24.8	31.9	24.1
LIBERIA	...	...	...	...	...	...	...
LIBYA	...	...	...	...	...	...	...
MADAGASCAR	1.2	4.1	25.0	10.1	18.2	3.2	9.6
MALAWI	8.1	12.1	4.1	−0.1	3.2	11.2	4.7
MALI	7.0	14.9	10.0	14.1	14.0	9.7	13.8
MAURITANIA	14.2	6.4	29.4	27.9	21.6	11.4	17.7
MAURITIUS	14.9	25.9	24.2	27.0	27.3	20.5	26.6
MOROCCO	16.5	22.9	22.3	25.7	26.2	19.3	21.9
MOZAMBIQUE	1.3	−8.7	18.0	26.7	22.1	0.5	9.0
NAMIBIA	21.2	29.4	26.3	29.8	27.5	19.7	25.4
NIGER	17.1	7.4	5.0	7.4	7.7	10.0	5.2
NIGERIA	23.3	29.5	25.9	15.4	23.7	15.4	18.6
RWANDA	8.8	3.6	12.6	11.5	8.6	8.8	7.0
SAO T. & PRINC.	−10.4	−9.3	23.0	6.1	18.2	−6.2	11.7
SENEGAL	−1.8	10.4	12.3	13.7	14.4	4.4	11.7
SEYCHELLES	11.5	20.0	22.8	6.8	14.1	16.6	17.4
SIERRA LEONE	3.6	−1.5	−1.8	−5.8	2.3	3.2	−3.6
SOMALIA	...	...	...	...	...	...	...
SOUTH AFRICA	33.9	19.1	15.2	16.1	15.3	23.9	16.0
SUDAN	−68.7	9.1	...	...	10.1	14.2	0.8
SWAZILAND	16.7	24.9	16.2	14.4	14.3	21.2	17.8
TANZANIA	20.7	20.9	12.3	14.5	11.4	16.7	11.1
TOGO	18.3	20.4	4.6	9.1	10.7	14.7	7.3
TUNISIA	24.6	21.6	23.1	21.8	22.3	22.6	22.2
UGANDA	42.4	5.9	12.8	14.9	15.8	16.6	12.6
ZAMBIA	11.8	14.8	0.7	3.9	5.7	8.9	6.6
ZIMBABWE	14.5	16.4	15.0	−0.9	−1.6	13.8	11.5
AFRICA	19.5	18.5	18.7	18.3	19.1	18.0	17.3

TABLE 2.4
GROSS DOMESTIC INVESTMENT
(PERCENTAGE OF GDP)

COUNTRY	1980	1990	2000	2003	2004	Annual Average 1980–1990	1991–2004
ALGERIA	39.1	28.9	23.0	29.8	28.8	33.7	27.9
ANGOLA	20.4	7.0	23.0	40.2	33.4	17.1	29.5
BENIN	35.6	14.2	18.7	20.3	18.2	19.8	17.6
BOTSWANA	40.4	37.8	19.0	25.5	27.2	32.4	27.3
BURKINA FASO	14.6	18.6	21.1	18.8	20.6	18.8	22.5
BURUNDI	16.9	13.5	8.4	11.3	12.4	17.5	10.6
CAMEROON	21.0	17.8	15.3	15.9	15.3	23.3	15.3
CAPE VERDE	38.7	24.4	19.7	18.1	17.5	43.7	25.9
CENT. AFR. REP.	12.3	6.1	9.5	6.0	6.8	9.9	9.1
CHAD	11.2	11.5	17.5	44.1	22.9	10.9	21.0
COMOROS	20.5	19.7	10.6	11.8	10.4	17.7	14.6
CONGO	20.8	15.9	21.0	23.2	22.9	25.5	27.7
CONGO (DRC)	24.7	34.4	12.3	12.3	12.3	31.0	13.5
COTE D'IVOIRE	22.8	6.7	10.5	9.6	8.5	15.0	10.4
DJIBOUTI	13.1	17.4	12.2	15.5	20.6	16.1	12.5
EGYPT	35.7	29.4	19.6	17.1	16.7	30.5	19.0
EQUAT. GUINEA	35.7	17.4	43.9	29.2	13.6	23.9	58.1
ERITREA	...	...	19.4	37.9	32.2	...	24.1
ETHIOPIA	12.6	12.0	15.9	20.5	19.5	13.9	16.2
GABON	32.9	21.7	22.6	29.7	29.5	36.8	26.8
GAMBIA	41.5	20.4	17.6	20.0	24.6	24.5	20.3
GHANA	5.6	26.7	24.0	23.2	24.8	9.9	23.3
GUINEA	13.4	12.7	22.0	9.9	10.7	14.3	18.0
GUINEA BISSAU	53.4	27.9	11.3	11.1	15.3	36.3	20.6
KENYA	22.8	24.2	15.4	12.9	13.7	22.8	17.1
LESOTHO	37.2	50.9	41.5	33.5	31.4	39.1	47.3
LIBERIA	...	...	...	...	...	...	...
LIBYA	25.3	18.6	12.9	10.5	12.6	22.3	13.1
MADAGASCAR	15.0	14.8	16.2	16.2	22.4	11.0	14.0
MALAWI	24.7	20.6	9.6	10.8	11.9	18.8	14.1
MALI	27.8	22.2	19.9	24.5	27.0	27.6	22.8
MAURITANIA	36.1	17.9	23.5	24.9	37.7	28.5	21.2
MAURITIUS	24.8	31.2	25.6	23.6	25.0	24.4	26.6
MOROCCO	24.2	25.3	23.7	23.2	22.8	24.4	22.2
MOZAMBIQUE	12.2	22.5	36.6	44.7	44.3	15.0	30.6
NAMIBIA	20.8	27.9	19.5	22.7	22.6	17.7	21.0
NIGER	28.1	11.0	11.4	14.2	15.4	14.9	10.6
NIGERIA	18.5	21.6	20.6	22.8	22.7	18.9	21.6
RWANDA	12.4	11.7	17.5	18.4	20.3	15.1	15.6
SAO T. & PRINC.	16.8	29.5	35.8	30.7	48.0	18.5	41.8
SENEGAL	24.1	14.6	20.8	19.5	20.2	19.8	17.6
SEYCHELLES	38.3	24.6	29.3	18.8	18.5	26.2	28.1
SIERRA LEONE	17.7	9.4	8.0	14.2	19.6	11.7	6.9
SOMALIA	...	...	...	...	...	...	...
SOUTH AFRICA	29.9	17.2	15.9	16.8	17.1	23.1	16.4
SUDAN	−3.6	7.3	17.9	18.2	20.4	3.5	19.1
SWAZILAND	40.7	19.1	21.3	18.6	19.2	27.1	20.9
TANZANIA	37.8	26.1	17.6	18.6	21.4	28.8	20.0
TOGO	33.4	25.0	14.8	14.5	13.3	25.0	13.3
TUNISIA	29.4	27.1	27.3	25.0	24.7	28.6	27.1
UGANDA	4.8	11.9	19.9	20.6	21.7	6.9	16.6
ZAMBIA	27.0	17.3	18.7	26.1	25.4	19.6	16.9
ZIMBABWE	18.8	17.4	7.0	1.9	3.1	18.2	14.9
AFRICA	26.3	21.6	18.9	20.0	20.1	23.7	19.7

TABLE 2.5
TERMS OF TRADE
(1995 = 100)

COUNTRY	1983	1993	1999	2003	2004	Annual Average Growth Rate (%) 1983–1993	1994–2004
ALGERIA	158.9	98.5	95.5	150.6	168.6	−3.0	7.1
ANGOLA	231.4	105.3	125.4	166.4	219.4	−5.3	10.1
BENIN	50.2	76.7	73.9	78.8	88.7	9.9	2.3
BOTSWANA	26.4	102.3	107.2	90.8	85.1	23.6	−1.6
BURKINA FASO	63.9	84.6	84.5	75.7	75.4	3.4	−0.7
BURUNDI	115.2	66.7	83.2	49.1	49.0	−0.6	−1.1
CAMEROON	179.7	97.7	77.6	109.1	111.8	−4.3	2.0
CAPE VERDE	288.8	101.7	70.1	68.6	68.3	−2.1	−3.1
CENT. AFR. REP.	111.6	101.1	92.8	93.2	86.0	1.2	−1.0
CHAD	58.9	67.4	91.9	154.4	205.2	4.1	12.0
COMOROS	291.4	170.3	110.6	564.1	564.0	−4.9	19.7
CONGO	187.8	113.4	109.0	189.6	210.1	−4.8	8.7
CONGO (DRC)	79.9	87.3	94.2	90.8	86.1	3.5	0.3
COTE D'IVOIRE	84.5	77.0	90.2	101.5	95.3	0.2	2.8
DJIBOUTI	384.9	114.3	147.3	137.9	144.9	−9.7	3.2
EGYPT	122.4	97.8	98.9	123.0	124.8	−1.5	2.5
EQUAT. GUINEA	107.3	104.0	109.3	122.1	194.8	1.4	11.8
ERITREA	..	98.3	97.3	79.9	79.9	−1.2	−1.7
ETHIOPIA	152.8	70.4	83.3	42.9	39.8	−2.2	−3.3
GABON	65.7	97.6	114.4	123.5	138.8	5.1	4.8
GAMBIA	84.6	104.8	82.2	73.0	58.5	2.5	−2.8
GHANA	99.2	78.6	98.8	98.8	91.9	−3.0	2.0
GUINEA	99.6	131.3	114.3	112.7	108.9	5.0	−1.3
GUINEA BISSAU	147.7	125.0	112.8	93.6	89.9	−0.3	−1.6
KENYA	138.5	79.6	91.0	83.2	76.9	−2.8	−0.1
LESOTHO	160.4	100.4	110.0	98.8	97.8	−3.9	0.1
LIBERIA	...	...	...	...	...	...	...
LIBYA	268.8	111.9	124.8	172.7	196.6	−5.1	7.0
MADAGASCAR	139.3	86.2	63.1	66.3	61.0	0.6	−2.0
MALAWI	94.3	86.8	101.3	89.8	88.6	0.4	0.4
MALI	93.9	73.6	104.2	94.2	100.9	−1.3	3.8
MAURITANIA	60.3	76.6	93.4	111.3	100.4	3.2	3.7
MAURITIUS	62.3	105.9	108.5	108.2	109.5	5.8	0.4
MOROCCO	108.0	95.2	110.1	100.8	97.9	−2.6	0.5
MOZAMBIQUE	81.2	99.8	82.2	93.4	93.9	4.3	−0.3
NAMIBIA	154.0	92.9	111.8	108.9	101.1	−1.8	1.4
NIGER	184.9	112.7	96.7	92.9	93.1	−2.6	−1.1
NIGERIA	153.5	107.3	116.5	162.9	195.0	0.0	7.8
RWANDA	140.8	72.9	90.1	73.3	66.0	−3.6	0.8
SAO T. & PRINC.	250.2	100.0	96.9	103.6	100.1	1.0	0.6
SENEGAL	98.0	99.5	104.6	104.0	102.0	0.6	0.4
SEYCHELLES	541.6	131.1	60.9	79.6	86.2	5.8	−1.2
SIERRA LEONE	96.5	99.2	110.4	88.9	87.1	0.3	−0.9
SOMALIA	115.8	100.2	99.6	99.2	99.2	−0.5	−0.1
SOUTH AFRICA	97.6	103.4	95.2	103.4	106.4	0.9	0.3
SUDAN	71.1	78.6	98.5	116.8	130.2	2.1	5.1
SWAZILAND	94.8	96.8	94.4	90.3	91.2	0.3	−0.5
TANZANIA	173.5	84.7	135.1	137.6	123.7	−6.5	4.1
TOGO	191.9	78.2	90.2	93.0	105.9	−6.4	4.2
TUNISIA	124.7	102.8	96.7	92.7	92.5	−2.0	−0.9
UGANDA	112.9	73.4	86.3	76.0	73.3	4.3	0.7
ZAMBIA	118.6	86.6	74.9	68.7	75.8	−0.6	−0.8
ZIMBABWE	67.1	90.1	103.1	99.8	99.5	5.0	1.0
AFRICA	123.2	99.1	101.1	117.4	125.3	−1.8	2.3

TABLE 2.6
CURRENT ACCOUNT BALANCE
(AS PERCENTAGE OF GDP)

COUNTRY	1983	1993	1999	2003	2004	Annual Average 1983–1993	Annual Average 1994–2004
ALGERIA	−0.2	1.6	0.0	13.4	13.1	0.4	5.7
ANGOLA	−6.8	−8.8	−27.8	−4.9	9.2	−4.3	−8.6
BENIN	−16.9	−4.5	−7.6	−8.5	−8.4	−5.7	−6.8
BOTSWANA	−16.7	10.3	12.3	11.0	6.4	2.9	9.3
BURKINA FASO	−3.2	−5.1	−10.8	−6.8	−8.4	−3.6	−8.3
BURUNDI	−13.1	−8.5	−6.1	−6.2	−15.1	−10.8	−8.0
CAMEROON	2.3	−5.4	−4.3	−2.5	−2.1	−1.9	−3.3
CAPE VERDE	−8.7	−9.1	−12.4	−8.9	−8.9	−4.5	−9.9
CENT. AFR. REP.	−13.2	−2.2	−1.6	−5.2	−2.8	−5.6	−3.3
CHAD	−4.9	−14.1	−15.9	−39.0	−18.3	−10.4	−20.2
COMOROS	0.4	−8.2	−6.4	−4.5	−2.2	−16.2	−7.9
CONGO	0.0	2.9	−17.1	−0.1	1.6	9.8	−13.4
CONGO (DRC)	−2.4	−3.5	−2.6	0.6	−3.0	−6.4	−3.1
COTE D'IVOIRE	−7.8	−10.3	−1.3	3.6	−0.2	−6.8	−0.7
DJIBOUTI	−18.8	−5.7	−0.4	−6.2	−10.7	−10.8	−4.9
EGYPT	−4.2	4.7	−1.9	2.4	3.2	−1.1	0.1
EQUAT. GUINEA	−22.6	−22.2	−43.6	−0.3	18.3	−21.3	−40.3
ERITREA	...	11.1	−28.2	−15.3	−9.9	...	−6.6
ETHIOPIA	−4.1	−3.3	−7.9	−4.7	−3.8	−2.6	−3.0
GABON	13.0	−1.1	8.4	9.6	11.6	−0.6	8.6
GAMBIA	−1.5	−4.6	−2.8	−5.2	−6.1	−1.4	−4.5
GHANA	−0.8	−9.4	−11.6	1.7	0.3	−3.0	−4.8
GUINEA	−0.2	−6.2	−7.6	−3.3	−2.9	−6.0	−6.0
GUINEA BISSAU	−25.4	−21.0	−12.0	−3.5	−2.2	−25.6	−12.0
KENYA	−0.7	2.9	−2.2	−2.5	−7.7	−2.8	−3.3
LESOTHO	−8.9	−27.3	−22.8	−11.1	−6.4	−19.3	−20.7
LIBERIA	...	...	...	...	...	...	...
LIBYA	−5.4	−4.5	5.4	13.6	21.3	−1.3	7.2
MADAGASCAR	−7.0	−7.8	−5.4	−6.0	−8.6	−7.1	−6.4
MALAWI	−8.5	−8.8	−8.2	−8.1	−10.0	−5.7	−9.0
MALI	−6.1	−4.1	−8.8	−4.2	−5.0	−5.4	−7.0
MAURITANIA	−28.3	−9.9	3.0	−10.0	−23.1	−11.4	−5.6
MAURITIUS	−5.0	−1.4	−1.5	2.6	2.6	−1.5	0.0
MOROCCO	−7.1	−1.9	−0.5	3.1	0.2	−4.7	0.3
MOZAMBIQUE	−12.7	−24.2	−22.4	−14.7	−9.3	−15.7	−18.0
NAMIBIA	0.0	3.2	6.9	4.0	5.5	2.4	4.5
NIGER	−3.5	−0.7	−6.5	−6.2	−7.9	−2.5	−6.5
NIGERIA	−13.9	−10.3	−8.4	−2.8	2.9	−4.9	−1.5
RWANDA	−5.5	−11.0	−7.7	−8.4	−6.8	−7.6	−6.7
SAO T. & PRINC.	−23.2	−62.8	−45.4	−36.1	−59.9	−43.1	−46.8
SENEGAL	−11.9	−8.9	−5.6	−6.4	−7.3	−8.6	−5.3
SEYCHELLES	−17.6	−8.9	−19.8	−2.8	1.0	−7.9	−11.1
SIERRA LEONE	−6.7	−8.6	−11.1	−7.6	−12.1	−6.2	−9.3
SOMALIA	−6.8	−10.1	−5.2	−2.3	−1.9	−8.7	−5.2
SOUTH AFRICA	−0.4	1.1	−0.4	−0.8	−2.0	1.7	−0.8
SUDAN	−10.1	−24.7	−15.8	−8.2	−6.8	−16.1	−14.5
SWAZILAND	0.0	−6.0	−2.6	−4.1	−6.0	3.2	−3.5
TANZANIA	−5.2	−7.0	−9.9	−2.4	−5.2	−4.3	−7.0
TOGO	−10.9	−5.9	−9.5	−11.7	−8.6	−6.0	−10.7
TUNISIA	−9.0	−8.8	−2.2	−2.9	−2.8	−5.9	−3.4
UGANDA	−0.7	−3.0	−7.4	−5.9	−1.2	−2.1	−4.5
ZAMBIA	−9.9	−2.7	−13.7	−13.3	−10.8	−6.2	−11.0
ZIMBABWE	−7.2	−2.1	2.5	−4.4	−7.1	−2.4	−3.1
AFRICA	−4.0	−1.8	−3.2	0.2	0.7	−2.3	−1.4

TABLE 2.7
BROAD MONEY SUPPLY (M2)
(PERCENTAGE ANNUAL CHANGE)

COUNTRY	1980	1990	2000	2003	2004	Annual Average 1980–1990	1991–2004
ALGERIA	17.4	11.4	13.2	16.0	4.9	14.4	18.2
ANGOLA	...	...	...	...	...	...	...
BENIN	48.9	28.6	26.0	−11.3	−6.8	12.7	9.6
BOTSWANA	19.0	−14.0	1.4	15.5	11.6	22.6	16.9
BURKINA FASO	15.1	−0.5	6.2	19.0	0.3	11.8	8.7
BURUNDI	1.4	9.6	4.3	15.8	−2.3	11.6	13.9
CAMEROON	21.4	−1.7	19.1	1.3	0.8	11.1	5.2
CAPE VERDE	30.6	14.6	13.7	9.0	3.2	18.7	11.4
CENT. AFR. REP.	35.0	−3.7	2.4	−8.0	2.6	8.4	5.1
CHAD	−15.3	−2.4	18.5	−3.1	2.6	8.4	9.2
COMOROS	...	3.9	14.5	−1.2	−2.5	12.7	6.4
CONGO	36.6	18.5	58.5	−2.4	0.0	14.0	5.8
CONGO (DRC)	...	...	...	...	...	...	...
COTE D'IVOIRE	2.8	−2.6	−1.9	−6.1	1.1	4.0	8.1
DJIBOUTI	...	3.6	1.1	17.8	3.2	7.6	2.4
EGYPT	51.4	28.7	11.6	21.3	4.4	25.7	12.4
EQUAT. GUINEA	...	−52.0	36.2	56.7	11.4	−9.0	36.5
ERITREA	...	...	17.3	15.1	2.7	...	21.6
ETHIOPIA	4.2	19.9	13.1	12.4	9.3	11.9	12.4
GABON	24.6	3.3	18.3	−1.2	3.2	8.6	6.3
GAMBIA	10.4	8.4	34.8	...	...	18.8	16.9
GHANA	33.8	13.3	54.2	34.2	0.5	42.2	36.9
GUINEA	...	...	...	33.2	12.8	...	14.6
GUINEA BISSAU	...	574.6	60.8	14.4	11.2	211.6	33.6
KENYA	0.8	20.1	4.5	11.9	3.9	12.7	16.4
LESOTHO	...	8.4	1.4	6.0	0.3	18.0	10.4
LIBERIA	...	...	...	...	...	...	...
LIBYA	26.6	19.0	3.1	7.8	4.3	7.2	5.3
MADAGASCAR	20.6	4.5	17.2	8.8	10.8	16.9	19.8
MALAWI	12.6	11.1	45.5	27.5	9.9	17.6	31.5
MALI	4.5	−4.9	12.2	22.7	4.7	8.1	14.0
MAURITANIA	12.5	11.5	16.1	10.5	3.6	13.0	5.5
MAURITIUS	23.2	21.2	9.2	10.9	5.1	21.0	13.2
MOROCCO	10.8	21.5	8.4	8.7	1.7	14.1	9.3
MOZAMBIQUE	...	37.2	38.3	18.3	−0.3	39.5	34.2
NAMIBIA	...	...	13.0	20.7	4.6	...	17.5
NIGER	20.8	−4.1	12.4	−13.2	7.0	7.5	0.5
NIGERIA	46.1	32.7	48.1	24.1	6.0	18.1	30.2
RWANDA	8.1	5.6	15.6	15.4	...	7.8	14.6
SAO T. & PRINC.	...	...	24.9	52.4	−7.9	...	38.4
SENEGAL	10.3	−4.8	10.7	14.6	2.4	7.6	9.2
SEYCHELLES	35.8	13.6	4.6	5.9	−0.4	12.1	13.0
SIERRA LEONE	21.6	74.0	12.1	21.9	7.9	51.8	27.9
SOMALIA	...	...	...	...	...	...	...
SOUTH AFRICA	22.8	11.4	7.2	12.5	5.9	17.2	13.2
SUDAN	29.4	48.8	36.9	30.3	12.2	38.0	51.9
SWAZILAND	13.7	0.6	−6.6	14.1	−1.4	17.1	11.7
TANZANIA	26.9	41.9	14.8	16.6	8.2	25.7	22.2
TOGO	9.1	9.5	15.2	5.9	14.1	9.0	5.2
TUNISIA	18.5	7.6	14.1	6.4	3.6	14.9	9.2
UGANDA	34.8	...	18.1	17.9	4.5	83.6	21.4
ZAMBIA	9.0	47.9	73.8	22.7	12.5	38.6	39.9
ZIMBABWE	29.3	15.1	68.9	430.0	81.2	16.8	83.4
AFRICA	23.2	20.6	17.9	18.0	15.6	19.3	22.7

TABLE 2.8
REAL EXCHANGE RATES INDICES (PERIOD AVERAGE)
(NATIONAL CURRENCY PER US $, 1995 = 100)

COUNTRY	CURRENCY	1980	1990	2000	2003	2004*	Average Percentage Growth 1990–2000	2001–2004
ALGERIA	DINAR	36.7	54.5	129.7	130.2	119.1	10.6	−2.0
ANGOLA	NEW KWANZA	...	31.1	98.4	74.7	54.9	22.7	−13.2
BENIN	CFA FRANC	...	80.5	133.9	108.1	98.1	5.3	−7.3
BOTSWANA	PULA	75.0	104.7	138.9	121.5	113.0	1.6	−4.1
BURKINA FASO	CFA FRANC	44.3	63.5	143.5	116.7	108.7	8.2	−6.6
BURUNDI	FRANC	67.3	101.4	136.0	189.1	188.2	4.2	8.6
CAMEROON	CFA FRANC	71.2	64.6	135.6	107.6	97.6	8.1	−7.7
CAPE VERDE	ESCUDO	...	113.1	139.8	117.9	106.9	1.6	−6.2
CENT. AFR. REP.	CFA FRANC	42.9	65.0	153.5	117.8	107.1	8.8	−8.3
CHAD	CFA FRANC	...	62.2	138.4	98.1	87.9	7.0	−10.6
COMOROS	FRANC	...	85.6	133.5	113.9	104.0	3.1	−5.6
CONGO	CFA FRANC	74.1	72.0	126.7	103.9	94.9	4.9	−6.6
CONGO (DRC)	FRANC	22.0	89.1	50.7	354.0	323.8	0.7	91.9
COTE D'IVOIRE	CFA FRANC	59.0	72.7	139.6	108.1	97.2	6.7	−8.4
DJIBOUTI	FRANC	...	110.4	99.8	101.1	101.6	−0.9	0.5
EGYPT	POUND	101.5	74.8	91.0	151.2	155.9	9.3	14.8
EQUAT. GUINEA	CFA FRANC	...	74.9	130.0	92.2	79.5	6.0	−11.3
ERITREA	NAKFA	...	...	108.6	100.7	94.1	...	−2.9
ETHIOPIA	BIRR	51.4	53.2	142.3	161.1	157.0	10.8	3.0
GABON	CFA FRANC	48.3	64.9	145.1	123.4	112.6	8.2	−5.9
GAMBIA	DALASI	66.1	99.1	132.4	237.9	255.5	2.7	18.0
GHANA	CEDI	14.3	75.3	169.8	150.1	143.3	8.9	−4.0
GUINEA	FRANC	...	93.9	161.6	170.8	170.9	5.7	1.5
GUINEA BISSAU	CFA FRANC	...	68.7	112.1	89.0	80.5	4.4	−7.7
KENYA	SHILLING	70.3	111.6	110.7	97.3	98.4	0.8	−2.7
LESOTHO	MALOTI	75.1	113.2	147.0	131.7	110.4	2.0	−4.5
LIBERIA	DOLLAR	163.5	131.5	2,878.0	3,049.2	2,595.2	356.9	−1.7
LIBYA	DINAR	...	138.4	124.4	351.3	355.4	−1.3	36.2
MADAGASCAR	FRANC	38.5	85.1	107.6	86.2	126.9	1.7	6.5
MALAWI	KWACHA	53.9	61.8	120.3	138.0	125.3	7.2	1.8
MALI	CFA FRANC	...	62.3	149.3	116.5	108.5	8.8	−7.4
MAURITANIA	OUGUIYA	...	75.1	163.7	166.4	162.0	7.3	−0.1
MAURITIUS	RUPEE	74.0	107.4	124.9	121.6	118.1	1.0	−1.2
MOROCCO	DIRHAM	67.4	110.9	128.2	117.9	111.5	1.1	−3.1
MOZAMBIQUE	METICAL	...	61.2	106.3	123.3	105.7	4.6	1.1
NAMIBIA	DOLLAR	68.2	106.6	146.0	130.2	109.8	2.5	−4.7
NIGER	CFA FRANC	36.9	66.9	141.4	114.9	108.9	8.0	−6.1
NIGERIA	NAIRA	66.4	241.3	298.3	268.8	240.2	21.0	−5.2
RWANDA	FRANC	79.5	121.0	123.6	163.4	163.2	4.4	7.3
SAO T. & PRINC.	DOBRA	...	34.0	144.2	138.5	140.5	14.3	−0.6
SENEGAL	CFA FRANC	56.2	65.1	153.5	124.7	114.1	8.2	−6.9
SEYCHELLES	RUPEE	106.0	104.1	118.3	105.1	103.4	0.9	−3.3
SIERRA LEONE	LEONE	85.9	110.3	122.7	138.4	157.6	3.9	6.7
SOMALIA	SHILLING	52.4	0.0	58.3	46.6	50.2	...	−3.3
SOUTH AFRICA	RAND	77.7	104.4	156.5	149.3	127.4	3.2	−2.7
SUDAN	POUND	45.2	23.8	10.0	9.0	8.7	32.4	−3.6
SWAZILAND	EMALANGENI	75.0	102.6	150.5	133.2	109.2	3.0	−5.3
TANZANIA	SHILLING	37.3	97.7	88.2	106.3	110.1	0.0	5.7
TOGO	CFA FRANC	53.7	76.4	148.4	124.1	112.7	6.3	−6.5
TUNISIA	DINAR	67.0	105.5	139.6	130.3	124.5	2.1	−2.7
UGANDA	SHILLING	...	93.7	147.6	173.6	158.4	10.0	2.0
ZAMBIA	KWACHA	69.1	92.8	114.8	103.3	90.7	3.3	−5.6
ZIMBABWE	DOLLAR	49.6	81.3	123.4	93.8	149.3	5.7	30.7

* estimates

TABLE 2.9
INTERNATIONAL RESERVES
(MILLIONS US DOLLARS)

COUNTRY	1980	1990	2000	2003	2004	Average Annual Growth (%) 1980–1990	1991–2004
ALGERIA	4,021.8	980.7	12,278.5	33,415.6	39,849.7	−4.3	39.6
ANGOLA	...	...	1,198.2	634.2	1,003.8	...	45.3
BENIN	8.6	69.1	458.1	509.8	411.3	116.0	20.5
BOTSWANA	334.0	3,331.5	6,318.2	5,339.8	5,210.9	29.2	3.4
BURKINA FASO	68.7	304.7	243.6	434.8	451.6	17.8	5.1
BURUNDI	104.7	111.6	37.7	67.4	55.7	8.4	7.4
CAMEROON	206.5	37.0	220.2	652.2	648.7	12.7	119.5
CAPE VERDE	42.4	77.0	28.3	93.6	120.1	6.8	27.6
CENT. AFR. REP.	61.5	122.6	136.3	137.1	142.9	10.3	3.4
CHAD	11.6	131.8	113.7	191.8	223.3	33.5	10.9
COMOROS	...	29.9	43.4	94.5	95.9	35.6	10.1
CONGO	92.5	9.9	225.0	39.4	25.7	−0.4	141.3
CONGO (DRC)	...	...	...	...	...	...	...
COTE D'IVOIRE	21.7	20.9	667.9	2,230.5	2,390.0	1.2	100.6
DJIBOUTI	...	93.6	67.8	100.1	102.3	14.8	1.3
EGYPT	1,149.0	3,324.6	13,628.6	14,219.7	14,167.9	19.5	14.2
EQUAT. GUINEA	...	0.7	23.0	237.7	609.3	98.8	319.7
ERITREA	...	...	36.0	24.7	40.1	...	13.1
ETHIOPIA	104.6	29.6	306.7	955.6	1,218.2	6.6	45.6
GABON	115.1	278.4	193.6	201.9	355.6	107.4	328.3
GAMBIA	5.7	55.4	109.4	...	...	...	6.4
GHANA	199.4	282.1	311.3	1,468.9	1,470.3	6.0	22.5
GUINEA	...	...	147.9	...	...	...	12.7
GUINEA BISSAU	...	18.2	66.7	164.4	217.0	...	29.2
KENYA	501.1	218.9	897.8	1,482.1	1,399.4	−4.9	45.0
LESOTHO	50.3	72.4	417.9	460.3	530.5	6.7	17.8
LIBERIA	...	...	...	...	...	...	...
LIBYA	13,220.4	5,991.2	12,655.0	19,778.2	22,992.7	5.9	17.9
MADAGASCAR	9.1	92.1	285.2	414.3	507.1	49.4	18.0
MALAWI	69.0	137.7	247.5	127.0	109.0	33.8	12.2
MALI	15.4	197.7	381.3	908.7	960.8	47.4	15.8
MAURITANIA	146.8	58.5	283.0	419.3	394.5	−2.3	18.6
MAURITIUS	95.3	742.6	909.8	1,598.4	1,584.0	62.4	7.3
MOROCCO	427.4	2,082.0	5,007.3	14,075.1	15,078.6	39.5	17.3
MOZAMBIQUE	...	231.7	725.1	998.5	997.4	32.1	13.1
NAMIBIA	...	...	260.0	325.2	276.3	...	22.2
NIGER	126.4	226.4	80.4	114.1	89.9	13.8	−1.4
NIGERIA	10,269.7	3,866.4	9,911.1	7,128.6	14,379.9	18.4	27.0
RWANDA	196.1	44.3	190.6	214.7	245.1	−8.2	20.3
SAO T. & PRINC.	...	...	11.6	25.5	23.9	...	25.3
SENEGAL	9.4	22.0	384.0	794.5	905.2	9.7	98.9
SEYCHELLES	18.4	16.6	43.8	67.4	29.2	10.7	10.6
SIERRA LEONE	30.6	5.4	49.2	66.6	85.8	−5.8	27.1
SOMALIA	...	...	...	...	...	...	...
SOUTH AFRICA	7,238.2	2,423.3	7,533.8	7,971.2	12,734.9	−1.2	20.0
SUDAN	48.7	11.4	247.3	847.5	1,187.8	17.2	66.3
SWAZILAND	158.7	216.5	351.8	277.5	308.7	8.9	5.0
TANZANIA	20.3	192.8	974.2	2,038.4	2,003.0	68.4	22.2
TOGO	78.1	357.9	152.3	182.5	257.0	20.4	2.4
TUNISIA	598.3	800.0	1,814.2	2,949.0	3,950.4	8.2	13.8
UGANDA	3.0	44.0	808.0	1,080.3	1,159.6	103.5	29.4
ZAMBIA	88.6	...	244.8	247.7	294.1	33.5	52.5
ZIMBABWE	326.4	218.8	238.5	...	...	−0.9	5.9
AFRICA	40,662.6	28,034.4	81,965.9	125,813.9	152,687.7	4.4	13.3

TABLE 2.10
CONSUMER PRICE INDICES (GENERAL)
(1995 = 100)

COUNTRY	1980	1990	2000	2003	2004*	Average Annual change (%) 1990–1999	2000–04
ALGERIA	11.6	29.3	135.6	149.1	155.1	18.1	2.3
ANGOLA	...	0.0	415,684.0	4,383,079.6	6,290,080.1	1,012.3	145.3
BENIN	...	59.8	120.0	129.9	130.5	7.7	2.5
BOTSWANA	20.2	55.2	148.9	189.4	197.9	10.9	7.4
BURKINA FASO	51.6	73.6	112.5	122.9	122.1	4.5	1.6
BURUNDI	29.0	60.0	239.7	286.0	305.9	13.9	10.0
CAMEROON	30.8	67.1	115.8	130.7	130.9	5.4	2.2
CAPE VERDE	...	74.6	122.3	130.3	131.7	7.3	1.2
CENT. AFR. REP.	53.3	71.9	106.1	115.0	112.6	3.9	2.0
CHAD	...	69.6	128.8	135.1	123.4	4.9	2.2
COMOROS	...	71.4	117.7	125.8	132.1	4.2	2.8
CONGO	26.5	48.4	129.7	131.5	135.9	8.0	1.3
CONGO (DRC)	0.0	0.0	104,674.8	196,791.3	212,259.0	3,380.1	142.6
COTE D'IVOIRE	38.8	64.1	115.2	130.0	130.2	5.9	3.0
DJIBOUTI	...	77.4	114.7	119.4	121.8	4.4	1.9
EGYPT	11.0	52.4	123.7	139.5	153.1	10.8	4.4
EQUAT. GUINEA	...	64.1	119.7	153.4	159.6	7.2	6.1
ERITREA	...	...	158.5	270.2	294.5	...	16.9
ETHIOPIA	35.3	54.4	104.9	107.6	115.6	7.4	3.0
GABON	41.6	73.2	107.0	114.0	113.2	5.5	0.5
GAMBIA	14.7	72.6	110.0	149.7	174.7	5.8	9.2
GHANA	0.8	28.3	302.3	582.9	657.0	27.6	22.4
GUINEA	...	61.0	123.5	141.5	160.4	8.7	6.9
GUINEA BISSAU	...	15.1	258.2	265.6	265.6	37.5	2.3
KENYA	11.1	34.0	140.1	179.0	199.7	16.9	7.8
LESOTHO	15.4	54.2	143.5	186.6	195.4	11.1	7.1
LIBERIA	33.1	65.2	...	235.1	258.6	9.7	12.6
LIBYA	...	42.0	282.5	106.3	108.6	11.7	-1.0
MADAGASCAR	7.0	35.3	163.7	203.7	213.9	17.6	7.6
MALAWI	5.6	24.7	365.6	582.0	617.1	30.5	17.3
MALI	...	75.2	108.6	112.5	107.3	4.2	-0.2
MAURITANIA	...	70.8	127.1	145.4	135.7	6.2	2.1
MAURITIUS	32.2	71.0	135.4	157.7	163.1	7.8	4.7
MOROCCO	37.0	74.6	109.7	114.8	116.5	4.5	1.6
MOZAMBIQUE	...	14.4	179.4	259.1	280.1	33.6	12.0
NAMIBIA	17.0	57.4	148.1	193.0	191.6	10.3	7.3
NIGER	62.0	76.4	113.9	119.9	117.8	5.0	1.3
NIGERIA	2.0	14.3	176.0	265.1	296.2	31.8	12.5
RWANDA	22.3	34.1	129.6	151.5	163.9	17.3	4.4
SAO T. & PRINC.	...	25.4	416.8	526.4	600.1	35.9	8.7
SENEGAL	40.7	71.8	107.2	110.5	112.4	4.2	1.5
SEYCHELLES	68.5	92.3	114.5	125.8	131.0	2.0	4.0
SIERRA LEONE	0.1	15.6	255.1	271.3	280.8	45.9	1.8
SOMALIA	0.2	27.5	193.2	258.5	258.5	35.0	11.5
SOUTH AFRICA	14.9	58.6	138.2	168.6	173.0	9.9	5.7
SUDAN	0.1	2.8	510.2	613.6	644.3	80.4	6.8
SWAZILAND	15.4	54.3	146.7	189.1	201.8	9.5	9.1
TANZANIA	2.0	29.5	181.1	203.4	215.0	22.9	5.0
TOGO	43.7	62.8	116.5	115.3	118.1	6.8	1.2
TUNISIA	34.6	75.5	117.2	126.2	130.8	4.9	2.8
UGANDA	...	40.5	125.4	140.9	143.6	16.5	2.0
ZAMBIA	0.1	3.0	354.0	640.4	754.4	76.4	21.9
ZIMBABWE	8.1	29.8	469.6	10,355.7	46,600.6	28.6	208.5
AFRICA	5.9	26.4	204.9	266.2	286.8	23.2	10.2

* estimates

TABLE 2.11
OVERALL GOVERNMENT DEFICIT (–) /SURPLUS (+) AS A PERCENTAGE OF GDP AT CURRENT PRICES
(PERCENTAGE)

COUNTRY	1980	1990	2000	2003	2004	Annual Average 1980–1990	Annual Average 1991–2004
ALGERIA	9.9	3.6	9.7	5.1	5.6	1.3	0.7
ANGOLA	–9.9	–23.7	–7.6	–7.4	–3.5	–10.2	–17.3
BENIN	–4.2	–4.1	–1.8	–2.6	–2.2	–4.7	–1.5
BOTSWANA	–0.5	9.9	9.0	0.3	–0.3	8.3	3.8
BURKINA FASO	–7.6	–4.1	–4.4	–2.9	–3.5	–4.9	–2.9
BURUNDI	–7.6	–2.7	–1.8	–6.3	18.3	–8.1	–2.7
CAMEROON	0.3	–7.6	4.4	1.8	0.8	–2.7	–1.3
CAPE VERDE	–8.0	–3.3	–19.5	–3.3	–4.6	–8.7	–9.1
CENT. AFR. REP.	–8.5	–6.8	–2.0	–3.7	–1.2	–2.8	–3.8
CHAD	6.4	–5.9	–6.9	–5.6	–4.1	–0.5	–5.6
COMOROS	–16.0	–1.7	–1.6	–4.1	–0.3	–8.4	–3.3
CONGO	–0.9	–6.6	1.1	0.4	5.0	1.3	–7.8
CONGO (DRC)	–0.4	–10.9	–6.0	–3.9	–4.8	–6.3	–7.8
COTE D'IVOIRE	–12.8	–19.3	–1.3	–2.9	–3.9	–7.7	–4.3
DJIBOUTI	6.3	–7.3	–1.8	–2.3	1.0	–4.4	–4.6
EGYPT	–9.6	–12.6	–3.9	–6.1	–6.0	–16.5	–4.6
EQUAT. GUINEA	–15.9	–5.3	7.8	23.3	28.5	–10.6	2.9
ERITREA	...	...	–41.9	–16.9	–22.1	...	–21.6
ETHIOPIA	–3.6	–9.7	–11.2	–8.4	–5.0	–6.0	–6.6
GABON	7.4	–4.1	11.7	7.4	8.8	–2.7	1.0
GAMBIA	–23.0	–1.7	–1.4	–4.7	–3.6	–7.4	–4.0
GHANA	–11.6	–2.1	–7.9	–3.5	–2.7	–4.0	–7.0
GUINEA	–0.5	–5.5	–3.2	–5.1	–2.5	–2.8	–3.4
GUINEA BISSAU	12.2	–5.9	–10.8	–13.9	–14.7	–5.3	–12.1
KENYA	–7.8	–6.8	1.7	–2.0	–1.7	–5.8	–4.1
LESOTHO	–10.1	–0.9	–1.8	0.7	2.4	–9.7	0.2
LIBERIA	...	...	...	...	...	...	...
LIBYA	–1.5	1.3	9.5	11.8	16.6	–12.9	4.1
MADAGASCAR	–14.2	–0.6	–2.8	–4.1	–3.3	–6.1	–5.0
MALAWI	–11.6	–2.8	–4.9	–5.3	–12.7	–7.1	–7.2
MALI	–3.9	–2.4	–3.0	–0.7	–2.9	–4.4	–2.8
MAURITANIA	–13.7	–5.0	–3.1	0.7	1.0	–7.2	1.9
MAURITIUS	–10.6	–2.1	–3.8	–6.2	–5.3	–6.3	–4.3
MOROCCO	–11.2	–0.6	–6.4	–2.5	–2.5	–7.8	–2.7
MOZAMBIQUE	–2.0	–5.9	–6.1	–4.9	–5.2	–7.7	–4.2
NAMIBIA	...	0.6	–1.2	–3.6	–2.1	0.2	–3.3
NIGER	–1.0	–7.0	–4.1	–2.7	–2.8	–3.7	–3.7
NIGERIA	–3.4	2.9	6.0	–1.4	7.4	–5.2	–0.5
RWANDA	–3.3	–7.2	1.9	–2.5	–0.1	–4.2	–4.0
SAO T. & PRINC.	–27.7	–42.2	–16.7	–13.5	–17.2	–26.7	–27.7
SENEGAL	–7.9	–0.5	0.1	–1.4	–2.4	–4.0	–0.8
SEYCHELLES	–6.6	5.6	–11.7	2.0	7.9	–7.0	–5.8
SIERRA LEONE	–12.1	–8.8	–9.3	–7.6	–5.9	–9.1	–7.1
SOMALIA	...	...	...	...	...	...	...
SOUTH AFRICA	–1.4	–2.3	–2.0	–2.4	–3.2	–3.5	–3.5
SUDAN	–8.9	–14.9	–0.8	0.9	–1.2	–11.1	–4.8
SWAZILAND	...	6.5	–1.5	–6.3	–6.6	–0.6	–1.9
TANZANIA	–5.7	–3.2	–1.8	–1.6	–2.9	–5.8	–1.8
TOGO	–6.6	–2.6	–4.4	1.3	0.0	–4.5	–3.8
TUNISIA	–3.3	–5.7	–2.4	–3.2	–1.5	–5.2	–3.4
UGANDA	–4.7	–4.1	–7.1	–4.3	–1.7	–5.7	–2.8
ZAMBIA	–18.5	–8.3	–0.5	–6.0	–3.9	–13.2	–3.9
ZIMBABWE	–9.6	–6.2	–20.7	–0.2	–9.7	–7.8	–7.5
AFRICA	–3.6	–4.4	–0.5	–1.4	0.0	–6.0	–3.0

TABLE 2.12
TOTAL EXTERNAL DEBT
(MILLIONS OF US DOLLARS)

COUNTRY	1983	1993	1999	2003	2004	Annual Average Growth Rate (%) 1983–1993	Annual Average Growth Rate (%) 1994–2004
ALGERIA	14,902	26,020	28,315	23,203	20,627	4.5	−1.8
ANGOLA	9,639	12,171	9,550	9,007	7,508	2.4	−3.7
BENIN	487	1,211	1,652	1,948	2,054	11.7	5.0
BOTSWANA	306	867	1,129	1,324	1,409	11.8	4.6
BURKINA FASO	326	1,012	1,547	1,806	1,846	11.0	5.9
BURUNDI	300	1,040	1,121	1,276	1,234	15.8	1.6
CAMEROON	1,206	9,058	8,303	6,026	5,862	22.0	−3.3
CAPE VERDE	71	144	365	628	690	9.4	15.5
CENT. AFR. REP.	257	817	855	1,122	1,236	12.5	4.2
CHAD	92	648	620	791	872	17.9	4.5
COMOROS	108	184	217	272	279	9.6	4.0
CONGO	0	4,576	5,452	6,989	2,192	6.1	−2.1
CONGO (DRC)	4,532	11,588	13,238	10,648	10,840	9.2	−0.3
COTE D'IVOIRE	6,632	17,107	11,156	10,586	11,562	12.3	−2.9
DJIBOUTI	39	266	337	428	448	29.9	5.0
EGYPT	31,300	30,282	28,224	29,093	30,144	0.1	0.1
EQUAT. GUINEA	101	249	244	225	219	9.9	−0.8
ERITREA	...	2	272	548	604	...	144.5
ETHIOPIA	1,401	10,956	6,485	5,705	5,982	28.0	−4.2
GABON	971	3,182	3,717	3,585	3,510	12.7	1.4
GAMBIA	242	299	508	568	567	1.4	6.1
GHANA	1,539	3,680	6,370	6,577	6,147	7.9	6.1
GUINEA	1,243	2,799	3,375	3,364	3,233	9.5	1.5
GUINEA BISSAU	511	842	791	862	907	5.0	0.9
KENYA	5,058	6,309	5,560	5,370	5,713	2.5	−0.8
LESOTHO	131	472	683	567	567	13.2	2.0
LIBERIA	...	...	...	...	...	...	...
LIBYA	4,780	4,691	5,743	5,702	5,830	1.9	2.1
MADAGASCAR	1,763	3,878	4,468	4,586	4,749	7.8	1.9
MALAWI	932	1,866	2,608	2,850	2,907	7.6	4.2
MALI	945	2,377	2,881	1,554	1,518	9.7	−3.4
MAURITANIA	1,297	2,117	2,089	1,960	1,993	6.6	−0.3
MAURITIUS	538	957	1,207	992	1,051	5.7	1.2
MOROCCO	12,011	21,131	19,766	16,171	15,655	5.7	−2.5
MOZAMBIQUE	2,007	5,132	4,818	5,259	5,373	10.7	3.5
NAMIBIA	0	93	74	98	108	−8.6	1.9
NIGER	633	1,224	1,604	1,571	1,651	7.5	3.2
NIGERIA	19,065	29,476	28,717	32,818	32,669	8.3	1.0
RWANDA	207	884	1,256	1,433	1,485	14.3	4.9
SAO T. & PRINC.	41	237	301	273	262	19.4	1.1
SENEGAL	1,971	3,502	3,505	3,889	4,229	8.0	2.2
SEYCHELLES	127	127	285	551	581	11.8	15.7
SIERRA LEONE	405	1,445	1,237	422	539	13.8	0.9
SOMALIA	1,187	2,324	3,155	3,737	3,881	7.6	4.8
SOUTH AFRICA	23,954	27,000	38,864	37,138	39,379	2.0	4.0
SUDAN	7,600	16,295	22,716	24,067	25,279	7.7	4.3
SWAZILAND	0	237	319	512	518	5.6	8.6
TANZANIA	3,907	6,963	7,379	6,119	6,225	6.6	−0.7
TOGO	771	1,234	1,207	2,012	1,993	4.9	5.3
TUNISIA	4,058	8,794	11,842	16,248	16,291	8.3	6.0
UGANDA	867	2,638	3,478	4,254	4,364	12.1	4.9
ZAMBIA	3,609	6,303	6,244	5,536	5,460	6.7	−1.1
ZIMBABWE	1,991	3,955	4,321	4,843	5,204	7.6	2.8
AFRICA	171,279	295,968	314,156	310,861	309,010	5.7	0.5

TABLE 2.13
DEBT SERVICE
(Millions of US Dollars)

COUNTRY	1983	1993	1999	2003	2004	Annual Average Growth Rate (%) 1983–1993	1994–2004
ALGERIA	4,720	8,970	4,985	4,660	4,991	6.7	−3.9
ANGOLA	290	1,577	2,353	2,005	1,278	28.0	3.8
BENIN	0	55	42	66	72	29.9	4.1
BOTSWANA	13	87	88	74	73	32.2	−0.4
BURKINA FASO	7	9	42	95	104	42.7	42.1
BURUNDI	13	30	23	53	253	11.9	46.7
CAMEROON	0	183	401	285	375	−0.5	31.5
CAPE VERDE	0	3	18	48	52	5.2	160.7
CENT. AFR. REP.	0	2	9	0	24	−2.1	32.6
CHAD	...	...	22	24	23	...	12.1
COMOROS	0	1	2	3	4	−94.4	28.2
CONGO	...	...	139	158	486	...	25.8
CONGO (DRC)	703	15	3	75	67	−20.0	162.4
COTE D'IVOIRE	385	837	1,064	272	1,101	14.4	24.1
DJIBOUTI	6	10	18	17	18	10.9	−7.9
EGYPT	3,660	2,464	1,598	2,240	2,382	0.1	0.4
EQUAT. GUINEA	3	26	89	59	46	78.8	9.4
ERITREA	...	...	4	24	24	...	81.0
ETHIOPIA	92	452	457	199	219	36.1	95.3
GABON	681	670	222	1,669	551	3.4	21.0
GAMBIA	55	21	49	42	66	1.0	15.5
GHANA	226	456	533	329	370	12.6	2.8
GUINEA	86	71	131	106	111	2.2	34.1
GUINEA BISSAU	1	4	3	6	6	19.8	50.8
KENYA	213	568	457	506	452	17.7	6.5
LESOTHO	0	26	45	45	54	5.3	10.6
LIBERIA	...	...	...	...	...	...	...
LIBYA	...	...	...	...	...	...	...
MADAGASCAR	319	393	120	185	96	7.0	21.9
MALAWI	53	20	0	94	99	3.1	7.1
MALI	20	79	106	70	83	16.9	2.9
MAURITANIA	2	129	79	74	69	0.4	−5.2
MAURITIUS	105	171	200	257	211	9.3	3.5
MOROCCO	1,229	3,129	2,988	2,605	2,226	10.3	−2.8
MOZAMBIQUE	99	111	214	312	395	44.2	13.4
NAMIBIA	0	21	21	33	35	−26.0	6.2
NIGER	...	...	29	73	50	...	166.7
NIGERIA	2,781	1,460	1,715	1,809	1,800	8.6	7.2
RWANDA	...	...	46	36	40	...	11.2
SAO T. & PRINC.	...	2	4	12	27	...	35.3
SENEGAL	178	178	202	258	383	1.8	17.8
SEYCHELLES	22	42	27	86	78	125.4	17.8
SIERRA LEONE	60	10	48	14	26	−6.2	34.8
SOMALIA	1	169	206	233	241	−11.7	3.3
SOUTH AFRICA	3,513	3,348	6,033	6,086	6,728	4.5	7.3
SUDAN	225	34	70	251	375	−7.5	27.4
SWAZILAND	...	...	...	...	...	...	...
TANZANIA	165	211	315	171	203	4.0	9.9
TOGO	72	18	53	1	122	−4.8	774.9
TUNISIA	555	1,324	1,612	1,641	2,366	9.3	6.7
UGANDA	0	116	110	151	161	−11.4	4.9
ZAMBIA	162	323	136	187	376	51.3	29.1
ZIMBABWE	278	307	565	44	54	4.4	−7.5
AFRICA	21,020	28,130	27,693	27,718	29,422	3.8	0.8

TABLE 3.1
LABOUR FORCE BY SECTOR
(PERCENT IN)

COUNTRY	AGRICULTURE				INDUSTRY				SERVICES			
	1980	1985	1990	1996	1980	1985	1990	1996	1980	1985	1990	1996
ALGERIA	31	25	19	14	27	29	32	35	42	46	49	51
ANGOLA	74	72	70	68	10	10	11	11	17	18	19	21
BENIN	70	65	59	54	7	7	8	10	23	28	32	36
BOTSWANA	70	61	52	42	13	19	28	41	17	20	20	17
BURKINA FASO	87	86	85	84	4	5	5	5	9	10	10	11
BURUNDI	93	92	92	91	2	3	3	3	5	5	5	6
CAMEROON	70	63	56	49	8	10	13	15	22	27	32	36
CAPE VERDE	52	46	40	35	23	27	31	36	26	27	29	29
CENT. AFR. REP.	72	67	61	56	6	8	10	12	21	25	29	32
CHAD	83	80	76	72	5	5	6	7	12	15	18	21
COMOROS	83	81	79	77	6	6	7	8	11	12	14	15
CONGO	62	61	60	58	12	12	12	13	26	27	28	29
CONGO (DRC)	71	68	64	60	13	14	16	17	16	18	20	23
COTE D'IVOIRE	65	60	54	49	8	10	12	14	27	30	34	37
DJIBOUTI	...	...	...	...	...	...	...	...	...	...	...	...
EGYPT	46	42	39	36	20	22	24	27	34	35	36	37
EQUAT. GUINEA	66	61	57	52	11	13	15	18	23	26	28	30
ERITREA	...	...	...	...	...	...	...	...	...	...	...	...
ETHIOPIA	80	77	74	72	8	9	10	12	12	14	15	16
GABON	75	73	71	69	11	12	12	13	14	15	16	18
GAMBIA	84	83	82	80	7	7	8	9	9	10	11	11
GHANA	56	54	53	52	18	18	19	19	26	27	28	29
GUINEA	81	78	76	74	9	10	11	13	10	11	12	13
GUINEA BISSAU	82	81	80	79	4	4	4	5	14	15	15	16
KENYA	81	79	77	75	7	7	8	9	12	13	14	16
LESOTHO	86	84	82	81	4	5	5	6	10	11	12	13
LIBERIA	74	73	71	70	9	9	9	9	16	18	20	21
LIBYA	18	14	11	8	29	30	32	34	53	55	57	58
MADAGASCAR	81	79	78	76	6	7	7	8	13	14	15	16
MALAWI	83	78	75	70	7	10	13	17	9	11	12	13
MALI	86	84	82	80	2	2	3	3	12	14	16	17
MAURITANIA	69	61	53	45	9	12	16	21	22	27	31	34
MAURITIUS	28	25	23	20	24	24	23	23	48	51	54	57
MOROCCO	46	40	35	30	25	29	35	40	29	31	31	30
MOZAMBIQUE	84	83	82	81	7	8	9	10	8	8	9	9
NAMIBIA	43	44	43	40	22	20	27	37	36	6	31	23
NIGER	91	89	88	86	2	2	2	2	7	9	10	12
NIGERIA	68	67	65	64	12	12	13	13	20	21	22	23
RWANDA	93	92	92	92	3	3	3	3	4	5	5	5
SAO T. & PRINC.	...	...	...	...	...	...	...	...	...	...	...	...
SENEGAL	81	79	78	77	6	7	7	7	13	14	15	16
SEYCHELLES	...	...	...	...	...	...	...	...	...	...	...	...
SIERRA LEONE	70	67	64	61	14	15	16	17	16	18	20	22
SOMALIA	76	74	72	70	8	9	10	11	16	17	18	19
SOUTH AFRICA	17	...	14	...	35	...	32	...	48	...	54	...
SUDAN	71	68	65	62	7	8	9	11	21	23	25	27
SWAZILAND	74	71	67	64	9	10	12	13	17	19	21	23
TANZANIA	86	84	81	79	5	5	6	7	10	11	12	14
TOGO	73	71	69	67	10	10	11	12	17	18	20	21
TUNISIA	35	31	28	25	36	43	49	56	29	26	23	19
UGANDA	86	84	82	81	4	5	6	6	10	11	12	13
ZAMBIA	73	71	70	68	10	11	11	12	17	18	19	20
ZIMBABWE	73	70	68	66	10	12	13	14	17	18	19	20
AFRICA	70	67	65	62	11	12	13	15	19	21	22	23

TABLE 3.2
LABOUR FORCE PARTICIPATION RATE
(Percentage of population of all ages in labour force)

COUNTRY	TOTAL				FEMALE				MALE			
	1980	1990	1995	2003	1980	1990	1995	2003	1980	1990	1995	2003
ALGERIA	26.0	27.9	30.8	36.4	21.4	21.2	24.3	29.7	78.6	78.8	75.7	70.3
ANGOLA	49.5	47.4	46.6	45.5	47.0	46.6	46.5	46.3	53.0	53.4	53.5	53.7
BENIN	47.9	45.1	45.2	45.6	47.0	48.3	48.3	48.3	53.0	51.7	51.7	51.7
BOTSWANA	43.3	42.8	44.1	45.1	48.9	46.6	46.1	45.2	51.1	53.4	54.0	54.8
BURKINA FASO	53.1	50.4	48.9	46.8	50.2	49.3	49.0	48.3	49.8	50.7	51.0	51.7
BURUNDI	54.9	53.8	53.0	52.7	50.2	49.2	49.2	48.9	49.8	50.8	50.8	51.1
CAMEROON	41.9	40.1	40.6	41.6	36.8	37.0	37.5	38.5	63.2	63.1	62.4	61.5
CAPE VERDE	32.5	35.2	37.3	41.0	34.0	37.4	37.7	38.4	66.0	62.6	62.3	61.6
CENT. AFR. REP.	52.2	48.8	47.9	46.8	48.4	47.1	46.9	46.4	51.6	52.9	53.1	53.5
CHAD	48.0	47.0	46.4	45.5	43.6	44.2	44.6	45.1	56.4	55.8	55.4	54.9
COMOROS	45.2	45.0	46.0	47.4	43.4	43.0	43.2	42.9	56.6	56.5	56.8	57.4
CONGO	42.0	41.6	41.2	40.5	41.9	42.5	42.8	43.0	58.1	57.5	57.2	57.0
CONGO (DRC)	44.3	42.7	42.4	41.7	44.6	44.0	43.7	43.2	55.4	56.0	56.3	56.8
COTE D'IVOIRE	40.9	39.0	39.6	40.8	31.6	31.4	32.2	33.3	68.4	68.6	67.8	66.7
DJIBOUTI	50.5	50.6	50.2	49.6	46.1	45.7	45.6	45.6	53.9	53.9	54.0	54.4
EGYPT	33.7	33.5	35.0	37.7	27.0	27.9	29.8	32.6	73.0	72.1	70.2	67.4
EQUAT. GUINEA	44.7	42.7	41.9	41.3	35.7	35.1	35.7	35.8	65.3	64.9	64.9	64.2
ERITREA	...	...	48.8	48.8	...	...	47.7	47.6	...	...	52.3	52.4
ETHIOPIA	45.8	44.6	43.9	43.7	42.5	42.4	42.1	42.0	57.5	57.6	57.9	58.0
GABON	48.6	44.5	44.4	44.9	45.0	44.3	44.5	44.7	55.0	55.7	55.7	55.4
GAMBIA	51.4	49.9	50.1	50.6	45.4	45.0	45.1	45.2	54.9	55.0	54.9	54.8
GHANA	46.4	46.4	47.7	50.1	50.9	50.9	50.7	50.2	49.1	49.1	49.3	49.8
GUINEA	51.8	50.0	49.7	49.3	47.2	47.5	47.3	47.1	52.8	52.6	52.7	52.9
GUINEA BISSAU	46.5	45.1	44.2	43.1	40.1	40.4	40.7	40.9	59.9	59.6	59.5	59.1
KENYA	47.2	47.5	49.5	52.4	46.3	46.4	46.7	47.1	53.7	53.6	53.3	52.9
LESOTHO	39.4	37.9	38.9	40.0	41.4	40.7	40.9	42.2	58.8	59.3	59.1	57.8
LIBERIA	40.7	39.4	38.9	38.0	39.5	40.1	40.3	40.3	60.5	59.9	59.7	59.7
LIBYA	31.0	29.5	31.8	35.3	18.6	18.4	20.8	24.6	81.4	81.6	79.2	75.4
MADAGASCAR	49.6	48.6	48.2	47.9	44.8	44.7	44.7	44.6	55.2	55.3	55.3	55.4
MALAWI	50.3	50.1	49.3	47.8	50.6	49.3	49.1	48.7	49.4	50.7	50.9	51.3
MALI	51.7	49.7	48.5	46.8	45.8	46.4	46.4	46.2	54.2	53.6	53.6	53.8
MAURITANIA	48.0	45.6	45.2	44.6	45.1	44.6	44.5	43.9	54.9	55.4	55.5	56.1
MAURITIUS	35.5	40.9	42.2	44.1	25.7	30.3	31.6	33.4	74.3	69.7	68.6	66.6
MOROCCO	35.9	37.1	38.8	41.4	33.5	34.5	34.6	35.1	66.5	65.5	65.4	64.9
MOZAMBIQUE	54.9	51.1	51.7	52.3	49.5	51.0	51.1	50.7	50.5	49.0	48.9	49.3
NAMIBIA	41.0	40.8	40.5	39.9	41.5	41.9	42.0	42.4	58.5	58.1	57.8	57.6
NIGER	48.1	47.2	46.7	45.8	43.8	43.2	43.2	43.3	56.2	56.8	56.8	56.7
NIGERIA	41.2	39.5	39.6	40.0	35.5	34.6	35.1	35.9	64.5	65.4	64.9	64.1
RWANDA	51.1	52.1	52.7	53.2	49.2	49.0	49.6	51.7	50.8	51.0	50.4	48.3
SAO T. & PRINC.	43.6	42.2	44.3	46.0	43.9	42.9	43.1	43.2	56.1	57.1	56.9	56.8
SENEGAL	45.9	44.0	44.3	44.9	42.2	42.8	43.1	43.3	57.8	57.2	57.0	56.7
SEYCHELLES	48.4	47.9	48.0	48.1	45.2	47.1	47.2	46.2	54.8	52.9	52.8	53.8
SIERRA LEONE	38.6	37.5	37.4	37.2	35.6	35.5	36.1	37.2	64.5	64.5	63.8	62.8
SOMALIA	45.2	43.7	43.3	42.5	43.4	43.3	43.3	43.4	56.6	56.6	56.7	56.6
SOUTH AFRICA	36.8	38.8	40.1	41.7	35.3	37.5	38.0	39.0	64.7	62.5	62.0	61.0
SUDAN	37.0	37.7	38.5	40.0	27.0	27.1	28.3	30.2	73.0	72.9	71.7	69.8
SWAZILAND	33.7	33.2	33.7	34.5	36.3	37.0	38.0	39.2	63.7	63.0	62.0	60.8
TANZANIA	51.2	51.1	51.0	51.2	49.8	49.7	49.6	49.2	50.2	50.3	50.4	50.8
TOGO	42.8	41.9	42.1	42.6	39.3	39.8	40.0	40.1	60.7	60.1	60.0	59.9
TUNISIA	34.0	34.5	37.2	41.8	29.0	29.2	30.6	32.7	71.0	70.8	69.4	67.3
UGANDA	51.7	50.7	49.5	47.8	47.6	47.8	47.9	47.6	52.4	52.2	52.1	52.4
ZAMBIA	42.8	43.3	42.8	42.1	44.2	44.0	44.0	43.7	55.8	56.0	56.0	56.3
ZIMBABWE	43.9	44.9	45.2	45.6	44.3	44.2	44.5	44.4	55.7	55.8	55.5	55.6
AFRICA	42.5	42.0	42.5	43.4	40.1	40.2	40.5	41.1	59.9	59.8	59.5	58.9

TABLE 3.3

COMPONENTS OF POPULATION CHANGE

COUNTRY	TOTAL FERTILITY RATE (PER WOMAN)			CRUDE BIRTH RATE (PER 1,000 POPULATION)			CRUDE DEATH RATE (PER 1,000 POPULATION)			RATE OF NATURAL INCREASE (PERCENT)		
	1980	1990	2004	1980	1990	2004	1980	1990	2004	1980	1990	2004
ALGERIA	6.7	4.4	2.7	42.4	30.9	22.3	11.6	7.1	5.4	3.1	2.4	1.7
ANGOLA	6.9	7.2	7.1	50.7	51.2	51.5	23.5	20.6	23.2	2.7	3.1	2.8
BENIN	7.1	6.6	5.5	51.5	47.0	40.8	19.2	15.2	14.1	3.2	3.2	2.7
BOTSWANA	6.1	5.1	3.5	44.7	38.2	29.4	10.2	8.2	25.1	3.5	3.0	0.4
BURKINA FASO	7.8	7.3	6.6	49.8	47.5	47.2	19.4	17.9	16.7	3.0	3.0	3.1
BURUNDI	6.8	6.8	6.7	45.8	46.3	44.9	18.3	20.4	20.1	2.8	2.6	2.5
CAMEROON	6.4	5.9	4.4	45.1	41.7	34.4	16.6	14.2	17.5	2.9	2.7	1.7
CAPE VERDE	6.5	4.2	3.1	37.2	34.7	26.9	10.4	8.2	5.2	2.7	2.6	2.2
CENT. AFR. REP.	5.8	5.6	4.8	43.2	41.5	37.1	19.4	18.0	21.9	2.4	2.3	1.5
CHAD	6.7	6.7	6.6	48.1	48.5	47.8	22.9	20.5	18.9	2.5	2.8	2.9
COMOROS	7.1	6.1	4.7	48.6	40.6	35.5	14.4	10.9	8.0	3.4	3.0	2.8
CONGO	6.3	6.3	6.2	44.7	44.5	43.7	16.3	14.9	14.8	2.8	3.0	2.9
CONGO (DRC)	6.6	6.7	6.6	48.0	48.0	49.5	16.8	15.0	20.7	3.1	3.3	2.9
COTE D'IVOIRE	7.4	6.2	4.5	50.8	41.4	34.7	16.4	14.6	19.5	3.4	2.7	1.5
DJIBOUTI	6.6	6.3	5.5	52.8	45.5	38.4	20.8	17.6	17.7	3.2	2.8	2.1
EGYPT	5.1	4.1	3.2	38.8	31.3	26.3	13.3	8.6	6.1	2.6	2.3	2.0
EQUAT. GUINEA	5.7	5.9	5.7	43.1	43.6	42.2	21.7	18.6	16.4	2.1	2.5	2.6
ERITREA	6.4	6.2	5.2	45.2	43.9	38.6	19.6	16.0	11.7	2.6	2.8	2.7
ETHIOPIA	6.8	6.9	6.0	46.3	46.2	41.8	20.9	18.8	17.3	2.5	2.7	2.4
GABON	4.5	5.1	3.8	33.0	36.4	30.5	18.5	16.6	11.1	1.4	2.0	1.9
GAMBIA	6.5	5.8	4.5	48.3	44.5	34.5	23.9	20.5	12.3	2.4	2.4	2.2
GHANA	6.8	5.6	3.9	45.9	38.9	30.9	13.8	11.5	9.7	3.2	2.7	2.1
GUINEA	7.0	6.5	5.6	51.5	45.1	41.7	24.5	19.9	15.4	2.7	2.5	2.6
GUINEA BISSAU	6.0	6.0	6.9	45.0	45.1	48.9	25.4	22.2	19.0	2.0	2.3	3.0
KENYA	7.7	5.9	3.8	50.8	41.3	31.6	13.3	10.7	17.1	3.7	3.1	1.5
LESOTHO	5.6	5.1	3.7	40.9	37.4	30.5	14.7	11.9	27.5	2.6	2.5	0.3
LIBERIA	6.8	6.8	6.7	47.2	42.0	49.3	16.8	19.7	21.3	3.0	2.2	2.8
LIBYA	7.3	4.7	2.9	46.3	27.6	23.0	11.6	4.9	4.2	3.5	2.3	1.9
MADAGASCAR	6.4	6.2	5.5	45.6	44.7	40.6	17.6	16.4	12.6	2.8	2.8	2.8
MALAWI	7.6	7.3	5.9	55.0	50.9	43.5	22.5	20.9	23.7	3.2	3.0	2.0
MALI	7.0	7.0	6.9	50.4	50.1	49.6	21.9	19.3	15.6	2.9	3.1	3.4
MAURITANIA	6.4	6.1	5.7	43.3	44.1	40.9	19.1	16.5	13.6	2.4	2.8	2.7
MAURITIUS	2.7	2.2	1.9	23.9	20.2	15.6	6.4	6.5	6.8	1.7	1.4	0.9
MOROCCO	5.6	4.2	2.7	38.0	30.6	22.7	12.0	8.1	5.9	2.6	2.2	1.7
MOZAMBIQUE	6.6	6.4	5.5	46.0	45.2	40.2	20.9	20.4	23.5	2.5	2.5	1.7
NAMIBIA	6.5	6.0	4.3	42.2	41.6	31.8	13.9	12.7	19.3	2.8	2.9	1.3
NIGER	8.2	8.0	7.9	56.7	55.5	54.3	24.6	22.6	18.4	3.2	3.3	3.6
NIGERIA	6.9	6.5	5.2	47.6	44.8	38.0	18.0	15.4	13.7	3.0	2.9	2.4
RWANDA	8.3	6.8	5.5	51.4	43.5	43.0	19.5	34.4	21.1	3.2	0.9	2.2
SAO T. & PRINC.	...	...	3.8	...	...	32.1	...	...	5.6	...	...	2.6
SENEGAL	6.8	6.2	4.8	48.0	43.0	36.1	20.4	16.0	11.7	2.8	2.7	2.4
SEYCHELLES	...	...	...	...	...	...	...	...	...	...	...	...
SIERRA LEONE	6.5	6.5	6.4	48.9	49.3	48.6	28.8	28.8	29.1	2.0	2.1	2.0
SOMALIA	7.3	7.3	7.1	51.8	51.9	51.1	22.4	23.2	16.7	2.9	2.9	3.4
SOUTH AFRICA	4.7	3.5	2.5	34.3	28.3	22.0	11.2	9.1	19.3	2.3	1.9	0.3
SUDAN	6.1	5.4	4.2	42.4	38.3	31.7	16.7	13.9	11.7	2.6	2.4	2.0
SWAZILAND	6.2	5.5	4.3	43.1	39.4	33.3	14.7	11.6	27.5	2.8	2.8	0.6
TANZANIA	6.7	6.1	4.9	46.6	43.5	38.3	15.2	12.9	17.9	3.1	3.1	2.0
TOGO	6.9	6.3	5.1	46.1	42.9	37.6	16.5	14.2	14.4	3.0	2.9	2.3
TUNISIA	5.2	3.5	2.0	35.2	27.4	16.9	9.0	6.7	5.5	2.6	2.1	1.1
UGANDA	7.1	7.1	7.0	50.4	50.5	50.1	18.3	20.7	15.5	3.2	3.0	3.5
ZAMBIA	7.0	6.3	5.5	46.3	44.8	41.5	15.4	16.5	27.2	3.1	2.8	1.4
ZIMBABWE	6.7	5.7	3.7	44.5	41.4	31.5	10.5	13.0	28.0	3.4	2.8	0.4
AFRICA	6.5	5.8	4.8	43.8	41.0	36.7	16.6	14.5	15.2	2.7	2.7	2.2

TABLE 3.4
MORTALITY INDICATORS

COUNTRY	INFANT MORTALITY RATE (PER 1,000)			LIFE EXPECTANCY AT BIRTH (YEARS)					
	1980	1990	2004	1980		1990		2004	
				M	F	M	F	M	F
ALGERIA	98	62	41	59	61	61	67	69	72
ANGOLA	161	159	136	40	43	43	46	39	41
BENIN	115	102	89	46	48	50	50	49	53
BOTSWANA	63	48	54	56	60	59	63	37	37
BURKINA FASO	131	113	90	45	51	46	54	46	47
BURUNDI	123	126	104	45	49	42	45	41	42
CAMEROON	108	86	85	48	51	51	54	44	46
CAPE VERDE	66	48	28	59	63	62	68	68	73
CENT. AFR. REP.	128	111	99	43	48	45	49	39	41
CHAD	149	131	112	40	44	43	46	44	46
COMOROS	110	88	63	50	54	54	58	60	63
CONGO	88	82	80	47	53	49	54	47	50
CONGO (DRC)	118	119	118	47	51	50	53	42	44
COTE D'IVOIRE	110	99	98	48	51	49	52	42	42
DJIBOUTI	137	119	99	43	46	46	49	45	46
EGYPT	114	72	38	54	57	61	64	67	72
EQUAT. GUINEA	142	122	98	42	45	46	49	48	50
ERITREA	119	93	70	43	46	47	51	52	54
ETHIOPIA	144	123	97	42	45	44	47	45	47
GABON	85	69	54	47	50	50	53	57	58
GAMBIA	143	106	77	39	42	42	45	54	56
GHANA	93	76	55	52	55	54	57	57	60
GUINEA	161	136	98	39	40	43	44	50	50
GUINEA BISSAU	169	145	116	37	40	41	44	44	47
KENYA	86	68	66	53	57	55	59	43	45
LESOTHO	114	101	89	51	55	56	58	32	36
LIBERIA	153	170	143	49	52	43	45	41	42
LIBYA	53	31	20	59	62	67	70	71	76
MADAGASCAR	119	111	88	47	49	48	50	53	56
MALAWI	165	143	111	44	45	44	45	38	38
MALI	164	135	115	45	47	48	50	49	50
MAURITANIA	124	112	93	45	48	48	51	52	55
MAURITIUS	32	22	15	63	69	66	73	69	76
MOROCCO	102	68	39	56	59	62	65	67	71
MOZAMBIQUE	143	139	118	42	45	42	45	37	39
NAMIBIA	88	68	57	52	55	54	56	42	43
NIGER	158	148	122	40	41	42	42	47	47
NIGERIA	119	99	76	47	48	50	51	51	51
RWANDA	128	128	107	44	47	31	32	40	41
SAO T. & PRINC.	60	53	30	...	...	...	...	68	73
SENEGAL	93	72	59	43	48	48	52	52	56
SEYCHELLES	...	...	...	...	...	...	...	...	...
SIERRA LEONE	190	188	172	34	37	34	37	33	35
SOMALIA	146	151	112	41	44	40	43	48	51
SOUTH AFRICA	66	50	46	53	60	56	64	44	47
SUDAN	116	97	74	47	50	51	54	54	57
SWAZILAND	101	81	75	49	54	54	58	32	33
TANZANIA	105	98	100	49	52	51	54	43	44
TOGO	110	90	78	48	49	50	52	49	51
TUNISIA	68	40	22	61	62	66	68	71	75
UGANDA	121	110	83	45	49	42	44	47	49
ZAMBIA	98	104	101	49	52	47	48	33	32
ZIMBABWE	68	59	56	57	61	52	53	33	32
AFRICA	115	96	79	48	51	51	54	50	52

Note : M and F refer to Male and Female respectively

TABLE 3.5
POPULATION WITH ACCESS TO SOCIAL INFRASTRUCTURES
(PERCENT OF POPULATION)

COUNTRY	SANITATION			SAFE WATER			HEALTH SERVICES		
	1985	1990	2002	1985	1990	2002	1985	1991	1992–99
ALGERIA	59	88	92	69	95	87	...	...	98
ANGOLA	18	30	30	28	32	50	70	24	24
BENIN	10	11	32	14	60	68	...	42	42
BOTSWANA	36	38	41	77	93	95	...	86	...
BURKINA FASO	9	13	12	35	39	51	70	...	90
BURUNDI	52	44	36	23	69	79	45	80	80
CAMEROON	36	21	48	36	50	63	20	15	80
CAPE VERDE	10	...	42	31	...	80	...	...	...
CENT. AFR. REP.	19	23	27	24	48	75	..	13	52
CHAD	14	6	8	31	20	34	30	26	30
COMOROS	...	23	23	63	89	94	82	...	...
CONGO	40	...	9	20	...	46	...	...	83
CONGO (DRC)	23	31	40	33	69	84	33	59	59
COTE D'IVOIRE	50	18	29	17	43	46	...	60	...
DJIBOUTI	37	48	50	43	78	80	...	...	...
EGYPT	80	54	68	75	94	98	99	99	99
EQUAT. GUINEA	...	...	53	...	...	44	...	...	...
ERITREA	...	8	9	...	40	57	...	...	...
ETHIOPIA	19	4	6	16	25	22	44	55	55
GABON	50	...	36	50	...	87	80	87	...
GAMBIA	...	...	53	45	...	82	90	...	93
GHANA	26	43	58	56	54	79	64	76	76
GUINEA	21	17	13	20	42	51	13	45	80
GUINEA BISSAU	25	...	34	31	...	59	64	...	40
KENYA	44	42	48	27	45	62	...	...	77
LESOTHO	22	37	37	36	...	76	50	80	80
LIBERIA	21	38	26	37	56	62	35	..	39
LIBYA	91	97	97	90	71	72	100	100	95
MADAGASCAR	3	12	33	31	40	45	65	65	38
MALAWI	60	36	46	32	41	67	54	80	35
MALI	21	36	45	17	34	48	35	...	40
MAURITANIA	...	28	42	37	41	56	30	...	63
MAURITIUS	97	99	99	99	100	100	100	99	99
MOROCCO	46	57	61	57	75	80	70	62	70
MOZAMBIQUE	20	...	27	15	...	42	40	30	39
NAMIBIA	14	24	30	52	58	80	72	...	59
NIGER	9	7	12	37	40	46	48	30	30
NIGERIA	35	39	38	36	49	60	66	67	67
RWANDA	58	37	41	49	58	73	80	...	80
SAO T. & PRINC.	15	...	24	42	...	79	...	...	...
SENEGAL	55	35	52	44	66	72	40	40	90
SEYCHELLES	99	...	...	95	...	87	99	99	99
SIERRA LEONE	21	...	39	24	...	57	36	...	38
SOMALIA	15	...	25	31	...	29	20	...	...
SOUTH AFRICA	...	63	67	...	83	87	...	...	...
SUDAN	5	33	34	40	64	69	70	70	70
SWAZILAND	...	...	52	54	...	52	...	55	55
TANZANIA	64	37	34	52	49	51	73	93	42
TOGO	14	75	80	35	77	82	61	...	...
TUNISIA	52	47	46	89	38	73	91	100	90
UGANDA	13	43	41	16	44	56	42	71	49
ZAMBIA	47	41	45	48	50	55	70	75	...
ZIMBABWE	26	49	57	52	77	83	71	...	85
AFRICA	35	39	43	42	58	64	61	66	67

TABLE 3.6
SCHOOL ENROLMENT RATIO

COUNTRY	PRIMARY						SECONDARY					
	1990			2001/02			1990			2001/02		
	Total	Male	Female	Total	Male	Female	Total	Male	Female	Total	Male	Female
ALGERIA	100	108	92	108	112	104	61	67	54	72	69	74
ANGOLA	92	95	88	...	...	...	12	15	10	19	21	17
BENIN	58	78	39	104	122	86	12	17	7	26	35	16
BOTSWANA	113	109	117	103	103	103	43	40	45	73	70	75
BURKINA FASO	33	41	26	44	51	36	7	9	5	10	12	8
BURUNDI	73	79	66	71	80	62	6	7	4	11	12	9
CAMEROON	101	109	93	107	115	99	28	33	23	33	36	29
CAPE VERDE	121	127	122	123	125	120	21	22	20	66	64	67
CENT. AFR. REP.	65	80	51	66	79	53	12	17	7	...	...	...
CHAD	54	75	34	73	90	57	8	13	3	11	18	...
COMOROS	75	87	63	90	98	81	18	21	14	28	30	25
CONGO	133	141	124	86	88	83	53	62	43	32	37	27
CONGO (DRC)	70	81	50	84	89	79	22	29	14	36	47	25
COTE D'IVOIRE	67	79	56	80	92	68	22	30	14	23	30	...
DJIBOUTI	38	45	32	40	46	35	12	14	9	20	24	15
EGYPT	94	101	86	97	100	94	76	84	68	88	91	85
EQUAT. GUINEA	...	....	...	126	132	120	...	...	...	30	38	22
ERITREA	23	23	22	61	67	54	15	15	14	28	33	22
ETHIOPIA	33	39	26	64	75	53	14	16	12	19	23	15
GABON	163	....	169	134	135	134	41	...	...	51	61	...
GAMBIA	64	76	52	79	82	75	19	25	11	34	40	28
GHANA	75	82	68	81	85	78	36	45	29	38	41	34
GUINEA	37	50	24	77	88	66	10	15	5	...	...	...
GUINEA BISSAU	56	72	42	...	...	...	9	13	6	20	26	...
KENYA	95	97	93	96	97	95	24	27	20	32	34	30
LESOTHO	112	100	123	124	123	125	25	20	30	34	30	38
LIBERIA	30	35	24	...	...	...	14	20	8	34	27	...
LIBYA	105	108	102	114	114	114	86	85	87	105	102	108
MADAGASCAR	103	103	103	104	106	102	18	17	16	...	...	...
MALAWI	68	74	62	146	149	143	8	10	3	34	39	29
MALI	27	34	19	57	65	49	7	9	4	...	...	...
MAURITANIA	49	56	41	86	88	85	14	19	9	22	25	19
MAURITIUS	109	109	109	106	106	106	53	53	53	80	81	78
MOROCCO	67	79	54	107	113	101	35	41	30	41	44	...
MOZAMBIQUE	67	77	57	99	110	87	8	10	6	13	16	10
NAMIBIA	129	123	135	106	106	106	44	39	49	61	57	65
NIGER	29	37	21	40	47	32	7	9	4	6	8	5
NIGERIA	91	104	79	96	107	86	25	26	19	...	...	...
RWANDA	70	70	69	117	118	116	8	9	7	14	15	14
SAO T. & PRINC.	...	....	...	126	130	122	...	...	...	39	42	36
SENEGAL	59	68	50	75	79	72	16	21	11	19	22	15
SEYCHELLES	96	....	...	116	116	115	...	...	...	110	107	113
SIERRA LEONE	50	60	41	...	...	...	17	22	13	26	29	...
SOMALIA	10	13	7	...	...	...	6	8	4	...	...	...
SOUTH AFRICA	122	123	121	105	107	103	74	63	73	86	83	90
SUDAN	53	60	45	59	63	54	24	25	20	32	22	...
SWAZILAND	111	114	109	100	103	98	44	44	44	45	45	45
TANZANIA	70	70	69	70	71	69	5	6	4	...	6	...
TOGO	109	132	86	124	136	112	24	35	12	79	54	...
TUNISIA	113	120	107	112	114	109	45	50	40	17	78	81
UGANDA	71	79	63	136	139	134	13	17	9	...	19	15
ZAMBIA	99	102	95	79	81	76	24	30	18	24	27	21
ZIMBABWE	116	117	115	99	100	98	50	53	46	43	45	40
	77	85	69	89	99	84	31	34	26	43	42	41

Explanatory Notes

The main objective of the notes below is to facilitate interpretation of the statistical data presented in Part III of the Report. Data shown for all African countries are annual totals or five year averages. Period average growth rates are calculated as the arithmetic average of annual growth rates over the period. These statistics are not shown in the tables when they are not significant or not comparable over years.

Section 1: Basic Indicators

This section contains one table (Table 1.1), which presents some basic indicators as background to the tables in this part of the Report. The table provides cross-country comparisons for area, population, GNI per capita, Consumer Price Inflation, life expectancy, infant mortality and adult literacy rates. The main sources of data in this table are the United Nations Organizations, the World Bank, Country reports and ADB Statistics Division's estimates.

Area refers to the total surface area of a country, comprising land area and inland waters. The data is obtained from the Food and Agriculture Organization (FAO). The population figures are mid–year estimates obtained from the United Nations Population Division.

GNI per capita figures are obtained by dividing GNI in current US dollars by the corresponding mid-year population. GNI measures the total domestic and foreign value added claimed by residents. It comprises GDP plus net factor income from abroad, which is the income residents receive from abroad for factor services less

similar payments made to nonresidents who contribute to the domestic economy. The data are obtained from the World Bank Atlas.

Life expectancy at birth is the number of years a new born infant would live, if patterns of mortality prevailing at the time of birth in the countries were to remain unchanged throughout his/her life. The infant mortality rate is the annual number of deaths of infants under one year of age per thousand live births. Adult literacy rate is the percentage of people aged 15 and above who can, with understanding, both read and write a short simple statement on their everyday life. The data are obtained from UNESCO.

Section 2: Macroeconomic Indicators

Table 2.1. Gross Domestic Product, real

National accounts estimates are obtained from regional member countries data, the World Bank, the IMF and the United Nations Statistical Division. In several instances, data are adjusted or supplemented with estimates made by the ADB Statistics Division. The concepts and definitions used for national accounts data are those of the United Nations 1993 System of National Accounts (SNA). Many countries continue to compile their national accounts in accordance with the 1968 SNA, but more and more are adopting the 1993 SNA.

Gross Domestic Product (GDP) measures the total final output of goods and services produced by a national economy, excluding provisions for depreciation. GDP figures are shown at constant 1995 market prices, and have been converted to US dollars using constant 1995 exchange rates provided by the IMF and the World Bank. For a few countries where the official exchange rate does not reflect effectively the rate applied to actual foreign exchange transactions, an alternative currency conversion factor has been used.

Aggregate growth rates for Africa are calculated as weighted averages of individual country growth rates using the share of the country's GDP in aggregate GDP based on the purchasing power parties (PPP) valuation of country GDPs.

Table 2.2. Gross Domestic Product, nominal

Data shown in this table are given at current market prices and are obtained by converting national currency series in current prices to US dollars at official exchange rates. Annual changes in GDP are presented in nominal terms.

Table 2.3. Gross National Savings

Gross National Savings (GNS) is calculated by deducting total consumption from GNI at current prices and adding net private transfers from abroad.

Table 2.4. Gross Capital Formation

Gross Capital Formation consists of gross domestic fixed capital formation plus net changes in the level of inventories.

Table 2.5. Terms of Trade

Terms of trade estimates are obtained from the IMF and supplemented by ADB Statistics Division estimates. These are obtained by dividing unit value indices of exports by unit value indices of imports. The terms of trade indices for the entire set of regional member countries are also ratios of the unit value of exports and the unit value of imports.

Table 2.6. Current Account Balance

Data in this table are obtained from the IMF, and based on the methodology of the fifth edition of the Balance of Payments Manual. The current account includes the trade balance valued f.o.b., net services and net factor income, and current transfer payments. The data is given as percentage of GDP.

Table 2.7. Broad Money Supply

Broad Money supply (M2) comprises currency outside banks, private sector demand deposits, (and, where applicable, post office and treasury checking deposits) and quasi-money.

Table 2.8. Real Exchange Rate Index

The real exchange rate index is defined broadly as the nominal exchange rate index adjusted for relative movements in national price or cost indicators of the home country and the United States of America.

Table 2.9. International Reserves

International Reserves consist of country's holdings of monetary gold, Special Drawing Rights (SDRs) and foreign exchange, as well as its reserve position in the International Monetary Fund (IMF).

Table 2.10. Consumer Price Index

Consumer price index shows changes in the cost of acquisition of a basket of goods and services purchased by the average consumer. Weights for the computation of the index numbers are obtained from household budget surveys.

Table 2.11. Overall Fiscal Deficit or surplus

The overall surplus/deficit is defined as current and capital revenue and official grants received, less total expenditure and lending minus repayments. The data is given as a percentage of GDP.

Tables 2.12–2.13. Total External Debt; Debt Service.

The main source of external debt data is the IMF. Total external debt covers outstanding and disbursed long-term debt, use of IMF credit, and short-term debt. Debt service is the sum of actual repayments of principal and actual payments of interest made in foreign exchange, goods, or services, on external public and publicly guaranteed debt.

Section 3: Labor Force and Social Indicators

This section presents data on labor force by sector (agriculture, industry and services) and also labor force participation rates, total and by sex.

Other tables in the section give data on components of population change (i.e. fertility, births, deaths and rate of natural increase), infant mortality rates, and life expectancy at birth, access to social infrastructure (sanitation, safe water and health services) and school enrolment ratios for primary and secondary levels.

Table 3.1. Labor Force by Sector

The labor force includes economically active persons aged 10 years and over. It includes the unemployed and the armed forces, but excludes housewives, students and other economically inactive groups. The agricultural sector consists of agriculture, forestry, hunting and fishing. Industry comprises mining and quarrying, manufacturing, construction, electricity, gas and water. Services include all other branches of economic activity and any statistical discrepancy in the origin of resources.

Table 3.2. Labor Force Participation Rates

The table shows the percentage of the population within each sex and age group that participates in economic activities (either employed or unemployed) from ILO data. Figures shown are ratios of the total economically-active population to the total population of all ages. Activity rates for females may be difficult to compare among countries because of the difference in the criteria adopted for determining the extent to which female workers are to be counted among the "economically active".

Table 3.3. Components of Population Change

Total fertility rate indicates the number of children that would be born per woman, if she were to live to the end of the child-bearing years; and bears children during those years in accordance with prevailing age-specific fertility rates. The crude birth rate represents the annual live births per thousand population. The crude death rate is the annual number of deaths per thousand population. Rate of Natural increase of the population is the difference between Crude Birth and Crude Death rates expressed as a percentage. The data in the table are obtained mainly from the United Nations Population Division, UNICEF and the World Bank.

Table 3.4. Mortality Indicators

The variables presented in this table — namely infant mortality rate and life expectancy at births — are as defined in Table 1.1. The sources of data are also the same.

Table 3.5. Population with Access to Social Infrastructures

The percentage of people with access to sanitation is defined separately for urban and rural areas. For urban areas, access to sanitation facilities is defined as urban population served by connections to public sewers or household systems, such as pit privies, pour-flush latrines, septic tanks, communal toilets, and other such

facilities. In the case of the rural population, the definition refers to those with adequate disposal, such as pit privies and pour-flush latrines. Applications of these definitions may vary from one country to another, and comparisons can therefore be inappropriate.

The population with access to safe water refers to the percentage of the population with reasonable access to safe water supply (which includes treated surface water, or untreated but uncontaminated water such as that from springs, sanitary wells, and protected boreholes). The threshold for the distance to safe water in urban areas is about 200 meters, while in rural areas it is reasonable walking distance to and from sources where water can be fetched.

The population with access to health services refers to the percentage of the population that can reach appropriate local health services by local means of transport in no more than one hour. Data in this table are obtained from the World Bank.

Table 3.6. School Enrolment

The primary school enrolment ratio is the total number of pupils enrolled at primary level of education, regardless of age, expressed as a percentage of the population corresponding to the official school age of primary education. School enrolment ratios may be more than 100 per cent in countries where some pupils' ages are different from the legal enrolment age. Data in this table are obtained from UNESCO.

The secondary school enrolment ratio is the total number of pupils enrolled at secondary level of education, regardless of age, expressed as a percentage of the population corresponding to the official school age of secondary education.

Data Sources

1.	**Basic Indicators**	Food and Agriculture Organization: FAOSTAT Database, 2004. United Nations Population Division: The 2002 revision. World Bank: Africa Live Database, February 2004. Regional Member Countries, ADB Statistics Division.
2.	**Macroeconomic Indicators**	
2.1–2.4	National Accounts	United Nations: National Accounts Yearbook, various years. World Bank: Africa Live Database, February 2004. IMF: World Economic Outlook data files, September 2004. ADB Statistics Division. Regional Member Countries.
2.5–2.6	External Sector	IMF: World Economic Outlook, Data files, September 2004.
2.7–2.10	Money Supply Exchange Rates and Prices	IMF: International Financial Statistics, December 2004, and International Financial Statistics, CD-ROM December 2004. ILO: Yearbook of Labor Statistics, various years. ADB Statistics Division, Regional Member Countries.
2.11	Government Finance	IMF: World Economic Outlook Data files, September 2004.
2.12–2.13	External Debt	IMF: World Economic Outlook, September 2004. ADB Statistics Division.
3.	**Labor Force and Social Indicators**	
3.1–3.2	Labor Force	Food and Agriculture Organization: FAOSTAT Database, 2004 World Bank: African Development Indicators, various issues ADB Statistics Division.
3.3–3.6	Social Indicators	UNICEF: The State of the World's Children, various years. World Bank: African Development Indicators, various issues. UN: Human Development Report, 2003 and 2004. UN: Population Division, The 2002 Revision. Regional Member Countries. ADB Statistics Division.

This publication was prepared by the Bank's Development Research Department (PDRE). Other publications of the Department are:

AFRICAN DEVELOPMENT REVIEW
A semi-annual professional journal devoted to the study and analysis of development issues in Africa

ECONOMIC RESEARCH PAPERS
A working paper series presenting the research findings, mainly by the research staff, on topics related to African development policy issues.

COMPENDIUM OF STATISTICS
An annual publication providing statistical information on the operational activities of the Bank Group.

GENDER, POVERTY AND ENVIRONMENTAL INDICATORS ON AFRICAN COUNTRIES
A biennial publication providing information on the broad development trends relating to gender, poverty and environmental issues in the 53 African countries.

SELECTED STATISTICS ON AFRICAN COUNTRIES
An annual publication, providing selected social and economic indicators for the 53 regional member countries of the Bank.

AFRICAN ECONOMIC OUTLOOK
An annual publication jointly produced by the African Development Bank and the OECD Development Centre, which analyses the comparative economic prospects for African countries.

Copies of these publications may be obtained from:

Development Research Department (PDRE)
African Development Bank

Headquarters	**Temporary Relocation Agency (TRA)**
01 BP 1387 Abidjan 01,	Angle des trois rues, Avenue du Ghana,
COTE D'IVOIRE	RUES PIERRE DE COUBERTIN
TELEFAX (225) 20 20 49 48	ET HEDI NOUIRA
TELEPHONE (225) 20 20 44 44	BP 323 — 1002 TUNIS BELVEDERE
TELEX 23717/23498/23263	TUNISIA
Web Site: www.afdb.org	TELEFAX (216) 71351933
EMAIL: afdb@afdb.org	TELEPHONE (216) 71333511
	Web Site: www.afdb.org
	EMAIL: afdb@afdb.org